Dynamic Asset Pricing Theory

Dynamic Asset Pricing Theory

Darrell Duffie

Princeton University Press
Princeton, New Jersey

Library of Congress Cataloging-in-Publication Data

Duffie, Darrell.
    Dynamic asset pricing theory / Darrell Duffie.
        p.   cm.
    Includes bibliographical references and indexes.
    ISBN 0-691-04302-7
    1. Capital assets pricing model. 2. Portfolio management.
    3. Uncertainty. I. Title.
HG4637.D84 1992
332.6–dc20   91-46738
                                        CIP

This book was composed with LaTeX by Archetype Publishing Inc.,
P.O. Box 6567, Champaign, IL 61821.

Princeton University Press books are printed on acid-free paper
and meet the guidelines for permanence and durability of the Committee
on Production Guidelines for Book Longevity of the Council on Library
Resources.

Printed in the United States

10 9 8 7 6 5 4 3 2 1

For Colin

Contents

Preface

THIS BOOK IS an introduction to the theory of portfolio choice and asset pricing in multiperiod settings under uncertainty. An alternate title might be *Arbitrage, Optimality, and Equilibrium*, since the book is built around the three basic constraints on asset prices: absence of arbitrage, single-agent optimality, and market equilibrium. The most important unifying principle is that any of these three conditions implies that there are "state prices," meaning positive discount factors, one for each state and date, such that the price of any security is merely the state-price weighted sum of its future payoffs. This idea can be traced to Kenneth Arrow's (1953) invention of the general equilibrium model of security markets. Identifying the state prices is the major task at hand. Technicalities are given relatively little emphasis so as to simplify these concepts and to make plain the similarities between discrete- and continuous-time models. All continuous-time models are based on Brownian motion, despite the fact that most of the results extend easily to the case of a general abstract information filtration.

To someone who came out of graduate school in the mid-eighties, the decade spanning roughly 1969–79 seems like a golden age of dynamic asset pricing theory. Robert Merton started continuous-time financial modeling with his explicit dynamic programming solution for optimal portfolio and consumption policies. This set the stage for his general equilibrium model of security prices (1973a), another milestone. His next major contribution was his continual development of the option pricing formula introduced by Fischer Black and Myron Scholes in 1973. The Black-Scholes model now seems to be by far the most important single breakthrough of this "golden decade," and ranks with the Modigliani-Miller Theorem (1958) and the CAPM of Sharpe (1964) and Lintner (1965) in its overall importance for financial theory and practice. A tremendously influential simplification of the Black-Scholes model appeared in the "binomial" option-pricing model of Cox, Ross, and Rubinstein (1979), who drew on an insight of Bill Sharpe.

Working with discrete-time models, LeRoy (1973), Rubinstein (1976), and Lucas (1978) developed multiperiod extensions of the CAPM. To this day, the "Lucas model" is the "vanilla flavor" of equilibrium asset pricing models. The simplest multiperiod representation of the CAPM finally appeared in Doug Breeden's continuous-time consumption-based CAPM, published in 1979. Although not published until 1985, the Cox-Ingersoll-Ross model of the term structure appeared in the mid-seventies and is still the premier textbook example of a continuous-time general equilibrium asset pricing model with practical applications. It also ranks as one of the key breakthroughs of that "golden decade" of 1969–79. Finally, extending the ideas of Cox and Ross (1976) and Ross (1978), Harrison and Kreps (1979) gave an almost definitive conceptual structure to the whole theory of dynamic security prices.

The decade or so since 1979 has, with relatively few exceptions, been a mopping-up operation. On the theoretical side, assumptions have been weakened, there have been some noteworthy extensions, and the various problems have become much more unified under the umbrella of the Harrison-Kreps model. On the applied side, markets have experienced an explosion of new valuation techniques, hedging applications, and security innovation, much of this based on the Black-Scholes and related arbitrage models. No major investment bank, for example, lacks the experts or computer technology required to implement advanced mathematical models of the term structure.

Although it is difficult to predict where the theory will go next, in order to promote faster progress by people coming into the field it seems wise to condense some of the basics into a textbook. This book is designed to be a streamlined course text, not a research monograph. Much generality is sacrificed for expositional reasons, and there is relatively little emphasis on mathematical rigor or on the existence of general equilibrium. As its title indicates, I am treating only the theoretical side of the story. Although it might be useful to tie the theory to the empirical side of asset pricing, others more qualified than myself will surely follow with books specializing on the estimation and testing of asset pricing models. (Singleton [1987] gives a useful survey.) Some important aspects of functioning security markets, such as asymmetric information, borrowing constraints, and transactions costs, have also been omitted. I have chosen to develop only some of the essential ideas of dynamic asset pricing, and even these are more than enough to put into one book or into a one-semester course. There are other books covering some of the topics treated here, such as those of Malliaris (1982), Ingersoll (1987), Jarrow (1988), Huang and Litzenberger (1988), Dothan

(1990), and Merton (1990b). Each has its own aims and themes. Survey articles have been written by Rothschild (1986), Constantinides (1989), and Merton (1990a). I hope that readers will find some advantage in having a distinctly different, unified, and newer perspective.

A reasonable way to teach a shorter course on continuous-time asset pricing out of this book is to begin with Chapter 1 as an introduction to the basic notion of state prices, and then to go directly to Chapters 5 through 9. Chapter 10, on numerical methods, could be skipped at some cost in the student's ability to implement the results. There is no direct dependence of any results in Chapters 5 through 9 on the first four chapters. While little beyond undergraduate calculus and linear algebra is assumed, a first reading will be easier with some background in basic microeconomics, say at the level of Kreps (1990) or Varian (1984). Familiarity with probability theory at a level approaching Billingsley (1986), for example, would also speed things along, although measure theory is not used heavily and undergraduate analysis, as in Bartle (1976), would be a good substitute. In any case, a series of appendixes supplies all of the required concepts and definitions in probability theory and stochastic processes.

Each chapter has exercises and notes to the literature. Students seem to learn best by doing problem exercises. I have tried to be thorough in giving sources for results whenever possible, and I plead that any cases in which I have mistaken or missed sources be brought to my attention for correction. The notation and terminology throughout is fairly standard. I use $\mathbb{R}$ to denote the real line and $\overline{\mathbb{R}} = \mathbb{R} \cup \{-\infty, +\infty\}$ for the extended real line. For any set Z and positive integer n, I use Z^n for the set of n-tuples of the form $(z_1, \ldots, z_n)$ with z_i in Z for all i. For example, think of $\mathbb{R}^n$. The conventions used for inequalities in any context are:

- $x \geq 0$ means that x is non-negative; for x in $\mathbb{R}^n$, this is equivalent to $x \in \mathbb{R}^n_+$;
- $x > 0$ means that x is non-negative and not zero, but not necessarily strictly positive in all coordinates;
- $x \gg 0$ means x is strictly positive in every possible sense. The phrase "x is strictly positive" means the same thing. For x in $\mathbb{R}^n$, this is equivalent to $x \in \mathbb{R}^n_{++} \equiv \text{int}(\mathbb{R}^n_+)$.

Although warnings will be given at appropriate times, it should be kept in mind that $X = Y$ will be used to mean equality almost everywhere or almost surely, as the case may be. The same caveat applies to each of the above inequalities. A function F on an ordered set (such as $\mathbb{R}^n$) is *increasing* if $F(x) \geq F(y)$ whenever $x \geq y$ and *strictly increasing* if $F(x) > F(y)$ whenever

$x > y$. When the domain and range of a function are implicitly obvious, the notation "$x \mapsto F(x)$" means the function that maps x to $F(x)$; for example, $x \mapsto x^2$ means the function $F : \mathbb{R} \to \mathbb{R}$ defined by $F(x) = x^2$.

I have many people to thank, in addition to those mentioned above who developed this theory. In 1982, Michael Harrison gave a class at Stanford that had a major effect on my understanding and research goals. I have referenced his lecture notes. Beside me in that class was Chi-fu Huang; we learned much of this material together, becoming close friends and collaborators. I owe him a lot. I am grateful to Niko and Vanna Skiadas, who treated me with overwhelming warmth and hospitality at their home on Skiathos, where parts of the first draft were written. Useful comments on subsequent drafts have been provided by Howie Corb, Rui Kan, John Overdeck, Christina Shannon, Philippe Henrotte, Chris Avery, Pinghua Young, Don Iglehart, Rohit Rahi, Shinsuke Kambe, Marco Scarsini, Kerry Back, Heracles Polemarchakis, John Campbell, Ravi Myneni, Michael Intriligator, Robert Ashcroft, Robert Merton, and Ayman Hindy. I thank Kingston Duffie, Ravi Myneni, and Paul Bernstein for coding and running some numerical examples. In writing the book, I have benefited from research collaboration over the years with George Constantinides, Larry Epstein, Wendell Fleming, Mark Garman, John Geanakoplos, Chi-fu Huang, Matt Jackson, Pierre-Louis Lions, Andreu Mas-Colell, Andy McLennan, Philip Protter, Tony Richardson, Wayne Shafer, Ken Singleton, Costis Skiadas, Richard Stanton, Bill Zame, and Thaleia Zariphopoulou. At Princeton University Press, Jack Repcheck, Sherry Wert, and Jane Low were friendly, helpful, and supportive. I owe a special debt to Costis Skiadas, whose generous supply of good ideas over the past three years has had a big influence on the result. The errors are my own responsibility, and I hope to hear of them and any other comments from readers.

I
Discrete-Time Models

This first part of the book takes place in a discrete-time setting with a discrete set of states. This should ease the development of intuition for the models to be found in Part II. The three pillars of the theory, *arbitrage, optimality,* and *equilibrium,* are developed repeatedly in different settings. Chapter 1 is the basic single-period model. Chapter 2 extends the results of Chapter 1 to many periods. Chapter 3 specializes Chapter 2 to a Markov setting, and illustrates dynamic programming as an alternate solution technique. The Ho-and-Lee and Black-Derman-Toy term-structure models are included as exercises. Chapter 4 is an infinite-horizon counterpart to Chapter 3 that has become known as the Lucas model.

The focus of the theory is the notion of state prices, which specify the price of any security as the state-price weighted sum or expectation of the security's state-contingent dividends. In a finite-dimensional setting, there exist state prices if and only if there is no arbitrage. The same fact is true in infinite-dimensional settings under mild regularity. Given an agent's optimal portfolio choice, a state-price vector is given by that agent's utility gradient. In an equilibrium with Pareto optimality, a state-price vector is likewise given by a representative agent's utility gradient at the economy's aggregate consumption process.

1

An Introduction to State Pricing

THIS CHAPTER INTRODUCES the basic ideas of the book in a finite-state one-period setting. In some sense, each subsequent chapter merely repeats this one from a new perspective. The objective is a characterization of security prices in terms of "state prices," one for each state of the world. The price of a given security is simply the state-price weighted sum of its payoffs in the different states. One can treat a state-price as the shadow price for wealth contingent on a given state of the world. We obtain a characterization of state prices, first based on the absence of arbitrage, then based on the first order conditions for optimal portfolio choice of a given agent, and finally from the first order conditions for Pareto optimality in an equilibrium with complete markets. State prices are connected with the "beta" model for excess expected returns, a special case of which is the Capital Asset Pricing Model. Many readers will find this chapter to be a review of standard results. In most cases, here and throughout the book, technical conditions are imposed that give up much generality so as to simplify the exposition.

A. Arbitrage and State Prices

Uncertainty is represented here by a finite set $\{1, \ldots, S\}$ of states, one of which will be revealed as true. The N securities are given by an $N \times S$ matrix D, with D_{ij} denoting the number of units of account paid by security i in state j. The security prices are given by some q in $\mathbb{R}^N$. A *portfolio* $\theta \in \mathbb{R}^N$ has *market value* $q \cdot \theta$ and *payoff* $D^\top \theta$. An *arbitrage* is a portfolio θ in $\mathbb{R}^N$ with $q \cdot \theta \leq 0$ and $D^\top \theta > 0$, or $q \cdot \theta < 0$ and $D^\top \theta \geq 0$. A *state-price* vector is a vector ψ in $\mathbb{R}^S_{++}$ with $q = D\psi$. We can think of ψ_j as the marginal cost of obtaining an additional unit of account in state j.

3

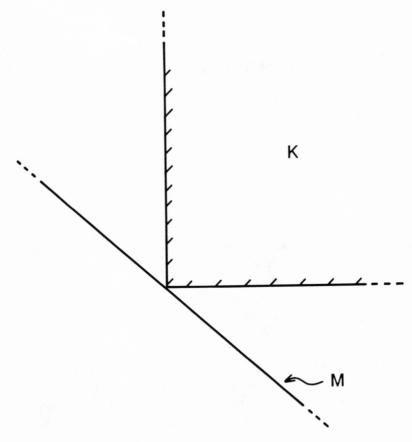

Figure 1.1.   *Separating a Cone from a Linear Subspace*

Theorem. *There is no arbitrage if and only if there is a state-price vector.*

Proof: The proof is an application of the Separating Hyperplane Theorem. Let $L = \mathbb{R} \times \mathbb{R}^S$ and $M = \{(-q \cdot \theta, D^\top \theta) : \theta \in \mathbb{R}^N\}$, a linear subspace of L. Let $K = \mathbb{R}_+ \times \mathbb{R}_+^S$, which is a cone (meaning that, if x is in K, then λx is in K for each strictly positive scalar λ.) Both K and M are closed and convex subsets of L. There is no arbitrage if and only if K and M intersect precisely at 0, as pictured in Figure 1.1.

Suppose $K \cap M = \{0\}$. The Separating Hyperplane Theorem (in a version for closed cones that is found in Appendix B) implies the existence of a linear functional $F : L \to \mathbb{R}$ such that $F(z) < F(x)$ for all z in M and nonzero x in K. Since M is a linear space, this implies that $F(z) = 0$ for all z in M and that $F(x) > 0$ for all nonzero x in K. The latter fact implies that

F is represented by some $\alpha > 0$ in $\mathbb{R}$ and $\psi \gg 0$ in $\mathbb{R}^S$ by $F(v, c) = \alpha v + \psi \cdot c$ for any $(v, c) \in L$. This implies that $-\alpha q \cdot \theta + \psi \cdot (D^\top \theta) = 0$ for all θ in $\mathbb{R}^N$. The vector ψ/α is therefore a state-price vector.

Conversely, if a state-price vector exists, then there is clearly no arbitrage. ∎

B. Risk-Neutral Probabilities

We can view any p in $\mathbb{R}^S_+$ with $p_1 + \cdots + p_S = 1$ as a vector of probabilities of the corresponding states. Given a state-price vector ψ for the dividend-price pair (D, q), let $\psi_0 = \psi_1 + \cdots + \psi_S$ and, for any state j, let $\hat{\psi}_j = \psi_j/\psi_0$. We now have a vector $(\hat{\psi}_1, \ldots, \hat{\psi}_S)$ of probabilities and can write, for an arbitrary security i,

$$\frac{q_i}{\psi_0} = \hat{E}(D_i) \equiv \sum_{j=1}^{S} \hat{\psi}_j D_{ij},$$

viewing the normalized price of the security as its expected payoff under specially chosen "risk-neutral" probabilities. If there exists a portfolio $\bar{\theta}$ with $D^\top \bar{\theta} = (1, 1, \ldots, 1)$, then $\psi_0 = \bar{\theta} \cdot q$ is the discount on riskless borrowing and, for any security i, $q_i = \psi_0 \hat{E}(D_i)$, showing any security's price to be its discounted expected payoff in this sense of artificially chosen probabilities.

C. Optimality and Asset Pricing

Suppose the dividend-price pair (D, q) is given and there is some portfolio θ with payoff $D^\top \theta > 0$. An *agent* is defined by a strictly increasing *utility function* $U : \mathbb{R}^S_+ \to \mathbb{R}$ and an *endowment* e in $\mathbb{R}^S_+$. This leaves the *budget-feasible set*

$$X(q, e) = \{ e + D^\top \theta \in \mathbb{R}^S_+ : \theta \in \mathbb{R}^N, \, q \cdot \theta = 0 \},$$

and the problem

$$\sup_{c \in X(q,e)} U(c). \tag{1}$$

Since there is a portfolio θ with $D^\top \theta > 0$, the solution is unaffected if we replace the budget constraint $q \cdot \theta = 0$ with the inequality constraint $q \cdot \theta \leq 0$.

Proposition. *If there is a solution to (1), then there is no arbitrage. If U is continuous and there is no arbitrage, then there is a solution to (1).*

Proof is left as an exercise.

Theorem. *Suppose that c^* is a strictly positive solution to (1) and that the vector $\partial U(c^*)$ of partial derivatives of U at c^* exists and is strictly positive. Then there is some scalar $\lambda > 0$ such that $\lambda \partial U(c^*)$ is a state-price vector.*

Proof: The first order condition for optimality is that, for any θ with $q \cdot \theta = 0$, the marginal utility for buying the portfolio θ is zero. This is expressed more precisely in the following way. The strict positivity of c^* implies that, for any portfolio θ, there is some scalar $k > 0$ such that $c^* + \alpha D^\top \theta \geq 0$ for all α in $[-k, k]$. Let $g_\theta : [-k, k] \to \mathbb{R}$ be defined by

$$g_\theta(\alpha) = U(c^* + \alpha D^\top \theta).$$

Suppose $q \cdot \theta = 0$. The optimality of c^* implies that g_θ is maximized at $\alpha = 0$. The first order condition for this is that $g'_\theta(0) = \partial U(c^*)^\top D^\top \theta = 0$. We can conclude that, if $q \cdot \theta = 0$, then $\partial U(c^*) D^\top \theta = 0$.

Conversely, if $\partial U(c^*) D^\top \theta = 0$, we claim that $q \cdot \theta = 0$. If not, and if we say $q \cdot \theta < 0$, we can choose a portfolio $\overline{\theta}$ with $D^\top \overline{\theta} > 0$ and $q \cdot (\theta + \overline{\theta}) = 0$. With this, the portfolio $\hat{\theta} = \theta + \overline{\theta}$ satisfies $\partial U(c^*)^\top D^\top \hat{\theta} > 0$ and $q \cdot \hat{\theta} = 0$, a contradiction of the optimality of c^*. If $q \cdot \theta > 0$, then $-\theta$ has the properties required for the same contradiction.

Thus, for any θ in $\mathbb{R}^N$, we have $q \cdot \theta = 0$ if and only if $\partial U(c^*)^\top D^\top \theta = 0$. This is true if and only if for some scalar $\lambda > 0$,

$$q = \lambda D \partial U(c^*). \tag{2}$$

Since $\partial U(c^*) \gg 0$, it follows that $\lambda \partial U(c^*)$ is a state price vector. ∎

Although we have assumed that U is strictly increasing, this does not necessarily mean that $\partial U(c^*) \gg 0$. If U is concave and strictly increasing, however, it is always true that $\partial U(c^*) \gg 0$.

Corollary. *If U is concave and differentiable, then a budget-feasible consumption choice $c^* \gg 0$ is optimal if and only if $\lambda \partial U(c^*)$ is a state-price vector for some scalar $\lambda > 0$.*

This follows from the sufficiency of the first order conditions for concave objective functions. The idea is illustrated in Figure 1.2. In that figure, there are only two states, and a state-price vector is a suitably normalized nonzero positive vector orthogonal to the budget set $X(q, e)$. The first order condition for optimality of c^* is that movement in any feasible direction away from c^* has negative or zero marginal utility, which is equivalent to the statement that the budget-feasible set is tangent at c^* to the preferred

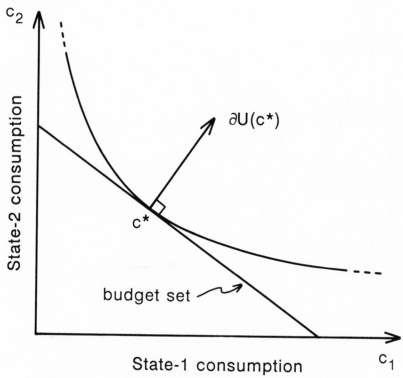

Figure 1.2. *First Order Conditions for Optimal Consumption Choice*

set $\{c : U(c) \geq U(c^*)\}$, as shown in the figure. This is equivalent to the statement that $\partial U(c^*)$ is orthogonal to $X(q, e)$ at c^*, consistent with the last corollary. Figure 1.3 illustrates a strictly suboptimal consumption choice c, at which the derivative vector $\partial U(c)$ is not co-linear with the state-price vector ψ.

We consider the special case of an *expected utility* function U, defined by a given vector p of probabilities and by some $u : \mathbb{R}_+ \to \mathbb{R}$ according to

$$U(c) = E[u(c)] \equiv \sum_{j=1}^{S} p_j u(c_j). \tag{3}$$

One can check that, for $c \gg 0$, if u is differentiable, then $\partial U(c)_j = p_j u'(c_j)$. For this expected utility function, (2) therefore applies if and only if

$$q = \lambda E[Du'(c^*)], \tag{4}$$

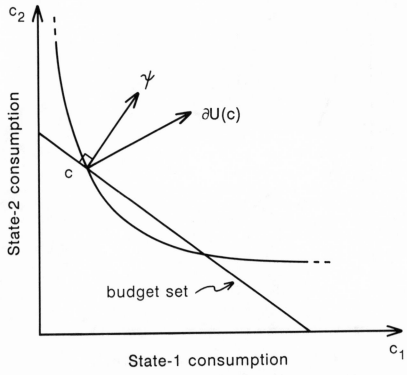

Figure 1.3. *A Strictly Suboptimal Consumption Choice*

with the obvious notational convention. As we saw in Section 1B, one can also write (2) or (4), with $\hat{\psi}_j = u'(c_j^*)p_j/E[u'(c^*)]$, as

$$\frac{q_i}{\psi_0} = \hat{E}(D_i) \equiv D\hat{\psi}. \tag{5}$$

D. Equilibrium, Pareto Optimality, and Complete Markets

Suppose there are m agents, defined as in Section 1C by strictly increasing utility functions $U_1, \ldots, U_m$ and by endowments $e^1, \ldots, e^m$. An *equilibrium* for the *economy* $[(U_i, e^i), D]$ is a collection $(\theta^1, \ldots, \theta^m, q)$ such that, given the security-price vector q, for each agent i, θ^i solves $\sup_\theta U_i(e^i + D^\top \theta)$ subject to $q \cdot \theta = 0$, and such that $\sum_{i=1}^m \theta^i = 0$. The existence of equilibrium is treated in the exercises and in sources cited in the notes.

With $\operatorname{span}(D) \equiv \{D^\top \theta : \theta \in \mathbb{R}^N\}$ denoting the set of possible portfolio payoffs, markets are *complete* if $\operatorname{span}(D) = \mathbb{R}^S$, and are otherwise *incomplete*.

Let $e = e^1 + \cdots + e^m$ denote the aggregate endowment. A consumption *allocation* $(c^1, \ldots, c^m)$ in $\left(\mathbb{R}_+^S\right)^m$ is *feasible* if $c^1 + \cdots + c^m \leq e$. A feasible allocation $(c^1, \ldots, c^m)$ is *Pareto optimal* if there is no feasible allocation $(\hat{c}^1, \ldots, \hat{c}^m)$ with $U_i(\hat{c}^i) \geq U_i(c^i)$ for all i and with $U_i(\hat{c}^i) > U_i(c^i)$ for some i. Complete markets and the Pareto optimality of equilibrium allocations are almost equivalent properties of any economy.

Proposition. *Suppose markets are complete and $(\theta^1, \ldots, \theta^m, q)$ is an equilibrium. Then the associated equilibrium allocation is Pareto optimal.*

This is sometimes known as *The First Welfare Theorem*. The proof, requiring only the strict monotonicity of utilities, is left as an exercise. We have established the sufficiency of complete markets for Pareto optimality. The necessity of complete markets for the Pareto optimality of equilibrium allocations does not always follow. For example, if the initial endowment allocation $(e^1, \ldots, e^m)$ happens by chance to be Pareto optimal, then any equilibrium allocation is also Pareto optimal, regardless of the span of securities. It would be unusual, however, for the initial endowment to be Pareto optimal. Although beyond the scope of this book, it can be shown that, with incomplete markets and under natural assumptions on utility, for almost every endowment, the equilibrium allocation is not Pareto optimal.

E. Pareto Optimality and the Representative Agent

Aside from its allocational implications, Pareto optimality is also a convenient property for the purpose of security pricing. In order to see this, consider, for each vector $\lambda \in \mathbb{R}_+^m$ of "agent weights," the utility function $U_\lambda : \mathbb{R}_+^S \to \mathbb{R}$ defined by

$$U_\lambda(x) = \sup_{(c^1, \ldots, c^m)} \sum_{i=1}^m \lambda_i U_i(c^i) \quad \text{subject to} \quad c^1 + \cdots + c^m \leq x. \quad (6)$$

Lemma. *Suppose that, for all i, U_i is concave. An allocation $(c^1, \ldots, c^m)$ that is feasible is Pareto optimal if and only if there is some nonzero $\lambda \in \mathbb{R}_+^m$ such that $(c^1, \ldots, c^m)$ solves (6) at $x = e = c^1 + \cdots + c^m$.*

Proof: Suppose that $(c^1, \ldots, c^m)$ is Pareto optimal. Let

$$\mathcal{U} = \{y \in \mathbb{R}^m : y_i = U_i(x^i) - U_i(c^i), \ x \in \mathcal{A}\},$$

where $\mathcal{A}$ is the set of feasible allocations. Let $J = \{y \in \mathbb{R}_+^m : y \neq 0\}$. Since $\mathcal{U}$ is convex (by the concavity of utility functions) and $J \cap \mathcal{U}$ is empty (by Pareto optimality), the Separating Hyperplane Theorem (Appendix B) implies that there is a nonzero vector λ such that $\lambda \cdot y \leq \lambda \cdot z$ for each y in $\mathcal{U}$ and each z in J. Since $0 \in \mathcal{U}$, we know that $\lambda \geq 0$, proving the first part of the result. The second part is easy to show as an exercise. ∎

Proposition. *Suppose that, for all i, U_i is concave. Suppose that markets are complete and that $(\theta^1, \ldots, \theta^m, q)$ is an equilibrium. Then there exists some nonzero $\lambda \in \mathbb{R}_+^m$ such that $(0, q)$ is a (no-trade) equilibrium for the single-agent economy $[(U_\lambda, e), D]$ defined by (6). Moreover, the equilibrium consumption allocation $(c^1, \ldots, c^m)$ solves the allocation problem (6) at the aggregate endowment. That is, $U_\lambda(e) = \sum_i \lambda_i U_i(c^i)$.*

Proof: Since there is an equilibrium, there is no arbitrage, and therefore there is a state-price vector ψ. Since markets are complete, this implies that the problem of any agent i can be reduced to

$$\sup_{c \in \mathbb{R}_+^S} \ U_i(c) \quad \text{subject to} \quad \psi \cdot c \leq \psi \cdot e^i.$$

We can assume that e^i is not zero, for otherwise $c^i = 0$ and agent i can be eliminated from the problem without loss of generality. By the Saddle Point Theorem of Appendix B, there is a Lagrange multiplier $\alpha_i \geq 0$ such that c^i solves the problem

$$\sup_{c \in \mathbb{R}_+^S} \ U_i(c) - \alpha_i \left(\psi \cdot c - \psi \cdot e^i \right).$$

(The Slater condition is satisfied since e^i is not zero and $\psi \gg 0$.) Since U_i is strictly increasing, $\alpha_i > 0$. Let $\lambda_i = 1/\alpha_i$. For any feasible allocation $(x^1, \ldots, x^m)$, we have

$$\sum_{i=1}^m \lambda_i U_i(c^i) = \sum_{i=1}^m \left[\lambda_i U_i(c^i) - \lambda_i \alpha_i \left(\psi \cdot c^i - \psi \cdot e^i \right) \right]$$

$$\geq \sum_{i=1}^m \lambda_i \left[U_i(x^i) - \alpha_i \left(\psi \cdot x^i - \psi \cdot e^i \right) \right]$$

$$= \sum_{i=1}^m \lambda_i U_i(x^i) - \psi \cdot \sum_{i=1}^m (x^i - e^i)$$

$$\geq \sum_{i=1}^m \lambda_i U_i(x^i).$$

This shows that $(c^1, \ldots, c^m)$ solves the allocation problem (6). We must also show that no trade is optimal for the single agent with utility function U_λ

and endowment e. If not, there is some x in $\mathbb{R}_+^S$ such that $U_\lambda(x) > U_\lambda(e)$ and $\psi \cdot x \le \psi \cdot e$. By the definition of U_λ, this would imply the existence of an allocation $(x^1, \ldots, x^m)$, not necessarily feasible, such that

$$\sum_{i=1}^m \lambda_i \left[U_i(x^i) - \psi \cdot (x^i - e^i) \right] > \sum_{i=1}^m \lambda_i \left[U_i(c^i) - \psi \cdot (c^i - e^i) \right],$$

which contradicts the fact that, for each agent i, (c^i, α_i) is a saddle point for that agent's problem. ∎

Corollary 1. *If, moreoever, U_λ is differentiable at e, then λ can be chosen so that $\partial U_\lambda(e)$ is a state-price vector, meaning*

$$q = D\partial U_\lambda(e). \tag{7}$$

Corollary 2. *Suppose there is a fixed vector p of state probabilities such that, for all i, $U_i(c) = E[u_i(c)] \equiv \sum_{j=1}^S p_j u_i(c_j)$, for some $u_i(\cdot)$. Then $U_\lambda(c) = E[u_\lambda(c)]$, where, for each y in $\mathbb{R}_+$,*

$$u_\lambda(y) = \max_{x \in \mathbb{R}_+^m} \sum_{i=1}^M \lambda_i u_i(x_i) \quad \text{subject to} \quad x_1 + \cdots + x_m \le y.$$

In this case, (7) is equivalent to $q = E[Du_\lambda'(e)]$.

Extensions of this *representative-agent* asset pricing formula will crop up frequently in later chapters. Conditions for the differentiability of U_λ are given in an exercise. It is enough that the equilibrium allocation $(c^1, \ldots, c^m)$ is strictly positive and that, for all i, U_i is of the expected utility form $U_i(c) = E[u_i(c)]$, where u_i is strictly concave and differentiable at c^i.

F. State-Price Beta Models

We fix a vector $p \gg 0$ in $\mathbb{R}^S$ of probabilities for this section, and for any x in $\mathbb{R}^S$ we write $E(x) = p_1 x_1 + \cdots + p_S x_S$. For any x and π in $\mathbb{R}^S$, we take $x\pi$ to be the vector $(x_1 \pi_1, \ldots, x_S \pi_S)$. The following version of the *Riesz Representation Theorem* can be shown as an exercise.

Lemma. *Suppose $F : \mathbb{R}^S \to \mathbb{R}$ is linear. Then there is a unique π in $\mathbb{R}^S$ such that, for all x in $\mathbb{R}^S$, we have $F(x) = E(\pi x)$. Moreover, F is strictly increasing if and only if $\pi \gg 0$.*

Corollary. *A dividend-price pair (D, q) admits no arbitrage if and only if there is some $\pi \gg 0$ in $\mathbb{R}^S$ such that $q = E(D\pi)$.*

Proof: Given a state-price vector ψ, let $\pi_s = \psi_s / p_s$. Conversely, if π has the assumed property, then $\psi_s = p_s \pi_s$ defines a state-price vector ψ. ∎

Given (D, q), we refer to any vector π given by this result as a *state-price deflator*. For example, the representative-agent pricing model of Corollary 2 of Section 1E shows that we can take $\pi_s = u'_\lambda(e_s)$.

For any x and y in $\mathbb{R}^S$, the *covariance* $\mathrm{cov}(x, y) \equiv E(xy) - E(x)E(y)$ is a measure of covariation between x and y that is useful in asset pricing applications. For any such x and y with $\mathrm{var}(y) \equiv \mathrm{cov}(y, y) \neq 0$, we can always represent x in the form $x = \alpha + \beta y + \epsilon$, where $\beta = \mathrm{cov}(y, x)/\mathrm{var}(y)$, where $\mathrm{cov}(y, \epsilon) = E(\epsilon) = 0$, and where α is a scalar. This *linear regression* of x on y is uniquely defined. The coefficient β is called the associated *regression coefficient*.

Suppose (D, q) admits no arbitrage. For any portfolio θ with $q \cdot \theta \neq 0$, the *return* on θ is the vector R^θ in $\mathbb{R}^S$ defined by $R^\theta_s = (D^\top \theta)_s / q \cdot \theta$. Fixing a state-price deflator π, for any such portfolio θ, we have $E(\pi R^\theta) = 1$. Suppose there is a *riskless portfolio*, meaning some portfolio θ with constant return R^0. We then call R^0 the *riskless return*. A bit of algebra shows that, for any portfolio θ with a return, we have

$$E(R^\theta) - R^0 = -\frac{\mathrm{cov}(R^\theta, \pi)}{E(\pi)}.$$

Thus, covariation with π has a negative effect on expected return, as one might expect from the interpretation of state prices as shadow prices for wealth.

The *correlation* between any x and y in $\mathbb{R}^S$ is zero if either has zero variance, and is otherwise defined by

$$\mathrm{corr}(x, y) = \frac{\mathrm{cov}(x, y)}{\sqrt{\mathrm{var}(x)\,\mathrm{var}(y)}}.$$

There is always a portfolio θ^* solving the problem

$$\sup_\theta \mathrm{corr}(D^\top \theta, \pi). \tag{8}$$

If there is such a portfolio θ^* with a return R^* having nonzero variance, then it can be shown as an exercise that, for any return R^θ,

$$E(R^\theta) - R^0 = \beta_\theta \left[E(R^*) - R^0 \right], \tag{9}$$

where

$$\beta_\theta = \frac{\mathrm{cov}(R^*, R^\theta)}{\mathrm{var}(R^*)}.$$

If markets are complete, then R^* is of course perfectly correlated with the state-price deflator.

Formula (9) is a *state-price beta model*, showing excess expected returns on portfolios to be proportional to the excess return on a portfolio having maximal correlation with a state-price deflator, where the constant of proportionality is the associated regression coefficient. The formula can be extended to the case in which there is no riskless return. Another exercise carries this idea, under additional assumptions, to the *Capital Asset Pricing Model*, or *CAPM*.

Exercises

1.1 The dividend-price pair (D, q) of Section 1A is defined to be *weakly arbitrage-free* if $q \cdot \theta \geq 0$ whenever $D^\top \theta \geq 0$. Show that (D, q) is weakly arbitrage-free if and only if there exists ("weak" state prices) $\psi \in \mathbb{R}_+^S$ such that $q = D\psi$. This fact is known as *Farkas's Lemma*.

1.2 Prove the assertion in Section 1A that (D, q) is arbitrage-free if and only if there exists some $\psi \in \mathbb{R}_{++}^S$ such that $q = D\psi$. Instead of following the proof given in Section 1A, use the following result, sometimes known as the *Theorem of the Alternative*.

Stiemke's Lemma. *Suppose A is an $m \times n$ matrix. Then one and only one of the following is true:*

    (a) There exists x in $\mathbb{R}_{++}^n$ with $Ax = 0$.
    (b) There exists y in $\mathbb{R}^m$ with $y^\top A > 0$.

1.3 Show, for $U(c) \equiv E[u(c)]$ as defined by (3), that (2) is equivalent to (4).

1.4 Prove the existence of an equilibrium as defined in Section 1D under these assumptions: There exists some portfolio θ with payoff $D^\top \theta > 0$ and, for all i, $e^i \gg 0$ and U_i is continuous, strictly concave, and strictly increasing. This is a demanding exercise, and calls for the following general result.

Kakutani's Fixed Point Theorem. *Suppose Z is a nonempty convex compact subset of $\mathbb{R}^n$ and, for each x in Z, $\varphi(x)$ is a nonempty convex compact subset of Z. Suppose also that $\{(x, y) \in Z \times Z : x \in \varphi(y)\}$ is closed. Then there exists x^* in Z such that $x^* \in \varphi(x^*)$.*

1.5 Prove Proposition 1D. Hint: The maintained assumption of strict monotonicity of $U_i(\cdot)$ should be used.

1.6 Suppose that the endowment allocation $(e^1, \ldots, e^m)$ is Pareto optimal.

(A) Show, as claimed in Section 1D, that any equilibrium allocation is Pareto optimal.

(B) Show that, in fact, $(e^1, \ldots, e^m)$ is itself an equilibrium allocation if U_i is concave for all i.

1.7 Prove Proposition 1C. Hint: A continuous real-valued function on a compact set has a maximum.

1.8 Prove Corollary 1 of Proposition 1E.

1.9 Prove Corollary 2 of Proposition 1E.

1.10 Suppose, in addition to the assumptions of Proposition 1E, that

   (a) $e = e^1 + \cdots + e^m$ is in $\mathbb{R}^S_{++}$;
   (b) for all i, U_i is concave and twice continuously differentiable in $\mathbb{R}^S_{++}$;
   (c) for all i, c^i is in $\mathbb{R}^S_{++}$ and the Hessian matrix $\partial^2 U(c^i)$, which is negative semi-definite by concavity, is in fact negative definite.

Property (c) can be replaced with the assumption of *regular preferences*, as defined in a source cited below in the Notes.

(A) Show that the assumption that $\partial U_\lambda(e)$ exists is justified and, moreover, that for each i there is a scalar $\gamma_i > 0$ such that $\partial U_\lambda(e) = \gamma_i \partial U_i(c^i)$. (This co-linearity is known as "equal marginal rates of substitution," a property of any Pareto optimal allocation.) Hint: Use the following:

Implicit Function Theorem. Suppose, for given m and n, that $f : \mathbb{R}^m \times \mathbb{R}^n \to \mathbb{R}^m \times \mathbb{R}^n$ is C^k (k times continuously differentiable) for some $k \geq 1$. Suppose also that the Jacobian matrix $\partial f(a, b)$ of f at some (a, b) is nonsingular. If $f(a, b) = 0$, then there exist scalars $\epsilon > 0$ and $\delta > 0$ and a C^k function $Z : \mathbb{R}^m \to \mathbb{R}^n$ such that: If $\|x - a\| < \epsilon$, then $f[x, Z(x)] = 0$ and $\|Z(x) - b\| < \delta$.

(B) Show that the negative definite part of condition (c) is satisfied if $e \gg 0$ and, for all i, U_i is an expected utility function of the form $U_i(c) = E[u_i(c)]$, where u_i is strictly concave with an unbounded derivative on $(0, \infty)$.

1.11 (Binomial Option Pricing) As an application of the results in Section 1A, consider the following two-state ($S = 2$) option-pricing problem.

There are $N = 3$ securities:

(a) a stock, with initial price $q_1 > 0$ and dividend $D_{11} = Gq_1$ in state 1 and dividend $D_{12} = Bq_1$ in state 2, where $G > B > 0$ are the "good" and "bad" gross returns, respectively;

(b) a riskless bond, with initial price $q_2 > 0$ and dividend $D_{21} = D_{22} = Rq_2$ in both states (that is, R is the riskless return and R^{-1} is the discount);

(c) a *call option* on the stock, with initial price $q_3 = C$ and dividend $D_{3j} = (D_{1j} - K)^+ \equiv \max(D_{1j} - K, 0)$ for both states $j = 1$ and $j = 2$, where $K \geq 0$ is the *exercise price* of the option. (The call option gives its holder the right, but not the obligation, to pay K for the stock, with dividend, after the state is revealed.)

(A) Show necessary and sufficient conditions on G, B, and R for the absence of arbitrage involving only the stock and bond.

(B) Assuming no arbitrage for the three securities, calculate the call-option price C explicitly in terms of q_1, G, R, B, and K. Find the state-price probabilities $\hat{\psi}_1$ and $\hat{\psi}_2$ referred to in Section 1B in terms of G, B, and R, and show that $C = R^{-1}\hat{E}(D_3)$, where $\hat{E}$ denotes expectation with respect to $(\hat{\psi}_1, \hat{\psi}_2)$.

1.12   (CAPM) In the setting of Section 1D, suppose $(c^1, \ldots, c^m)$ is an equilibrium consumption allocation. For any agent i, suppose utility is of the expected-utility form $U_i(c) = E[u_i(c)]$. For any agent i, suppose there are fixed positive constants $\bar{c}$ and b_i such that, for any state j, we have $c_j^i < \bar{c}$ and $u_i(x) = x - b_i x^2$ for all $x \leq \bar{c}$.

(A) In the context of Corollary 2 of Section 1E, show that $u_\lambda'(e) = k - Ke$ for some positive constants k and K. From this, derive the CAPM:

$$q = AE(D) - B\mathrm{cov}(D, e), \qquad (10)$$

for positive constants A and B, where $\mathrm{cov}(D, e) \in \mathbb{R}^N$ is the vector of covariances between the security dividends and the aggregate endowment.

Suppose, for a given portfolio θ, that each of the following is well defined:

- the return $R^\theta \equiv D^\top \theta / q \cdot \theta$;
- the return R^M on a portfolio M with payoff $D^\top M = e$;
- the return R^0 on any portfolio θ^0 with $\mathrm{cov}(D^\top \theta^0, e) = 0$;
- $\beta_\theta = \mathrm{cov}(R^\theta, R^M)/\mathrm{var}(R^M)$.

The return R^M is sometimes called the *market return*. The return R^0 is called the *zero-beta return*, and is the return on a riskless bond if one exists. Prove the "beta" form of the CAPM:

$$E(R^\theta - R^0) = \beta_\theta E(R^M - R^0). \tag{11}$$

(B) Part (A) relies on the completeness of markets. Without any such assumption, but assuming that the equilibrium allocation $(c^1, \ldots, c^m)$ is strictly positive, show that the same beta form (11) applies, provided we extend the definition of the market return R^M to be the return on any portfolio solving:

$$\sup_{\theta \in \mathbb{R}^N} \operatorname{corr}(R^\theta, e). \tag{12}$$

For complete markets, $\operatorname{corr}(R^M, e) = 1$, so the result of part (A) is a special case.

(C) The CAPM applies essentially as stated without the quadratic expected-utility assumption provided that each agent i is *strictly variance-averse*, in that $U_i(x) > U_i(y)$ whenever $E(x) = E(y)$ and $\operatorname{var}(x) < \operatorname{var}(y)$. Formalize this statement by providing a reasonable set of supporting technical conditions.

We remark that a common alternative formulation of the CAPM allows security portfolios in initial endowments $\hat{\theta}^1, \ldots, \hat{\theta}^m$ with $\sum_{i=1}^m \hat{\theta}^i_j = 1$ for all j. In this case, with the total endowment e redefined by $e = \sum_{i=1}^m e^i + D^\top \theta^i$, the same CAPM (11) applies. If $e^i = 0$ for all i, then even in incomplete markets, $\operatorname{corr}(R^M, e) = 1$, since (12) is solved by $\theta = (1, 1, \ldots, 1)$. The Notes below provide references.

1.13 An *Arrow-Debreu equilibrium* for $[(U_i, e^i), D]$ is a nonzero vector ψ in $\mathbb{R}^S_+$ and a feasible consumption allocation $(c^1, \ldots, c^m)$ such that, for each i, c^i solves $\sup_c U_i(c)$ subject to $\psi \cdot c^i \le \psi \cdot e^i$. Suppose that markets are complete, in that $\operatorname{span}(D) = \mathbb{R}^S$. Show that $(c^1, \ldots, c^m)$ is an Arrow-Debreu consumption allocation if and only if it is an equilibrium consumption allocation in the sense of Section 1D.

1.14 Suppose (D, q) admits no arbitrage. Show that there is a unique state-price vector if and only if markets are complete.

1.15 (Aggregation)   For the "representative-agent" problem (6), suppose, for all i, that $U_i(c) = E[u(c)]$, where $u(c) = c^\gamma/\gamma$ for some nonzero scalar $\gamma < 1$.

(A) Show, for any nonzero agent weight vector $\lambda \in \mathbb{R}_+^S$, that $U_\lambda(c) = E[kc^\gamma/\gamma]$ for some scalar $k > 0$, and that (6) is solved by $c^i = k_i c$ for some scalar $k_i \geq 0$ that is nonzero if and only if λ_i is nonzero.

(B) With this special utility assumption, prove Proposition 1E after replacing the assumption that markets are complete with the assumption that $e^i \in$ span (D) for all i. Calculate the equilibrium and show that the equilibrium consumption allocation is Pareto optimal.

1.16 (State-Price Beta Model) This exercise is to prove and extend the state-price beta model (9) of Section 1F.

(A) Show problem (8) is solved by any portfolio θ such that $\pi = D^\top \theta + \epsilon$, where $\text{cov}(\epsilon, D^j) = 0$ for any security j, where $D^j \in \mathbb{R}^S$ is the payoff of security j.

(B) Given a solution θ to (8) such that R^θ is well defined with nonzero variance, prove (9).

(C) Reformulate (9) for the case in which there is no riskless return by redefining R^0 to be the expected return on any portfolio θ such that R^θ is well defined and $\text{cov}(R^\theta, \pi) = 0$, assuming such a portfolio exists.

1.17 Prove the Riesz representation lemma of Section 1F. The following hint is perhaps unnecessary in this simple setting, but allows the result to be extended to a broad variety of spaces called *Hilbert spaces*. Given a vector space L, a function $(\cdot \mid \cdot) : L \times L \to \mathbb{R}$ is called an *inner product* for L if, for any x, y, and z in L and any scalar α, we have the five properties:

    (a) $(x \mid y) = (y \mid x)$
    (b) $(x + y \mid z) = (x \mid z) + (y \mid z)$
    (c) $(\alpha x \mid y) = \alpha(x \mid y)$
    (d) $(x \mid x) \geq 0$
    (e) $(x \mid x) = 0$ if and only if $x = 0$.

Suppose a finite-dimensional vector space L has an inner product $(\cdot \mid \cdot)$. (This defines a special case of a Hilbert space.) Two vectors x and y are defined to be *orthogonal* if $(x \mid y) = 0$. For any linear subspace H of L and any x in L, it can be shown that there is a unique y in H such that $(x - y \mid z) = 0$ for all z in H. This vector y is the orthogonal projection in L of x onto H, and solves the problem $\min_{h \in H} \|x - h\|$. Let $L = \mathbb{R}^S$. For any x and y in L, let $(x \mid y) = E(xy)$. We must show that, given a linear functional F, there is a unique π with $F(x) = (\pi \mid x)$ for all x. Let $J = \{x : F(x) = 0\}$. If

$J = L$, then F is the zero functional, and the unique representation is $\pi = 0$. If not, there is some z such that $F(z) = 1$ and $(z \mid x) = 0$ for all x in J. Show this using the idea of orthogonal projection. Then show that $\pi = z/(z \mid z)$ represents F, using the fact that, for any x, we have $x - F(x)z \in J$.

Notes

The basic approach of this chapter follows Arrow (1953). The state-pricing implications of no arbitrage found in Section 1A originate with Ross (1978). The idea of "risk-neutral" probabilities apparently originates in Arrow (1970: 131), a version of Arrow (1953). Proposition 1D is the First Welfare Theorem of Arrow (1951) and Debreu (1954). The generic inoptimality of incomplete markets equilibrium allocations can be gleaned from sources cited by Geanakoplos (1990). Werner (1991) treats constrained optimality.

The "representative-agent" approach goes back, at least, to Negishi (1960). The existence of a representative agent is no more than an illustrative simplification in this setting, and should not be confused with the more demanding notion of aggregation of Gorman (1953) found in Exercise 1.15. In Chapter 9, the existence of a representative agent with smooth utility, based on Exercise 1.11, is important for technical reasons.

Debreu (1972) provides preference assumptions that substitute for the existence of a negative-definite Hessian matrix of each agent's utility function at the equilibrium allocation. For more on regular preferences and the differential approach to general equilibrium, see Mas-Colell (1985) and Balasko (1989). Kreps (1988) reviews the theory of choice and utility representation of preferences.

The CAPM is due to Sharpe (1964) and Lintner (1965). The version without a riskless asset is due to Black (1972). For Farkas's and Stiemke's Lemmas, and other forms of the Theorem of the Alternative, see Gale (1960).

Arrow and Debreu (1954) and, in a slightly different model, McKenzie (1954) are responsible for a proof of the existence of complete markets equilibria. Debreu (1982) surveys the existence problem. Standard introductory treatments of general equilibrium theory are given by Debreu (1959) and Hildenbrand and Kirman (1989). In this setting, with incomplete markets, Polemarchakis and Siconolfi (1991) address the failure of existence unless one has a portfolio θ with payoff $D^\top\theta > 0$. Geanakoplos (1990) surveys other literature on the existence of equilibria in incomplete markets, some of which takes the alternative of defining security payoffs in nominal units of account, while allowing consumption of multiple commodities. Most of the literature allows for an initial period of consumption before the realization of the uncertain state. Hellwig (1991), Mas-Colell and Monteiro (1991), and Monteiro (1991) have recently shown existence with a continuum of states. Geanakoplos and Polemarchakis (1986) show a failure, in incomplete markets equilibrium, of even constrained Pareto optimality (in a certain sense). (See, however, Mas-Colell [1987].) Geanakoplos and Polemarchakis (1986) and Chae (1988) show existence in a model closely related to that studied in this chapter. Grodal and Vind (1988) and Yamazaki (1991) show existence with alternative formulations. With multiple commodities or multiple periods, existence is not guaranteed under any natural conditions, as shown by Hart (1975), who gives a counterexample. For these more delicate cases, the literature on generic existence is cited in the Notes to Chapter 2 below. Nielsen (1990a,b) addresses the existence of equilibrium in the CAPM. Balasko and Cass (1986) and Balasko, Cass, and Siconolfi (1990) treat equilibrium with constrained participation in security trading.

The binomial option-pricing formula of Exercise 1.11 is from an early edition of William Sharpe's text, *Investments* (1985), and is extended in Chapter 2 to a multiperiod setting. The hint given for the demonstration of the Riesz representation exercise is condensed from the proof given by Luenberger (1969) of the *Riesz-Frechet Theorem*: For any Hilbert space H with inner product $(\cdot \mid \cdot)$, any continuous linear functional $F : H \to \mathbb{R}$ has a unique π in H such that $F(x) = (\pi \mid x)$, $x \in H$. The Fixed Point Theorem of Exercise 1.4 is from Kakutani (1941).

2

The Basic Multiperiod Model

THIS CHAPTER EXTENDS the results of Chapter 1 on arbitrage, optimality, and equilibrium to a multiperiod setting. A connection is drawn between state prices and martingales for the purpose of representing security prices. The exercises include the consumption-based capital asset pricing model and the multiperiod "binomial" option pricing model.

A. Uncertainty

As in Chapter 1, there is some finite set, say Ω, of states. In order to handle multiperiod issues, however, we will treat uncertainty a bit more formally as a *probability space* $(\Omega, \mathcal{F}, P)$, with $\mathcal{F}$ denoting the *tribe* of subsets of Ω that are *events* (and can therefore be assigned a probability), and with P a *probability measure* assigning to any event B in $\mathcal{F}$ its probability $P(B)$. Those not familiar with the definition of a probability space can consult Appendix A.

There are $T + 1$ dates: $0, 1, \ldots, T$. At each of these, a tribe $\mathcal{F}_t \subset \mathcal{F}$ denotes the set of events corresponding to the information available at time t. That is, if an event B is in $\mathcal{F}_t$, then at time t this event is known to be true or false. (A definition of tribes in terms of "partitions" of Ω is given in Exercise 2.11.) We adopt the usual convention that $\mathcal{F}_t \subset \mathcal{F}_s$ whenever $t \leq s$, meaning that events are never "forgotten." For simplicity, we also take it that every event in $\mathcal{F}_0$ has probability 0 or 1, meaning roughly that there is no information at time $t = 0$. Taken altogether, the *filtration* $\mathbb{F} = \{\mathcal{F}_0, \ldots, \mathcal{F}_T\}$ represents how information is revealed through time. For any random variable Y, we let $E_t(Y) = E(Y \mid \mathcal{F}_t)$ denote the conditional expectation of Y given $\mathcal{F}_t$. (Appendix A provides definitions of random variables and of conditional expectation.) An *adapted process* is a sequence $X = \{X_0, \ldots, X_T\}$ such that, for each t, X_t is a random variable with respect to $(\Omega, \mathcal{F}_t)$. Informally, this means that at time t, the outcome of X_t is known.

An adapted process X is a *martingale* if, for any times t and $s > t$, we have $E_t(X_s) = X_t$. As we shall see, martingales are useful in the characterization of security prices. In order to simplify things, for any two random variables Y and Z, we always write $Y = Z$ if the probability that $Y \neq Z$ is zero.

B. Security Markets

A security is a claim to an adapted *dividend process*, say δ, with δ_t denoting the dividend paid by the security at time t. Each security has an adapted *security-price process* S, so that S_t is the price of the security, *ex dividend*, at time t. That is, at each time t, the security pays its dividend δ_t and is then available for trade at the price S_t. This convention implies that δ_0 plays no role in determining ex-dividend prices. The *cum-dividend* security price at time t is $S_t + \delta_t$.

Suppose there are N securities defined by the $\mathbb{R}^N$-valued adapted dividend process $\delta = (\delta^1, \ldots, \delta^N)$. These securities have some price process $S = (S^1, \ldots, S^N)$. A *trading strategy* is an adapted process θ in $\mathbb{R}^N$. Here, $\theta_t = (\theta_t^1, \ldots, \theta_t^N)$ represents the portfolio held after trading at time t. The dividend process δ^θ *generated* by a trading strategy θ is defined by

$$\delta_t^\theta = \theta_{t-1} \cdot (S_t + \delta_t) - \theta_t \cdot S_t, \tag{1}$$

with "θ_{-1}" taken to be zero by convention.

C. Arbitrage, State Prices, and Martingales

Given a dividend-price pair (δ, S) for N securities, a trading strategy θ is an *arbitrage* if $\delta^\theta > 0$. Let Θ denote the space of trading strategies. For any θ and φ in Θ and scalars a and b, we have $a\delta^\theta + b\delta^\varphi = \delta^{a\theta + b\varphi}$. Thus the *marketed subspace* $M = \{\delta^\theta : \theta \in \Theta\}$ of dividend processes generated by trading strategies is a linear subspace of the space L of adapted processes.

Proposition. There is no arbitrage if and only if there is a strictly increasing linear function $F : L \to \mathbb{R}$ such that $F(\delta^\theta) = 0$ for any trading strategy θ.

Proof: The proof is almost identical to the first part of the proof of Theorem 1A. Let $L_+ = \{c \in L : c \geq 0\}$. There is no arbitrage if and only if the cone L_+ and the linear subspace M intersect precisely at zero. Suppose there is no arbitrage. The Separating Hyperplane Theorem, in a form given in Appendix B for cones, implies the existence of a nonzero linear functional F such that $F(x) < F(y)$ for each x in M and each nonzero y in L_+. Since M

is a linear subspace, this implies that $F(x) = 0$ for each x in M, and thus that $F(y) > 0$ for each non-zero y in L_+. This implies that F is strictly increasing. The converse is immediate. ∎

The following result gives a convenient *Riesz representation* of a linear function on the space of adapted processes. Proof is left as an exercise, extending the single-period Riesz representation lemma of Section 1F.

Lemma. *For each linear function $F : L \to \mathbb{R}$ there is a unique π in L, called the Riesz representation of F, such that*

$$F(x) = E\left(\sum_{t=0}^{T} \pi_t x_t\right), \quad x \in L.$$

If F is strictly increasing, then π is strictly positive.

For convenience, we call any strictly positive adapted process a *deflator*. A deflator π is a *state-price deflator* if, for all t,

$$S_t = \frac{1}{\pi_t} E_t\left(\sum_{j=t+1}^{T} \pi_j \delta_j\right). \tag{2}$$

For $t = T$, the right-hand side of (2) is zero, so $S_T = 0$ whenever there is a state-price deflator. The notion here of a state-price deflator is thus a natural extension of that of Chapter 1. It can be shown as an exercise that π is a state-price deflator if and only if, for any trading strategy θ,

$$\theta_t \cdot S_t = \frac{1}{\pi_t} E_t\left(\sum_{j=t+1}^{T} \pi_j \delta_j^{\theta}\right), \quad t < T, \tag{3}$$

meaning roughly that the market value of a trading strategy is, at any time, the state-price discounted expected future dividends generated by the strategy.

The *gain process* G for (δ, S) is defined by $G_t = S_t + \sum_{j=1}^{t} \delta_j$. Given a deflator γ, the *deflated gain process* G^γ is defined by $G_t^\gamma = \gamma_t S_t + \sum_{j=1}^{t} \gamma_j \delta_j$. We can think of deflation as a change of numeraire. One can show as an easy exercise that π is a state-price deflator if and only if $S_T = 0$ and the state-price-deflated gain process G^π is a martingale.

Theorem. *The dividend-price pair (δ, S) admits no arbitrage if and only if there is a state-price deflator.*

Proof: Suppose there is no arbitrage. Then $S_T = 0$, for otherwise the strategy θ is an arbitrage when defined by $\theta_t = 0$, $t < T$, $\theta_T = -S_T$. The previous proposition implies that there is some strictly increasing linear function $F : L \to \mathbb{R}$ such that $F(\delta^\theta) = 0$ for any strategy θ. By the previous lemma, there is some deflator π such that $F(x) = E(\sum_{t=0}^{T} x_t \pi_t)$ for all x in L. This implies that $E(\sum_{t=0}^{T} \delta_t^\theta \pi_t) = 0$ for any strategy θ.

We must prove (2), or equivalently, that G^π is a martingale. From Appendix A, an adapted process X is a martingale if and only if $E(X_\tau) = X_0$ for any stopping time $\tau \le T$. Consider, for an arbitrary security n and an arbitrary stopping time $\tau \le T$, the trading strategy θ defined by $\theta^k = 0$ for $k \ne n$ and $\theta_t^n = 1$, $t < \tau$, with $\theta_t^n = 0$, $t \ge \tau$. Since $E(\sum_{t=0}^{T} \pi_t \delta_t^\theta) = 0$, we have

$$E\left(-S_0^n \pi_0 + \sum_{t=0}^{\tau} \pi_t \delta_t^n + \pi_\tau S_\tau^n \right) = 0,$$

implying that the deflated gain process $G^{n\pi}$ of security n satisfies $G_0^{n\pi} = E(G_\tau^{n\pi})$. Since τ is arbitrary, $G^{n\pi}$ is a martingale, and since n is arbitrary, G^π is a martingale.

This shows that absence of arbitrage implies the existence of a state-price deflator. The converse is easy. ∎

D. Individual Agent Optimality

We introduce an agent, defined by a strictly increasing utility function U on the set L_+ of non-negative adapted "consumption" processes, and by an endowment process e in L_+. Given (δ, S), a trading strategy θ leaves the agent with the total consumption process $e + \delta^\theta$. Thus the agent has the *budget-feasible consumption set*

$$X = \{e + \delta^\theta \in L_+ : \theta \in \Theta\},$$

and the problem

$$\sup_{c \in X} U(c). \tag{4}$$

The existence of a solution to (4) implies the absence of arbitrage. Conversely, it is shown as an exercise that if U is continuous, then the absence of arbitrage implies that there exists a solution to (4). (For purposes of checking continuity or the closedness of sets in L, we will say that c_n converges to c if $c_n(\omega, t) \to c(\omega, t)$ for all ω and t. Then U is continuous if $U(c_n) \to U(c)$ whenever $c_n \to c$.)

Suppose that (4) has a strictly positive solution c^* and U is differentiable at c^*. We can use the first order conditions for optimality (which can be reviewed in Appendix B) to characterize security prices in terms of the derivatives of the utility function U at c^*. Specifically, for any c in L, the derivative of U at c^* in the direction c is the derivative $g'(0)$, where $g(\alpha) = U(c^* + \alpha c)$ for any scalar α sufficiently small in absolute value. That is, $g'(0)$ is the marginal rate of improvement of utility as one moves in the direction c away from c^*. This derivative is denoted $\nabla U(c^*; c)$. By saying that U is differentiable at c^*, we mean that this derivative exists for any c in L. In this case, we say that $\nabla U(c^*)$ exists and treat it as a linear function on L into $\mathbb{R}$. Since δ^θ is a budget-feasible direction of change for any trading strategy θ, the first order conditions for optimality of c^* imply that

$$\nabla U(c^*; \delta^\theta) = 0, \quad \theta \in \Theta.$$

We now have the characterization of a state-price deflator.

Proposition. *Suppose that (4) has a strictly positive solution c^* and that $\nabla U(c^*)$ exists and is strictly increasing. Then there is no arbitrage and a state-price deflator is given by the Riesz representation π of $\nabla U(c^*)$:*

$$\nabla U(c^*; x) = E\left(\sum_{t=0}^{T} \pi_t x_t\right), \quad x \in L.$$

Despite our standing assumption that U is strictly increasing, $\nabla U(c^*)$ need not in general be strictly increasing, but is so if U is concave.

As an example, suppose U has the *additive* form

$$U(c) = E\left[\sum_{t=0}^{T} u_t(c_t)\right], \quad c \in L_+, \tag{5}$$

for some $u_t : \mathbb{R}_+ \to \mathbb{R}$, $t \geq 0$. It is then an exercise to show that, if $\nabla U(c)$ exists, then

$$\nabla U(c; x) = E\left[\sum_{t=0}^{T} u_t'(c_t) x_t\right]. \tag{6}$$

If, for all t, u_t is concave with an unbounded derivative and e is strictly positive, then any solution c^* to (4) is strictly positive.

Corollary. *Suppose U is defined by (5). Under the conditions of the Proposition, for any times t and $\tau \geq t$,*

$$S_t = \frac{1}{u_t'(c_t^*)} E_t\left[S_\tau u_\tau'(c_\tau^*) + \sum_{j=t+1}^{\tau} \delta_j u_j'(c_j^*)\right].$$

Extending this classical result for additive utility, the exercises include other utility examples such as *habit-formation* utility and *recursive* utility. As in Chapter 1, we now turn to the multi-agent case.

E. Equilibrium and Pareto Optimality

Suppose there are m agents; agent i is defined as above by a strictly increasing utility function $U_i : L_+ \to \mathbb{R}$ and an endowment process $e^i \in L_+$. An *equilibrium* is a collection $(\theta^1, \ldots, \theta^m, S)$, where S is a security-price process and, for each i, θ^i is a trading strategy solving

$$\sup_{\theta \in \Theta} \ U_i(c) \quad \text{subject to} \quad c = e^i + \delta^\theta \in L_+, \tag{7}$$

with $\sum_{i=1}^m \theta^i = 0$.

We define markets to be *complete* if, for each process x in L, there is some trading strategy θ with $\delta_t^\theta = x_t$, $t \geq 1$. Complete markets thus means that any consumption process x can be obtained by investing some amount at time 0 in a trading strategy that generates the dividend x_t in each period t after 0. With the same definition of Pareto optimality, Proposition 1C carries over to this multiperiod setting. Any equilibrium $(\theta^1, \ldots, \theta^m, S)$ has an associated feasible consumption allocation $(c^1, \ldots, c^m)$ defined by letting $c^i - e^i$ be the dividend process generated by θ^i.

Proposition. *Suppose $(\theta^1, \ldots, \theta^m, S)$ is an equilibrium and markets are complete. Then the associated consumption allocation is Pareto optimal.*

The completeness of markets depends on the security-price process S itself. Indeed, the dependence of the marketed subspace on S makes the existence of an equilibrium a nontrivial issue. We ignore existence here and refer to the Notes for some relevant sources.

F. Equilibrium Asset Pricing

Again following the ideas in Chapter 1, we define for each λ in $\mathbb{R}_+^m$ the utility function $U_\lambda : L_+ \to \mathbb{R}$ by

$$U_\lambda(x) = \sup_{(c^1, \ldots, c^m)} \ \sum_{i=1}^m \lambda_i \, U_i(c^i) \quad \text{subject to} \quad c^1 + \cdots + c^m \leq x. \tag{8}$$

Proposition. *Suppose, for all i, that U_i is concave and strictly increasing. Suppose that $(\theta^1, \ldots, \theta^m, S)$ is an equilibrium and that markets are complete. Then there exists some nonzero $\lambda \in \mathbb{R}_+^m$ such that $(0, S)$ is a (no-trade) equilibrium for the* *one-agent economy* $[(U_\lambda, e), \delta]$, *where* $e = e^1 + \cdots + e^m$. *With this* λ *and with* $x = e = e^1 + \cdots + e^m$, *problem (8) is solved by the equilibrium consumption allocation.*

Proof is assigned as an exercise. The result is essentially the same as Proposition 1D. A method of proof, as well as the intuition for this proposition, is that, with complete markets, a state-price deflator π represents Lagrange multipliers for consumption in the various periods and states for all of the agents simultaneously, as well as for the *representative agent* (U_λ, e).

Corollary 1. *If, moreover, U_λ is differentiable at e, then λ can be chosen so that, for any times t and $\tau \geq t$, there is a state-price deflator π equal to the Riesz representation of $\nabla U_\lambda(e)$.*

Differentiability of U_λ at e can be shown by exactly the arguments used in Exercise 1.10.

Corollary 2. *Suppose, for each i, that U_i is of the additive form:*

$$U_i(c) = E\left[\sum_{t=0}^{T} u_{it}(c_t) \right].$$

Then U_λ is also additive, with

$$U_\lambda(c) = E\left[\sum_{t=0}^{T} u_{\lambda t}(c_t) \right],$$

where

$$u_{\lambda t}(y) = \sup_{x \in \mathbb{R}_+^m} \sum_{i=1}^{m} \lambda_i \, u_{it}(x_i) \text{ subject to } x_1 + \cdots + x_m \leq y.$$

In this case, the differentiability of U_λ at e implies that, for any times t and $\tau \geq t$,

$$S_t = \frac{1}{u'_{\lambda t}(e_t)} \, E_t\left[u'_{\lambda \tau}(e_\tau) S_\tau + \sum_{j=t+1}^{\tau} u'_{\lambda j}(e_j)\delta_j \right]. \tag{9}$$

G. Arbitrage and Equivalent Martingale Measures

This section shows the equivalence between the absence of arbitrage and the existence of a probability measure Q with the property, roughly speaking, that discounted gain processes are martingales under Q.

There is *short-term riskless borrowing* at a given time $t < T$ if there is a trading strategy θ with:

(a) $\delta_s^\theta = 0$, $s < t$;
(b) $\delta_{t+1}^\theta = 1$; and
(c) $\delta_s^\theta = 0$, $s > t + 1$.

In that case, the *discount* at period t is defined as $d_t = -\delta_t^\theta$.

Let us suppose throughout this section that, for each $t < T$, there is short-term riskless borrowing at a strictly positive discount d_t. We can define, for any times t and $\tau > T$,

$$R_{t,\tau} = (d_t d_{t+1} \cdots d_{\tau-1})^{-1},$$

the payback at time τ of one unit of account borrowed risklessly at time t and rolled over in short-term borrowing repeatedly until date τ.

It would be a simple situation, both computationally and conceptually, if any security's price were merely the expected discounted dividends of the security. Of course, this is unlikely to be the case in a market with risk-averse investors. We can nevertheless come close to this sort of characterization of security prices by adjusting the original probability measure P. For this, we define a new probability measure Q to be *equivalent* to P if Q and P assign zero probabilities to the same events. An equivalent probability measure Q is an *equivalent martingale measure* if

$$S_t = E_t^Q \left(\sum_{j=t+1}^{T} \frac{\delta_j}{R_{t,j}} \right), \quad t < T.$$

It is easy to show that Q is an equivalent martingale measure if and only if, for any trading strategy θ,

$$\theta_t \cdot S_t = E_t^Q \left(\sum_{j=t+1}^{T} \frac{\delta_j^\theta}{R_{t,j}} \right), \quad t < T. \tag{10}$$

If interest rates are deterministic, (10) is merely the total discounted expected dividends, after substituting Q for the original measure P. We will show that the absence of arbitrage is equivalent to the existence of an equivalent martingale measure.

We already know from Proposition 2C that the absence of arbitrage is equivalent to the existence of a state-price deflator π. Let Q be the probability measure defined, as explained in Appendix A, by the Radon-Nikodym derivative given by

$$\xi_T = \frac{\pi_T R_{0,T}}{\pi_0}.$$

Since ξ_T is strictly positive, Q and P are equivalent probability measures. The *density process* ξ for Q is defined by $\xi_t = E_t(\xi_T)$. Relation (A.2) of Appendix A implies that, for any times t and $j > t$ and any $\mathcal{F}_j$-measurable random variable Z_j,

$$E_t^Q(Z_j) = \frac{1}{\xi_t} E_t(\xi_j Z_j). \tag{11}$$

Fixing some time $t < T$, consider a trading strategy θ that invests one unit of account at time t and repeatedly rolls the value over in short-term riskless borrowing until time T, with final value $R_{t,T}$. Since $\theta_t \cdot S_t = 1$ and $\delta_T^\theta = R_{t,T}$, relation (3) implies that

$$\pi_t = E_t(\pi_T R_{t,T}) = \frac{E_t(\pi_T R_{0,T})}{R_{0,t}} = \frac{E_t(\xi_T \pi_0)}{R_{0,t}} = \frac{\xi_t \pi_0}{R_{0,t}}. \tag{12}$$

From (11), (12), and the definition of a state-price deflator, (10) is satisfied, so Q is indeed an equivalent martingale measure. We have shown the following result.

Theorem. *There is no arbitrage if and only if there exists an equivalent martingale measure. Moreover, π is a state-price deflator if and only if an equivalent martingale measure Q has the density process ξ defined by $\xi_t = R_{0,t}\pi_t/\pi_0$.*

Proposition. *Suppose that $\mathcal{F}_T = \mathcal{F}$ and there is no arbitrage. Then markets are complete if and only if there is a unique equivalent martingale measure.*

Proof: Suppose that markets are complete and let Q_1 and Q_2 be two equivalent martingale measures. We must show that $Q_1 = Q_2$. Let A be any event. Since markets are complete, there is a trading strategy θ with dividend process δ^θ such that $\delta_T^\theta = R_{0,T} 1_A$ and $\delta_t^\theta = 0$, $0 < t < T$. By (10), we have $\theta_0 \cdot S_0 = Q_1(A) = Q_2(A)$. Since A is arbitrary, $Q_1 = Q_2$.

Exercise 2.18 outlines a proof of the converse part of the result. ∎

This martingale approach simplifies many asset-pricing problems that might otherwise appear to be quite complex, such as the American option-pricing problem to follow in Section I. This martingale approach also applies much more generally than indicated here. For example, the assumption of short-term borrowing is merely a convenience. More generally, one can typically obtain an equivalent martingale measure after normalizing prices and dividends by the price of some particular security.

H. Valuation of Redundant Securities

Suppose that the given dividend-price pair (δ, S) is arbitrage-free, with an associated state-price deflator π. Now consider the introduction of a new security with dividend process $\hat{\delta}$ and price process $\hat{S}$. We say that $\hat{\delta}$ is *redundant* given (δ, S) if there exists a trading strategy θ, with respect to only the original securities, that *replicates* $\hat{\delta}$, in the sense that $\delta_t^\theta = \hat{\delta}_t$, $t \geq 1$. The absence of arbitrage implies that

$$\hat{S}_t = V_t \equiv \frac{1}{\pi_t} E_t \left(\sum_{j=t+1}^T \pi_j \hat{\delta}_j \right), \quad t < T.$$

If this were not the case, there would be an arbitrage, as follows. We take τ to be the stopping time $\inf\{t : \hat{S}_t > V_t\}$, and we define the strategy:

(a) Sell the redundant security $\hat{\delta}$ at time τ for $\hat{S}_\tau$, and hold this position until T.

(b) Invest $\theta_\tau \cdot S_\tau$ at time τ in the replicating strategy θ, and follow this strategy until T.

Since the dividends generated by this combined strategy (a)–(b) after τ are zero, the only dividend is at τ for the amount $\hat{S}_\tau - V_\tau > 0$, which means that this is an arbitrage if the event $\{\tau \leq T\}$ has positive probability. Likewise, if $\hat{S}_\tau < V_\tau$ for some nontrivial stopping time τ, the opposite strategy is an arbitrage. We have shown the following.

Proposition. *Suppose (δ, S) is arbitrage-free with state-price deflator π. Let $\hat{\delta}$ be a redundant dividend process with price process $\hat{S}$. Then the combined dividend-price pair $[(\delta, \hat{\delta}), (S, \hat{S})]$ is arbitrage-free if and only if it has π as a state-price deflator.*

In applications, it is often assumed that (δ, S) generates complete markets, in which case any additional security is redundant. Exercise 2.1 gives an example in which the redundant security is an option on one of the original securities.

I. Valuation and Optimal Exercise Policies

Given an adapted process X and a stopping time τ, consider the dividend process δ^τ defined by $\delta_t^\tau = 0$, $t \neq \tau$, and $\delta_\tau^\tau = X_\tau$. In this context, X defines what is known as an *American security*. A stopping time is an *exercise policy*, determining the time at which to accept payment. The exercise policy τ is selected by the holder of the security. A good example is an American put option on a security with price process Y. The American put gives the holder of the option the right, but not the obligation, to sell the underlying security for a fixed exercise price at any time before a given expiration date. In this case, if the option has an exercise price K and expiration date $\bar{\tau} < T$, then $X_t = (K - Y_t)^+$, $t \leq \bar{\tau}$, and $X_t = 0$, $t > \bar{\tau}$.

Putting aside the American security X, suppose that the given securities have an arbitrage-free dividend-price process (δ, S) with state-price deflator π. We also suppose that the American security defined by X is redundant given (δ, S) in that, for any stopping time τ, the dividend process δ^τ is redundant given (δ, S). From Proposition 2.H, given any stopping time τ, δ^τ has an associated cum-dividend price process, say V^τ, that is given in the absence of arbitrage by

$$V_t^\tau = \frac{1}{\pi_t} E_t \left(\pi_\tau X_\tau \right), \quad t < \tau.$$

Consider the associated stopping-time problem

$$V_0^* \equiv \sup_{\tau \in \mathcal{T}} V_0^\tau, \tag{13}$$

where $\mathcal{T}$ is the set of stopping times. A solution τ^* to (13) is a *rational exercise policy* for the American security X, in the sense that it maximizes the initial arbitrage-free value of the security.

The initial arbitrage-free value V_0 of the American security must be V_0^*, the value of the security with a rational exercise strategy. In order to see this, suppose, for example, that $V_0^* > V_0$. Then one could buy the American security, adopt for it a rational exercise policy τ, and also adopt a trading strategy replicating $-\delta^\tau$. The net effect is an initial profit of $V_0^* - V_0 > 0$ and no further dividends, an arbitrage. Conversely, suppose that $V_0 > V_0^*$. Then one could sell the American security for V_0. By assumption, the dividend process δ^τ determined by the holder of the security can be replicated by a trading strategy whose initial cost is $V_0^\tau < V_0^*$, yielding an initial profit of $V_0 - V_0^\tau > 0$ and no further dividends, an arbitrage.

We have swept some difficulties associated with American securities under the rug. First, the dividend process associated with an American security is not necessarily uniquely determined, since there could be more than one rational exercise policy. The real difficulties with analyzing American securities begin with incomplete markets. In that case, the choice of exercise policy may play a role in determining the marketed subspace M, and therefore a role in pricing securities. It could even be that there is no rational exercise policy, or that there are different state-price deflators generating different rational exercise policies with different initial values for the American option.

Moreover, any "attempted arbitrage" involving sale of the American security leaves the choice of exercise policy τ up to the holder of the American security. If the holder chooses an exercise policy based on private information (or randomizes, independent of the given filtration), then additional analysis is required. Even if the American security's dividend process is redundant for a given state-price deflator and for any rational exercise policy, it is not obvious whether the American security is priced by arbitrage considerations alone. Suppose, for example, that $V_0 > V_0^*$. If the holder of the security chooses an exercise policy τ with $\tau \leq \tau^*$ for some rational exercise policy τ^*, then the price process V^* of the American security with an optimal exercise policy τ^* satisfies $V_\tau^* \geq X_\tau$, which can be shown as an exercise. An arbitrage would follow. If, on the other hand, for any rational exercise policy τ^*, the holder of the American security chooses an exercise policy τ that is "late," meaning $\tau > \tau^*$, with positive probability, further analysis is required.

With the equivalent martingale measure Q defined in Section 2.G, we can also write the optimal stopping problem (13) in the form

$$V_0^* = \sup_{\tau \in \mathcal{T}} \ E^Q \left(\frac{X_\tau}{R_{0,\tau}} \right).$$

Based on this idea, Exercise 2.1 gives a simple example of American security valuation in a complete-markets setting. Chapter 3 extends the idea to a Markovian setting, which offers computational advantages in solving for the rational exercise policy τ^* and value V_0^*.

Exercises

2.1 Suppose, in the setting of Section 2.B, that S is the price process of a security with zero dividends before T. We assume that

$$S_{t+1} = S_t H_{t+1}; \quad t \geq 0; \quad S_0 > 0, \tag{14}$$

where H is an adapted process such that, for all $t \geq 1$, H_t has only two possible outcomes $U > 0$ and $D > 0$, each with positive conditional probability given $\mathcal{F}_{t-1}$. Suppose β is the price process of a security, also with no dividends before T, such that

$$\beta_{t+1} = \beta_t R; \quad t \geq 1; \quad \beta_0 > 0,$$

where $R > 1$ is a constant. We can think of β as the price process of a riskless bond. Consider a third security, a *European call option* on S with *expiration* at some fixed date $\tau < T$ and exercise price $K \geq 0$. This means that the price process C^τ of the third security has expiration value

$$C_\tau^\tau = (S_\tau - K)^+ \equiv \max (S_\tau - K, 0), \tag{15}$$

with $C_t^\tau = 0$, $t > \tau$. That is, the option gives its holder the right, but not the obligation, to purchase the stock at time τ at price K.

(A) Assuming no arbitrage, show that, for $0 \leq t < \tau$,

$$C_t^\tau = \frac{1}{R^{\tau-t}} \sum_{i=0}^{\tau-t} b(i; \tau - t, p)(U^i D^{\tau-t-i} S_t - K)^+, \tag{16}$$

where $p = (R - D)/(U - D)$ and where

$$b(i; n, p) = \frac{n!}{i!(n - i)!} p^i (1 - p)^{n-i} \tag{17}$$

is the probability of i successes, each with probability p, out of n independent binomial trials. One can thus view (16) as the discounted expected exercise value of the option, with expectation under some probability measure constructed from the stock and bond returns. In order to model this viewpoint, let $\hat{S}$ be the process defined by

$$\hat{S}_{t+1} = \hat{S}_t \hat{H}_{t+1}; \quad t \geq 0; \quad \hat{S}_0 = S_0, \tag{18}$$

where $\{\hat{H}_0, \hat{H}_1, \ldots\}$ is a sequence of independent random variables with outcomes U and D of probability p and $1 - p$, respectively. Then (18) implies that

$$C_0^\tau = E \left[\frac{(\hat{S}_\tau - K)^+}{R^\tau} \right]. \tag{19}$$

(B) We take it that $\mathbb{F}$ is the filtration generated by the return process H, meaning that for all $t \geq 1$, $\mathcal{F}_t$ is the tribe generated by $\{H_1, \ldots, H_t\}$. We extend the definition of the option described in part (A) by allowing the expiry date τ to be a stopping time. Show that (19) is still implied by the absence of arbitrage.

(C)   An *American call option* with expiration date $\bar{\tau} < T$ is merely an option of the form described in part (A), with the exception that the exercise date τ is a stopping time selected by the holder of the option from the set $\mathcal{T}(\bar{\tau})$ of all stopping times bounded by $\bar{\tau}$. Show that the rational exercise problem

$$\sup_{\tau \in \mathcal{T}(\bar{\tau})} C_0^{\tau} \tag{20}$$

is solved by $\tau = \bar{\tau}$. In other words, the holder of the American call option maximizes its value by holding the option to expiration. Hint: Jensen's Inequality states that, for f a convex function, X a random variable on $(\Omega, \mathcal{F}, P)$, and $\mathcal{G}$ a sub-tribe of $\mathcal{F}$, we have $E[f(X) \mid \mathcal{G}] \geq f[E(X \mid \mathcal{G})]$.

(D)   Show that the unique arbitrage-free price of the American call described in part (C) is at any time t equal to $C_t^{\bar{\tau}}$, which is the corresponding European call price.

(E)   A *European put option* is defined just as is the European call, with the exception that the exercise value is $(K - S_{\tau})^+$ rather than $(S_{\tau} - K)^+$. That is, the put gives its holder the right, but not the obligation, to sell (rather than buy) the stock at τ for the exercise price K. Let F^{τ} denote the European put price process for expiration at τ. The *American put* with expiration $\bar{\tau}$, analogous to the case of calls, has an exercise date τ selected by the holder from the set $\mathcal{T}(\bar{\tau})$ of stopping times bounded by $\bar{\tau}$. Show by counterexample that the problem

$$\sup_{\tau \in \mathcal{T}(\bar{\tau})} F_0^{\tau} \tag{21}$$

is not, in general, solved by $\tau = \bar{\tau}$, and that the arbitrage-free American put price process is not generally the same as the corresponding arbitrage-free European put price process $F^{\bar{\tau}}$, contrary to the case of American call options on stocks with no dividends before expiration. An easy algorithm for computing the value of the American put in this setting is given in Chapter 3.

2.2   Suppose, in the context of problem (4), that (δ, S) admits no arbitrage and that U is continuous. Show the existence of a solution. Hint: A continuous function on a compact set has a maximum. In this setting, a set is compact if it is closed and bounded.

2.3   Suppose, in the context of problem (4), that $e \gg 0$ and that U has the additive form (5), where, for each t, u_t is concave with an unbounded derivative. Show that any solution c^* is strictly positive. Show that the same conclusion follows if the assumption that $e \gg 0$ is replaced with the assumption that markets are complete and that e is not zero.

2.4 Prove Lemma 2C. Hint: For any x and y in L, let

$$(x \mid y) = E \left(\sum_{t=0}^{T} x_t y_t \right).$$

Then follow the hint given for Exercise 1.17, remembering that we write $x = y$ whenever $x_t = y_t$ for all t almost surely.

2.5 For U of the additive form (5), show that the gradient $\nabla U(c)$, if it exists, is represented as in (6).

2.6 Suppose $(c^1, \ldots, c^m)$ is a strictly positive equilibrium consumption allocation and that, for all i, U_i is of the additive form: $U_i(c) = E[\sum_{t=0}^{T} u_{it}(c_t)]$. Assume there is a constant $\bar{c}$ larger than c_t^i for all i and t such that, for all i and t, $u_{it}(x) = A_{it}x - B_{it}x^2$, $x \leq \bar{c}$, for some positive constants A_{it} and B_{it}. That is, utility is quadratic in the relevant range.

(A) In the context of Corollary 2 of Section 2F, show that, for each t, there are some constants k_t and K_t such that $u'_{\lambda t}(e_t) = k_t + K_t e_t$. Suppose, for a given trading strategy θ and time t, that the following are well defined:

- $R_t^\theta = \theta_{t-1} \cdot (S_t + \delta_t) / \theta_{t-1} \cdot S_{t-1}$, the return on θ at time t;
- R_t^M, the return at time t on a strategy φ maximizing $\mathrm{corr}_{t-1}(R_t^\varphi, e_t)$, where $\mathrm{corr}_t(\,\cdot\,)$ denotes $\mathcal{F}_t$-conditional correlation;
- $\beta_{t-1}^\theta = \mathrm{cov}_{t-1}(R_t^\theta, R_t^M)/\mathrm{var}_{t-1}(R_t^M)$, the conditional beta of the trading strategy θ with respect to the market return, where $\mathrm{cov}_t(\,\cdot\,)$ denotes $\mathcal{F}_t$-conditional covariance and $\mathrm{var}_t(\,\cdot\,)$ denotes $\mathcal{F}_t$-conditional variance;
- R_t^0, the return at time t on a strategy η with $\mathrm{corr}_{t-1}(R_t^\eta, e_t) = 0$.

Derive the following beta-form of the *consumption-based CAPM*:

$$E_{t-1}(R_t^\theta - R_t^0) = \beta_{t-1}^\theta E_{t-1}(R_t^M - R_t^0). \tag{22}$$

(B) Prove the same beta-form (22) of the CAPM holds in equilibrium even without assuming complete markets.

(C) Extend the state-price beta model of Section 1F to this setting, as follows, without using the assumptions of the CAPM. Let π be a state-price deflator. For each t, suppose R_t^* is the return on a trading strategy solving

$$\sup_\theta \mathrm{corr}_{t-1}(R_t^\theta, \pi_t).$$

Assume that $\text{var}_{t-1}(R_t^*)$ is nonzero almost surely. Show that, for any return R_t^θ,

$$E_{t-1}(R_t^\theta - R_t^0) = \beta_{t-1}^\theta E_{t-1}(R_t^* - R_t^0), \tag{23}$$

where $\beta_{t-1}^\theta = \text{cov}_{t-1}(R_t^\theta, R_t^*)/\text{var}_{t-1}(R_t^*)$ and $\text{corr}_{t-1}(R_t^0, \pi_t) = 0$.

2.7   Prove Proposition 2E.

2.8   In the context of Section 2D, suppose that U is the *habit-formation* utility function defined by $U(c) = E[\sum_{t=0}^T u(c_t, h_t)]$, where $u : \mathbb{R}_+ \times \mathbb{R} \to \mathbb{R}$ is differentiable on the interior of its domain and, for any t, the "habit" level of consumption is defined by $h_t = \sum_{j=0}^{t-1} \alpha_j c_{t-j}$ for some $\alpha \in \mathbb{R}^T$. For example, we could take $\alpha_j = \gamma^j$ for $\gamma \in (0, 1)$, which gives geometrically declining weights on past consumption. Calculate the Riesz representation of the gradient of U at a strictly positive consumption process c.

2.9   Consider a utility function U defined by $U(c) = V_0$, where the *utility process* V is defined recursively, backward from T in time, by $V_T = J(c_T, 0)$ and, for $t < T$, by $V_t = J(c_t, E_t[h(V_{t+1})])$, where $J : \mathbb{R}_+ \times \mathbb{R} \to \mathbb{R}$ is continuously differentiable on the interior of its domain and $h : \mathbb{R} \to \mathbb{R}$ is continuously differentiable. This is a special case of what is known as *recursive utility*, and also a special case of what is known as *Kreps-Porteus* utility. Note that the utility function can depend nontrivially on the filtration $\mathbb{F}$, which is not true for additive or habit-formation utility functions.

(A)   Give an expression for the gradient of U at a strictly positive consumption process c.

(B)   Suppose that h is concave and that $(c, v) \mapsto J[c, h(v)]$ is concave. Show that U is concave.

(C)   Suppose that J and h are strictly increasing. Show that U is strictly increasing.

(D)   Consider the special case $h(v) = v^\alpha$ and $J(c, v) = (c^\beta + \rho v^{\beta/\alpha})^{1/\beta}$ for constants α and β in $(0, 1]$. Obtain an expression for the gradient of the associated utility function.

2.10   In the setting of Section 2E, an Arrow-Debreu equilibrium is a feasible consumption allocation $(c^1, \ldots, c^m)$ and a nonzero linear function $\Psi : L \to \mathbb{R}$ such that, for all i, c^i solves $\max_{c \in L_+} U_i(c)$ subject to $\Psi(c^i) \le \Psi(e^i)$. Suppose that $(c^1, \ldots, c^m)$ and Ψ form an Arrow-Debreu equilibrium and that π is the Riesz representation of Ψ. Let S be defined by $S_T = 0$ and by taking π to be a state-price deflator. Suppose, given (δ, S), that markets are complete.

Show the existence of trading strategies $\theta^1, \ldots, \theta^m$ such that $(\theta^1, \ldots, \theta^m, S)$ is an equilibrium with the same consumption allocation $(c^1, \ldots, c^m)$.

2.11 Given a finite set Ω of states, a *partition* of Ω is a collection of disjoint non-empty subsets of Ω whose union is Ω. For example, a partition of $\{1, 2, 3\}$ is given by $\{\{1\}, \{2, 3\}\}$. The tribe on a finite set Ω generated by a given partition p of Ω, denoted $\sigma(p)$, is the smallest tribe $\mathcal{F}$ on Ω such that $p \subset \mathcal{F}$. Conversely, for any tribe $\mathcal{F}$ on Ω, the partition $\mathcal{P}(\mathcal{F})$ generated by $\mathcal{F}$ is the smallest partition p of Ω such that $\mathcal{F} = \sigma(p)$. Since partitions and tribes on a given finite set Ω are in one-to-one correspondence, we could have developed the results of Chapter 2 in terms of an increasing sequence $p_0, p_1, \ldots, p_T$ of partitions of Ω rather than a filtration of tribes, $\mathcal{F}_0, \mathcal{F}_1, \ldots, \mathcal{F}_T$. (In the infinite-state models of Part II, however, it is more convenient to use tribes than partitions.)

Given a subset B of Ω and a partition p of Ω, let $n(B, p)$ denote the minimum number of elements of p whose union contains B. In a sense, this is the number of distinct non-empty events that might occur if B is to occur. For $t < T$, let

$$n_t = \max_{B \in p_t} n(B, p_{t+1}).$$

Finally, the *spanning number* of the filtration $\mathbb{F}$ generated by $p_0, \ldots, p_T$ is $n(\mathbb{F}) \equiv \max_{t < T} n_t$. In a sense, $n(\mathbb{F})$ is the maximum number of distinct events that could be revealed between two periods.

Show that complete markets requires at least $n(\mathbb{F})$ securities, and that given the filtration $\mathbb{F}$, there exists a set of $n(\mathbb{F})$ dividend processes and associated arbitrage-free security-price processes such that markets are complete. This issue is further investigated in sources indicated in the Notes.

2.12 Given securities with a dividend-price pair (δ, S), extend Theorem 2G to show, in the presence of riskless borrowing at a strictly positive discount at each date, the equivalence of these statements:

(a) There exists a state-price deflator.
(b) There exists a deflator π such that (3) holds for any strategy θ.
(c) $S_T = 0$ and there exists a deflator π such that the deflated gain process G^π is a martingale.
(d) There is no arbitrage.
(e) There is an equivalent martingale measure.

2.13 Show, from (11) and (12), that (10) is indeed satisfied, confirming that Q is an equivalent martingale measure.

2.14 Show, as claimed in Section I, that if τ^* is a rational exercise policy for the American security X and if V^* is the price process for the American security with this rational exercise policy, then $V_\tau^* \geq X_\tau$ for any stopping time τ with $\tau \leq \tau^*$.

2.15 (Aggregation Revisited)   Suppose, in the context of problem (8), that $x \gg 0$ and, for all i, $U_i(c) = E[\sum_{t=0}^{T} u_t(c_t)]$, where, for all t, $u_t(x) = k_t x^{\gamma(t)}/\gamma(t)$, where k_t and $\gamma(t) < 1$, $\gamma(t) \neq 0$, are constants (depending on t). Show that U_λ is of the same form. Replace the assumption of complete markets in Proposition 2F with the assumption that $e \gg 0$ and, for all i, there is a trading strategy θ such that $\delta_t^\theta = e_t^i$, for $t \geq 1$. Demonstrate the same conclusion. Show that the equilibrium consumption allocation is Pareto optimal.

2.16 (Put-Call Parity)   In the general setting explained in Section 2B, suppose there exist the following securities:

(a) a "stock," with price process X;
(b) a European call option on the stock with exercise price K and expiration date τ;
(c) a European put option on the stock with exercise price K and expiration date τ;
(d) a τ-period zero-coupon riskless bond.

Let X_0, C_0, P_0, and B_0 denote the initial respective prices of the securities. Solve for C_0 explicitly in terms of X_0, P_0, and B_0.

2.17 (Futures-Forward Price Equivalence)   This exercise defines (in ideal terms) a *forward contract* and a *futures contract*, and gives simple conditions under which the *futures price* and the *forward price* coincide. We adopt the setting of Section B, in the absence of arbitrage. Fixed throughout are a *delivery date* τ and a settlement amount W_τ (an $\mathcal{F}_\tau$-measurable random variable).

Informally speaking, the associated forward contract made at time t is a commitment to pay an amount F_t (the forward price), which is agreed upon at time t and paid at time τ, in return for the amount W_τ at time τ. Formally speaking, this means that the forward contract is a security whose price process is zero and whose dividend process δ is defined by $\delta_t = 0$, $t \neq \tau$, and $\delta_\tau = W_\tau - F_t$.

(A) Suppose that Q is an equivalent martingale measure and that there is riskless short-term borrowing at any date t at a discount d_t that is deterministic. Show that $\{F_0, F_1, \ldots, F_\tau\}$ is a Q-martingale, in that $F_t = E_t^Q(F_\tau)$ for all $t \leq \tau$.

A futures contract differs from a forward contract in several practical ways that depend on institutional details. One of the details that is particularly important for pricing purposes is *resettlement*. For theoretical modeling purposes, we can describe resettlement as follows. A futures-price process $\Phi = \{\Phi_0, \ldots, \Phi_\tau\}$ for delivery of W_τ at time τ is taken as given. At any time t, an investor can adopt a position of θ futures contracts by agreeing to accept the resettlement payment $\theta(\Phi_{t+1} - \Phi_t)$ at time $t+1$, $\theta(\Phi_{t+2} - \Phi_{t+1})$ at time $t+2$, and so on, until the position is changed (or eliminated). This process of paying or collecting any changes in the futures price, period by period, is called *marking to market*, and serves in practice to reduce the likelihood or magnitude of potential defaults. Formally, all of this means simply that the dividend process δ of the futures contract is defined by $\delta_t = \Phi_t - \Phi_{t-1}$, $1 \leq t \leq \tau$.

For our purposes, it is natural to assume that the delivery value Φ_τ is contractually equated with W_τ. (In a more detailed model, we could equate Φ_τ and W_τ by the absence of *delivery arbitrage*.)

(B) Suppose Q is an equivalent martingale measure and show that, for all $t \leq \tau$, $\Phi_t = E_t^Q(W_\tau)$.

It follows from puts (A) and (B) that, with deterministic interest rates and the absence of arbitrage, futures and forward prices coincide.

We now suppose that W_τ is the market value S_τ of a security with dividend process δ.

(C) Suppose that δ and the discount process $d = \{d_1, \ldots, d_T\}$ on riskless borrowing are both deterministic. Calculate the futures and forward prices, Φ_t and F_t, explicitly in terms of S_t, d, and δ.

2.18 Provide details fleshing out the following outline of a proof of the converse part of Proposition 2G.

Let $J = \{(x_1, \ldots, x_T) : x \in L\}$ and $H = \{(\delta_1^\theta, \ldots, \delta_T^\theta) : \theta \in \Theta\}$. Markets are complete if and only if $J = H$. By Theorem 2G, there is a unique equivalent martingale measure if and only if there is a unique state-price deflator π such that $\pi_0 = 1$. Suppose $H \neq J$. Since H is a linear subspace of J, there is some nonzero y in J "orthogonal" to H, in the sense that $E(\sum_{t=1}^T y_t h_t) = 0$ for all h in H. Let $\hat{\pi} \in L$ be defined by $\hat{\pi}_0 = 1$ and $\hat{\pi}_t = \pi_t + \alpha y_t$, $t \geq 1$, where $\alpha > 0$ is a scalar small enough that $\hat{\pi} \gg 0$. Then $\hat{\pi}$ is a distinct state-price deflator with $\hat{\pi}_0 = 1$. This shows that if there is a unique state-price deflator π with $\pi_0 = 1$, then markets must be complete. Hint: Let

$$(y \mid h) \equiv E\left(\sum_{t=1}^{T} y_t h_t\right), \quad h \in H$$

define an inner $(\cdot \mid \cdot)$ for H in the sense of Exercise 1.17.

Notes

The model of uncertainty and information is standard. The model of uncertainty is equivalent to that originated in the general equilibrium model of Debreu (1953), which appears in Chapter 7 of Debreu (1959). For more details in a finance setting, see Dothan (1990). The connection between arbitrage and martingales given in Sections 2C and 2G is from the more general model of Harrison and Kreps (1979). The spirit of the results on optimality and state prices is also from Harrison and Kreps (1979). The habit-formation utility model was developed by Dunn and Singleton (1986) and in continuous time by Ryder and Heal (1973). The recursive-utility model, in various forms, is due to Selden (1978), Kreps and Porteus (1978), and Epstein and Zin (1989), and is surveyed by Epstein (1991). Koopmans (1960) presented an early precursor. The recursive-utility model allows for preference for earlier or later resolution of uncertainty (which have no impact on additive utility). This is relevant, for example, in the context of the remarks by Ross (1989). For a more general form of recursive utility than that appearing in Exercise 2.9, the von Neumann-Morgenstern function h can be replaced with a function of the conditional distribution of next-period utility. Examples are the local-expected-utility model of Machina (1982) and the *betweenness certainty equivalent* model of Chew (1983, 1989) and Dekel (1987). For further justification and properties of recursive utility, see Chew and Epstein (1991) and Skiadas (1991). For further implications for asset pricing, see Epstein and Zin (1991), Giovannini and Weil (1989), and Epstein (1991).

Radner (1967, 1972) originated the sort of dynamic equilibrium model treated in this chapter. The basic approach to existence given in Exercise 2.11 is suggested by Kreps (1981), and is shown to work for "generic" dividends and endowments, under technical regularity conditions, in McManus (1984), Repullo (1986), and Magill and Shafer (1990), provided the number of securities is at least as large as the spanning number of the filtration $\mathbb{F}$ (as suggested in Exercise 2.11). This literature is reviewed in depth by Geanakoplos (1990). See Duffie and Huang (1985) for the definition of spanning number in more general settings and for a continuous-time version of a similar result. Duffie and Shafer (1986) show generic existence of equilibrium in incomplete markets; Hart (1975) gives a counterexample. Bottazzi (1991) has a somewhat more advanced version of this result in its single-period multiple-commodity version. If one defines security dividends in nominal terms, rather than in units of consumption, then equilibria always exist under standard technical conditions on preferences and endowments, as shown by Cass (1984), Werner (1985), and Duffie (1987), although equilibrium may be indeterminate, as shown by Cass (1989) and Geanakoplos and Mas-Colell (1989). On this point, see also Mas-Colell (1991) and Cass (1991). American option pricing is brought up again in later chapters.

The optimality of portfolio and consumption choices in incomplete markets in this setting is given a dual interpretation by He and Pearson (1991b).

The representative agent state-pricing model for this setting was shown by Constantinides (1982). Kraus and Litzenberger (1975) and Stapleton and Subrahmanyam (1978) present parametric examples of equilibrium. Hansen and Richard (1987) explore the state-price beta model in a much more general multiperiod setting. Ross (1987) and Prisman (1985) show the impact of taxes and transactions costs on the state-pricing model. The consumption-based CAPM of Exercise 2.6 is found, in a different form, in Rubinstein (1976). The aggregation result of Exercise 2.15 is based on Rubinstein (1974b). Rubinstein (1974a) has a detailed treatment of asset pricing results in the setting of this chapter. Rubinstein (1987) is a useful expository treatment of derivative asset pricing in this setting.

3

The Dynamic Programming
Approach

THIS CHAPTER PRESENTS portfolio choice and asset pricing in the framework of dynamic programming, a technique for solving dynamic optimization problems with a recursive structure. The asset-pricing implications go little beyond those of the previous chapter, but there are computational advantages. After introducing the idea of dynamic programming in a deterministic setting, we review the basics of a finite-state Markov chain. The Bellman equation is shown to characterize optimality in a Markov setting. The first order condition for the Bellman equation, often called the "stochastic Euler equation," is then shown to characterize equilibrium security prices. This is done with additive utility in the main body of the chapter, and extended to more general recursive forms of utility in the exercises. The last sections of the chapter show the computation of arbitrage-free derivative security values in a Markov setting, including an application of Bellman's equation for optimal stopping to the valuation of American securities such as the American put option. An exercise presents algorithms for the numerical solution of term-structure derivative securities in a simple binomial setting.

A. The Bellman Approach

To get the basic idea, we start in the T-period setting of the previous chapter, with no securities except those permitting short-term riskless borrowing at any time t at the discount $d_t > 0$. The endowment process of a given agent is e. Given a consumption process c, it is convenient to define the agent's *wealth process* W^c by $W_0^c = 0$ and

$$W_t^c = \frac{W_{t-1}^c + e_{t-1} - c_{t-1}}{d_t}, \quad t \geq 1. \tag{1}$$

43

Given a utility function $U : L_+ \rightarrow \mathbb{R}$ on the set L of non-negative adapted processes, the agent's problem can be rewritten as

$$\sup_c \; U(c) \quad \text{subject to (1) and } c_T \leq W_T^c + e_T. \tag{2}$$

Dynamic programming is only convenient with special types of utility functions. One example is an additive utility function U, defined by

$$U(c) = E\left[\sum_{t=0}^{T} u_t(c_t)\right], \tag{3}$$

with $u_t : \mathbb{R}_+ \rightarrow \mathbb{R}$ strictly increasing and continuous for each t. Given this utility function, it is natural to consider the problem at any time t of maximizing the "remaining utility," given current wealth $W_t^c = w$. In order to keep things simple at first, we take the case in which there is no uncertainty, meaning that $\mathcal{F}_t = \{\Omega, \emptyset\}$ for all t. The maximum remaining utility at time t is then written, for each w in $\mathbb{R}$, as

$$V_t(w) = \sup_{c \in L_+} \; \sum_{s=t}^{T} u_s(c_s),$$

subject to $W_t^c = w$, the wealth dynamic (1), and $c_T \leq W_T^c + e_T$. If there is no budget-feasible consumption choice (because w is excessively negative), we write $V_t(w) = -\infty$.

Clearly $V_T(w) = u_T(w + e_T)$, $w \geq -e_T$, and it is shown as an exercise that, for $t < T$,

$$V_t(w) = \sup_{\bar{c} \in \mathbb{R}_+} \; u_t(\bar{c}) + V_{t+1}\left(\frac{w + e_t - \bar{c}}{d_t}\right), \tag{4}$$

the *Bellman equation.* It is also left as an exercise to show that an optimal consumption policy c is defined inductively by $c_t = C_t(W_t^c)$, where $C_t(w)$ denotes a solution to (4) for $t < T$, and where $C_T(w) = w + e_T$. From (4), the *value function* V_{t+1} thus summarizes all information regarding the "future" of the problem that is required for choice at time t.

B. First Order Conditions of the Bellman Equation

Throughout this section, we take the additive model (3) and assume in addition that, for each t, u_t is strictly concave and differentiable on $(0, \infty)$. Extending Exercise 2.2, there exists an optimal consumption policy c^*. We assume that c^* is strictly positive. Let W^* denote the wealth process associated with c^* by (1).

Lemma. *For any* t, V_t *is strictly concave and continuously differentiable at* W_t^*, *with* $V_t'(W_t^*) = u_t'(c_t^*)$.

Proof is left as Exercise 3.3, which gives a broad hint. The first order conditions for the Bellman equation (4) then imply, for any $t < T$, that the one-period discount is

$$d_t = \frac{u_{t+1}'(c_{t+1}^*)}{u_t'(c_t^*)}. \tag{5}$$

The same equation is easily derived from the general characterization of equilibrium security prices given by equation (2.9). More generally, the price $\Lambda_{t,\tau}$ at time t of a unit riskless bond maturing at any time $\tau > t$ is

$$\Lambda_{t,\tau} \equiv d_t\, d_{t+1} \cdots d_{\tau-1} = \frac{u_\tau'(c_\tau^*)}{u_t'(c_t^*)}, \tag{6}$$

which, naturally, is the marginal rate of substitution of consumption between the two dates.

Since the price of a coupon-bearing bond, the only kind of security in a deterministic setting, is merely the sum of the prices of its coupons and principal, (6) provides a complete characterization of security prices in this setting.

C. Markov Uncertainty

We start with the easiest kind of Markov uncertainty, a *time-homogeneous Markov chain*. Let the elements of a fixed set $Z = \{1, \ldots, k\}$ be known as *shocks*. For any shocks i and j, let $q_{ij} \in [0, 1]$ be thought of as the probability, for any t, that shock j occurs in period $t + 1$ given that shock i occurs in period t. Of course, for each i, $q_{i1} + \cdots + q_{ik} = 1$. The $k \times k$ *transition matrix* q is thus a complete characterization of transition probabilities. This idea is formalized with the following construction of a probability space and filtration of tribes. It is enough to consider a state of the world as some particular sequence $(z_0, \ldots, z_T)$ of shocks that might occur. We therefore let $\Omega = Z^{T+1}$ and let $\mathcal{F}$ be the set of all subsets of Ω. For each t, let $X_t : \Omega \to Z$ (the random shock at time t) be the random variable defined by $X_t(z_0, \ldots, z_T) = z_t$. Finally, for each i in Z, let P_i be the probability measure on $(\Omega, \mathcal{F})$ uniquely defined by two conditions:

$$P_i(X_0 = i) = 1 \tag{7}$$

and, for all $t < T$,

$$P_i[X(t+1) = j \mid X(0),\, X(1),\, X(2), \ldots, X(t)] = q_{X(t),j}. \tag{8}$$

Relations (7) and (8) mean that, under probability measure P_i, X starts at i with probability 1 and has the transition probabilities previously described informally. In particular, (8) means that $X = \{X_0, \ldots, X_T\}$ is a Markov process: the conditional distribution of X_{t+1} given $X_0, \ldots, X_t$ depends only on X_t. To complete the formal picture, for each t, we let $\mathcal{F}_t$ be the tribe generated by $\{X_0, \ldots, X_t\}$, meaning that the information available at time t is that obtained by observing the shock process X until time t.

Lemma. *For any time t, let $f : Z^{T-t+1} \to \mathbb{R}$ be arbitrary. Then there exists a fixed function $g : Z \to \mathbb{R}$ such that, for any i in Z,*

$$E^i \left[f(X_t, \ldots, X_T) \mid \mathcal{F}_t \right] = E^i[f(X_t, \ldots, X_T) \mid X_t] = g(X_t),$$

where E^i denotes expectation under P_i.

This lemma gives the complete flavor of the Markov property.

D. Markov Asset Pricing

Taking the particular Markov source of uncertainty described in Section 3C, we now consider the prices of securities in a single- or representative-agent setting with additive utility of the form (3), where, for all t, u_t has a strictly positive derivative on $(0, \infty)$. Suppose, moreover, that for each t there are functions $f_t : Z \to \mathbb{R}^N$ and $g_t : Z \to \mathbb{R}$ such that the dividend is $\delta_t = f_t(X_t)$ and the endowment is $e_t = g_t(X_t)$. Then Lemma 3C and the general gradient solution (2.9) for equilibrium security prices imply the following characterization of the equilibrium security price process S. For each t there is a function $\mathcal{S}_t : Z \to \mathbb{R}^N$ such that $S_t = \mathcal{S}_t(X_t)$. In particular, for any initial shock i and any time $t < T$,

$$\mathcal{S}_t(X_t) = \frac{1}{\pi_t} E^i \left(\pi_{t+1} \left[f_{t+1}(X_{t+1}) + \mathcal{S}_{t+1}(X_{t+1}) \right] \,\Big|\, X_t \right), \tag{9}$$

where π is the state-price deflator given by $\pi_t = u'_t[g_t(X_t)]$. This has been called the *stochastic Euler equation* for security prices.

E. Security Pricing by Markov Control

We will demonstrate (9) once again, under stronger conditions, using instead Markov control methods. Suppose that $\{X_t\}$ is the shock process already described. For notational simplicity, we take it that the transition matrix q is strictly positive and that, for all t,

- u_t is continuous, strictly concave, increasing, and differentiable on $(0, \infty)$;
- $e_t = g_t(X_t)$ for some $g_t : Z \to \mathbb{R}_{++}$; and
- $\delta_t = f_t(X_t)$ for some $f_t : Z \to \mathbb{R}^N_{++}$.

We assume, naturally, that $\mathcal{S}_t : Z \to \mathbb{R}^N_{++}$, $t < T$, and that there is no arbitrage. For each $t \leq T$, consider the value function $V_t : Z \times \mathbb{R} \to \mathbb{R}$ defined by

$$V_t(i, w) = \sup_{(c, \theta) \in L_+ \times \Theta} E \left[\sum_{j=t}^{T} u_j(c_j) \mid X_t = i \right], \tag{10}$$

subject to

$$W_j^\theta = \theta_{j-1} \cdot [\mathcal{S}_j(X_j) + f(X_j)], \quad j > t; \quad W_t^\theta = w, \tag{11}$$

and

$$c_j + \theta_j \cdot \mathcal{S}_j(X_j) \leq W_j^\theta + g(X_j), \quad t \leq j \leq T.$$

The conditional expectation in (10), which is well defined since $q \gg 0$, does not depend on the initial state X_0 according to Lemma 3C, so we abuse the notation by simply ignoring the initial state in this sort of expression. For sufficiently negative w, there is no solution, in which case we take $V_t(i, w) = -\infty$. For initial wealth $w = 0$ and time $t = 0$, (10) is equivalent to problem (2.4) with $S_j = \mathcal{S}_j(X_j)$ for all j.

We now define a sequence $F_0, \ldots, F_T$ of functions on $Z \times \mathbb{R}$ into $\overline{\mathbb{R}}$ that will eventually be shown to coincide with the value functions $V_0, \ldots, V_T$. We first define $F_{T+1} \equiv 0$. For $t \leq T$, we let F_t be given by the Bellman equation

$$F_t(i, w) = \sup_{(\overline{\theta}, \overline{c}) \in \mathbb{R}^N \times \mathbb{R}_+} G_{it}(\overline{\theta}, \overline{c}) \text{ subject to } \overline{c} + \overline{\theta} \cdot \mathcal{S}_t(i) \leq w + g(i), \tag{12}$$

where

$$G_{it}(\overline{\theta}, \overline{c}) = u_t(\overline{c}) + E \left[F_{t+1} \left(X_{t+1}, \overline{\theta} \cdot [\mathcal{S}_{t+1}(X_{t+1}) + f_{t+1}(X_{t+1})] \right) \mid X_t = i \right].$$

The following technical conditions extend those of Lemma 3B, and have essentially the same proof.

Proposition. For any i in Z and $t \leq T$, the function $F_t(i, \cdot) : \mathbb{R} \to \overline{\mathbb{R}}$, restricted to its domain of finiteness $\{w : F_t(i, w) > -\infty\}$, is strictly concave and increasing. If $(\overline{c}, \overline{\theta})$ solves (12) and $\overline{c} > 0$, then $F_t(i, \cdot)$ is continuously differentiable at w with derivative $F_{tw}(i, w) = u_t'(\overline{c})$.

It can be shown as an exercise that, unless the constraint is infeasible, a solution to (12) always exists. In this case, for any i, t, and w, let $[\Phi_t(i, w), C_t(i, w)]$ denote a solution. We can then define the associated wealth process W^* recursively by $W_0^* = 0$ and

$$W_t^* = \Phi_{t-1}(X_{t-1}, W_{t-1}^*) \cdot [S_t(X_t) + f_t(X_t)], \quad t \geq 1.$$

Let (c^*, θ^*) be defined, at each t, by $c_t^* = C_t(X_t, W_t^*)$ and $\theta_t^* = \Phi_t(X_t, W_t^*)$. The fact that (c^*, θ^*) solves (10) for $t = 0$ and $w = 0$ can be shown as follows. Let (c, θ) be an arbitrary feasible policy. We have, for each t from the Bellman equation (12),

$$F_t(X_t, W_t^\theta) \geq u_t(c_t) + E\left[F_{t+1}\left(X_{t+1}, \theta_t \cdot [S_{t+1}(X_{t+1}) + f_{t+1}(X_{t+1})]\right) \,\bigg|\, X_t\right].$$

Rearranging this inequality and applying the law of iterated expectations,

$$E[F_t(X_t, W_t^\theta)] - E\left[F_{t+1}\left(X_{t+1}, W_{t+1}^\theta\right)\right] \geq E[u_t(c_t)]. \tag{13}$$

Adding equation (13) from $t = 0$ to $t = T$ shows that $F_0(X_0, W_0) \geq U(c)$. Repeating the same calculations for the special policy $(c, \theta) = (c^*, \theta^*)$ allows us to replace the inequality in (13) with an equality, leaving $F_0(X_0, W_0) = U(c^*)$. This shows that $U(c^*) \geq U(c)$ for any feasible (θ, c), meaning that (θ^*, c^*) indeed solves equation (10) for $t = 0$. An optimal policy can thus be captured in *feedback* form in terms of the functions C_t and Φ_t, $t \leq T$. We also see that, for all $t \leq T$, $F_t = V_t$, so V_t inherits the properties of F given by the last proposition.

We can now recover the stochastic Euler equation (9) directly from the first order conditions to (12), rather than from the more general first order conditions developed in Chapter 2 based on the gradient of U.

Theorem. A feasible policy (c^*, θ^*) with c^* strictly positive solves (10) for $t = 0$ and $w = 0$ if and only if, for all $t < T$,

$$S_t(X_t) = \frac{1}{u_t'(c_t^*)} E\left[u_{t+1}'\left(c_{t+1}^*\right)[S_{t+1}(X_{t+1}) + f_{t+1}(X_{t+1})] \,\big|\, X_t\right]. \tag{14}$$

The theorem follows from the necessity and sufficiency of the first order conditions for (12), relying on the last proposition for the fact that
$F_{t+1,w}(X_{t+1}, W_{t+1}^*) = u_{t+1}'(c_{t+1}^*)$.

In a single-agent model, we define a sequence $\{S_0, \ldots, S_T\}$ of security-
price functions to be a *single-agent equilibrium* if $(e, 0)$ (no trade) solves (10)
for $t = 0$, $w = 0$, and any initial shock i.

Corollary. $\{S_0, \ldots, S_T\}$ *is a single-agent equilibrium if and only if* $S_T = 0$ *and,
for all* $t < T$, *the stochastic Euler equation* (9) *is satisfied.*

F. Arbitrage-Free Valuation in a Markov Setting

Taking the setting of Markov uncertainty described in Section 3C, but assuming no particular optimality properties or equilibrium, suppose that security
prices and dividends are given, at each t, by functions S_t and f_t on Z into $\mathbb{R}^N$.
It can be shown as an exercise that the absence of arbitrage is equivalent
to the existence of a state-price deflator π given by $\pi_t = \psi_t(X_t)$ for some
$\psi_t : Z \to \mathbb{R}$. With this, we have, for $0 < t \le T$,

$$S_{t-1}(X_{t-1}) = \frac{1}{\psi_{t-1}(X_{t-1})} E\left(\psi_t(X_t)\left[f_t(X_t) + S_t(X_t)\right] \big| X_{t-1}\right). \qquad (15)$$

In the special setting of Section 3D, for example, (9) tells us that we can
take $\psi_t(i) = u_t'[g(i)]$.

Since $Z = \{1, \ldots, k\}$ for some integer k, we can abuse the notation by
treating any function such as $S_t : Z \to \mathbb{R}$ interchangeably as a vector in $\mathbb{R}^k$
denoted S_t, with i-th element $S_t(i)$. In this sense, (15) can also be written

$$S_{t-1} = \Pi_{t-1}(f_t + S_t), \qquad (16)$$

where Π_{t-1} is the $k \times k$ matrix with (i, j)-element $q_{ij}\psi_t(j)/\psi_{t-1}(i)$. For each
t and $s > t$, we let $\Pi_{t,s} = \Pi_t\Pi_{t+1}\cdots\Pi_{s-1}$. Then (16) is equivalent to: For
any t and $\tau > t$,

$$S_t = \Pi_{t,\tau}S_\tau + \sum_{s=t+1}^{\tau} \Pi_{t,s}f_s. \qquad (17)$$

As an example, consider the "binomial" model of Exercise 2.1. We
can let $Z = \{0, 1, \ldots, T\}$, with shock i having the interpretation: "There

have so far occurred i 'up' returns on the stock." From the calculations in Exercise 2.1, it is apparent that, for any t, we may choose $\Pi_t = \Pi$, where

$$\Pi_{ij} = \frac{p}{R}, \quad j = i + 1,$$

$$= \frac{1 - p}{R}, \quad j = i,$$

$$= 0, \quad \text{otherwise},$$

where $p = (R - D)/(U - D)$. For a given initial stock price x and any $i \in Z$, the stock-price process S of Exercise 2.1 can indeed be represented at each time t by $S_t : Z \to \mathbb{R}$, where $S_t(i) = xU^iD^{t-i}$.

We can recover the "binomial" option-pricing formula (2.16) by noting that the European call option with strike price K and expiration time τ may be treated as a security with dividends only at time τ given by the function $g : Z \to \mathbb{R}$, with $g(i) = [S_\tau(i) - K]^+$. From (17), the arbitrage-free value of the option at time t is $C_t^\tau = \Pi^{\tau-t}g$, where Π^t denotes the t-th power of Π. This same valuation formula applies to an arbitrary security paying a dividend at time τ defined by some payoff function $g : Z \to \mathbb{R}$.

G. Early Exercise and Optimal Stopping

In the setting of Section 3F, consider an "American" security, defined by some payoff functions $g_t : Z \to \mathbb{R}$, $t \in \{0, \ldots, T\}$. As explained in Section 2.I, the security is a claim to the dividend $g_\tau(X_\tau)$ at any stopping time τ selected by the owner. Expiration of the security at some time $\bar{\tau}$ is handled by defining g_t to be zero for $t > \bar{\tau}$. Given the state-price deflator π defined by $\pi_t = \psi(X_t)$, as outlined in the previous section, the rational exercise problem (2.13) for the American security, with initial shock i, is given by

$$J_0(i) \equiv \sup_{\tau \in \mathcal{T}} \frac{1}{\psi_0(i)} E^i\left[\psi_\tau(X_\tau)g(X_\tau)\right], \tag{18}$$

where $\mathcal{T}$ is the set of stopping times. As explained in Section 2.I, if the American security is redundant and there is no arbitrage, then $J_0(i)$ is its cum-dividend value at time 0 with initial shock i. Provided the transition matrix q is strictly positive, the Bellman equation for (18) is

$$J_t(i) \equiv \max\left(g_t(i), \frac{1}{\psi_t(i)} E\left[\psi_{t+1}(X_{t+1})J_{t+1}(X_{t+1})\big|X_t = i\right]\right). \tag{19}$$

If q is not strictly positive, a slightly more complicated expression applies. It is left as an exercise to show that J_0 is indeed determined inductively, backward in time from T, by (19) and $J_T = 0$. Moreover, (18) is solved by the stopping time

$$\tau^* = \min\left[t : J_t(X_t) = g_t(X_t)\right]. \tag{20}$$

In our alternate notation that treats J_t as a vector in $\mathbb{R}^k$, we can rewrite the Bellman equation (19) in the form

$$J_t = \max\left(g_t, \Pi_t J_{t+1}\right), \tag{21}$$

where, for any x and y in $\mathbb{R}^k$, $\max(x, y)$ denotes the vector in $\mathbb{R}^k$ that has $\max(x_i, y_i)$ as its i-th element. This form (21) of the Bellman equation applies even if q is not strictly positive.

Equation (21) leads to a simple recursive solution algorithm for the American put valuation problem of Exercise 2.1. Given an expiration time $\bar{\tau} < T$ and exercise price K, we have $J_T = 0$ and

$$J_t = \max\left[(K - S_t)^+, \; \Pi_t J_{t+1}\right], \tag{22}$$

or more explicitly: For any t and $i \leq t$,

$$J_t(i) = \max\left([K - S_t(i)]^+, \; \frac{p J_{t+1}(i+1) + (1-p) J_{t+1}(i)}{R}\right), \tag{23}$$

where $S_t(i) = x U^i D^{t-1}$ and $p = (R - D)/(U - D)$.

More generally, consider an *American security* defined by dividend functions $h_0, \ldots, h_T$ and exercise payoff functions $g_0, \ldots, g_T$. For a given expiration time $\bar{\tau}$, we have $h_t = g_t = 0$, $t > \bar{\tau}$. The owner of the security chooses a stopping time τ at which to exercise, generating the dividend process δ^τ defined by

$$\begin{aligned}
\delta_t^\tau &= h_t(x_t), && t < \tau, \\
&= g_t(X_t), && t = \tau, \\
&= 0, && t > \tau.
\end{aligned}$$

Assuming that δ^τ is redundant for any exercise policy τ, the security's arbitrage-free cum-dividend value is defined recursively by $J_T = 0$ and the extension of (21):

$$J_t = \max\left(g_t, \; h_t + \Pi_t J_{t+1}\right). \tag{24}$$

Exercises

3.1 Prove the Bellman equation (4).

3.2 For each t and each w such that there exists a feasible policy, let $C_t(w)$ solve equation (4). Let W^* be determined by equation (1) with $c_{t-1} = C_{t-1}(W^*_{t-1})$ for $t > 0$. Show that an optimal policy c^* is given by $c^*_t = C_t(W^*_t)$, $t < T$, and $c^*_T = e_T + W^*_T$.

3.3 Prove Lemma 3B. Hint: If $f : \mathbb{R} \to \mathbb{R}$ is concave, then for each x there is a number β such that $\beta(x - y) \geq f(x) - f(y)$ for all x and y. If f is also differentiable at x, then $\beta = f'(x)$. If f is differentiable and strictly concave, then f is continuously differentiable. Let $w^* = W^*_t$. If $c^*_t > 0$, there is an interval $I = (\underline{w}, \overline{w}) \subset \mathbb{R}$ with $w^* \in I$ such that $v : I \to \mathbb{R}$ is well defined by

$$v(w) = u_t(c^*_t + w - w^*) + V_{t+1}(W^*_{t+1}).$$

Now use the differentiability of v, the definition of a derivative, and the fact that $v(w) \leq V_t(w)$ for all $w \in I$.

3.4 Prove equation (9).

3.5 Prove Proposition 3E.

3.6 Prove Theorem 3E and its Corollary.

3.7 Consider the case of securities in positive supply, which can be taken without loss of generality to be a supply of 1 each. Equilibrium in the context of Section 3E is thus redefined by: $\{S_0, \ldots, S_T\}$ is an equilibrium if (c^*, θ^*) solves (10) at $t = 0$ and $w = \mathbf{1} \cdot [S_0(X_0) + f_0(X_0)]$, where $\mathbf{1} = (1, \ldots, 1)$ and, for all t, $\theta^*_t = \mathbf{1}$, and $c^*_t = g_t(X_t) + \mathbf{1} \cdot f_t(X_t)$. Demonstrate a new version of the stochastic Euler equation (9) that characterizes equilibrium in this case.

3.8 (Recursive Utility Revisited) The objective in this exercise is to extend the basic results of the chapter to the case of a recursive-utility function that generalizes additive utility. Rather than assuming a typical additive-utility function U of the form

$$U(c) = E\left[\sum_{t=0}^{T} \rho^t u(c_t)\right], \tag{25}$$

we adopt instead the more general recursive definition of utility given by $U(c) = Y_0$, where Y is a process defined by $Y_{T+1} = 0$ and, for any $t \leq T$,

$$Y_t = J\left(c_t, E_t[h(Y_{t+1})]\right), \tag{26}$$

where $J : \mathbb{R}_+ \times \mathbb{R} \to \mathbb{R}$ and $h : \mathbb{R} \to \mathbb{R}$. This is the special case treated in Exercise 2.9 of what is known as recursive utility. (In an even more general recursive-utility model, the von Neumann-Morgenstern criterion $E[h(\cdot)]$ is replaced by a general functional on distributions, but we do not deal with this further generalization.) Note that the special case $J(q, w) = u(q) + \rho w$ and $h(y) = y$ gives us the additively separable criterion (25). The conventional additive utility has the disadvantage that the elasticity of intertemporal substitution (as measured in a deterministic setting) and relative risk aversion are fixed in terms of one another. The recursive criterion, however, allows one to examine the effects of varying risk aversion while holding fixed the utility's elasticity of intertemporal substitution in a deterministic setting.

(A) (Dynamic Programming) Provide an extension of the Bellman equation (12) for optimal portfolio and consumption choice, substituting the recursive utility for the additive utility. That is, state a revised Bellman equation and regularity conditions on the utility primitives (J, h) under which a solution to the Bellman equation implies that the associated feedback policies solving the Bellman equation generate optimal consumption and portfolio choice. (State a theorem with proof.) Also, include conditions under which there exists a solution to the Bellman equation. For simplicity, among your conditions you may wish to impose the assumptions that J and h are continuous and strictly increasing.

(B) (Asset Pricing Theory) Suppose that J and h are differentiable, increasing, and concave, with either h or J (or both) strictly concave. Provide any additional regularity conditions that you feel are called for in order to derive an analogue to the stochastic Euler equation (9) for security prices.

(C) (An Investment Problem) Let $G : Z \times \mathbb{R}_+ \to \mathbb{R}_+$ and consider the capital-stock investment problem defined by

$$\sup_{c \in L_+} U(c) \tag{27}$$

subject to $0 \leq c_t \leq K_t$ for all t, where $K_0, K_1, \ldots$, is a capital-stock process defined by $K_t = G(X_t, K_{t-1} - c_{t-1})$, and where $X_0, \ldots, X_T$ is the Markov process defined in Section 3C. The utility function U is the recursive function defined above in terms of (J, h). Provide reasonable conditions on (J, h, G) under which there exists a solution. State the Bellman equation.

(D) (Parametric Example) For this part, in order to obtain closed-form solutions, we depart from the assumption that the shock takes only a finite number of possible values, and replace this with a normality assumption. Solve the problem of part (C) in the following case:

   (a) X is the real-valued shock process defined by $X_{t+1} = A + BX_t + \epsilon_{t+1}$, where A and B are scalars and $\epsilon_1, \epsilon_2, \ldots$ is an $i.i.d.$ sequence of normally distributed random variables with $E(\epsilon_t) = 0$ and $\text{var}(\epsilon_t) = \sigma^2$.

   (b) $G(x, a) = a^\gamma e^x$ for some $\gamma \in (0, 1)$.

   (c) $J(q, w) = \log(q) + \rho \log(w^{1/\alpha})$ for some $\alpha \in (0, 1)$.

   (d) $h(v) = e^{\alpha v}$ for $v \geq 0$.

Hint: You may wish to conjecture a solution to the value function of the form $V_t(x, k) = A_1(t) \log(k) + A_2(t)x + A_3(t)$, for time-dependent coefficients A_1, A_2, and A_3. This example is unlikely to satisfy the regularity conditions that you imposed in part (C).

(E)   (Term Structure)   For the consumption endowment process e defined by the solution to part (D), return to the setting of part (B), and calculate the price $\Lambda_{t,s}$ at time t of a pure discount bond paying one unit of consumption at time $s > t$. Note that α is a measure of risk tolerance that can be studied independently of the effects of intertemporal substitution in this model, since, for deterministic consumption processes, utility is independent of α, with $J[q, h(v)] = \log(q) + \rho \log(v)$. Does higher risk tolerance imply higher, lower, or an ambiguous change in short-term interest rates? (Justify your answer.)

3.9   Show equation (5) directly from equation (2.9).

3.10   Consider, as in the setup described in Section 3F, securities defined by the dividend-price pair (δ, S), where, for all t, there are functions f_t and S_t on Z into $\mathbb{R}^N$ such that $\delta_t = f_t(X_t)$ and $S_t = S_t(X_t)$. Show that there is no arbitrage if and only if there is a state-price deflator π such that, for each time t, $\pi_t = \psi_t(X_t)$ for some function $\psi_t : Z \to (0, \infty)$.

3.11   Verify that problem (18) is solved by the stopping time τ^* defined by (20), where J_t is defined by $J_T = 0$ and the Bellman equation (19).

3.12   (Binomial Term-Structure Algorithms)   This exercise asks for a series of numerical solutions of term-structure valuation problems in a setting with binomial changes in short-term interest rates. In the setting of Section 3F, suppose that short-term riskless borrowing is possible at any time t

at the discount d_t. The one-period interest rate at time t is denoted r_t, and is given by its definition:

$$d_t = \frac{1}{1 + r_t}.$$

The underlying shock process X has the property that either $X_t = X_{t-1} + 1$ or $X_t = X_{t-1}$. That is, in each period, the new shock is the old shock plus a 0-1 binomial trial. An example is the binomial stock-option pricing model of Exercise 2.1, which is reconsidered in Section 3F. As opposed to that example, we do not necesarily assume here that interest rates are constant. Rather, we allow, at each time t, a function $\rho_t : Z \to \mathbb{R}$ such that $r_t = \rho_t(X_t)$. For simplicity, however, we take it that at any time t the pricing matrix Π_t defined in Section 3F is of the form

$$(\Pi_t)_{ij} = \frac{p}{1 + \rho_t(i)}, \quad j = i + 1,$$

$$= \frac{1 - p}{1 + \rho_t(i)}, \quad j = i,$$

$$= 0, \quad \text{otherwise},$$

where $p \in (0, 1)$ is the "risk-neutral" probability that $X_{t+1} - X_t = 1$. Literally, there is an equivalent martingale measure Q under which, for all t, we have

$$Q(X_{t+1} - X_t = 1 \mid X_0, \ldots, X_t) = p.$$

It may help to imagine the calculation of security prices at the nodes of the "tree" illustrated in Figure 3.1. The horizontal axis indicates the time periods; the vertical axis corresponds to the possible levels of the shock, assuming that $X_0 = 0$. At each time t and at each shock level i, the price of a given security at the (i, t)-node of the tree is given by a weighted sum of its value of the two succesor nodes $(i + 1, t + 1)$ and $(i, t + 1)$. Specifically,

$$S_t(i) = \frac{1}{1 + \rho_t(i)} \left[p S_{t+1}(i + 1) + (1 - p) S_{t+1}(i) \right].$$

Two typical models for the short rate are obtained by taking $p = 1/2$ and either

(a) the *Ho and Lee model*: For each t, $\rho_t(i) = a_t + b_t i$ for some constants a_t and b_t; or

(b) the *Black-Derman-Toy model*: For each t, $\rho_t(i) = a_t \exp(b_t i)$ for some constants a_t and b_t.

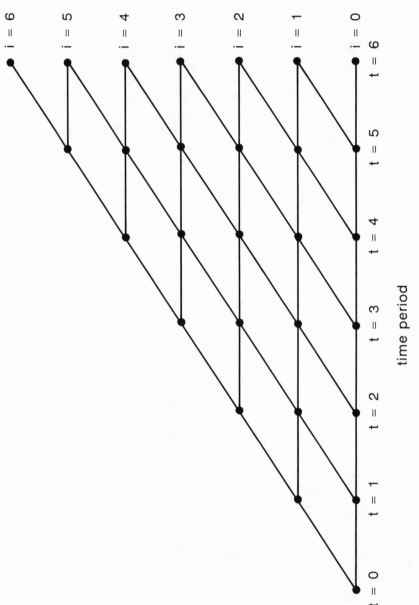

shock level

time period

Figure 3.1. *A Binomial Tree*

(A)   For both cases (a) and (b), prepare computer code to calculate the arbitrage-free price $\Lambda_{0,t}$ of a zero-coupon bond of any given maturity t, given the coefficients a_t and b_t for each t. Prepare an example taking $b_t = 0.01$ for all t and $a_0, a_1, \ldots, a_T$ such that $E^Q(r_t) = 0.01$ for all t. (These parameters are of a typical order of magnitude for monthly periods.) Solve for the price $\Lambda_{0,t}$ of a unit zero-coupon riskless bond maturing at time t, for all t in $\{1, \ldots, 50\}$.

(B) Consider, for any i and t, the price $\psi(i, t)$ at time 0 of a security that pays one unit of account at time t if and only if $X_t = i$.

Show that ψ can be calculated recursively by the forward difference equation

$$\psi(i, t+1) = \frac{\psi(i, t)}{2[1 + \rho_t(i)]} + \frac{\psi(i-1, t)}{2[1 + \rho_t(i-1)]}, \qquad 0 < i < t+1, \qquad (28)$$

and, for $i = 0$ or $i = t+1$,

$$\psi(i, t+1) = \frac{\psi(i, t)}{2[1 + \rho_t(i)]}. \qquad (29)$$

The initial condition is $\psi(0, 0) = 1$.

Knowledge of this "shock-price" function ψ is useful. For example, the arbitrage-free price at time 0 of a security that pays the dividend $f(X_t)$ at time t (and nothing otherwise) is given by $\sum_{i=0}^{t} \psi_t(i) f(i)$.

(C) In practice, the coefficients a_t and b_t are often fitted to match the initial term structure $\Lambda_{0,1}, \ldots, \Lambda_{0,T}$, given the "volatility" coefficients $b_0, \ldots, b_T$. The following algorithm has been suggested for this purpose, using the fact that $\Lambda_{0,t} = \sum_{i=0}^{t} \psi_t(i)$.

   (a) Let $\psi(0, 0) = 1$ and let $t = 1$.
   (b) Fixing ψ_{t-1} and b_t, let $\lambda_t(a_t) = \sum_{i=0}^{t} \psi_t(i)$, where ψ_t is given by the forward difference equation (28)–(29). Only the dependence of the t-maturity zero-coupon bond price $\lambda_t(a_t)$ on a_t is notation-ally explicit. Since $\lambda_t(a_t)$ is strictly monotone in a_t, we can solve numerically for that coefficient a_t such that $\Lambda_{0,t} = \lambda_t(a_t)$. (A Newton-Raphson search will suffice.)
   (c) Let t be increased by 1. Return to step (b) if $t \leq T$. Otherwise, stop.

Prepare computer code for this algorithm (a)–(b)–(c). Given $b_t = 0.01$ for all t, solve for a_t for all t, for both the Ho and Lee and the Black-Derman-Toy models, given an initial term structure that is given by $\Lambda_{0,t} = \alpha^t$, where $\alpha = 0.99$.

(D)   Extend your code as necessary to give the price of American call options on coupon bonds of any given maturity. For the coefficients $a_0, \ldots, a_T$ that you determined from part (C), calculate the initial price of an American option on a bond that pays coupons of 0.011 each period until its maturity at time 20, at which time it pays 1 unit of account in addition to its coupon. The option has an exercise price of 1.00 and expiration at time 10. Do this for both the Ho and Lee model and the Black-Derman-Toy model.

Notes

Bellman's principle of optimality is due to Bellman (1957). Freedman (1983) covers the theory of Markov chains. For general treatments of dynamic programming in a discrete-time Markov setting, see Bertsekas (1976) and Bertsekas and Shreve (1978). The proof for Lemma 3B that is sketched in Exercise 3.3, on the differentiability of the value function, is from Benveniste and Scheinkman (1979), and easily extends to general state spaces; see, for example, Duffie (1988b) and Stokey and Lucas (1989). The *semigroup* pricing approach implicit in equation (17) is from Duffie and Garman (1985). Exercise 3.8, treating asset pricing with the recursive utility of Exercise 2.9, is extended to the infinite-horizon setting of Epstein and Zin (1989) in Exercise 4.12. See Epstein (1991) for more on recursive utility, and Streufert (1991a,b,c) for more on dynamic programming with a recursive-utility function.

The extensive exercise on binomial term-structure valuation algorithms is based almost entirely on Jamshidian (1991), who emphasizes the connection between the solution ψ of the difference equation (28)–(29) and *Green's function*. This connection is reconsidered in Chapters 7 and 10 for continuous-time applications. The two particular term-structure models appearing in this exercise are based, respectively, on Ho and Lee (1986) and Black, Derman, and Toy (1990). The parametric form shown here for the Ho and Lee model is slightly more general than the form actually appearing in Ho and Lee (1986). Most authors take the convention that X_{t+1} is $X_t + 1$ or $X_t - 1$, which generates a slightly different form for the same model. The two forms are equivalent after a change of the parameters. Continuous-time versions of these models are considered in Chapter 7. Chapter 10 also deals in more detail with algorithms designed to match the initial term structure. Exercise 10.5 demonstrates convergence, with a decreasing length of time period, of the discrete-time Black-Derman-Toy model to its continuous-time version. Jamshidian (1991) considers a larger class of examples.

4

The Infinite-Horizon Setting

THIS CHAPTER PRESENTS infinite-period analogues of the results of Chapters 2 and 3. Although it requires additional technicalities and produces few new insights, this setting is often deemed important for reasons of elegance or for serving the large-sample theory of econometrics, which calls for an unbounded number of observations. We start directly with a Markov dynamic programming extension of the finite-horizon results of Chapter 3, and only later consider the implications of no arbitrage or optimality for security prices without using the Markov assumption. Finally, we return to the stationary Markov setting to review briefly the large-sample approach to estimating asset pricing models. Only Sections 4A and 4B are essential; the remainder could be skipped on a first reading.

A. The Markov Dynamic Programming Solution

Suppose $X = \{X_1, X_2, \ldots\}$ is a time-homogeneous Markov chain of shocks valued in a finite set Z, defined exactly as in Section 3C, with the exception that there is an infinite number of time periods. Sources given in the Notes explain the existence of a probability space $(\Omega, \mathcal{F}, P_i)$, for each initial shock i, satisfying the defining properties $P_i(X_0 = i) = 1$ and

$$P_i(X_{t+1} = i \mid X_0, \ldots, X_t) = q_{X(t), j},$$

where q is the given transition matrix. As in Chapter 3, $\mathcal{F}_t$ denotes the tribe generated by $\{X_0, \ldots, X_t\}$. This is the first appearance in the book of a set Ω of states that need not be finite, but because there is only a finite number of events in $\mathcal{F}_t$ for each t, most of this chapter can be easily understood without referring to Appendix C for a review of general probability spaces.

Let L denote the space of sequences of random variables of the form $c = \{c_0, c_1, c_2, \ldots\}$ such that there is a constant k with the property that, for all t, c_t is $\mathcal{F}_t$-measurable with $|c_t| \le k$. In other words, L is the space of bounded adapted processes. Agents choose a consumption process from the set L_+ of non-negative processes in L. There are N securities; security n is defined by a dividend process δ^n in L and has a price process S^n in L. A trading strategy is some $\theta = (\theta^1, \ldots, \theta^N) \in \Theta \equiv L^N$. Each strategy θ in Θ generates a dividend process δ^θ in L defined, just as in Chapter 2, by

$$\delta_t^\theta = \theta_{t-1} \cdot (S_t + \delta_t) - \theta_t \cdot S_t, \quad t \ge 0,$$

with "θ_{-1}" $= 0$ by convention. A given agent has an endowment process e in L_+ and, given a particular initial shock i, a utility function $U^i : L_+ \to \mathbb{R}$. The agent's problem is

$$\sup_{\theta \in \Theta(e)} \quad U^i(e + \delta^\theta),$$

where $\Theta(e) = \{\theta \in \Theta : e + \delta^\theta \ge 0\}$.

In order to develop a time-homogeneous Markov model, we restrict ourselves initially to utility functions, endowments, and security dividends with special time-homogeneous properties. Given an initial shock i, consider the utility function $U^i : L_+ \to \mathbb{R}$ defined by a discount $\rho \in (0, 1)$ and a strictly increasing, bounded, concave, and continuous $u : \mathbb{R}_+ \to \mathbb{R}$ according to

$$U^i(c) = E^i \left[\sum_{t=0}^{\infty} \rho^t u(c_t) \right], \tag{1}$$

where E^i denotes expectation under the probability measure P_i associated with the initial shock $X_0 = i$. Suppose that $g : Z \to \mathbb{R}_{++}$ and $f : Z \to \mathbb{R}_{++}^N$ are such that, for all t, the endowment is $e_t = g(X_t)$ and the dividend vector is $\delta_t = f(X_t)$. Finally, suppose that security prices are given by some fixed $S : Z \to \mathbb{R}_{++}^N$ so that, for all t, $S_t = S(X_t)$.

We fix a portfolio b in $\mathbb{R}_{++}^N$ and think of $-b$ as a lower bound on short positions. This restriction will later be removed. For now, however, wealth is bounded below by

$$\underline{w} = \min_{i \in Z} -b \cdot [S(i) + f(i)].$$

Let $D = Z \times [\underline{w}, \infty)$. A function $F : D \to \mathbb{R}$ is defined to be in the space denoted $B(D)$ if, for each i in Z, $F(i, \cdot) : [\underline{w}, \infty) \to \mathbb{R}$ is bounded, continuous, and concave. We are looking for some V in $B(D)$ as the *value* of the agent's control problem. That is, we want some V in $B(D)$ with

$$V(i, w) = \sup_{(c,\theta) \in L_+ \times \Theta} U^i(c), \tag{2}$$

subject to

$$W_0^\theta = w, \tag{3}$$

$$W_t^\theta = \theta_{t-1} \cdot [\mathcal{S}(X_t) + f(X_t)], \quad t \geq 1, \tag{4}$$

$$c_t + \theta_t \cdot \mathcal{S}(X_t) \leq W_t^\theta + g(X_t), \quad t \geq 0, \tag{5}$$

$$\theta_t \geq -b, \quad t \geq 0. \tag{6}$$

We will solve for the value function V by taking an arbitrary F in $B(D)$ and, from this candidate, construct a new candidate denoted $\mathcal{U}F$ that is described below. Our method will show that if $F = \mathcal{U}F$, then $F = V$. In fact, this approach also leads to an algorithm for calculating V called *value iteration*, which is also laid out below. For any F in $B(D)$, let $\mathcal{U}F : D \to \mathbb{R}$ be defined by

$$\mathcal{U}F(i, w) = \sup_{(\bar{\theta}, \bar{c}) \in \mathbb{R}^N \times R_+} \rho\, u(\bar{c}) + \rho\, E^i \left[F\left(X_2, \bar{\theta} \cdot [\mathcal{S}(X_2) + f(X_2)] \right) \right], \tag{7}$$

subject to

$$\bar{c} + \bar{\theta} \cdot \mathcal{S}(i) \leq w + g(i), \tag{8}$$

$$\bar{\theta} \geq -b. \tag{9}$$

In other words, $\mathcal{U}F(i, w)$ is the supremum utility that can be achieved at (i, w), assuming that the value function in the next period is F. Proofs of the next three results are left as exercises.

Fact. *If F is in $B(D)$, then $\mathcal{U}F$ is in $B(D)$.*

For any F and G in $B(D)$, let

$$d(F, G) = \sup\{|F(i, w) - G(i, w)| : (i, w) \in D\},$$

giving a notion of the *distance* between any two such functions. Clearly $F = G$ if and only if $d(F, G) = 0$.

Lemma. *For any F and G in $B(D)$, $d(\mathcal{U}F, \mathcal{U}G) \leq \rho\, d(F, G)$.*

Using this lemma, we can construct the unique solution F to the equation $\mathcal{U}F = F$. The solution F is called the *fixed point* of $\mathcal{U}$ and, as shown by the following result, can be constructed as the limit of the finite-horizon versions of the value functions as the horizon goes to infinity.

Proposition. *Let $F_{-1}(i, w) = 0$ for all (i, w) in D, and let $F_t = \mathcal{U} F_{t-1}$, $t \geq 0$. Then $F(i, w) \equiv \lim_{t \to \infty} F_t(i, w)$ exists for all (i, w) in D and defines the unique function F in $B(D)$ satisfying $F = \mathcal{U} F$.*

Let $C : D \to \mathbb{R}_+$ and $\Phi : D \to \mathbb{R}^N$ be functions defined by letting $[C(i, w), \Phi(i, w)]$ solve (7)–(9). Given the initial conditions (i, w) of (2)–(6), let W^* be defined by $W_0^* = w$ and $W_t^* = \Phi(W_{t-1}^*, X_{t-1})$, $t \geq 1$. Then let (c^*, θ^*) be defined by $c_t^* = C(W_t^*, X_t)$ and $\theta_t^* = \Phi(W_t^*, X_t)$, $t \geq 0$. We refer to (θ^*, c^*) as the *optimal feedback policy*.

Theorem. *The value function V of (2)–(6) is the unique fixed point of $\mathcal{U}$. The optimal feedback policy (c^*, θ^*) solves (2)–(6).*

Proof: Let F be the unique solution of the Bellman equation. Fix any initial shock i in Z and initial wealth w in $[\underline{w}, \infty)$. Let (θ, c) be an arbitrary feasible policy. For any time t, by the Bellman equation (7)–(9),

$$F(X_t, W_t^\theta) \geq \rho u(c_t) + \rho E^i \left[F(X_{t+1}, W_{t+1}^\theta) \mid X_t \right].$$

Multiplying through by ρ^{t-1} and rearranging,

$$\rho^{t-1} F(X_t, W_t^\theta) - \rho^t E^i \left[F(X_{t+1}, W_{t+1}^\theta) \mid X_t \right] \geq \rho^t u(c_t). \tag{10}$$

Taking expectations on each side, and using the law of iterated expectations,

$$E^i \left[\rho^{t-1} F(X_t, W_t^\theta) \right] - \rho^t E^i \left[F(X_{t+1}, W_{t+1}^\theta) \right] \geq E^i [\rho^t u(c_t)].$$

Calculating the sum of this expression from $t = 0$ to $t = T$, for any time $T \geq 1$, causes telescopic cancellation on the left-hand side, leaving only

$$E^i \left[F(X_0, W_0^\theta) \right] - \rho^T E^i \left[F(X_{T+1}, W_{T+1}^\theta) \right] \geq E^i \left[\sum_{t=0}^{T} \rho^t u(c_t) \right].$$

Since F is a bounded function and $\rho \in (0, 1)$, the limit of the left-hand side as $T \to \infty$ is $F(i, w)$. By the Dominated Convergence Theorem (Appendix C), the limit of the right-hand side is $U^i(c)$. Thus $F(i, w) \geq U^i(c)$, implying that $F(i, w) \geq V(i, w)$ for any i and w. All of the above calculations apply for the feedback policy (c^*, θ^*), for which we can replace the inequality in (10) with an equality, using the definition of C and Φ. This leaves $F(i, w) = U^i(c^*)$. It follows, since (i, w) is arbitrary, that V is indeed the value function and that (c^*, θ^*) is an optimal policy, proving the result. ∎

B. Markov Dynamic Programming and Equilibrium

Section 4A shows the existence of optimal control in feedback form, given by *policy functions* C and Φ that specify optimal consumption and portfolio choices in terms of the current shock–wealth pair (i, w). In order to characterize an equilibrium by the same approach, we adopt stronger utility conditions for this section. In addition to our standing assumption that u is strictly increasing, bounded, concave, and continuous, we add the following regularity condition.

Assumption A.   *The function u is strictly concave and differentiable on $(0, \infty)$.*

We define S to be a single-agent *Markov equilibrium* if associated optimal feedback policies C and Φ can be chosen so that, for any shock i, $C(i, 0) = g(i)$ and $\Phi(i, 0) = 0$. With this, the consumption and security markets always clear if the agent is originally endowed with no wealth beyond that of his or her private endowment. The short sales restriction on portfolios is superfluous in equilibrium since this short sales constraint is not binding at the solution $(e, 0)$, and since the equilibrium shown (which is the unique equilibrium) does not depend on the particular lower bound $-b$ chosen. (It is assigned as an exercise to verify this fact.) Our main objective is to demonstrate the following characterization of equilibrium.

Proposition. *S is a Markov equilibrium if and only if, for all i,*

$$S(i) = \frac{1}{u'[g(i)]} E^i \left(\sum_{t=1}^{\infty} \rho^t u'[g(X_t)] f(X_t) \right). \tag{11}$$

The law of iterated expectations implies the following equivalent form of (11), sometimes called the stochastic Euler equation.

Corollary. *S is a Markov equilibrium if and only if, for any time t and any initial shock i,*

$$S(X_t) = \frac{1}{u'[g(X_t)]} E^i \left(\rho u'[g(X_{t+1})] \left[S(X_{t+1}) + f(X_{t+1}) \right] \, \middle| \, X_t \right). \tag{12}$$

We will demonstrate these results by exploiting the properties of the value function V.

Fact 1. *For each i, $V(i, \cdot) : [\underline{w}, \infty) \to \mathbb{R}$ is increasing and strictly concave.*

Fact 2. *Fixing S arbitrarily, let (C, Φ) be the optimal feedback policies, as above. Suppose at a given i and $\hat{w} > \underline{w}$, that $\hat{c} = C(i, \hat{w}) > 0$. Then $V(i, \cdot)$ is continuously differentiable at $\hat{w}$ with derivative $V_w(i, \hat{w}) = \rho \, u'(\hat{c})$.*

These two facts, proved in a manner similar to their analogues in Chapter 3, imply, from the first order conditions of the Bellman equation (7) and the fact that V solves the Bellman equation, that C and Φ can be chosen with $C(i,0) = g(i)$ and $\Phi(i,0) = 0$ for all i if and only if

$$S(i) = \frac{1}{u'[g(i)]} E^i \left(\rho \, u'[g(X_2)] \left[S(X_2) + f(X_2) \right] \right), \quad i \in Z. \tag{13}$$

Then (13) is equivalent to (11) and (12), proving the Proposition and Corollary.

C. Arbitrage and State Prices

We turn away from the special case of Markov uncertainty in order to investigate the implications of lack of arbitrage and of optimality for security prices in an abstract infinite-horizon setting. Suppose Ω is a set, $\mathcal{F}$ is a tribe on Ω, and, for each non-negative integer t, $\mathcal{F}_t$ is a finite sub-tribe with $\mathcal{F}_t \subset \mathcal{F}_s$ for $s \geq t$. We also fix a probability measure P on $(\Omega, \mathcal{F})$. As usual, we assume that $\mathcal{F}_0$ includes only events of probability 0 or 1. We again denote by L the space of bounded adapted processes. There are N securities; security n is defined by a dividend process δ^n in L and has a price process S^n in L. A trading strategy is some $\theta = (\theta^1, \ldots, \theta^N) \in \Theta \equiv L^N$.

An *arbitrage* is a trading strategy θ with $\delta^\theta > 0$. If there is no arbitrage, then for any T, there is no *T-period arbitrage*, meaning an arbitrage θ with $\theta_t = 0$, $t \geq T$. Fixing T momentarily, if there is no T-period arbitrage, then the results of Chapter 2 imply that there is a *T-period state-price deflator*, a strictly positive process π^T in L with $\pi_0^T = 1$ such that, for any trading strategy θ with $\theta_t = 0$, $t \geq T$, we have $E(\sum_{t=0}^{T} \pi_t^T \delta_t^\theta) = 0$. Likewise, there is a $(T+1)$-period state-price deflator π^{T+1}. It can be checked that the process $\hat{\pi}$ defined by $\hat{\pi}_t = \pi_t^T$, $t \leq T$, and $\hat{\pi}_t = \pi_t^{T+1}$, $t > T$, is also a $(T+1)$-period state-price deflator. By induction in T, this means that there is a strictly positive adapted process π such that, for any trading strategy θ with $\theta_t = 0$ for all t larger than some T, we have $E(\sum_{t=0}^{\infty} \pi_t \delta_t^\theta) = 0$. In particular, π has the property that, for any times t and $\tau \geq t$, we have the well-worn state-pricing relationship

$$S_t = \frac{1}{\pi_t} E_t \left(\pi_\tau S_\tau + \sum_{j=t+1}^{\tau} \pi_j \delta_j \right). \tag{14}$$

Equation (14) even holds when τ is a bounded stopping time. Unfortunately, there is no reason (yet) to believe that there is a state-price deflator, a strictly positive adapted process π such that (14) holds for τ an unbounded stopping time, or that, for any t,

$$S_t = \frac{1}{\pi_t} E_t \left(\sum_{j=t+1}^{\infty} \pi_j \delta_j \right). \tag{15}$$

Indeed, the right-hand side of (15) may not even be well defined. We need some restriction on π!

We call an adapted process x *mean-summable* if $E\left(\sum_{t=0}^{\infty} |x_t|\right) < \infty$, and let L^* denote the space of mean-summable processes. If $\pi \in L^*$ and $c \in L$, then the Dominated Convergence Theorem (Appendix C) implies that $E\left(\sum_{t=0}^{\infty} \pi_t c_t\right)$ is well defined and finite, so L^* may be a natural space of candidate state-price deflators if (15) is to work.

D. Optimality and State Prices

An agent is defined by an endowment process e in the space L_+ of non-negative processes in L, and by a strictly increasing utility function $U : L_+ \to \mathbb{R}$. Given the dividend-price pair $(\delta, S) \in L^N \times L^N$, the agent has the budget-feasible set $X(S, e) = \{e + \delta^\theta \in L_+ : \theta \in \Theta\}$ and faces the problem

$$\sup_{c \in X(S,e)} U(c). \tag{16}$$

We say that the utility function U is L^*-*smooth* at c if the gradient $\nabla U(c)$ exists and moreover has a unique Riesz representation π in L^* defined by

$$\nabla U(c; x) = E \left(\sum_{t=0}^{\infty} \pi_t x_t \right),$$

for any feasible direction x in L. (See Appendix B for the definition of the gradient and feasible directions.) For example, suppose that U is defined by $U(c) = E\left[\sum_{t=0}^{\infty} \rho^t u(c_t)\right]$, where $u : \mathbb{R}_+ \to \mathbb{R}$ is strictly increasing and continuously differentiable on $(0, \infty)$, and where $\rho \in (0, 1)$. Then, for any c in L_+ that is bounded away from zero, U is L^*-smooth at c, any x in L is a feasible direction at c, and

$$\nabla U(c; x) = E \left[\sum_{t=0}^{\infty} \rho^t u'(c_t) x_t \right], \quad x \in L. \tag{17}$$

These facts leave us with the following characterization of state-price deflators.

Proposition. *Suppose c^* solves (16), c^* is bounded away from zero, and U is L^*-smooth at c^*. Then the Riesz representation π of $\nabla U(c^*)$ is a state-price deflator.*

Corollary. *Suppose, moreover, that U is defined by $U(c) = E\left[\sum_{t=0}^{\infty} \rho^t u(c_t)\right]$, where $\rho \in (0,1)$ and u has a strictly positive derivative on $(0,\infty)$. Then π, defined by $\pi_t = \rho^t u'(c_t^*)$, is a state-price deflator and, for any time t and stopping time $\tau > t$,*

$$
S_t = \frac{1}{u'(c_t^*)} E_t \left[\rho^{\tau - t} u'(c_\tau^*) S_\tau + \sum_{j=t+1}^{\tau} \rho^{j-t} u'(c_j^*) \delta_j \right].
$$

This corollary gives a necessary condition for optimality that, when specialized to the case of equilibrium, recovers the stochastic Euler equation (12) as a necessary condition on equilibrium without relying on Markov uncertainty or dynamic programming. For sufficiency, we should give conditions under which the stochastic Euler equation implies that S is an equilibrium. For this, we define S to be a single-agent equilibrium if e solves (16) given S.

Theorem. *Suppose that U is strictly increasing, concave, and L^*-smooth at the endowment process e. Suppose that the endowment process e is bounded away from zero. Let $\pi \in L^*$ be the Riesz representation of $\nabla U(e)$. It is necessary and sufficient for S to be a single-agent equilibrium that π is a state-price deflator.*

The assumption that e is bounded away from zero is automatically satisfied in the Markovian example of Section 4A. Proof of the Theorem is assigned as an exercise.

E. Method-of-Moments Estimation

Although it is not our main purpose to delve into econometrics, it seems worthwhile to illustrate here why the infinite-horizon setting is deemed useful for empirical modeling.

Suppose that $B \subset \mathbb{R}^m$ is a set of parameters; each b in B corresponds to a different Markov economy with the same state space Z. In particular, the transition matrix $q(b)$ of the Markov process X may vary with b. For instance, we could take a single agent with utility given by a discount factor $\rho \in (0,1)$ and a reward function $u_\alpha(x) = x^\alpha/\alpha$ for $\alpha < 1$ (with $u_0(x) = \log x$). We could then take $m = 2$ and $b = (\rho, \alpha) \in B = (0,\infty) \times (-\infty, 1)$. In this example, the transition matrix $q(b)$ does not depend on b.

We fix some b_0 in B, to be thought of as the "true" parameter vector governing the economy. Our approach will be to estimate the unknown parameter vector b_0 with the generalized method of moments. Suppose that there is some integer $\ell \geq 0$ such that, for each time t, the econometrician observes at time $t + \ell$ the data $h(Y_t)$, where $Y_t = (X_t, X_{t+1}, \ldots, X_{t+\ell})$ and $h : Z^{\ell+1} \to \mathbb{R}^n$. For example, the data could be in the form of security prices, dividends, endowments, or functions of these.

For simplicity, we will assume that the transition matrix $q(b_0)$ of X is strictly positive. With this, a result known as the *Frobenius-Perron Theorem* implies that there is a unique vector $p \in \mathbb{R}^k_{++}$ whose elements sum to 1 with the property that $q(b_0)^\top p = p$. Letting $q(b_0)^t$ denote the t-fold product of $q(b_0)$, we see that $P_i(X_t = j) = q(b_0)^t_{ij}$, so that $q(b_0)^t$ is the t-period transition matrix. It can be shown that p is given by any row of $\lim_t q(b_0)^t$. Thus, regardless of the initial shock i, $\lim_t P_i(X_t = j) = p_j$. Indeed, the convergence to the "steady-state" probability vector p is exponentially fast, in the sense that there is a constant $\beta > 1$ such that, for any i and j,

$$\beta^t [p_j - P_i(X_t = j)] \to 0. \tag{18}$$

From this, it follows immediately that, for any $H : Z \to \mathbb{R}$, we have $E^i[H(X_t)] \to \sum_{i=1}^k p_i H(i)$, and again convergence is exponentially fast. The *empirical distribution vector* p_T of X at time T is defined by

$$p_{Ti} = \frac{1}{T} \#\{t < T : X_t = i\},$$

where $\#A$ denotes the number of elements in a finite set A. That is, p_{Ti} is the average fraction of time, up to T, spent in state i. From the law of large numbers for *i.i.d.* sequences of random variables, it is not hard to show that p_T converges almost surely to the steady-state distribution vector p. Proof of this fact is assigned as Exercise 4.14, which includes a broad hint. From this, we have the following form of the *law of large numbers for Markov chains*.

The Strong Law of Large Numbers for Markov Chains. *For any $H : Z \to \mathbb{R}$, the empirical average $\sum_{t=0}^T H(X_t)/T$ converges almost surely to the steady-state mean $\sum_{i=1}^k p_i H(i)$.*

Proof: Since $\sum_{t=0}^T H(X_t)/T = \sum_{i=1}^k p_{Ti} H(i)$, the result follows from the fact that $p_T \to p$ almost surely. ∎

All of these properties follow even if $q(b_0)$ is not strictly positive provided the t-period transition matrix $q(b_0)^t$ is strictly positive for some t. From this fact, Y inherits the same convergence properties as X, since Y can be treated as a Markov process whose $(\ell+1)$-period transition matrix is strictly positive. In particular, for any $G : Z^{\ell+1} \to \mathbb{R}$, the empirical average $\sum_{t=1}^T G(Y_t)/T$ converges almost surely to the corresponding steady-state mean, which is also equal to $\lim_t E^i[G(Y_t)]$, a quantity that is independent of the initial shock i.

We now specify some *test moment function* $F : \mathbb{R}^n \times B \to \mathbb{R}^M$ with the property that, for all t, $E_t\left(F[h(Y_t), b_0]\right) = 0$. For a simple example, we could take the single-agent Markov equilibrium described by the stochastic Euler equation (13), where the utility function is specified as above by the unknown parameter vector $b_0 = (\rho_0, \alpha_0)$. For this example, we can let $Y_t = (X_t, X_{t+1})$ and let $h(Y_t) = (R_{t+1}, e_{t+1}, e_t)$, where $e_t = g(X_t)$ is the current endowment and R_t is the $\mathbb{R}^N$-valued return vector defined by

$$R_{it} = \frac{S_i(X_t) + f_i(X_t)}{S_i(X_{t-1})}, \quad i \in \{1, \ldots, N\}.$$

With $M = N$ and $b = (\rho, \alpha)$, we can let

$$F_i[h(Y_t), b] = \frac{\rho e_{t+1}^{\alpha-1} R_{i,t+1}}{e_t^{\alpha-1}} - 1. \tag{19}$$

From (13), we confirm that $E_t[F(Y_t, b_0)] = 0$.

We know from the strong law of large numbers that, for each b in B, the empirical average $\overline{F}_T(b) \equiv \sum_{t=1}^T F(Y_t, b)/T$ converges almost surely to a limit denoted $\overline{F}_\infty(b)$. By the law of iterated expectations, for any initial state i,

$$E^i[F(Y_t, b_0)] = E^i(E_t[F(Y_t, b_0)]) = 0.$$

From this, we know that $\overline{F}_\infty(b_0) = 0$ almost surely. A natural estimator of b_0 at time t is then given by the problem

$$\inf_{b \in B} \; \| \overline{F}_t(b) \| . \tag{20}$$

Under conditions, one can show that if b_t solves (20) for each t, then $\{b_t\}$ is a *consistent estimator*, in the sense that $b_t \to b_0$ almost surely. The sequence $\{b_t\}$, if it exists, is called a *generalized-method-of-moments*, or *GMM*, estimator of b_0. A sufficient set of technical conditions is as follows.

GMM Regularity Conditions. *The parameter set B is compact. For any b in B other than b_0, $\overline{F}_\infty(b) \neq 0$. The function F is Lipschitz with respect to b, in the sense that there is a constant k such that, for any y in $Z^{\ell+1}$ and any b_1 and b_2 in B, we have*

$$\| F(y, b_1) - F(y, b_2) \| \leq k \, \| b_1 - b_2 \| .$$

Theorem. *Under the GMM regularity conditions, a GMM estimator exists and any GMM estimator is consistent.*

The proof follows immediately from the following proposition.

Uniform Strong Law of Large Numbers. *Under the GMM regularity conditions,*

$$\sup_{b \in B} |\overline{F}_T(b) - \overline{F}_\infty(b)| \to 0 \quad \text{almost surely.}$$

Proof: The following proof is adapted from a source indicated in the Notes. Without loss of generality for the following arguments, we can take $M = 1$. Since B is a compact set and F is Lipschitz with respect to b, for each $\epsilon \in (0, \infty)$ there is a finite set $B_\epsilon \subset B$ with the following property: For any b in B there is some b_ϵ and b^ϵ in B_ϵ satisfying, for all y,

$$F(y, b_\epsilon) \leq F(y, b) \leq F(y, b^\epsilon), \qquad |F(y, b_\epsilon) - F(y, b^\epsilon)| \leq \epsilon. \tag{21}$$

As is customary, for any sequence $\{x_n\}$ of numbers we let

$$\underline{\lim}_n x_n = \sup_n \inf_{k \geq n} x_k.$$

For a given $\epsilon > 0$,

$$\underline{\lim}_t \inf_b \left[\overline{F}_t(b) - \overline{F}_\infty(b) \right] \geq \underline{\lim}_t \inf_b \left[\overline{F}_t(b_\epsilon) - \overline{F}_\infty(b) \right]$$

$$\geq \underline{\lim}_t \inf_b \left[\overline{F}_t(b_\epsilon) - \overline{F}_\infty(b_\epsilon) \right]$$

$$+ \inf_b \left[\overline{F}_\infty(b_\epsilon) - \overline{F}_\infty(b) \right]$$

$$\geq -\epsilon \quad \text{a.s.,}$$

by the strong law of large numbers, (21), and the fact that B_ϵ is finite. Let $A_\epsilon \subset \Omega$ be the event of probability 1 on which this inequality holds, and let $A = A_1 \cap A_{1/2} \cap A_{1/3} \cdots$. Then A also has probability 1, and on A we have

$$\underline{\lim}_t \inf_b \left[\overline{F}_t(b) - \overline{F}_\infty(b) \right] \geq 0. \tag{22}$$

Likewise, by using b^ϵ in place of b_ϵ and $-\overline{F}$ in place of $\overline{F}$, we have

$$\underline{\lim}_t \inf_b \left[-\overline{F}_t(b) + \overline{F}_\infty(b) \right] \geq 0 \quad \text{a.s.} \tag{23}$$

The claim follows from (22) and (23). ∎

The Notes cite papers that prove the consistency of GMM estimators under weaker conditions and analyze the theoretical properties of this estimator. Included in these are conditions for the normality of the limit of the distribution of $(b_t - b_0)/\sqrt{t}$ and the form of covariance matrix Σ of this asymptotic distribution. As shown in these references, the efficiency properties of the GMM estimator, in terms of this asymptotic covariance matrix Σ, can be improved by replacing the criterion function $b \mapsto \| \overline{F}_t(b) \|$ in (20) with the criterion function $b \mapsto \overline{F}_t(b)^\top W_t \overline{F}_t(b)$, for a particular adapted sequence $\{W_t\}$ of positive semi-definite matrices. Other papers cited in the Notes apply GMM estimators in a financial setting.

Exercises

4.1   Prove Fact 4A.

4.2   Prove Lemma 4A.

4.3   Prove Proposition 4A.

4.4   Prove Fact 1 of Section 4B.

4.5   Prove Fact 2 of Section 4B.

4.6   Show that (13) is necessary and sufficient for optimality of $C(i,0) = g(i)$ and $\Phi(i,0) = 0$, that is, for equilibrium.

4.7   Show that (11), (12), and (13) are equivalent.

4.8   Show that the constraint (9), placing a lower bound on portfolios, is not binding in a Markov equilibrium.

4.9   Suppose there is a single security with price process $S \equiv 1$ and with dividend process δ satisfying $\delta_t > -1$ for all t. The utility function U is defined by (1), where $u(x) = x^\alpha/\alpha$ for $\alpha < 1$ and $\alpha \neq 0$. The endowment process e is given by $e_t = 0$, $t > 1$, and $e_0 = w > 0$. Let $\mathcal{L}_+$ denote the space of non-negative adapted processes. With a non-negative wealth constraint and no other bounding restrictions, the agent's problem is modified to

$$\sup_{c \in \mathcal{L}_+} \; U(c) \;\; \text{subject to} \;\; W_t^c \geq 0, \; t \geq 0, \tag{24}$$

where $W_0^c = w$ and $W_t^c = (W_{t-1}^c - c_{t-1})(1 + \delta_t)$, $t > 1$.

(A)   Suppose $\delta_t = \epsilon$ for all t, where $\epsilon > -1$ is a constant. Provide regularity conditions on α, ρ, and ϵ under which there exists a solution to (24). Solve for the value function and the optimal consumption policy. Hint: Use dynamic programming and conjecture that the value function is of the form $V(w) = kw^\alpha/\alpha$ for some constant k. Solve the Bellman equation explicitly for V, and then show that the Bellman equation characterizes optimality by showing that $V(w) \geq U(c)$ for any feasible c, and that $V(w) = U(c^*)$, where c^* is your candidate policy. Note that this will require a demonstration that $\rho^t V(W_t^c) \to 0$ for any feasible c.

(B) Suppose that δ is an *i.i.d.* process. Provide regularity conditions on $\beta = \rho E[(1 + \delta_1)^\alpha]$, ρ, and α under which there exists a solution to (24). Solve for the value function and the optimal consumption policy.

(C) Solve parts (A) and (B) once again for $u(x) = \log(x)$, $x > 0$, and $u(0) = -\infty$. The utility function U may now take $-\infty$ as a value.

4.10 Extend the solutions to parts (D) and (E) of Exercise 3.8 to the infinite-horizon case, adding any additional regularity conditions on the parameters $(\gamma, \alpha, \rho, A, B, \sigma^2)$ that you feel are called for.

4.11 Demonstrate the Riesz representation (17) of the gradient of the additive discounted utility function. Hint: Use the Dominated Convergence Theorem.

4.12 Prove Theorem 4D.

4.13 Prove relation (18), showing exponential convergence of probabilities to their steady-state counterparts.

4.14 Prove the version of the strong law of large numbers shown in Section 4E. Hint: Prove the almost sure convergence of the empirical distribution vector p_T to p by using the strong law of large numbers for *i.i.d.* random variables with finite expectations. For this, given any $l \in Z$, let $\tau_n(l)$ be the n-th time $t \geq 0$ that $X_t = l$. Note that

$$Q_{nlj} \equiv \#\{t : X_t = j, \ \tau_n(l) \leq t < \tau_{n+1}\}$$

has a distribution that does not depend on n or the initial state i, and that, for each l and j, the sequences $\{Q_{1lj}, Q_{2lj}, \ldots\}$ and $\{t_n\}$, with $t_n = \tau_{n+1}(l) - \tau_n(l)$, are each *i.i.d.* with distributions that do not depend on the initial state i. Complete the proof from this point, considering the properties, for each l and j in Z, of

$$\frac{N^{-1} \sum_{n=1}^{N} Q_{nlj}}{N^{-1} \sum_{n=1}^{N} t_n}.$$

Notes

Freedman (1983) covers the theory of Markov chains. Revuz (1975) is a treatment of Markov processes on a general state space. Sections 4A and 4B are based on Lucas (1978), although the details here are different. LeRoy (1973) gives a precursor of this model. The probability space, on which the Markov process X is defined, is constructed in Bertsekas and Shreve (1978). The fixed-point approach of Section 4A is based on Blackwell (1965); Lemma 4A is, in more general guises, called Blackwell's Theorem. The results extend easily to a general compact metric space Z of shocks, as, for example, in Lucas (1978), Duffie (1988), or Stokey and Lucas (1989). Corresponding results can be shown for production, as in Brock (1979, 1982) and Duffie (1988b); and for more general utilities, as in the recursive-utility model of Epstein and Zin (1989). See also Ma (1991a), Kan (1991), and Streufert (1991a, b, c). Wang (1991a, b) shows the generic ability to distinguish between additive and nonadditive recursive utility from security-price data. Sections 4C and 4D are slightly unconventional, and are designed merely to bridge the gap from the finite-dimensional results of Chapter 2 to this infinite-dimensional setting. Strong assumptions are adopted here in order to guarantee the "transversality" conditions. Much weaker conditions suffice. See, for example, Kocherlakota (1990).

Kandori (1988) gives a proof of Pareto optimality and a representative agent in a complete-markets general equilibrium model. Examples are given by Abel (1986), Campbell (1984), Donaldson, Johnson, and Mehra (1987), and Dumas and Luciano (1989). Further characterization of equilibrium is given by Prescott and Mehra (1980) and Donaldson and Mehra (1984). Levine (1985) shows conditions for the existence of equilibrium with incomplete markets. Conditions for the existence of a stationary Markov equilibrium (with incomplete markets and heterogeneous agents) are given by Duffie, Geanakoplos, Mas-Colell, and McLennan (1988).

A recent spate of literature has addressed the issue of asset pricing with heterogeneous agents and incomplete markets, partly spurred by the *equity premium puzzle* pointed out by Mehra and Prescott (1985), showing the difference in expected returns between equity and riskless bonds to be far in excess of what one would find from a typical representative-agent model. Bewley (1982) and Mankiw (1986) have seminal examples of the effects of incomplete markets. The more recent literature includes Scheinkman (1989), Aiyagari and Gertler (1990), Mehrling (1990), Constantinides and Duffie (1991), Duffie (1991), Heaton and Lucas (1991), Marcet and Singleton (1991), Lucas (1991), and Telmer (1990). Others have attempted to resolve the perceived equity premium puzzle by turning to more general utility functions, such as the habit-formation model (see, for example, Constantinides [1990a] and Hansen and Jaganathan [1990]) or the recursive model (see Epstein and Zin [1989, 1991]).

Section 4E gives a "baby version" of the estimation technique used in Hansen and Singleton (1982, 1983). Brown and Gibbons (1985) give an alternative exposition of this model. The generalized method of moments, in a much more general setting than that of Section 4E, is shown by Hansen (1982) to be consistent. We have used the exponential convergence of probabilities given by equation (18) to avoid the assumption that the shock process X is stationary. This extends to a more general Markov setting under regularity conditions. The proof given for the uniform strong law of large numbers is based on Pollard (1984). A general treatment of method-of-moments estimation can be found in Gallant and White (1988). Duffie and Singleton (1989) extend the GMM to a setting with simulated estimation of moments. General treatments of dynamic programming are given by Bertsekas and Shreve (1978) and Dynkin and Yushkevich (1979). Exercise 4.11 is based on Samuelson (1969) and Levhari and Srinivasan (1969), and is extended by Hakansson (1970), Blume, Easley, and O'Hara (1982), and others. Many further results in the vein of Chapter 4 can be found in Duffie (1988b) and, especially, Stokey and Lucas (1989).

II

Continuous-Time Models

Part II is a continuous-time counterpart to Part I in which uncertainty is generated by Brownian motion. The results are somewhat richer and more delicate than those in Part I, with a greater dependence on mathematical technicalities. It is wiser to focus on the parallels than on these technicalities. Once again, the three basic forces behind the theory are arbitrage, optimality, and equilibrium.

Chapter 5 introduces the continuous-trading model and develops the Black-Scholes partial differential equation (PDE) for arbitrage-free prices of derivative securities. The Harrison-Kreps model of equivalent martingale measures is presented in Chapter 6 in parallel with the theory of state prices in continuous time. Chapter 7 applies to the results of Chapter 6 to futures, forwards, American options, and the term structure, including Cox-Ingersoll-Ross and Heath-Jarrow-Morton term-structure models. Chapter 8 is a summary of optimal continuous-time portfolio choice, using both dynamic programming and an approach involving equivalent martingale measures or state prices. Chapter 9 is a summary of security pricing in an equilibrium setting. Included are such well-known models as Breeden's consumption-based capital asset pricing model and the general-equilibrium version of the Cox-Ingersoll-Ross model of the term structure of interest rates. Chapter 10 outlines three numerical methods for calculating derivative security prices in a continuous-time setting: binomial approximation, Monte Carlo simulation of a discrete-time approximation of security prices, and finite-difference solution of the associated PDE for the asset price or the Green's function.

5

The Black-Scholes Model

THIS CHAPTER PRESENTS the basic Black-Scholes model of arbitrage pricing in continuous time, as well as extensions to a nonparametric multivariate Markov setting. We first introduce the Brownian model of uncertainty and continuous security trading, and then derive partial differential equations for the arbitrage-free prices of derivative securities. The classic example is the Black-Scholes option-pricing formula. Chapter 6 extends to a non-Markovian setting using new techniques.

A. Trading Gains for Brownian Prices

We fix a probability space $(\Omega, \mathcal{F}, P)$. A *process* is a measurable function on $\Omega \times [0, \infty)$ into $\mathbb{R}$. (For a definition of measurability with respect to a product space of this variety, see Appendix C.) The value of a process X at time t is the random variable variously written as X_t, $X(t)$, or $X(\cdot, t) : \Omega \to \mathbb{R}$. A *standard Brownian motion* is a process B defined by these properties:

(a) $B_0 = 0$ almost surely;
(b) for any times t and $s > t$, $B_s - B_t$ is normally distributed with mean zero and variance $s - t$;
(c) for any times $t_0, \ldots, t_n$ such that $0 \le t_0 < t_1 < \cdots < t_n < \infty$, the random variables $B(t_0)$, $B(t_1) - B(t_0)$, $\ldots, B(t_n) - B(t_{n-1})$ are independently distributed; and
(d) for each ω in Ω, the *sample path* $t \mapsto B(\omega, t)$ is continuous.

It is a nontrivial fact, whose proof has a colorful history, that the probability space $(\Omega, \mathcal{F}, P)$ can be constructed so that there exist standard Brownian motions. By 1900, in perhaps the first scientific work involving Brownian motion, Louis Bachelier proposed Brownian motion as a model of stock prices. We will follow his lead for the time being and suppose that a given standard Brownian motion B is the price process of a security. Later we consider more general classes of price processes.

The tribe $\mathcal{F}_t^B$ generated by $\{B_s : 0 \leq s \leq t\}$ is, on intuitive grounds, a reasonable model of the information available at time t for trading the security, since $\mathcal{F}_t^B$ includes every event based on the history of the price process B up to that time. For technical reasons, however, one must be able to assign probabilities to the *null sets* of Ω, the subsets of events of zero probability. For this reason, we will fix instead the *standard filtration* $\mathbb{F} = \{\mathcal{F}_t : t \geq 0\}$ of B, with $\mathcal{F}_t$ defined as the tribe generated by the union of $\mathcal{F}_t^B$ and the null sets. The probability measure P is also extended by letting $P(A) = 0$ for any null set A. This *completion* of the probability space is defined in more detail in Appendix C.

A *trading strategy* is an adapted process θ specifying at each state ω and time t the number $\theta_t(\omega)$ of units of the security to hold. If a strategy θ is a constant, say $\bar{\theta}$, between two dates t and $s > t$, then the total gain between those two dates is $(B_s - B_t)\bar{\theta}$, the price change multiplied by the quantity held. So long as the strategy is piecewise constant, we would have no difficulty in defining the total gain between any two times. In order to make for a good model of trading gains when we do not necessarily require piecewise constant trading, a trading strategy θ is required to satisfy $\int_0^T \theta_t^2 \, dt < \infty$ almost surely for each T. Let $\mathcal{L}^2$ denote the space of adapted processes satisfying this integrability restriction. For each θ in $\mathcal{L}^2$ there is an adapted process with continuous sample paths, denoted $\int \theta \, dB$, that is called the *stochastic integral* of θ with respect to B. The definition of $\int \theta \, dB$ is outlined in Appendix D. The value of the process $\int \theta \, dB$ at time T is usually denoted $\int_0^T \theta_t \, dB_t$, and represents the total gain generated up to time T by trading the security with price process B according to the trading strategy θ.

An interpretation of $\int_0^T \theta_t \, dB_t$ can be drawn from the discrete-time analogue $\sum_{t=0}^T \theta_t \Delta^1 B_t$, where $\Delta^1 B_t \equiv B_{t+1} - B_t$, that is, the sum (over t) of the shares held at t multiplied by the change in price between t and $t+1$. More generally, let $\Delta^n B_t = B_{(t+1)/n} - B_{t/n}$. In a sense that we shall not make precise, $\int_0^T \theta_t \, dB_t$ can be thought of as the limit of $\sum_{t=0}^{Tn} \theta_{t/n} \Delta^n B_t$, as the number n of trading intervals per unit of time goes to infinity. This statement is literally true, for example, if θ has continuous sample paths, taking "limit" to mean limit in probability. The definition of $\int_0^T \theta_t \, dB_t$ as a limit in probability of the discrete-time analogue extends to a larger class of θ, but not large enough to capture some of the applications in later chapters. The definition of $\int_0^T \theta_t \, dB_t$ given in Appendix D therefore admits any θ in $\mathcal{L}^2$.

The stochastic integral has some of the properties that one would expect from the fact that it is a good model of trading gains. For example, suppose a trading strategy θ is piecewise constant on $[0, T]$ in that, for some stopping times $t_0, \ldots, t_N$ with $0 = t_0 < t_1 < \cdots < t_N = T$, and for any n, we have $\theta(t) = \theta(t_{n-1})$ for all $t \in [t_{n-1}, t_n)$. Then

$$\int_0^T \theta_t \, dB_t = \sum_{n=1}^N \theta(t_{n-1})[B(t_n) - B(t_{n-1})].$$

One of the advantages of the continuous-time model is that it allows us to consider trading strategies that are not necessarily piecewise constant. A second natural property of stochastic integration as a model for trading gains is linearity: For any θ and φ in $\mathcal{L}^2$ and any scalars a and b, the process $a\theta + b\varphi$ is also in $\mathcal{L}^2$, and

$$\int_0^T (a\theta_t + b\varphi_t) \, dB_t = a \int_0^T \theta_t \, dB_t + b \int_0^T \varphi_t \, dB_t.$$

B. Martingale Trading Gains

The properties of standard Brownian motion imply that B is a martingale. (This follows basically from the property that its increments are independent and of zero expectation, but a proof is not offered here.) A process θ is bounded if there is a fixed constant k such that $|\theta(\omega, t)| \leq k$ for all (ω, t). For any bounded θ in $\mathcal{L}^2$, the law of iterated expectations and the "martingality" of B imply, for any integer times t and $\tau > t$, that $E_t(\sum_{s=t}^\tau \theta_s \Delta^1 B_s) = 0$. This means that the discrete-time gain process X, defined by $X_0 = 0$ and $X_t = \sum_{s=0}^{t-1} \theta_s \Delta^1 B_s$, is itself a martingale with respect to the discrete-time filtration $\{\mathcal{F}_0, \mathcal{F}_1, \ldots\}$, an exercise for the reader. The same is also true in continuous time: For any bounded θ in $\mathcal{L}^2$, $\int \theta \, dB$ is a martingale. This is natural; it should be impossible to generate an expected profit by trading a security that never experiences an expected price change. If one places no bounding restriction on θ, however, the expectation of $\int_0^T \theta_t \, dB_t$ may not even exist. The following proposition assists in determining whether the expectation or the variance of $\int_0^T \theta_t \, dB_t$ is finite, and whether $\int \theta \, dB$ is indeed a martingale. Consider the spaces

$$\mathcal{H}^1 = \left\{ \theta \in \mathcal{L}^2 : E\left[\left(\int_0^T \theta_t^2 \, dt \right)^{1/2} \right] < \infty, \ T > 0 \right\}$$

$$\mathcal{H}^2 = \left\{ \theta \in \mathcal{L}^2 : E\left(\int_0^T \theta_t^2 \, dt \right) < \infty, \ T > 0 \right\}.$$

Proposition. *If θ is in $\mathcal{H}^1$ or $\mathcal{H}^2$, then $\int \theta\, dB$ is a martingale. If θ is in $\mathcal{H}^2$, then*

$$\text{var}\left(\int_0^T \theta_t\, dB_t\right) = E\left(\int_0^T \theta_t^2\, dt\right) < \infty. \tag{1}$$

A proof is cited in the Notes.

C. Ito Prices and Gains

As a model of security-price processes, standard Brownian motion is too restrictive for most purposes. Consider, instead, a process of the form

$$S_t = x + \int_0^t \mu_s\, ds + \int_0^t \sigma_s\, dB_s, \quad t \geq 0, \tag{2}$$

where x is a real number, σ is in $\mathcal{L}^2$, and μ is in $\mathcal{L}^1$, meaning that μ is an adapted process such that $\int_0^t |\mu_s|\, ds < \infty$ almost surely for all t. We call a process S of this form (2) an *Ito process*, a sufficiently general type of security-price process for all that follows in this chapter. It is common to write (2) in the informal "differential" form

$$dS_t = \mu_t\, dt + \sigma_t\, dB_t; \quad S_0 = x.$$

One often thinks intuitively of dS_t as the "increment" of S at time t, made up of two parts, the "dt" part and the "dB_t" part. In order to further interpret this differential representation of an Ito process, suppose that σ and μ are in $\mathcal{H}^2$. It is then literally the case that, for any time t,

$$\frac{d}{d\tau} E_t\left(S_\tau\right)\bigg|_{\tau=t} = \mu_t \quad \text{almost surely} \tag{3}$$

and

$$\frac{d}{d\tau} \text{var}_t\left(S_\tau\right)\bigg|_{\tau=t} = \sigma_t^2 \quad \text{almost surely}, \tag{4}$$

where the derivatives are taken from the right, and where, for any random variable X with finite variance, $\text{var}_t(X) \equiv E_t(X^2) - [E_t(X)]^2$ is the $\mathcal{F}_t$-conditional variance of X. In this sense of (3) and (4), we can interpret μ_t as the conditional expected rate of change of S at time t and σ_t^2 as the rate of change of the conditional variance of S at time t. One sometimes reads the associated abuses of notation "$E_t(dS_t) = \mu_t\, dt$" and "$\text{var}_t(dS_t) = \sigma_t^2\, dt$." Of course, dS_t is not even a random variable, so this sort of characterization is not rigorously justified and is used purely for its intuitive content. We will refer to μ and σ as the *drift* and *diffusion* processes of S, respectively. Many authors reserve the term "diffusion" for σ_t^2 or other related quantities.

For an Ito process S of the form (2), let $\mathcal{L}(S)$ denote the space consisting of any adapted process θ with $\{\theta_t \mu_t : t \geq 0\}$ in $\mathcal{L}^1$ and $\{\theta_t \sigma_t : t \geq 0\}$ in $\mathcal{L}^2$. For θ in $\mathcal{L}(S)$, we define the stochastic integral $\int \theta \, dS$ as the Ito process given by

$$\int_0^T \theta_t \, dS_t = \int_0^T \theta_t \mu_t \, dt + \int_0^T \theta_t \sigma_t \, dB_t, \quad T \geq 0. \tag{5}$$

We also refer to $\int \theta \, dS$ as the *gain process generated by θ*, given the price process S. If θ is such that $\{\theta_t \mu_t : t \geq 0\}$ and $\{\theta_t \sigma_t : t \geq 0\}$ are in $\mathcal{H}^2$, we write that θ is in $\mathcal{H}^2(S)$; this condition guarantees that the gain $\int \theta \, dS$ is a finite-variance process.

We will have occasion to refer to adapted processes θ and φ that are equal *almost everywhere*, by which we mean that $E(\int_0^\infty |\theta_t - \varphi_t| \, dt) = 0$. In fact, we shall write "$\theta = \varphi$" whenever $\theta = \varphi$ almost everywhere. This is a natural convention, for suppose that X and Y are Ito processes with $X_0 = Y_0$ and with $dX_t = \mu_t \, dt + \sigma_t \, dB_t$ and $dY_t = a_t \, dt + b_t \, dB_t$. Since stochastic integrals are defined for our purposes as continuous sample path processes, it turns out that $X_t = Y_t$ for all t almost surely if and only if $\mu = a$ almost everywhere and $\sigma = b$ almost everywhere. We call this the *unique decomposition property* of Ito processes.

D. Ito's Lemma

More than any other result, *Ito's Lemma* is the basis for explicit solutions to asset pricing problems in a continuous-time setting.

Ito's Lemma. Suppose X is an Ito process with $dX_t = \mu_t \, dt + \sigma_t \, dB_t$, and let $f : \mathbb{R}^2 \to \mathbb{R}$ be twice continuously differentiable. Then the process Y, defined by $Y_t = f(X_t, t)$, is an Ito process with

$$dY_t = \left[f_x(X_t, t)\mu_t + f_t(X_t, t) + \frac{1}{2} f_{xx}(X_t, t)\sigma_t^2 \right] dt + f_x(X_t, t)\sigma_t \, dB_t. \tag{6}$$

A generalization of Ito's Lemma appears later in the chapter. Expression (6) is known as *Ito's formula*.

E. The Black-Scholes Option-Pricing Formula

Consider a security, to be called a *stock*, with price process

$$S_t = x \exp(\alpha t + \sigma B_t), \quad t \geq 0, \tag{7}$$

where $x > 0$, α, and σ are constants. Such a process, called a *geometric Brownian motion*, is often called *log-normal* because, for any t, $\log(S_t) = \log(x) + \alpha t + \sigma B_t$ is normally distributed. Moreover, since $X_t \equiv \alpha t + \sigma B_t = \int_0^t \alpha\, ds + \int_0^t \sigma\, dB_s$ defines an Ito process X with constant drift α and diffusion σ, and since $y \mapsto x\, e^y$ is a C^2 function, Ito's Lemma implies that S is an Ito process and that

$$dS_t = \mu S_t\, dt + \sigma S_t\, dB_t; \quad S_0 = x,$$

where $\mu = \alpha + \sigma^2/2$. From (3) and (4), at any time t, S has the conditional expected rate of change μS_t and conditional rate of change of variance $\sigma^2 S_t^2$, so that, per dollar invested in this security at time t, one may think of μ as the "instantaneous" expected rate of return, and σ as the "instantaneous" standard deviation of the rate of return. This sort of characterization abounds in the literature, and one often reads the associated abuses of notation "$E(dS_t/S_t) = \mu\, dt$" and "$\mathrm{var}(dS_t/S_t) = \sigma^2\, dt$." The coefficient σ is also known as the *volatility* of S. In any case, a geometric Brownian motion is a natural two-parameter model of a security-price process because of these simple interpretations of μ and σ.

Consider a second security, to be called a *bond*, with the price process β defined by

$$\beta_t = \beta_0\, e^{rt}, \quad t \geq 0, \tag{8}$$

for some constants $\beta_0 > 0$ and r. We have the obvious interpretation of r as the *continually compounding interest rate*, that is, the exponential rate at which riskless deposits accumulate with interest. Throughout, we will also refer to r as the *short rate*. Since $\{rt : t \geq 0\}$ is trivially an Ito process, β is also an Ito process with

$$d\beta_t = r\beta_t\, dt. \tag{9}$$

We can also view (9) as an ordinary differential equation with initial condition β_0 and solution (8).

We allow any trading strategies a in $\mathcal{H}^2(S)$ for the stock and b in $\mathcal{H}^2(\beta)$ for the bond. Such a trading strategy (a, b) is said to be *self-financing* if it generates no dividends (either positive or negative), meaning that, for all t,

$$a_t S_t + b_t \beta_t = a_0 S_0 + b_0 \beta_0 + \int_0^t a_\tau\, dS_\tau + \int_0^t b_\tau\, d\beta_\tau. \tag{10}$$

The self-financing condition (10) is merely a statement that the current portfolio value (on the left-hand side) is precisely the initial investment plus any trading gains, and therefore that no dividend "inflow" or "outflow" is generated.

Now consider a third security, an *option*. We begin with the case of a European call option on the stock, giving its owner the right, but not the obligation, to buy the stock at a given exercise price K on a given expiry date T. The option's price process Y is as yet unknown except for the fact that $Y_T = (S_T - K)^+ \equiv \max(S_T - K, 0)$, which follows from the fact that the option is rationally exercised if and only if $S_T > K$. (See Exercise 2.1 for a discrete-time analogue.)

Suppose there exists a self-financing trading strategy (a, b) in the stock and bond with $a_T S_T + b_T \beta_T = Y_T$. If $a_0 S_0 + b_0 \beta_0 < Y_0$, then one could sell the option for Y_0, make an initial investment of $a_0 S_0 + b_0 \beta_0$ in the trading strategy (a, b), and at time T liquidate the entire portfolio $(-1, a_T, b_T)$ of option, stock, and bond with payoff $-Y_T + a_T S_T + b_T \beta_T = 0$. The initial profit $Y_0 - a_0 S_0 - b_0 \beta_0 > 0$ is thus riskless, so the trading strategy $(-1, a, b)$ would be an arbitrage. Likewise, if $a_0 S_0 + b_0 \beta_0 > Y_0$, the strategy $(1, -a, -b)$ is an arbitrage. Thus, if there is no arbitrage, $Y_0 = a_0 S_0 + b_0 \beta_0$. The same arguments applied at each date t imply that, in the absence of arbitrage, $Y_t = a_t S_t + b_t \beta_t$. A full definition of continuous-time arbitrage is given in Chapter 6, but for now we can proceed without much ambiguity at this informal level. Our objective now is to show the following.

The Black-Scholes Formula. *If there is no arbitrage, then, for all* $t < T$, $Y_t = C(S_t, t)$, *where*

$$C(x, t) = x\Phi(z) - e^{-r(T-t)} K\Phi\left(z - \sigma\sqrt{T - t}\right), \qquad (11)$$

with

$$z = \frac{\log(x/K) + (r + \sigma^2/2)(T - t)}{\sigma\sqrt{T - t}}, \qquad (12)$$

where Φ *is the cumulative standard normal distribution function.*

F. A First Attack on the Black-Scholes Formula

We will eventually see many different ways to arrive at the Black-Scholes formula (11)–(12). Although it is not the shortest argument, the following is perhaps the most obvious and constructive. We start by assuming that $Y_t = C(S_t, t)$, $t < T$, without knowledge of the function C aside from the assumption that it is twice continuously differentiable on $(0, \infty) \times [0, T)$ (allowing an application of Ito's Lemma). This will lead us to deduce (11)–(12), justifying the assumption and proving the result at the same time.

Based on our assumption that $Y_t = C(S_t, t)$ and Ito's Lemma,

$$dY_t = \mu_Y(t)\, dt + C_x(S_t, t)\sigma S_t\, dB_t, \quad t < T, \tag{13}$$

where

$$\mu_Y(t) = C_x(S_t, t)\mu S_t + C_t(S_t, t) + \frac{1}{2}C_{xx}(S_t, t)\sigma^2 S_t^2.$$

Now suppose there is a self-financing trading strategy (a, b) with

$$a_t S_t + b_t \beta_t = Y_t, \quad t \in [0, T], \tag{14}$$

as outlined in Section E. This assumption will also be justified shortly. Equations (10) and (14), along with the linearity of stochastic integration, imply that

$$dY_t = a_t\, dS_t + b_t\, d\beta_t = (a_t \mu S_t + b_t \beta_t r)\, dt + a_t \sigma S_t\, dB_t. \tag{15}$$

One way to choose the trading strategy (a, b) so that both (13) and (15) are satisfied is to "match coefficients separately in both dB_t and dt." In fact, the unique decomposition property of Ito processes explained at the end of Section 5C implies that this is the only way to ensure that (13) and (15) are consistent. Specifically, we choose a_t so that $a_t \sigma S_t = C_x(S_t, t)\sigma S_t$; for this, we let $a_t = C_x(S_t, t)$. From (14) and $Y_t = C(S_t, t)$, we then have $C_x(S_t, t)S_t + b_t \beta_t = C(S_t, t)$, or

$$b_t = \frac{1}{\beta_t}\left[C(S_t, t) - C_x(S_t, t)S_t\right]. \tag{16}$$

Finally, "matching coefficients in dt" from (13) and (15) leaves, for $t < T$,

$$-rC(S_t, t) + C_t(S_t, t) + rS_t C_x(S_t, t) + \frac{1}{2}\sigma^2 S_t^2 C_{xx}(S_t, t) = 0. \tag{17}$$

In order for (17) to hold, it is enough that C satisfies the *partial differential equation (PDE)*: For all $(x, t) \in (0, \infty) \times [0, T)$,

$$-rC(x, t) + C_t(x, t) + rxC_x(x, t) + \frac{1}{2}\sigma^2 x^2 C_{xx}(x, t) = 0. \tag{18}$$

The fact that $Y_T = C(S_T, T) = (S_T - K)^+$ supplies the *boundary condition*:

$$C(x, T) = (x - K)^+, \quad x \in (0, \infty). \tag{19}$$

By direct calculation of derivatives, one can show as an exercise that (11)–(12) is a solution to (18)–(19). All of this seems to confirm that $C(S_0, 0)$, with C defined by the Black-Scholes formula (11)–(12), is a good candidate for the initial price of the option. In order to make this solid, suppose that $Y_0 > C(S_0, 0)$. Consider the strategy $(-1, a, b)$ in the option, stock, and bond, with $a_t = C_x(S_t, t)$ and b_t given by (16) for $t < T$. We can choose a_T and b_T arbitrarily so that (14) is satisfied; this does not affect the self-financing condition (10) because the value of the trading strategy at a single point in time has no effect on the stochastic integral. (For this, see the implications of equality "almost everywhere" at the end of Section 5C.) The result is that (a, b) is self-financing by construction and that $a_T S_T + b_T \beta_T = Y_T = (S_T - K)^+$. This strategy therefore nets an initial riskless profit of

$$Y_0 - a_0 S_0 - b_0 \beta_0 = Y_0 - C(S_0, 0) > 0,$$

which defines an arbitrage. Likewise, if $Y_0 < C(S_0, 0)$, the trading strategy $(+1, -a, -b)$ is an arbitrage. Thus, it is indeed a necessary condition for the absence of arbitrage that $Y_0 = C(S_0, 0)$. Sufficiency is a more delicate matter. We shall see in Chapter 6 that the Black-Scholes formula for the option price is also sufficient for the absence of arbitrage. One last piece of business is to show that the "option-hedging" strategy (a, b) is such that a is in $\mathcal{H}^2(S)$ and b is in $\mathcal{H}^2(\beta)$. This is true, and is left to show as an exercise.

Transactions costs play havoc with the sort of reasoning just applied. For example, if brokerage fees are any positive fixed fraction of the market value of stock trades, the stock-trading strategy a constructed above would call for infinite total brokerage fees, since, in effect, the number of shares traded is infinite! This fact and the literature on transactions costs in this setting is reviewed in the Notes.

G. The PDE for Arbitrage-Free Derivative Security Prices

The expression $dS_t = \mu S_t \, dt + \sigma S_t \, dB_t$ for the log-normal stock-price process S of Section E is a special case of a *stochastic differential equation* (SDE) of the form

$$dS_t = \mu(S_t, t) \, dt + \sigma(S_t, t) \, dB_t; \quad S_0 = x, \tag{20}$$

where $\mu : \mathbb{R} \times [0, \infty) \to \mathbb{R}$ and $\sigma : \mathbb{R} \times [0, \infty) \to \mathbb{R}$ are given functions. Under regularity conditions on μ and σ reviewed in Appendix E, there is a unique Ito process S solving (20) for each starting point x in $\mathbb{R}$. Assuming that such a solution S defines a stock-price process, consider the bond-price process β defined by

$$\beta_t = \beta_0 \exp \left[\int_0^t r(S_u, u) \, du \right], \tag{21}$$

where $r : \mathbb{R} \times [0, \infty) \to \mathbb{R}$ is well enough behaved for the existence of the integral in (21). A trivial application of Ito's Lemma implies that

$$d\beta_t = \beta_t r(S_t, t) \, dt; \quad \beta_0 > 0. \tag{22}$$

Rather than restricting attention to the option payoff $Y_T = (S_T - K)^+$, consider a *derivative security* defined by the payoff $Y_T = g(S_T)$ at time T, for some continuous $g : \mathbb{R} \to \mathbb{R}$. Arguments like those in Section F lead one to formulate the arbitrage-free price process Y of the derivative security as $Y_t = C(S_t, t)$, $t \in [0, T]$, where C solves the PDE:

$$- r(x, t) C(x, t) + C_t(x, t) + r(x, t) x C_x(x, t) + \frac{1}{2} \sigma(x, t)^2 C_{xx}(x, t) = 0, \tag{23}$$

for $(x, t) \in \mathbb{R} \times [0, T)$, with the boundary condition

$$C(x, T) = g(x), \quad x \in \mathbb{R}. \tag{24}$$

In order to tie things together, suppose that C solves (23)–(24). If $Y_0 \neq C(S_0, 0)$, then an obvious extension of our earlier arguments implies that there is an arbitrage. (This extension is left as an exercise.) This is true even if C is not twice continuously differentiable, but merely $C^{2,1}(\mathbb{R} \times [0, T))$, meaning that the derivatives C_x, C_t, and C_{xx} exist and are continuous in $\mathbb{R} \times (0, T)$, and extend continuously to $\mathbb{R} \times [0, T)$. (Ito's Lemma also applies to any function in this class.)

This PDE characterization of the arbitrage-free price of derivative securities is useful if there are convenient methods for solving PDEs of the form (23)–(24). Numerical solution techniques are discussed in Chapter 10. One of these techniques is based on a probabilistic representation of solutions given in the next section.

H. The Feynman-Kac Solution

A potential simplification of the PDE problem (23)–(24) is obtained as follows. For each (x, t) in $\mathbb{R} \times [0, T]$, let $Z^{x,t}$ be the Ito process defined by $Z_s^{x,t} = x$, $s \leq t$, and

$$dZ_s^{x,t} = r(Z_s^{x,t}, s) Z_s^{x,t} \, ds + \sigma(Z_s^{x,t}, s) \, dB_s, \quad s > t. \tag{25}$$

That is, $Z^{x,t}$ starts at x at time t and continues from there by following the SDE (25).

Condition FK. *The functions* σ, r, *and* g *satisfy one of the technical sufficient conditions given in Appendix E for Feynman-Kac solutions.*

The "technical conditions" called for in Appendix E by condition FK are truly just technical, and can be viewed as smoothness conditions limiting how quickly the functions σ, r, and g can grow or change direction. Referring to Appendix E, we have the following solution to the PDE (23)–(24) as an expectation of the discounted payoff of the derivative security, modified by replacing the original price process S with a *pseudo-price process* $Z^{x,t}$ whose expected rate of return is the riskless interest rate. This is sometimes known as *risk-neutral valuation.* This is not to say that agents are risk-neutral, but rather that risk neutrality applies to an adjusted security-price process.

The Feynman-Kac Solution. *Under Condition FK, if there is no arbitrage, then the derivative security defined by the payoff* $g(S_T)$ *at time* T *has the price process* Y *with* $Y_t = C(S_t, t)$, *where* C *is the solution to (23)–(24) given by*

$$C(x, t) = E\left(\exp\left[-\int_t^T r(Z_s^{x,t}, s)\, ds\right] g\left(Z_T^{x,t}\right)\right), \quad (x, t) \in \mathbb{R} \times [0, T]. \quad (26)$$

It can be checked as an exercise that (26) recovers the Black-Scholes option-pricing formula (11). Calculating this expectation directly is a simpler way to solve the corresponding PDE (17)–(18) than is the Fourier transform method originally used in discovering the Black-Scholes formula. Chapter 10 presents numerical methods for solving (23)–(24), one of which involves Monte Carlo simulation of the Feynman-Kac solution (26), which bears a close resemblance to the discrete-time equivalent-martingale-measure arbitrage-free price representation of Chapter 2. This is more than a coincidence, as we shall see in Chapter 6.

I. The Multidimensional Case

Suppose that $B^1, \ldots, B^d$ are d independent standard Brownian motions on a probability space $(\Omega, \mathcal{F}, P)$. The process $B = (B^1, \ldots, B^d)$ is known as a *standard Brownian motion in* $\mathbb{R}^d$. The standard filtration $\mathbb{F} = \{\mathcal{F}_t : t \geq 0\}$ of B is defined just as in the one-dimensional case. Given $\mathbb{F}$, the subsets $\mathcal{L}^1$, $\mathcal{L}^2$, $\mathcal{H}^1$, and $\mathcal{H}^2$ of adapted processes are also as defined in Sections A and B.

In this setting, X is an Ito process if, for some x in $\mathbb{R}$, some μ in $\mathcal{L}^1$, and some $\theta^1, \ldots, \theta^d$ in $\mathcal{L}^2$,

$$X_t = x + \int_0^t \mu_s\, ds + \sum_{i=1}^d \int_0^t \theta_s^i\, dB_s^i, \quad t \geq 0. \quad (27)$$

For convenience, (27) is also written

$$X_t = x + \int_0^t \mu_s \, ds + \int_0^t \theta_s \, dB_s, \quad t \geq 0, \tag{28}$$

or in the convenient stochastic differential form

$$dX_t = \mu_t \, dt + \theta_t \, dB_t; \quad X_0 = x. \tag{29}$$

If $X^1, \ldots, X^N$ are Ito processes, then we call $X = (X^1, \ldots, X^N)$ an *Ito process in* $\mathbb{R}^N$, which can be written

$$X_t = x + \int_0^t \mu_s \, ds + \int_0^t \theta_s \, dB_s, \quad t \geq 0, \tag{30}$$

or

$$dX_t = \mu_t \, dt + \theta_t \, dB_t; \quad X_0 = x \in \mathbb{R}^N, \tag{31}$$

where μ and θ are valued in $\mathbb{R}^N$ and $\mathbb{R}^{N \times d}$, respectively. (Here, $\mathbb{R}^{N \times d}$ denotes the space of real matrices with N rows and d columns.) Ito's Lemma extends as follows.

Ito's Lemma. *Suppose X is the Ito process in $\mathbb{R}^N$ given by (30) and f is in $C^{2,1}(\mathbb{R}^N \times [0, \infty))$. Then $\{f(X_t, t) : t \geq 0\}$ is an Ito process and, for any time t,*

$$f(X_t, t) = f(X_0, 0) + \int_0^t \mathcal{D}_X f(X_s, s) \, ds + \int_0^t f_x(X_s, s)\theta_s \, dB_s,$$

where

$$\mathcal{D}_X f(X_t, t) = f_x(X_t, t)\mu_t + f_t(X_t, t) + \frac{1}{2}\mathrm{tr}\left[\theta_t \theta_t^\top f_{xx}(X_t, t)\right].$$

Here, f_x, f_t, and f_{xx} denote the obvious partial derivatives of f valued in $\mathbb{R}^N$, $\mathbb{R}$, and $\mathbb{R}^{N \times N}$ respectively, and $\mathrm{tr}(A)$ denotes the *trace* of a square matrix A (the sum of its diagonal elements).

If X and Y are real-valued Ito processes with $dX_t = \mu_X(t) \, dt + \sigma_X(t) \, dB_t$ and $dY_t = \mu_Y(t) \, dt + \sigma_Y(t) \, dB_t$, then Ito's Lemma (for $N = 2$) implies that the product $Z = XY$ is an Ito process, with drift μ_Z given by

$$\mu_Z(t) = X_t \mu_Y(t) + Y_t \mu_X(t) + \sigma_X(t) \cdot \sigma_Y(t). \tag{32}$$

Provided that μ_X, μ_Y, σ_X, and σ_Y are all in $\mathcal{H}^2$, an application of Fubini's Theorem (Appendix C) implies that

$$\frac{d}{d\tau} \mathrm{cov}_t(X_s, Y_s)\Big|_{s=t} = \sigma_X(t) \cdot \sigma_Y(t) \quad \text{almost surely}, \tag{33}$$

where the derivative is taken from the right, extending the intuition developed with (3) and (4).

If X is an Ito process in $\mathbb{R}^N$ with $dX_t = \mu_t \, dt + \sigma_t \, dB_t$ and $\theta = (\theta^1, \ldots, \theta^N)$ is a vector of adapted processes such that $\theta \cdot \mu$ is in $\mathcal{L}^1$ and, for each i, $\theta \cdot \sigma^i$ is in $\mathcal{L}^2$, then we say that θ is in $\mathcal{L}(X)$, which implies that

$$\int_0^T \theta_t \, dX_t \equiv \int_0^T \theta_t \cdot \mu_t \, dt + \int_0^T \theta_t^\top \sigma_t \, dB_t, \quad T \geq 0,$$

is well defined as an Ito process. If $\theta \cdot \mu$ is in $\mathcal{H}^2$ and, for each i, $\theta \cdot \sigma^i$ is also in $\mathcal{H}^2$, then we say that θ is in $\mathcal{H}^2(X)$, which implies that $\int \theta \, dX$ is a finite-variance process.

Suppose that $S = (S^1, \ldots, S^N)$ is an Ito process in $\mathbb{R}^N$ specifying the prices of N given securities, and that S satisfies the stochastic differential equation:

$$dS_t = \mu(S_t, t) \, dt + \sigma(S_t, t) \, dB_t; \quad S_0 = x \in \mathbb{R}^N, \tag{34}$$

where $\mu : \mathbb{R}^N \times [0, \infty) \to \mathbb{R}^N$ and $\sigma : \mathbb{R}^N \times [0, \infty) \to \mathbb{R}^{N \times d}$ satisfy enough regularity (conditions are given in Appendix E) for existence and uniqueness of a solution to (34). Let

$$\beta_t = \beta_0 \exp \left[\int_0^t r(S_u, u) \, du \right]; \quad \beta_0 > 0, \tag{35}$$

define the price process of a bond, where $r : \mathbb{R}^N \times [0, \infty) \to \mathbb{R}$ defines a continuously compounding short rate, sufficiently well-behaved that (35) is a well-defined Ito process. We can also use Ito's Lemma to write

$$d\beta_t = \beta_t r(S_t, t) \, dt; \quad \beta_0 > 0. \tag{36}$$

Finally, let some continuous $g : \mathbb{R}^N \to \mathbb{R}$ define the payoff $g(S_T)$ at time T of a derivative security whose price at time zero is to be determined.

Once again, the arguments of Section F can be extended to show that, under technical regularity conditions and in the absence of arbitrage, the price process Y of the derivative security is given by $Y_t = C(S_t, t)$, where C solves the PDE:

$$\mathcal{D}_Z C(x, t) - r(x, t) C(x, t) = 0, \quad (x, t) \in \mathbb{R}^N \times [0, T), \tag{37}$$

with boundary condition

$$C(x, T) = g(x), \quad x \in \mathbb{R}^N, \tag{38}$$

where

$$\mathcal{D}_Z C(x, t) = C_x(x, t) r(x, t) x + C_t(x, t)$$
$$+ \frac{1}{2} \operatorname{tr} \left[\sigma(x, t) \sigma(x, t)^\top C_{xx}(x, t) \right]. \tag{39}$$

We exploit once again the technical condition FK on r, σ, and g reviewed in Appendix E for existence of a probabilistic representation of solutions to the PDE (37)–(38).

The Feynman-Kac Solution. *Under Condition FK, if there is no arbitrage, then the derivative security with payoff $g(S_T)$ at time T has the price process Y given by $Y_t = C(S_t, t)$, where C is the solution to the PDE (37)–(38) given by*

$$C(x, t) = E \left[\exp \left(-\int_t^T r(Z_s^{x,t}, s) \, ds \right) g \left(Z_T^{x,t} \right) \right], \quad (x, t) \in \mathbb{R}^N \times [0, T], \tag{40}$$

where $Z^{x,t}$ is the Ito process defined by $Z_s^{x,t} = x$, $s \le t$, and

$$dZ_s^{x,t} = r(Z_s^{x,t}, s) Z_s^{x,t} \, ds + \sigma(Z_s^{x,t}, s) \, dB_s, \quad s \ge t. \tag{41}$$

The exercises provide applications and additional extensions of this approach to the arbitrage-free valuation of derivative securities, allowing for intermediate dividends and for an underlying Markov-state process. Chapter 6 further extends arbitrage-free pricing to a non-Markovian setting using martingale methods. Chapter 7 gives further applications, including futures, forwards, American options, and the term structure of interest rates.

Exercises

5.1 Fixing a probability space and a filtration $\{\mathcal{F}_t : t \ge 0\}$, a process X is *Markov* if, for any time t and any integrable random variable Y that is measurable with respect to the tribe generated by $\{X_s : s \ge t\}$, we have $E(Y \mid \mathcal{F}_t) = E(Y \mid X_t)$ almost surely. In particular, for any measurable $f : \mathbb{R} \to \mathbb{R}$ such that $f(X_t)$ has finite expectation, we have $E[f(X_t) \mid \mathcal{F}_s] = E[f(X_t) \mid X_s]$ for $s \le t$. It is a fact, which we shall not prove, that standard Brownian motion B is a Markov process with respect to its standard filtration. Use this fact to show that B is a martingale with respect to its standard filtration. Suppose that θ is a bounded adapted process. Show, as stated in Section B, that the discrete-time process X defined by $X_0 = 0$ and $X_t = \sum_{s=0}^{t-1} \theta_s \Delta^1 B_s$, $t \ge 1$, is a martingale with respect to $\{\mathcal{F}_0, \mathcal{F}_1, \ldots\}$.

5.2 Suppose that S is defined by (7). Use Ito's Lemma to show that, as claimed, $dS_t = \mu S_t \, dt + \sigma S_t \, dB_t$, where $\mu = \alpha + \sigma^2/2$.

5.3 Verify that the ordinary differential equation (9), with initial condition β_0, is solved by (8).

5.4 Verify by direct calculation of the derivatives that the PDE (18)–(19) is solved by the Black-Scholes formula (11).

5.5 Derive the PDE (23) for the arbitrage-free value of the derivative security. Hint: Use arguments analogous to those used to derive the PDE (18) for the Black-Scholes formula.

5.6 Suppose the PDE (37) for the arbitrage-free value of the derivative security is not satisfied, in that the initial price Y_0 of the security is not equal to $C(S_0, 0)$, where C solves (37)–(38). Construct an arbitrage that nets an initial risk-free profit of m units of account, where m is an arbitrary number chosen by you.

5.7 Suppose that the stock, whose price process S is given by (20), pays dividends at a rate $\delta(S_t, t)$ at time t, where $\delta : \mathbb{R} \times [0, \infty) \to \mathbb{R}$ defines a *cumulative dividend process* D by $D_t = \int_0^t \delta(S_\tau, \tau) \, d\tau$. The total gain process G for the security is defined by $G_t = S_t + D_t$, and a trading strategy θ in $\mathcal{L}(G)$ generates the gain process $\int \theta \, dG$, the sum of capital and dividend gains. Derive a new PDE generalizing (23) for the arbitrage-free value of the derivative security defined by g. Provide regularity conditions for the associated Feynman-Kac solution, extending (25)–(26).

5.8 Suppose that S is a stock-price process defined by (20), β is a bond-price process defined by (21), and a derivative security is defined by the lump-sum payoff $g(S_T)$ at time T, as in Section G, and also by the cumulative dividend process H defined by $H_t = \int_0^t h(S_\tau, \tau) \, d\tau$, where $h : \mathbb{R} \times [0, T] \to \mathbb{R}$. By definition, a trading strategy (a, b) in $\mathcal{H}^2(S, \beta)$ *finances* this derivative security if

$$a_t S_t + b_t \beta_t = a_0 S_0 + b_0 \beta_0 + \int_0^t a_\tau \, dS_\tau + \int_0^t b_\tau \, d\beta_\tau - H_t, \quad t \le T, \quad (42)$$

and

$$a_T S_T + b_T \beta_T = g(S_T). \quad (43)$$

Relation (42) means that the current value of the portfolio is, at any time, the initial value, plus trading gains to date, less the payout to date of the derivative dividends. If (a, b) finances the derivative security in this sense and the derivative security's initial price Y_0 is not equal to $a_0 S_0 + b_0 \beta_0$, then there is an arbitrage. For example, if $Y_0 > a_0 S_0 + b_0 \beta_0$, then the strategy $(-1, a, b)$ in derivative security, stock, and bond generates the cumulative dividend process $-H + H = 0$ and the final payoff $-g(S_T) + g(S_T) = 0$, with the initial riskless profit $Y_0 - a_0 S_0 - b_0 \beta_0 > 0$. Derive an extension of the PDE (23)–(24) for the derivative security price, as well as an extension of the Feynman-Kac solution (25)–(26).

5.9 Suppose that X is the Ito process in $\mathbb{R}^K$ solving the SDE

$$dX_t = \mu(X_t, t) \, dt + \sigma(X_t, t) \, dB_t; \quad X_0 = x.$$

We could refer to X, by analogy with Chapter 3, as the "shock process." Suppose the price process S for the N "stocks" is defined by $S_t = \mathcal{S}(X_t, t)$, where $\mathcal{S}$ is in $C^{2,1}(\mathbb{R}^K \times [0, \infty))$, and that the bond-price process β is the Ito process defined by $d\beta_t = \beta_t r(X_t, t) \, dt$, $\beta_0 > 0$, where $r : \mathbb{R}^K \times [0, \infty) \to \mathbb{R}$ is sufficiently well behaved for this purpose.

(A)   State regularity conditions that you find appropriate in order to derive a PDE analogous to (37)–(38) for the price of an additional security defined by the payoff $g(X_T)$ at time T, where $g : \mathbb{R}^K \to \mathbb{R}$. Then provide the Feynman-Kac solution, analogous to (40)–(41), including a sufficient set of technical conditions based on Appendix E.

(B)   Extend part (A) to the case in which the stocks pay a cumulative dividend process D that is an Ito process in $\mathbb{R}^N$ well defined by $D_t = \int_0^t \delta(X_s, s) \, ds$, where $\delta : \mathbb{R}^K \times [0, \infty) \to \mathbb{R}^N$, and in which the additional security has the lump-sum payoff of $g(X_T)$ at time T, as well as a cumulative dividend Ito process H well defined by $H_t = \int_0^t h(X_s, s) \, ds$, where $h : \mathbb{R}^K \times [0, T] \to \mathbb{R}$.

5.10 Suppose the short-rate process r is given by a bounded continuous function $r : [0, T] \to \mathbb{R}$. Consider a security with price process S defined by

$$dS_t = \mu(S_t) \, dt + \sigma(S_t) \, dB_t,$$

where μ and σ satisfy a Lipschitz condition. Suppose this security has the cumulative dividend process D defined by $D_t = \int_0^t \delta_\tau S_\tau \, d\tau$, where $\delta : [0, T] \to \mathbb{R}$ is a bounded continuous function. (Such a function δ is often called the "dividend yield.")

(A)   (Put-Call Parity)   Suppose there are markets for European call and put options on the above security with exercise price K and expiry date T. Let C_0 and P_0 denote the call and put prices at time zero. Give an explicit expression for P_0 in terms of C_0, in the absence of arbitrage and transactions costs.

(B) Suppose, for all t, that $r_t = 0.10$ and that $\delta_t = 0.08$. Consider a European option expiring in $T = 0.25$ years. Suppose that $K = 50$ and $S_0 = 45$. If the call sells for 3.75, what is the put price? (Give a specific dollar price, to the nearest penny, showing how you calculated it.)

(C) Suppose, instead, that the dividend process D is defined by $D_t = \int_0^t \delta_\tau \log(S_\tau) S_\tau \, d\tau$. Suppose $\sigma(x) = \epsilon x$, for some constant $\epsilon > 0$. Solve part (A) again. Then calculate the price of a European call with exercise price $K = 35$ given initial stock price $S_0 = 40$, assuming, for all t, that $\delta_t = 0.08$, $r_t = 0.10$, and $\epsilon = 0.20$. Assume expiry in 0.25 years. Justify your answer.

5.11 Suppose the price of haggis (an unusually nasty food served in Scotland) follows the process H defined by

$$dH_t = H_t \mu_H \, dt + H_t \sigma_H \, dB_t; \quad H_0 > 0,$$

in British pounds per pint, where μ_H is a constant, σ_H is a constant vector in $\mathbb{R}^2$, and B is a standard Brownian motion in $\mathbb{R}^2$. A trader at a Wall Street investment bank, Gold in Sacks, Incorporated, has decided that, since there are options on almost everything else, there may as well be options on haggis. Of course, there is the matter of selling the options in the United States, denominated in U.S. dollars. It has been noted that the price of the U.S. dollar, in British pounds per dollar, follows the process

$$dD_t = D_t \mu_D \, dt + D_t \sigma_D \, dB_t; \quad D_0 > 0,$$

where μ_D is a constant and σ_D is a constant vector in $\mathbb{R}^2$. The continuously compounding short rate in U.S. funds is r_D, a constant. Although there are liquid markets in Edinburgh for haggis and for U.S. dollars, there is not a liquid market for haggis options. Gold in Sacks has therefore decided to sell call options on haggis at a U.S. dollar strike price of 6.50 per pint expiring in 3 months, and cover its option position with a replicating strategy in the other instruments, so as to earn a riskless profit equal to the markup in the sale price of the options over the initial investment cost to Gold in Sacks for the replicating strategy.

(A) What replicating strategy would you recommend?

(B) If the options are sold at a 10 percent profit markup, give an explicit formula for the option price Gold in Sacks should charge its customers.

(C) Suppose borrowing in U.S. funds is too clumsy, since the other two parts of the strategy (dollar and haggis trading) are done at Gold in Sacks's Edinburgh office. If the British pound borrowing rate is r_P, a constant, can you still answer parts (A) and (B), using British pound borrowing (and lending) rather than U.S. dollar borrowing (and lending)? If so, do so. If not, say why not. If you find it useful, you may use any arbitrage conditions relating the various coefficients $(\mu_H, \mu_D, \sigma_H, \sigma_D, r_D, r_P)$, if indeed there are any such coefficients precluding arbitrage.

5.12 Show, in the setting of Section E, that (26) recovers the Black-Scholes formula (11)–(12).

5.13 Show that the Black-Scholes option-hedging strategy (a, b) of Section F is such that $a \in \mathcal{H}^2(S)$ and $b \in \mathcal{H}^2(\beta)$, as assumed.

Notes

The material in this chapter is standard. The Black-Scholes (1973) formula was extended by Merton (1973b, 1977) and subsequently given literally hundreds of further extensions and applications. Cox and Rubinstein (1985) is a standard reference on options, while Hull (1989) has further applications and references. The basic approach of using continuous-time self-financing strategies as the basis for making arbitrage arguments is due to Merton (1977) and Harrison and Kreps (1979). The basic idea of risk-neutral valuation, via adjustment of the underlying stock-price process, is due to Cox and Ross (1976). This is extended to the notion of equivalent martingale measures, found in Chapter 6, by Harrison and Kreps (1979). The impact of variations in the "volatility" on the Black-Scholes option-pricing formula is shown, in two different senses, by Reisman (1986), Johnson and Shanno (1987), and El Karoui, Jeanblanc-Picqué, and Viswanathan (1991).

Part (C) of Exercise 5.10 was related to the author by Bruce Grundy. The line of exposition in this chapter is based on Gabay (1982) and Duffie (1988a). On the implications of transactions costs in the Black-Scholes setting, see Leland (1985), Davis and Panas (1990), Henrotte (1991), and Bergman (1991).

6

State Prices and Equivalent
Martingale Measures

THIS CHAPTER SUMMARIZES the theory of arbitrage-free security prices in the continuous time setting introduced in Chapter 5. The main idea is the equivalence between no arbitrage, the existence of state prices, and the existence of an equivalent martingale measure, paralleling the discrete-state theory of Chapter 2. This extends the Markovian results of Chapter 5, which are based on PDE methods. For those interested mainly in applications, the first section of Chapter 7 summarizes the major conclusions of this chapter as a "black box," making it possible to skip this chapter on a first reading.

The existence of a state-price deflator is shown to imply the absence of arbitrage. Then a state-price "beta" model of expected returns is derived. Turning to equivalent martingale measures, we begin with the sufficiency of an equivalent martingale measure for the absence of arbitrage. Girsanov's Theorem (Appendix D) gives conditions under which there exists an equivalent martingale measure. This approach generates yet another proof of the Black-Scholes formula. State prices are then connected with equivalent martingale measures; the two concepts are more or less the same. Technical conditions are given under which the absence of arbitrage leads to the existence of an equivalent martingale measure, showing the essential equivalence of these two properties. (They are literally equivalent in the analogous finite-state model of Chapter 2, and the distinction here is purely technical.) The last few sections are relatively difficult; it is up to the reader where to stop.

A. Arbitrage

We fix a standard Brownian motion $B = (B^1, \ldots, B^d)$ in $\mathbb{R}^d$, restricted to some time interval $[0, T]$, on a given probability space $(\Omega, \mathcal{F}, P)$. We also fix the standard filtration $\mathbb{F} = \{\mathcal{F}_t : t \in [0, T]\}$ of B, as defined in Section 5I. For simplicity, we take $\mathcal{F}$ to be $\mathcal{F}_T$. Suppose the price processes of N given securities form an Ito process $X = (X^1, \ldots, X^N)$ in $\mathbb{R}^N$. We assume that $\text{var}(X_t^i) < \infty$ for all i and t.

We restrict attention to trading strategies in $\mathcal{H}^2(X)$. As indicated in Section 5I, this technical condition guarantees that the gain $\int \theta \, dX$ is a finite-variance process for any trading strategy θ. Recall that a trading strategy θ is *self-financing* if

$$\theta_t \cdot X_t = \theta_0 \cdot X_0 + \int_0^t \theta_s \, dX_s, \quad t \leq T. \tag{1}$$

A self-financing strategy θ in $\mathcal{H}^2(X)$ is an arbitrage if $\theta_0 \cdot X_0 < 0$ and $\theta_T \cdot X_T \geq 0$, or $\theta_0 \cdot X_0 \leq 0$ and $\theta_T \cdot X_T > 0$.

It is implicit here that there are no dividends paid by the securities during the interval $[0, T)$, and that X_T is the vector of cum-dividend security prices at time T. We later extend the model to treat the case of intermediate dividends.

If there is some process r with the property that, for some self-financing trading strategy θ,

$$\theta_t \cdot X_t = \exp\left(\int_0^t r_s \, ds \right), \quad t \in [0, T],$$

then we call r the *short-rate process*. In the simplest example of this, one of the security-price processes, say X^1, is of the form $X_t^1 = \exp(\int_0^t r_s \, ds)$. In this case, $dX_t^1 = r_t X_t^1 \, dt$, allowing us to view r_t as the riskless short-term continuously compounding rate of interest, in an instantaneous sense.

B. Numeraire Invariance

It is often convenient to renormalize all security prices, sometimes relative to a particular price process. This section shows that this renormalization has essentially no economic effects. A *deflator* is a strictly positive Ito process. We can deflate the previously given security price process X by a deflator Y to get the new price process X^Y defined by $X_t^Y = X_t Y_t$. Changing a numeraire should have no real economic effects. For technical reasons that will become clear, however, we define a *regular deflator* to be a deflator Y with the property that the space $\mathcal{H}^2(X)$ of predeflation admissible trading strategies is the same as the space $\mathcal{H}^2(XY)$ of postdeflation trading strategies.

Numeraire Invariance Theorem. *Suppose Y is a regular deflator. Then a trading strategy θ is self-financing with respect to X if and only if θ is self-financing with respect to X^Y.*

Proof: Let $W_t = \theta_0 \cdot X_0 + \int_0^t \theta_s \, dX_s$, $t \in [0, T]$. Let W^Y be the process defined by $W_t^Y = W_t Y_t$. Since W and Y are Ito processes, Ito's Lemma implies, letting σ_X, σ_W, and σ_Y denote the respective diffusions of X, W, and Y, that

$$
\begin{aligned}
dW_t^Y &= Y_t \, dW_t + W_t \, dY_t + \sigma_W(t) \cdot \sigma_Y(t) \, dt \\
&= Y_t \theta_t \, dX_t + (\theta_t \cdot X_t) \, dY_t + [\theta_t^\top \sigma_X(t)]\sigma_Y(t) \, dt \\
&= \theta_t \cdot [Y_t \, dX_t + X_t \, dY_t + \sigma_X(t)\sigma_Y(t) \, dt] \\
&= \theta_t \, dX_t^Y.
\end{aligned}
$$

Thus, $\theta_t \cdot X_t^Y = \theta_0 \cdot X_0^Y + \int_0^t \theta_s \, dX_s^Y$, completing the proof. ∎

Corollary. *Suppose Y is a regular deflator. There is no arbitrage given the price process X if and only if there is no arbitrage given the deflated price process X^Y.*

Proof: This is immediate from the Numeraire Invariance Theorem, the strict positivity of Y, and the definition of an arbitrage. ∎

C. Arbitrage and State-Price Deflators

Once again, we fix the setup of Section A.

Paralleling the terminology of Section 2C, a *state-price deflator* is a deflator π with the property that the deflated price process X^π is a martingale. We shall eventually see that, under some regularity, there is a state-price deflator if and only if there is no arbitrage. First we look at the necessity of no arbitrage, given a state-price deflator.

Proposition. *If there is a regular state-price deflator, then there is no arbitrage.*

Proof: Suppose π is a regular state-price deflator. Let θ be any self-financing trading strategy. Since X^π is a martingale and $\theta \in \mathcal{H}^2(X^\pi)$, Proposition 5B implies that $E\left(\int_0^T \theta_t \, dX_t^\pi\right) = 0$. By numeraire invariance, θ is self-financing with respect to X^π, and we have

$$
\theta_0 \cdot X_0^\pi = E\left(\theta_T \cdot X_T^\pi - \int_0^T \theta_t \, dX_t^\pi\right) = E\left(\theta_T \cdot X_T^\pi\right).
$$

If $\theta_T \cdot X_T^\pi \geq 0$, then $\theta_0 \cdot X_0^\pi \geq 0$. Likewise, if $\theta_T \cdot X_T^\pi > 0$, then $\theta_0 \cdot X_0^\pi > 0$. It follows that θ cannot be an arbitrage for X^π. Since θ is arbitrary, the Corollary to the Numeraire Invariance Theorem implies that there is no arbitrage for X. ∎

D. State-Price Restrictions on Expected Rates of Return

Suppose that π is a state-price deflator for X, and consider an arbitrary security with price process S. Since a state-price deflator is an Ito process, we can write

$$d\pi_t = \mu_\pi(t)\, dt + \sigma_\pi(t)\, dB_t,$$

for appropriate μ_π and σ_π. Since S is an Ito process, we can also write $dS_t = \mu_S(t)\, dt + \sigma_S(t)\, dB_t$ for some μ_S and σ_S. Since S^π is a martingale, its drift is zero. It follows from Ito's Lemma that, almost everywhere,

$$0 = \mu_\pi(t)S_t + \mu_S(t)\pi_t + \sigma_S(t) \cdot \sigma_\pi(t).$$

We suppose that S is a strictly positive process, and can therefore rearrange to get

$$\frac{\mu_S(t)}{S_t} = \frac{-\mu_\pi(t)}{\pi_t} - \frac{\sigma_S(t) \cdot \sigma_\pi(t)}{\pi_t S_t}. \tag{2}$$

The *cumulative-return process* of this security is the Ito process R defined by $R_0 = 0$ and

$$dR_t = \mu_R(t)\, dt + \sigma_R(t)\, dB_t \equiv \frac{\mu_S(t)}{S_t}\, dt + \frac{\sigma_S(t)}{S_t}\, dB_t.$$

We can now write $dS_t = S_t\, dR_t$. Looking back at equations (5.3) and (5.4), μ_R may be viewed as the conditional expected rate of return, and $\sigma_R(t) \cdot \sigma_R(t)$ as the rate of change in the conditional variance of the return. We re-express (2) as

$$\mu_R(t) - r_t = -\frac{1}{\pi_t}\sigma_R(t) \cdot \sigma_\pi(t), \tag{3}$$

where $r_t = -\mu_\pi(t)/\pi_t$. In the sense of equation (5.32), $\sigma_R(t) \cdot \sigma_\pi(t)$ is a notion of "instantaneous covariance" of the increments of R and π. Thus (3) is reminiscent of the results of Section 1F. If $\sigma_R(t) = 0$, then $\mu_R(t) = r_t$, so we may view r_t as the short-term riskless interest rate. In sum, (3) implies a sense in which excess expected rates of return are proportional to the "instantaneous" conditional covariance between returns and state prices. The constant of proportionality, $-1/\pi_t$, does not depend on the security. This interpretation is a bit loose, but (3) itself is unambiguous.

We have been unnecessarily restrictive in deriving (3) only for a particular security. The same formula applies in principle to the return on an arbitrary self-financing trading strategy θ in $\mathcal{H}^2(X)$. In order to define this return, let W^θ denote the associated *market-value process*, defined by $W_t^\theta = \theta_t \cdot X_t$. If one can define an Ito process R^θ by

$$R_t^\theta = \int_0^t \frac{1}{W_s^\theta}\, dW_s^\theta, \quad t \in [0, T],$$

then R^θ represents the cumulative-return process for θ. In this case, it can be verified as an exercise that the drift μ_θ and diffusion σ_θ of R^θ satisfy the return restriction extending (3) given by

$$\mu_\theta(t) - r_t = -\frac{1}{\pi_t}\sigma_\theta(t) \cdot \sigma_\pi(t).$$

E. State-Price Beta Models

Continuing with the setup of the previous section, we can always find adapted processes φ and ϵ valued in $\mathbb{R}^N$ and $\mathbb{R}^d$ respectively such that

$$\sigma_\pi(t) = \sigma_X(t)^\top \varphi_t + \epsilon_t \quad \text{and} \quad \sigma_X(t)\epsilon_t = 0, \quad t \in [0, T], \tag{4}$$

where σ_X is the $\mathbb{R}^{N \times d}$-valued diffusion of the price process X. For each (ω, t) in $\Omega \times [0, T]$, the vector $\sigma_X(\omega, t)^\top \varphi(\omega, t)$ is the orthogonal projection in $\mathbb{R}^N$ of $\sigma_\pi(\omega, t)$ onto the span of the rows of the matrix $\sigma_X(\omega, t)$. Suppose $\theta = (\theta^1, \ldots, \theta^N)$ is a self-financing trading strategy with $\sigma_X^\top \theta = \sigma_X^\top \varphi$. (For example, if $X_t^1 = \exp(\int_0^t r_s\, ds)$ for a short-rate process r, we can construct θ by letting $\theta_t^j = \varphi_t^j, j > 1$, and by choosing θ^1 so that the self-financing condition is met.) The market-value process W^θ of θ is an Ito process since θ is self-financing. If W^θ is also strictly positive, we can define the associated return process $R^* \equiv R^\theta$ by

$$dR_t^* = \frac{1}{W_t^\theta}\, dW_t^\theta; \quad R_0^* = 0.$$

Since the diffusion of W^θ is $\sigma_X^\top \varphi$, the diffusion of R^* is $\sigma^* \equiv \sigma_X^\top \varphi / W^\theta$. For an arbitrary Ito return process R, (3) implies that

$$\mu_R(t) - r_t = -\frac{1}{\pi_t}\sigma_R(t) \cdot \sigma_\pi(t)$$

$$= -\frac{1}{\pi_t}\sigma_R(t) \cdot [\sigma_X(t)^\top \varphi_t + \epsilon_t]$$

$$= -\frac{W_t^\theta}{\pi_t}\sigma_R(t) \cdot \sigma_t^*,$$

using the fact that $\sigma_R(t)$ is (in each state ω) a linear combination of the rows of $\sigma_X(t)$. This in turn implies that $\sigma_R(t) \cdot \epsilon_t = 0$. In particular, for the return process R^*, we have

$$\mu_t^* - r_t = \frac{-W_t^\theta}{\pi_t} \sigma_t^* \cdot \sigma_t^*,$$

where μ^* is the drift (expected rate of return) of R^*. Substituting back into (3) the resulting expression for W_t^θ / π_t leaves the *state-price beta model of returns* given by

$$\mu_R(t) - r_t = \beta_R(t)\,(\mu_t^* - r_t), \tag{5}$$

where

$$\beta_R(t) = \frac{\sigma_R(t) \cdot \sigma_t^*}{\sigma_t^* \cdot \sigma_t^*}. \tag{6}$$

In the "instantaneous sense" in which $\sigma_t^* \cdot \sigma_t^*$ stands for the conditional variance for dR_t^* and $\sigma_R(t) \cdot \sigma_t^*$ stands for the conditional covariance between dR_t and dR_t^*, we can view (5) as the continuous-time analogue to the state-price beta models of Section 1F and Exercise 2.6(C). Likewise, we can loosely think of R^* as a return process having maximal conditional correlation with the state-price deflator π.

F. Equivalent Martingale Measures

A probability measure Q on $(\Omega, \mathcal{F})$ is said to be *equivalent* to P provided $Q(A) > 0$ if and only if $P(A) > 0$, for any event A. An equivalent probability measure Q is an *equivalent martingale measure* for X if X is a martingale with respect to Q, and if the Radon-Nikodym derivative $\frac{dQ}{dP}$ (defined in Appendix C) has finite variance.

In the finite-state setting of Chapter 2, it was shown that the existence of a state-price deflator is equivalent, after deflation by some convenient numeraire, to the existence of an equivalent martingale measure. Later in this chapter, technical conditions will be given that sustain that equivalence in this continuous-time setting. Aside from offering a conceptual simplification of some asset-pricing and investment problems, the use of equivalent martingale measures is justified by the large body of known properties of martingales.

First, we establish the sufficiency of an equivalent martingale measure for the absence of arbitrage. The last section of this chapter gives a result that is almost a converse, supplying conditions under which the absence of arbitrage implies the existence of an equivalent martingale measure. Aside from technical issues, the arguments are the same as those used to show this equivalence in Chapter 2.

Theorem. *If the price process X admits an equivalent martingale measure, then there is no arbitrage.*

Proof: The proof is quite similar to that of Proposition 6C. Let Q be an equivalent martingale measure. Let θ be any self-financing trading strategy. We first consider the case in which θ is bounded. The fact that X is a martingale under Q implies that $E^Q(\int_0^T \theta_t \, dX_t) = 0$. The self-financing condition (1) therefore implies that

$$\theta_0 \cdot X_0 = E^Q \left(\theta_T \cdot X_T - \int_0^T \theta_t \, dX_t \right) = E^Q(\theta_T X_T).$$

Thus, if $\theta_T \cdot X_T \geq 0$, then $\theta_0 \cdot X_0 \geq 0$. Likewise, if $\theta_T \cdot X_T > 0$, then $\theta_0 \cdot X_0 > 0$. An arbitrage is therefore impossible using bounded trading strategies.

For the general case of any self-financing trading strategy $\theta \in \mathcal{H}^2(X)$, additional technical arguments are needed to show that $E^Q(\int_0^T \theta_t \, dX_t) = 0$. Since X is an Ito process, we can write $dX_t = \mu_t \, dt + \sigma_t \, dB_t$ for appropriate μ and σ. By the Diffusion Invariance Principle (Appendix D), there is a standard Brownian motion $\hat{B}$ in $\mathbb{R}^d$ under Q such that $dX_t = \sigma_t \, d\hat{B}_t$. Let $Y = \int_0^T \|\theta_t \sigma_t\|^2 \, dt$. Since θ is in $\mathcal{H}^2(X)$, Y has finite expectation under P. Since the product of two random variables of finite variance is of finite expectation, $\frac{dQ}{dP}\sqrt{Y}$ is also of finite expectation under P. Thus, relative to Q, we know that $\theta \in \mathcal{H}^1(X)$. Since $dX_t = \sigma_t \, d\hat{B}_t$, this implies by Proposition 5B that $\int \theta_t \, dX_t$ is a Q-martingale, so $E^Q(\int_0^T \theta_t \, dX_t) = 0$. The remainder of the proof is now covered by the arguments used for bounded θ. ∎

In most cases, we apply the theorem via the following result, which follows from the corollary to the Numeraire Invariance Theorem in Section 6B.

Corollary. *If there is a regular deflator Y such that the deflated price process X^Y admits an equivalent martingale measure, then there is no arbitrage.*

G. Equivalent Martingale Measures and Girsanov's Theorem

We now look for convenient conditions on X supporting the existence of an equivalent martingale measure. Such conditions can be found in Girsanov's Theorem (Appendix D), using the following line of analysis.

Since X is an Ito process, we can write $dX_t = \mu_t \, dt + \sigma_t \, dB_t$ and consider the linear equations

$$\sigma_t \eta_t = \mu_t, \quad t \in [0, T], \tag{7}$$

to be solved for an $\mathbb{R}^d$-valued process η with components in $\mathcal{L}^2$. If such a solution to (7) exists, we say that X is *reducible*. There may be more than one solution. If X is reducible, however, we can single out the solution to (7) defined as follows. Let Σ_t and $\hat{\mu}_t$ be obtained, respectively, by eliminating (ω by ω) as many linearly dependent rows from σ_t as possible and by eliminating the corresponding elements of μ_t. Regardless of how this is done, if X is reducible, then a particular solution η^X to (7) is uniquely defined by

$$\eta_t^X = \Sigma_t^\top \left(\Sigma_t \Sigma_t^\top \right)^{-1} \hat{\mu}_t. \tag{8}$$

If X is reducible let $\nu(X) = \int_0^T \eta_t^X \cdot \eta_t^X \, dt/2$, and let

$$\xi(X) = \exp \left[- \int_0^T \eta_t^X \, dB_t - \nu(X) \right]. \tag{9}$$

If X is reducible, $\exp[\nu(X)]$ has a finite expectation, and $\xi(X)$ has finite variance, we say that X is L^2-*reducible*. All of this sets up L^2-reducibility as a convenient condition for the existence of an equivalent martingale measure. For example, if η^X is bounded, then X is L^2-reducible.

Theorem. *If X is L^2-reducible, then there is an equivalent martingale measure and no arbitrage.*

Proof: If X is L^2-reducible, then Girsanov's Theorem (Appendix D) implies that Q is an equivalent martingale measure when defined by $dQ/dP = \xi(X)$. The lack of arbitrage follows from the theorem in Section 6F. ∎

H. Black-Scholes, One More Time

Suppose the given security-price process is $X = (\beta, S^1, \ldots, S^{N-1})$, where

$$dS_t = \mu_t \, dt + \sigma_t \, dB_t$$

and

$$d\beta_t = r_t \beta_t \, dt; \quad \beta_0 > 0,$$

where μ, σ, and r are adapted processes (valued in $\mathbb{R}^{N-1}$, $\mathbb{R}^{(N-1)\times d}$, and $\mathbb{R}$ respectively). If the short-rate process r is bounded, then β^{-1} is a convenient regular deflator. Let $Z_t = S_t/\beta_t$, $t \in [0, T]$. By Ito's Lemma,

$$dZ_t = \left(-r_t Z_t + \frac{\mu_t}{\beta_t} \right) dt + \frac{\sigma_t}{\beta_t} \, dB_t. \tag{10}$$

In order to apply Theorem 6G to the deflated price process $\hat{X} = (1, Z)$, one needs to check that Z is L^2-reducible. Given this, there would be an equivalent martingale measure Q and no arbitrage. Suppose, for the moment, that this is the case. By the Diffusion Invariance result of Appendix D, there is a standard Brownian motion $\hat{B}$ in $\mathbb{R}^d$ under Q such that

$$dZ_t = \frac{\sigma_t}{\beta_t} \, d\hat{B}_t.$$

Since $S_t = \beta_t Z_t$, $t \in [0, T]$, another application of Ito's Lemma yields

$$dS_t = r_t \, S_t \, dt + \sigma_t \, d\hat{B}_t. \tag{11}$$

Equation (11) is an important intermediate result for arbitrage-free asset pricing, giving an explicit expression for security prices under a probability measure Q with the property that the "discounted" price process S/β is a martingale. For example, this leads to an easy recovery of the Black-Scholes formula, for suppose that $S_T^2 = (S_T^1 - K)^+$, defining an option payoff on S^1. Since S^2/β is a martingale under Q, the option-price process S^2 is given by

$$S_t^2 = \beta_t E_t^Q \left(\frac{S_T^2}{\beta_T} \right) = E_t^Q \left[\exp \left(-\int_t^T r_s \, ds \right) (S_T^1 - K)^+ \right]. \tag{12}$$

The reader is asked to verify as an exercise that this is the Black-Scholes formula for the case of $d = 1$, $N = 3$, $S_0^1 > 0$, and with constants $\bar{r}$ and $\bar{\sigma}$ such that, for all t, $r_t = \bar{r}$ and $\sigma_t^1 = \bar{\sigma} \, S_t^1$. Indeed, in this case, Z is L^2-reducible, an exercise, so the assumption of an equivalent martingale measure is justified. To be more precise, it is sufficient for the absence of arbitrage that the option-price process is given by (12). The necessity of (12) for the absence of arbitrage and related issues is brought up in the next section.

The detailed calculations of Girsanov's Theorem appear nowhere in the actual solution (11) for arbitrage-free security prices, which can be given by inspection in terms of σ and r only. The results extend to the case of an infinite horizon under technical conditions given in sources cited in the Notes.

I. Complete Markets and Redundant Security Prices

In this setting, *complete markets* means that any random variable Y with finite variance can be obtained as the terminal value $\theta_T \cdot X_T$ of some self-financing trading strategy θ. For this section, let the price process X be (β, S) as in

Section 6H, for a bounded short-rate process r. Section 6H gave sufficient conditions for the absence of arbitrage in the Black-Scholes setting. This section gives necessary conditions based on the completeness of markets in the Black-Scholes model. First, we provide a spanning condition for complete markets in the presence of an equivalent martingale measure.

Proposition. *Suppose there is an equivalent martingale measure for the deflated price process S/β. Markets are complete if and only if $\text{rank}(\sigma) = d$ almost everywhere.*

Proof: Suppose that $\text{rank}(\sigma) = d$ almost everywhere. Let Y be an arbitrary random variable with finite variance. Let $Z = S/\beta$ as in Section 6H, let Q be an equivalent martingale measure for Z, and let $\hat{B}$ be a standard Brownian motion in $\mathbb{R}^d$ under Q satisfying (11). By the Martingale Representation Theorem of Appendix D, there is some η in $\mathcal{L}(\hat{B})$ such that $Y/\beta_T = E^Q(Y/\beta_T) + \int_0^T \eta_t \, d\hat{B}_t$. By the rank assumption on σ, there are some adapted processes $\theta^1, \ldots, \theta^{N-1}$ solving

$$(\theta_t^1, \ldots, \theta_t^{N-1})\sigma_t = \beta_t \eta_t^\top, \quad t \in [0, T]. \tag{13}$$

Let θ^0 be defined by

$$\theta_t^0 = E^Q\left(\frac{Y}{\beta_T}\right) + \sum_{i=1}^N \left(\int_0^t \theta_t^i \, dZ_t^i - \theta_t^i Z_t^i\right).$$

Then a simple calculation shows that $\theta = (\theta^0, \ldots, \theta^{N-1})$ is self-financing with respect to the price process $(1, Z)$ and that $\theta_T \cdot (1, Z_T) = Y/\beta_T$. By the Numeraire Invariance Theorem, taking β as a deflator, θ is also self-financing with respect to (β, S) and $\theta_T \cdot (\beta_T, S_T) = Y$, proving the completeness of markets.

Conversely, suppose that it is not true that $\text{rank}(\sigma) = d$ almost everywhere. We will show that markets are not complete. By the rank assumption on σ, there is some bounded $\eta \in \mathcal{L}(\hat{B})$ with the property that there is no solution $\theta^1, \ldots, \theta^{N-1}$ to (13). It is then easy to see that there is no trading strategy θ that is self-financing with respect to $(1, Z)$ such that $\theta_T \cdot (1, Z_T) = \int_0^T \eta_t \, d\hat{B}_t$. By the Numeraire Invariance Theorem, there is no trading strategy θ self-financing with respect to (β, S) with $\theta_T \cdot (\beta_T, S_T) = \beta_T \int_0^T \eta_t \, d\hat{B}_t$. ∎

We return to the Black-Scholes example of Section 6H, with $N = 2$, $d = 1$, $S_0^1 > 0$, and assume that, for all t, we have $\sigma_t^1 = \bar{\sigma} S_t^1$ and $r_t = \bar{r}$, for constants $\bar{\sigma}$ and $\bar{r}$. Since $\text{rank}(\sigma^1) = d$ almost everywhere, the existence of an equivalent martingale measure implies that there is no arbitrage and that markets are complete, even if we restrict trading to the two securities ("bond and stock") with price process (β, S^1). The construction in the last proof implies that, given the option payoff $(S_T^1 - K)^+$, there is a self-financing trading strategy (θ^0, θ^1) whose value at any time t is $Y_t \equiv E_t^Q[e^{-\bar{r}(T-t)}(S_T^1 - K)^+]$. In Section 6H, we showed that $S^2 = Y$ is sufficient for the absence of arbitrage with respect to (β, S^1, S^2), where S^2 is the call-option price process. Now we show that $S^2 = Y$ is also necessary for the absence of arbitrage. (This was already shown, in effect, in Chapter 5, but the following argument leads to a more general theorem.) Suppose, to set up a contradiction, that $S^2 \neq Y$. Then there is some constant $\epsilon > 0$ such that at least one of the events A^+ or A^- has strictly positive probability, with A^+ denoting the event that $S_t^2 - Y_t \geq \epsilon$ for some t in $[0, T]$ and A^- the event that $Y_t - S_t^2 \geq \epsilon$ for some t in $[0, T]$. Without loss of generality, suppose A^+ has strictly positive probability, and let $\tau = \inf\{t : S_t^2 - Y_t \geq \epsilon\}$, a stopping time that is valued in $[0, T]$ with strictly positive probability. Let φ be the trading strategy defined by $\varphi_t = 0$, $t < \tau$, and $\varphi_t = (\theta_t^0 + e^{\bar{r}(t-\tau)}\epsilon, \theta_t^1, -1)$, $t \geq \tau$, where (θ^0, θ^1) is the option-replicating strategy described above. It can be checked that φ is self-financing and that $\varphi_T \cdot (\beta_T, S_T^1, S_T^2) > 0$, implying that φ is an arbitrage.

By generalizing the above arguments, one can prove the following result concerning a *redundant security*, a security with price process Y such that there exists a self-financing trading strategy θ with terminal value $\theta_T \cdot (\beta_T, S_T) = Y_T$. Complete markets implies that any security is redundant.

Theorem. *Suppose S/β admits an equivalent martingale measure Q. Consider a redundant security with price process Y. Then $(\beta, S^1, \ldots, S^{N-1}, Y)$ admits no arbitrage if and only if Y/β is a Q-martingale.*

J. State Prices and Equivalent Martingale Measures

We now investigate the relationship between equivalent martingale measures and state-price deflators. They turn out to be effectively the same concept. We take as given the setup of Section 6A, including a price process X for N securities. Suppose that Q is an equivalent martingale measure after deflation by Y, where $Y_t = \exp(-\int_0^t r_s \, ds)$ for a bounded short-rate process r. The *density process* ξ for Q is the martingale defined by

$$\xi_t = E_t\left(\frac{dQ}{dP}\right), \quad t \in [0, T],$$

where $\frac{dQ}{dP}$ is the Radon-Nikodym derivative of Q with respect to P. As stated in Appendix C, for any times t and $s > t$, and any $\mathcal{F}_s$-measurable random variable W such that $E^Q(|W|) < \infty$,

$$E_t^Q(W) = \frac{E_t(\xi_s W)}{\xi_t}, \quad t \in [0, T]. \tag{14}$$

We will show that a state-price deflator π is given by $\pi_t = Y_t \xi_t$. Conversely, given a state-price deflator π with $\mathrm{var}(\pi_T) < \infty$, we will show that an equivalent martingale measure is given by defining its density process ξ according to

$$\xi_t = \exp\left(\int_0^t r_s \, ds\right) \frac{\pi_t}{\pi_0}, \quad t \in [0, T]. \tag{15}$$

In order to verify this relationship between state-price deflators and equivalent martingale measures, suppose Q is an equivalent martingale measure for X^Y with density process ξ, and let $\pi_t = \xi_t Y_t$. Then, for any times t and $s > t$, using (14),

$$E_t(\pi_s X_s) = E_t(\xi_s X_s^Y) = \xi_t E_t^Q(X_s^Y) = \xi_t X_t^Y = \pi_t X_t. \tag{16}$$

This shows that X^π is a martingale, so π is a state-price deflator. The same calculations in reverse show the converse. The general equivalence between state-price deflators and equivalent martingale measures was shown in the simpler setting of Chapter 2 without technical qualification. An exercise further pursues the equivalence in this setting.

K. Arbitrage Pricing with Dividends

This section and the following two extend the basic approach to securities with dividends paid during $[0, T]$. Consider an Ito process D for the *cumulative dividend* of a security. This means that the cumulative total amount of dividends paid by the security until time t is D_t. For example, if $D_t = \int_0^t \delta_s \, ds$, then δ represents the *dividend-rate process*, as treated in Exercises 5.7, 5.8, and 5.9. Given a cumulative-dividend process D and the associated security-price process X, the *gain process* $G = X + D$ measures the total (capital plus dividend) gain generated by holding the security. A trading strategy is now defined to be a process θ in $\mathcal{H}^2(G)$. Here, $\int \theta \, dG$ represents the total gain generated by θ. By the linearity of stochastic integrals, if $\int \theta \, dX$ and $\int \theta \, dD$ are well defined, then $\int \theta \, dG = \int \theta \, dX + \int \theta \, dD$, once again the sum of capital gains and dividend gains.

Suppose we are given N securities defined by the price process $X = (X^1, \ldots, X^N)$ and cumulative-dividend process $D = (D^1, \ldots, D^N)$, with the associated gain process $G = X + D$. We assume, for each j, that X^j and D^j are finite-variance Ito processes. A trading strategy $\theta \in \mathcal{H}^2(G)$ is *self-financing*, extending our earlier definition, if

$$\theta_t \cdot X_t = \theta_0 \cdot X_0 + \int_0^t \theta_s \, dG_s, \quad t \in [0, T].$$

As before, an *arbitrage* is a self-financing trading strategy θ with $\theta_0 \cdot X_0 \leq 0$ and $\theta_T \cdot X_T > 0$, or with $\theta_0 \cdot X_0 < 0$ and $\theta_T \cdot X_T \geq 0$.

We can extend our earlier results characterizing security prices in the absence of arbitrage. An equivalent martingale measure for the dividend-price pair (D, X) is defined as an equivalent probability measure Q under which $G = X + D$ is a martingale, and such that $\frac{dQ}{dP}$ has finite variance. The existence of an equivalent martingale measure implies, by the same arguments as those given in the proof of Theorem 6F, that there is no arbitrage.

Given a trading strategy $\theta \in \mathcal{H}^2(G)$, if there is an Ito process D^θ such that

$$D_t^\theta = \theta_0 \cdot X_0 + \int_0^t \theta_s \, dG_s - \theta_t \cdot X_t, \quad t \in [0, T],$$

then we say that D^θ is the cumulative dividend process *generated* by θ. Suppose there exists an equivalent martingale measure Q for (D, X), and consider an additional security defined by the cumulative dividend process H and price process V; both H and V are assumed to be Ito processes of finite variance. Suppose that the additional security is *redundant*, in that there exists some trading strategy θ with respect to (D, X) such that $D^\theta = H$ and $\theta_T \cdot X_T = V_T$. The absence of arbitrage involving all $N + 1$ securities implies that, for all t, we have $V_t = \theta_t \cdot X_t$ almost surely. From this, the gain process $V + H$ of the redundant security is also a martingale under Q. The proof is a simple extension of that of Theorem 6I.

Under an equivalent martingale measure Q for (D, X), we have, for any time $t \in [0, T]$,

$$X_t + D_t = G_t = E_t^Q(G_T) = E_t^Q(X_T + D_T),$$

which implies that $X_t = E_t^Q(X_T + D_T - D_t)$. For example, if D is defined by $D_t = \int_0^t \delta_s \, ds$, then

$$X_t = E_t^Q \left(X_T + \int_t^T \delta_s \, ds \right). \tag{17}$$

Given the dividend-price pair (D, X), there should be no economic effect, in principle, from a change of numeraire given by a deflator Y.

We can write $dY_t = \mu_Y(t)\,dt + \sigma_Y(t)\,dB_t$ for appropriate μ_Y and σ_Y, and $dD_t = \mu_D(t)\,dt + \sigma_D(t)\,dB_t$ for appropriate μ_D and σ_D. The *deflated cumulative dividend process* D^Y is defined by $dD_t^Y = Y_t\,dD_t + \sigma_D(t)\cdot\sigma_Y(t)\,dt$. The *deflated gain process* G^Y is defined by $G_t^Y = D_t^Y + S_tY_t$. If the dividend process D^θ generated by θ with respect to (D, X) is an Ito process, then its deflated version is the dividend process generated by θ with respect to (X^Y, D^Y), a form of numeraire invariance. In this setting, a regular deflator is a deflator Y with the property that $\mathcal{H}^2(G) = \mathcal{H}^2(G^Y)$. If Y is a regular deflator, it follows that there is no arbitrage with respect to (X, Y) if and only if there is no arbitrage with respect to (X^Y, D^Y). These facts can be shown as exercises.

The term "$\sigma_D(t)\cdot\sigma_Y(t)\,dt$" in dD_t^Y might seem puzzling at first. This term is in fact dictated by numeraire invariance. In all applications that appear in this book, however, we have either $\sigma_D = 0$ or $\sigma_Y = 0$, implying the more "obvious" definition $dD_t^Y = Y_t\,dD_t$, which can be intuitively treated as the dividend "increment" dD_t deflated by Y_t.

Suppose that $X = (\beta, S)$, with $S = (S^1, \ldots, S^{N-1})$ and

$$\beta_t = \beta_0 \exp\left(\int_0^t r_s\,ds\right); \quad \beta_0 > 0,$$

where r is a bounded short-rate process. Consider the regular deflator Y defined by $Y_t = \beta_t^{-1}$. If, after deflation by Y, there is an equivalent martingale measure Q, then (17) implies the convenient pricing formula:

$$S_t = E_t^Q\left[\exp\left(\int_t^T -r_u\,du\right)S_T + \int_t^T \exp\left(\int_t^s -r_u\,du\right)dD_s\right]. \qquad (18)$$

Proposition 6I and Theorem 6I extend in the obvious way to this setting.

L. Lumpy Dividends and the Term Structure

By means going beyond the scope of this book, one can extend (18) to the case of finite-variance cumulative-dividend process of the form $D = Z + V - W$, for an Ito process Z and increasing adapted processes V and W that are right continuous. By *increasing*, we mean that $V_s \geq V_t$ whenever $s \geq t$. By *right continuous*, we mean that, for any t, $\lim_{s\downarrow t} V_s = V_t$. (By convention, $V_{0-} = V_0 = 0$.) The *jump* ΔV_t of V at time t, as depicted in Figure 6.1, is defined by $\Delta V_t = V_t - V_{t-}$, where $V_{t-} \equiv \lim_{s\uparrow t} V_s$ denotes the left limit. The *jump* $\Delta D_t \equiv D_t - D_{t-}$ of the total dividend process D represents the lump-sum dividend paid at time t.

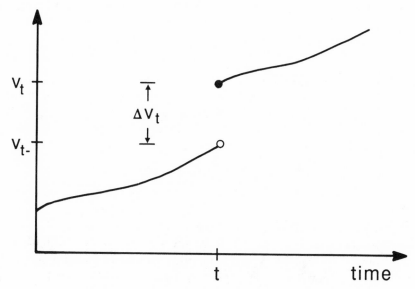

Figure 6.1. *A Right-Continuous Increasing Sample Path*

Each of the above implications of the absence of arbitrage for security prices has a natural extension to this case of "lumpy" dividends. In particular, (18) applies as stated, with $\int \theta \, dD$ defined by $\int \theta \, dZ + \int \theta \, dV - \int \theta \, dW$ whenever all three integrals are well defined, the first as a stochastic integral and latter two as *Stieltjes integrals*. A reader unfamiliar with the Stieltjes integral may consult sources given in the Notes. Happily, the stochastic integral and the Stieltjes integral coincide whenever both are well defined. In this book, we only consider applications that involve two trivial examples of the Stieltjes integral $\int \theta \, dV$.

(a) For the first example of a Stieltjes integral, we let $V = \int \delta_t \, dt$ for some δ in $\mathcal{L}^1$, in which case $\int_0^t \theta_s \, dV_s = \int_0^t \theta_s \delta_s \, ds$.

(b) In the second case, for some stopping time τ, we have $V_t = 0$, $t < \tau$, and $V_t = v$, $t \geq \tau$, where $v = \Delta V_\tau$ is the jump of V at time τ. For this second case, we have $\int_0^t \theta_s \, dV_s = 0$, $t < \tau$, and $\int_0^t \theta_s \, dV_s = \theta_\tau \Delta V_\tau$, $t \geq \tau$, which is natural for our purposes.

Because of the possibility of jumps in dividends, it is now necessary to take an explicit stance on whether security prices will be measured ex dividend or cum dividend. We opt for the former method, which means that, for a dividend-price pair (D, X), a trading strategy θ is self-financing if

$$\theta_t \cdot (X_t + \Delta D_t) = \theta_0 \cdot X_0 + \int_0^t \theta_s \, dG_s, \quad t \in [0, T],$$

always taking the convention that $\Delta D_0 = 0$ (which is without loss of generality). With this, an *arbitrage* is defined as self-financing trading strategy θ with $\theta_0 \cdot X_0 \leq 0$ and $\theta_T \cdot (X_T + \Delta D_T) > 0$, or with $\theta_0 \cdot X_0 < 0$ and $\theta_T \cdot (X_T + \Delta D_T) \geq 0$.

Extending our earlier definition to allow for lumpy dividends, a trading strategy θ finances a dividend process D^θ if

$$\theta_t \cdot (X_t + \Delta D_t) = \theta_0 \cdot X_0 + \int_0^t \theta_s \, dG_s - D^\theta_{t-}, \quad t \in [0, T],$$

with $\Delta D^\theta_T = \theta_T \cdot (X_T + \Delta D_T)$.

With these new definitions in place, the *term structure* can be characterized from (18) as follows. Given a bounded short-rate process r, suppose that Q is an equivalent martingale measure after deflation by Y, where $Y_t = \exp(-\int_0^t r_s \, ds)$. A unit zero-coupon riskless bond maturing at time τ is defined by the cumulative-dividend process H with $H_s = 0$, $s < \tau$, and $H_s = 1$, $s \geq \tau$. Since $dH_s = 0$ for $s \neq \tau$, and since $\Delta H_\tau = 1$, we know from case (b) above of the Stieltjes integral that

$$\int_t^T \exp\left(\int_t^s -r_u \, du\right) dH_s = \exp\left(\int_t^\tau -r_u \, du\right).$$

Then (18) implies that the price at time t of a unit zero-coupon riskless bond maturing at time $\tau > t$ is given by

$$\Lambda_{t,\tau} = E_t^Q \left[\exp\left(\int_t^\tau -r_u \, du\right)\right]. \tag{19}$$

The solution for the term structure given by (19) is based on the implicit assumption that the price of a bond after its maturity date is zero. This is also consistent with our earlier analysis of option prices, where we have implicitly equated the terminal cum-dividend price of an option with its terminal dividend payment. For example, with an option expiring at T on a price process S with exercise price K, we set the terminal option price at its expiration value $(S_T - K)^+$. This seems innocuous. If had we actually allowed for the possibility that the terminal cum-dividend option price might be something other than $(S_T - K)^+$, however, we would have needed a more complicated model and further analysis to conclude from the absence of arbitrage that the $(S_T - K)^+$ is indeed the cum-dividend expiration value.

This issue of terminal security prices is further pursued in a source cited in the Notes.

M. Equivalent Martingale Measures Implied by No Arbitrage

So far, we have exploited the existence of an equivalent martingale measure as a sufficient condition for the absence of arbitrage. Now we turn to the converse issue: Does the absence of arbitrage imply the existence of an equivalent martingale measure? In the finite-dimensional setting of Chapter 2, we know that the answer is always: "After a change of numeraire, yes." Only technicalities stand between this finite-dimensional equivalence and the infinite-dimensional case we face here. Because of these technicalities, the remainder of the chapter is somewhat advanced and can be skipped on a first reading.

Given a dividend-price pair (D, X), with associated gain process G, let Θ denote the space of self-financing trading strategies in $\mathcal{H}^2(G)$. The *marketed subspace* is

$$M = \{\theta_T \cdot (X_T + \Delta D_T) : \theta \in \Theta\}.$$

We assume there is no arbitrage. For each $Z = \theta_T \cdot (X_T + \Delta D_T)$ with θ in Θ, let $\psi(Z) = \theta_0 \cdot X_0$ denote the unique initial investment required to obtain the payoff Z. We know that this function $\psi : M \to \mathbb{R}$ is well defined since, if there are two trading strategies θ and φ in Θ with $\theta_T \cdot (X_T + \Delta D_T) = \varphi_T \cdot (X_T + \Delta D_T)$ and $\theta_0 \cdot X_0 > \varphi_0 \cdot X_0$, then $\varphi - \theta$ is an arbitrage. The function ψ is linear since stochastic integration is linear. Finally, ψ is strictly increasing, again following from the absence of arbitrage. Let $L^2(P)$ denote the space of random variables with finite variance. The marketed subspace M is a subset of $L^2(P)$ because all trading strategies are in $\mathcal{H}^2(G)$. Moreover, M is a *linear subspace*, in this sense: Whenever $Z = \theta_T \cdot (X_T + \Delta D_T)$ and $W = \varphi_T \cdot (X_T + \Delta D_T)$ are in M, $aZ + bW$ is also in M for any constants a and b, since $a\theta + b\varphi$ is a self-financing strategy (from the linearity of stochastic integration).

We adopt the usual *mean-square norm* for $L^2(P)$, defined by $\|Z\| \equiv [E(Z^2)]^{1/2}$. We say that a sequence $\{Z_n\}$ in $L^2(P)$ converges to Z, denoted $Z_n \to Z$, if $\| Z_n - Z \| \to 0$. The marketed subspace M is *closed* if, for any sequence $\{Z_n\}$ in M and Z in $L^2(P)$ such that $Z_n \to Z$, it follows that Z is in M. Moreover, $\psi : M \to \mathbb{R}$ is *continuous* provided $\psi(Z_n) \to \psi(Z)$ whenever $Z^n \to Z$.

The next result, from a source cited in the Notes, states conditions under which we can extend ψ from M to the whole space $L^2(P)$, maintaining its useful properties. The assumptions are so strong as to make the result of little direct use, but will later be relaxed.

Lemma. *Suppose J is a closed linear subspace of $L^2(P)$ and $\psi : J \to \mathbb{R}$ is strictly increasing, linear, and continuous. Then there is some continuous, linear, and strictly increasing $\Psi : L^2(P) \to \mathbb{R}$ such that $\Psi(Z) = \psi(Z)$ for each Z in J.*

This extension result, an infinite-dimensional analogue of Theorem 1A, is the key to the existence of an equivalent martingale measure, as shown in the following continuous-time analogue to Theorem 2G. In order to simplify things, we revert to the setting of Section 6A, in which prices are implicitly measured cum dividend, and in which $D_t = 0$ for $t < T$. The case of general dividends can be handled with minor alterations as an exercise.

Theorem. *Suppose $X^1 \equiv 1$, ψ is continuous, and the marketed subspace M is closed. Then there is no arbitrage if and only if there is an equivalent martingale measure.*

Proof: Suppose there is no arbitrage. The preceding lemma implies that ψ has a strictly increasing continuous linear extension Ψ. Since Ψ is continuous and linear, the Riesz Representation Theorem for $L^2(P)$ (Exercise 6.8) implies that there is a unique π in $L^2(P)$ such that

$$\Psi(Z) = E(\pi Z), \quad Z \in L^2(P).$$

Since $X^1 \equiv 1$, we have $E(\pi X_T^1) = X_0^1 = 1$, so $E(\pi) = 1$. Let Q be the probability measure defined by $dQ/dP = \pi$. Since Ψ is strictly increasing, $\pi \gg 0$, so Q is equivalent to P.

Obviously X^1 is a martingale. To show that X^i is a Q-martingale for each $i > 1$, let τ be an arbitrary stopping time valued in $[0, T]$, and let θ be the trading strategy defined by:

(a) $\theta^j = 0, j \neq i, j \neq 1$;
(b) $\theta_t^i = 1, t \leq \tau; \theta_t^i = 0, t > \tau$;
(c) $\theta_t^1 = 0, t \leq \tau; \theta_t^1 = X_\tau^i, t > \tau$.

It is easily seen that $\theta \in \Theta$ and that $\theta_T \cdot X_T = X_\tau^i$, with initial investment $X_0^i = \psi(X_\tau^i) = E(\pi X_\tau^i) = E^Q(X_\tau^i)$. This characterizes X^i as a Q-martingale.

Conversely, if there is an equivalent martingale measure, then there is no arbitrage by Theorem 6F. ∎

In the presence of a bounded short-rate process r, the result extends to obtain the existence of an equivalent martingale measure for the deflated price process X^Y, where $Y_t = \exp(-\int_0^t r_s \, ds)$.

The previous results depend on the assumption of a continuous pricing function ψ and a closed marketed subspace M. We already commented that these assumptions are so strong as to be of little direct use, and in any case they are difficult to verify even under additional conditions. If M is not closed or ψ is not continuous, we can resort to defining an *approximate arbitrage* to be a sequence $\{x_n\}$ in M, with $\psi(x_n) \leq 0$ for all n, such that $x_n \to x > 0$ and $\lim_n \psi(x_n) \leq 0$. If we strengthen the assumption of no arbitrage to the assumption of no approximate arbitrage, we can then recover the existence of an equivalent martingale measure by essentially the same arguments used for the previous two results.

Proposition. *Suppose $X^0 \equiv 1$. Then there is no approximate arbitrage if and only if there is an equivalent martingale measure.*

Proof: Let $\overline{M}$ be the closure of M. That is, x is in $\overline{M}$, by definition, if x is in M or if $x_n \to x$, where $\{x_n\}$ is a sequence in M. The absence of approximate arbitrage implies that ψ can be extended to a strictly positive continuous linear function $\overline{\psi}$ on $\overline{M}$. The previous lemma implies that $\overline{\psi}$ can be extended to a strictly increasing continuous linear function $\Psi : L^2(P) \to \mathbb{R}$. Then the proof of the previous theorem applies. ∎

Exercises

6.1 Verify relations (10) and (11).

6.2 Consider the case given in Section 6H of $d = 1$, $N = 2$, $S_0^1 > 0$, and with constants $\bar{r}$ and $\bar{\sigma}$ such that, for all t, $r_t = \bar{r}$ and $\sigma_t^1 = \bar{\sigma} S_t^1$. For the option-price process S^2 given by (12), show that $Z = (S^1/\beta, S^2/\beta)$ is L^2-reducible, justifying the assumption of an equivalent martingale measure and the absence of arbitrage.

6.3 Show, in the context of the previous exercise, that (12) defines the Black-Scholes option-pricing formula.

6.4 Prove Theorem 6I.

6.5 Suppose that the return process R^θ for a self-financing trading strategy θ is well defined as an Ito process, as at the end of Section 6D. Show, as claimed there, that R^θ satisfies the state-price restriction (3).

6.6 Extend the arguments of Section 6I to the case of intermediate dividends, as follows. First, consider a particular security with a dividend-rate process δ in $\mathcal{H}^2$. The cumulative-dividend process H is thus defined by $H = \int_0^t \delta_s \, ds$, $t \in [0, T]$. Suppose that the security's price process V satisfies $V_T = 0$. Suppose that Q is an equivalent martingale measure with density ξ.

Let π be defined by $\pi_0 = 1$ and (15). The fact that $H^Y + V^Y$ is a Q-martingale is equivalent to:

$$V_t = \frac{1}{Y_t} E_t^Q \left(\int_t^T Y_s \delta_s \, ds \right), \quad t \in [0, T].$$

(A) From the definition of ξ, Fubini's Theorem, the law of iterated expectations, and the fact that ξ is a martingale, show each of the equalities:

$$V_t = \frac{1}{\xi_t Y_t} E_t \left(\xi_T \int_t^T Y_s \delta_s \, ds \right)$$

$$= \frac{1}{\xi_t Y_t} E_t \left(\int_t^T \xi_T Y_s \delta_s \, ds \right)$$

$$= \frac{1}{\xi_t Y_t} \int_t^T E_t(\xi_T Y_s \delta_s) \, ds$$

$$= \frac{1}{\xi_t Y_t} \int_t^T E_t[E_s(\xi_T Y_s \delta_s)] \, ds$$

$$= \frac{1}{\xi_t Y_t} \int_t^T E_t(\xi_s Y_s \delta_s) \, ds$$

$$= \frac{1}{\xi_t Y_t} E_t \left(\int_t^T \xi_s Y_s \delta_s \, ds \right)$$

$$= \frac{1}{\pi_t} E_t \left(\int_t^T \pi_s \delta_s \, ds \right).$$

This calculation shows that $H^\pi + V^\pi$ is a martingale, consistent with the definition of π as a state-price deflator. Reversing the calculations shows that if π is a state-price deflator and $\text{var}(\pi_T) < \infty$, then $H^Y + V^Y$ is a Q-martingale, where Q is the probability measure defined by its density process ξ from (15).

(B) Extend to the case of V_T not necessarily zero. That is, suppose Q is an equivalent probability measure whose density process ξ is of finite variance. Show that $V^Y + H^Y$ is a Q-martingale if and only if $V^\pi + H^\pi$ is a P-martingale.

(C) Extend to the case of a cumulative-dividend process H that is a bounded Ito process. (Although beyond the scope of this book, an extension of Ito's Lemma applying to general dividend processes that are not necessarily Ito processes shows that one need not assume that H is an Ito process.)

6.7 Extend Exercise 6.5 to allow for cumulative-dividend processes, as follows. Recall that the cumulative-dividend process D^θ generated by a trading strategy θ is defined by $\Delta D_T = W_T^\theta$ and $W_t^\theta = W_0^\theta + \int_0^t \theta_s \, dG_s - D_{t-}^\theta$, where $W_t^\theta = \theta_t \cdot (X_t + \Delta D_t)$ and G is the gain process of the given securities. Let G^θ denote the gain process generated by θ, defined by $G_t^\theta = W_t^\theta + D_t^\theta$. Assuming that an Ito return process R^θ for θ is well defined by $dR_t^\theta = (W_t^\theta)^{-1} \, dG_t^\theta$, show that R^θ satisfies the return restriction (3).

6.8 Prove the Riesz Representation Theorem for $L^2(P)$, as follows. For any continuous linear functional $F : L^2(P) \to \mathbb{R}$, there is a unique π in $L^2(P)$ such that $F(x) = E(\pi x)$ for all x in $L^2(P)$. Hint: Follow the hint given for Exercise 1.17.

6.9 Extend the proof of Theorem 6M to allow for general dividend processes. Add technical conditions as necessary.

Notes

The basic approach of this chapter is from Harrison and Kreps (1979) and Harrison and Pliska (1981), who coined most of the terms and developed most of the techniques and basic results. Huang (1985a, b) generalized the basic theory. The development here differs in some minor ways. Müller (1985) reviews some of the results. Huang and Pagès (1991) give an extension to the case of an infinite-time horizon. The Stieltjes integral, mentioned in Section 6L, can be found in an analysis text such as Royden (1968).

In order to see a sense in which the absence of arbitrage implies that terminal ex-dividend prices are zero, see Ohashi (1991). This issue is especially delicate in non-Brownian information settings, since the event that $X_T^n > 0$ can, in some informational sense not explored here, be suddenly revealed at time T, and therefore be impossible to exploit with a simultaneous trade. For further discussion of the terminal arbitrage issue, see Ohashi (1991).

The results of Section 6M, inspired by Kreps (1981), are based on Clark (1990); related results can be found in Harrison and Kreps (1979), Kreps (1981), Duffie and Huang (1986), Stricker (1990), Ansel and Stricker (1991), El Karoui and Quenez (1991), and Delbaen (1991). Dybvig and Huang (1988) replace the $\mathcal{H}^2(X)$ integrability condition used in this chapter with a lower-bound condition on wealth, and recover similar arbitrage-free pricing implications. Hindy (1991) shows the implications of a non-negative wealth constraint. Further references are found in Duffie (1988b). Most of the results in this chapter extend to an abstract filtration, not necessarily generated by Brownian motion. For various notions of counterexamples, see Stricker (1990) and Back and Pliska (1991). The notion of an approximate arbitrage is a slight variation on the notion of a *free lunch*, introduced by Kreps (1981).

On the relationship between complete markets and equivalent martingale measures, see Müller (1985), Artzner and Heath (1990), and Jarrow and Madan (1990). Carr and Jarrow (1990) show a connection between *local time* and the Black-Scholes model.

General treatments of some of the issues covered in this chapter can be found in Christensen (1987), Christensen (1991), Conze and Viswanathan (1991), and Jouini and Kallal (1991).

7

Applications to Derivative Pricing

THIS CHAPTER APPLIES arbitrage-free pricing techniques from Chapter 6 to derivative securities that are not as easily treated by the direct PDE approach of Chapter 5. After summarizing the essential results from Chapter 6 for this purpose, we study the pricing of forwards and futures, American options, and term-structure derivatives. These three topics can be read independently of each other.

A. Equivalent Martingale Measures in a Black Box

Skipping over the theory developed in Chapter 6, this section reviews the properties of an equivalent martingale measure, a convenient "black-box" approach to derivative asset pricing in the absence of arbitrage. Once again, we fix a standard Brownian motion $B = (B^1, \ldots, B^d)$ in $\mathbb{R}^d$ restricted to some time interval $[0, T]$, on a given probability space $(\Omega, \mathcal{F}, P)$. The standard filtration $\mathbb{F} = \{\mathcal{F}_t : 0 \le t \le T\}$ of B is as defined in Section 5I.

We take as given an adapted short-rate process r and an Ito security-price process S in $\mathbb{R}^N$ with

$$dS_t = \mu_t \, dt + \sigma_t \, dB_t,$$

for appropriate μ and σ. It was shown in Chapter 6 that, aside from technical conditions, the absence of arbitrage is equivalent to the existence of a probability measure Q with special properties, called an equivalent martingale measure. Among its properties, under Q there is a standard Brownian motion $\hat{B}$ in $\mathbb{R}^d$ such that, if the given securities pay no dividends before T, then

$$dS_t = r_t S_t \, dt + \sigma_t \, d\hat{B}_t, \tag{1}$$

which repeats equation (6.11). After substitution of this "risk-neutralizing" measure Q for P, one can treat every security as though its "instantaneous

117

expected rate of return" is the short rate r. More generally, suppose the securities with price process S are claims to a cumulative-dividend process D. (That is, D_t is the vector of cumulative dividends paid by the N securities up through time t.) In this case, we have

$$S_t = E_t^Q \left[\exp \left(\int_t^T -r_s \, ds \right) S_T + \int_t^T \exp \left(\int_t^s -r_u \, du \right) dD_s \right], \qquad (2)$$

which repeats (6.18). For example, suppose that $D_t = \int_0^t \delta_s \, ds$ for some dividend-rate process δ. Then (2) implies that

$$dS_t = (r_t S_t - \delta_t) \, dt + \sigma_t \, d\hat{B}_t, \qquad (3)$$

generalizing (1). For another example, consider a unit zero-coupon riskless bond maturing at any time s. The cumulative-dividend process, say H, of this security is characterized by $dH_\tau = 0$ for $\tau \neq s$ and $dH_s = 1$, so the price of this bond at any time $t < s$ is given from (2) as

$$\Lambda_{t,s} \equiv E_t^Q \left[\exp \left(\int_t^s -r_u \, du \right) \right].$$

This doubly-indexed process Λ is sometimes known as the *discount function*, or more loosely as the *term structure of interest rates*.

By the definition of an equivalent martingale measure given in Chapter 6, any random variable that has finite variance with respect to P has finite expectation with respect to Q. Moreover, for any such random variable Z,

$$E_t^Q(Z) = \frac{1}{\xi_t} E_t(\xi_T Z), \qquad (4)$$

where

$$\xi_t = \exp \left(-\int_0^t \eta_s \, dB_s - \frac{1}{2} \int_0^t \eta_s^\top \eta_s \, ds \right),$$

and where, with (1), η is a particular solution to the linear equations

$$\sigma_t \eta_t = \mu_t - r_t S_t, \quad t \in [0, T].$$

The remainder of this chapter applies these concepts to the calculation of derivative asset prices, going beyond the simple cases treated in Chapter 5.

B. Forward Prices

This section and the next two address the pricing of forward and futures contracts. A discrete-time primer on this topic is given in Exercise 2.17. The forward contract is the simpler of these two closely related securities. Let W be an $\mathcal{F}_T$-measurable finite-variance random variable underlying the claim payable to a holder of the forward contract at its delivery date T. The forward-price process F is an Ito process defined by the fact that one forward contract at time t is a commitment to pay the net amount $F_t - W$ at time T, with no other cash flows at any time. In particular, the true price of a forward contract is zero.

We fix a bounded short-rate process r and an equivalent martingale measure Q after deflation by Y, defined as usual by $Y_t = \exp\left(-\int_0^t r_s \, ds\right)$. The dividend process H defined by the forward contract made at time t is given by $H_s = 0$, $s < T$, and $H_T = W - F_t$. Since the true price of a forward contract is zero, (2) implies that

$$0 = E_t^Q \left[\exp\left(-\int_t^T r_s \, ds\right)(W - F_t) \right].$$

Solving for the forward price,

$$F_t = \frac{E_t^Q \left[\exp\left(-\int_t^T r_s \, ds\right) W \right]}{E_t^Q \left[\exp\left(-\int_t^T r_s \, ds\right) \right]}.$$

If we assume that there exists at time t a zero-coupon riskless bond maturing at time T, then

$$F_t = \frac{1}{\Lambda_{t,T}} E_t^Q \left[\exp\left(-\int_t^T r_s \, ds\right) W \right]. \tag{5}$$

In any case, it can be verified as an exercise that the forward-price process F is indeed an Ito process.

If r and W are statistically independent with respect to Q, we have the simplified expression $F_t = E_t^Q(W)$, implying that the forward price is a Q-martingale. This would be true, for instance, if the short-rate process r is deterministic.

As an example, suppose that the forward contract is for delivery at time T of one unit of a particular security with price process S and dividend process D. In particular, $W = S_T$. We can obtain a more concrete representation of the forward price than (5), as follows. From (5) and (2),

$$F_t = \frac{1}{\Lambda_{t,T}} \left(S_t - E_t^Q \left[\int_t^T \exp\left(-\int_t^s r_u\, du \right) dD_s \right] \right). \tag{6}$$

If the short-rate process r is deterministic, we can simplify further to

$$F_t = \frac{S_t}{\Lambda_{t,T}} - E_t^Q \left[\int_t^T \exp\left(\int_s^T r_u\, du \right) dD_s \right], \tag{7}$$

which is known as the *cost-of-carry formula* for forward prices.

For deterministic r and D, the cost-of-carry formula (7) can be recovered from a direct and simple arbitrage argument. As an alternative to buying a forward contract at time t, one could instead buy the underlying security at t and borrow the required cost S_t by selling riskless zero-coupon bonds maturing at T. If one lends out the dividends as they are received by buying riskless bonds maturing at T, the net payoff to this strategy at time T is the value S_T of the underlying security, less the maturity value $S_t/\Lambda_{t,T}$ of the bonds sold at t, plus the total maturity value $\int_t^T \Lambda_{s,T}^{-1}\, dD_s$ of all of the bonds purchased with the dividends received between t and T. The total is $S_T - S_t/\Lambda_{t,T} + \int_t^T \Lambda_{s,T}^{-1}\, dD_s$. The payoff of the forward contract is $S_T - F_t$. Since these two strategies have no payoffs except at T, and since both F_t and $S_t/\Lambda_{t,T} - \int_t^T \Lambda_{s,T}^{-1}\, dD_s$ are known at time t, there would be an arbitrage unless F_t and $S_t/\Lambda_{t,T} - \int_t^T \Lambda_{s,T}^{-1}\, dD_s$ are equal.

We have put aside the issue of calculating the equivalent martingale measure Q. The simplest case is that in which the forward contract is redundant, for in this case, the equivalent martingale measure does not depend on the forward price. The forward contract is automatically redundant if the underlying asset is a security with deterministic dividends between the contract date t and the delivery date T, provided there is at time t a complete set of bonds maturing at all dates between t and T. In that case, the forward contract can be replicated by a strategy similar to that used to directly verify the cost-of-carry formula. Construction of the strategy is assigned as an exercise.

C. Futures Contracts and Continuous Resettlement

As with a forward contract, a futures contract with delivery date T is keyed to some delivery value W, an $\mathcal{F}_T$-measurable random variable with finite variance. The contract is completely defined by a *futures-price process* Φ with the property that $\Phi_T = W$. As we shall see, the contract is literally a security whose price process is zero and whose cumulative dividend process is Φ. In other words, changes in the futures price are credited to the holder of the contract as they occur. See Exercise 2.17 for an explanation in discrete time.

This definition is an abstraction of the traditional notion of a futures contract, which calls for the holder of one contract at the delivery time T to accept delivery of some asset (whose spot market value is represented here by W) in return for simultaneous payment of the current futures price Φ_T. Likewise, the holder of -1 contract, also known as a *short position* of 1 contract, is traditionally obliged to make delivery of the same underlying assset in exchange for the current futures price Φ_T. This informally justifies the property $\Phi_T = W$ of the futures price process Φ given in the definition above. Roughly speaking, if Φ_T is not equal to W (and if we continue to neglect transactions costs and other details), there is a delivery arbitrage. We will not explicitly define a delivery arbitrage here since it only complicates the analysis of futures prices that follows. Informally, however, in the event that $W > \Phi_T$, one could buy at time T the deliverable asset for W, simultaneously sell one futures contract, and make immediate delivery for a profit of $W - \Phi_T$. Thus the potential of delivery arbitrage will naturally equate Φ_T with the delivery value W. This is sometimes known as the principle of *convergence*.

Many modern futures contracts have streamlined procedures that avoid the delivery process. For these, the only link that exists with the notion of delivery is that the terminal futures price Φ_T is contractually equated to some such variable W, which could be the price of some commodity or security, or even some abstract variable of general economic interest such as a price deflator. This procedure, finessing the actual delivery of some asset, is known as *cash settlement*. In any case, whether based on cash settlement or on the absence of delivery arbitrage, we shall always take it by definition that the delivery futures price Φ_T is equal to the given delivery value W.

The institutional feature of futures markets that is central to our analysis of futures prices is resettlement, the process that generates daily or even more frequent payments to and from the holders of futures contracts based on changes in the futures price. As with the expression "forward price," the term "futures price" can be misleading in that the futures price Φ_t at time t is not the price of the contract at all. Instead, at each resettlement time t, an investor who has held $\bar{\theta}$ futures contracts since the last resettlement time, say s, receives the resettlement payment $\bar{\theta}(\Phi_t - \Phi_s)$, following the simplest resettlement recipe. More complicated resettlement arrangements often apply in practice. The continuous-time abstraction is to take the futures-price process Φ to be an Ito process and a *futures-position process* to be some θ

in $\mathcal{H}^2(\Phi)$ generating the resettlement gain $\int \theta \, d\Phi$ as a cumulative-dividend process. In particular, as we have already stated in its definition, the futures-price process Φ is itself, formally speaking, the cumulative-dividend process associated with the contract. The true price process is zero, since (again ignoring some of the detailed institutional procedures) there is no payment against the contract due at the time a contract is bought or sold.

D. Arbitrage-Free Characterization of Futures Prices

The futures-price process Φ can now be characterized as follows. We take a setting in which there is a bounded short-rate process r and an equivalent martingale measure Q after deflation by Y, where $Y_t = \exp(\int_0^t -r_s \, ds)$. Since Φ is strictly speaking the cumulative-dividend process associated with the futures contract, and since the true price process of the contract is zero, the deflated gain process for the contract is $\Phi^Y = \int Y \, d\Phi$, which is therefore a Q-martingale. Since Y is a strictly positive bounded process that is bounded away from zero, $\int Y \, d\Phi$ is a Q-martingale if and only if Φ is also a Q-martingale. (This seems obvious; proof is assigned as an exercise.) Since $\Phi_T = W$, we have deduced a convenient representation for the futures-price process:

$$\Phi_t = E_t^Q(W), \quad t \in [0, T]. \tag{8}$$

If r and W are statistically independent under Q, the futures-price process Φ given by (8) and the forward-price process F given by (5) are thus identical. In particular, if r is deterministic, the cost-of-carry formula (7) applies as well to futures prices.

As for how to calculate an equivalent martingale measure Q, it is most convenient if the futures contract is redundant, for then a suitable Q can be calculated directly from the other available securities. We shall work on this approach, originating with an article cited in the Notes, and fix for the remainder of the section an equivalent martingale measure Q for the Y-deflated versions of all securities other than the futures contract. Aside from the case of complete markets, it is not obvious how to establish the redundancy of a futures contract since the futures-price process Φ is itself the cumulative-dividend process of the contract, so any argument might seem circular. Suppose, however, that there is a self-financing strategy (in securities other than the futures contract) whose value at the delivery date T is

$$Z_T = W \exp\left(\int_t^T r_s \, ds\right).$$

We will give an example of such a strategy shortly. From the definition of Q, the market value of this strategy at time t is $Z_t = E_t^Q(W)$. We claim that if Φ_t is not equal to Z_t, then there is an arbitrage. In order to show this, we will construct a trading strategy, involving only the futures contract and borrowing or lending at the short rate, such that the strategy pays off exactly Z_T at time T and requires the investment of Φ_t at time t. It will be clear from this that the absence of arbitrage equates Φ_t and Z_t. The strategy is constructed as follows. Let θ be the futures-position process defined by $\theta_s = 0, s < t$, and $\theta_s = \exp\left(\int_t^s r_u \, du\right), s \geq t$. Let V_t be the amount invested at the short rate at time t, determined as follows. Let $V_s = 0, s < t$, and $V_t = \Phi_t$. After t, let all dividends generated by the futures position be invested at the short rate and "rolled over." That is, let

$$dV_s = r_s V_s \, ds + \theta_s \, d\Phi_s, \quad s \in [t, T].$$

The total market value at any time $s \geq t$ of this self-financing strategy in futures and investment at the short rate is the amount V_s invested at the short rate, since the true price of the futures contract is zero. We can calculate by Ito's Lemma that

$$V_T = \Phi_T \exp\left(\int_t^T r_s \, ds\right) = W \exp\left(\int_t^T r_s \, ds\right) = Z_T, \qquad (9)$$

which verifies the claim that the futures contract is redundant.

Summarizing, the futures-price process is uniquely defined by (8) provided there is a self-financing strategy with value $Z_T = W \exp\left(\int_t^T r_s \, ds\right)$ at the delivery date T. It remains to look for examples in which Z_T is indeed the value at time T of some self-financing strategy. That is the case, for instance, if the futures contract delivers a security that pays no dividends before T and if the short-rate process is deterministic. With this, the purchase of $\exp(\int_t^T r_s \, ds)$ units of the underlying security at time 0 would suffice. More general examples can easily be constructed.

There is one loose end to tidy up. The assumption that the futures-price process Φ is an Ito process played a role in our analysis, yet we have not confirmed that the solution (8) for Φ is actually an Ito process. This can be shown as an application of Girsanov's Theorem (Appendix D).

E. American Security Valuation

Again taking the setup given in Section 6A, consider an American security defined by an adapted process X. The American security is a claim to the payoff X_τ at a stopping time τ chosen by the holder of the security. In this sense, we call a stopping time an *exercise policy*, following the discrete-time treatment in Chapter 2. Our objective is to calculate the price process V of the American security. The classic example is the case of a put option on a stock in the Black-Scholes setting of log-normal stock prices and constant short rates. In that case, we have $X_t = (K - S_t)^+$, where K is the exercise price and S is a log-normal stock-price process.

We suppose that, given any exercise policy τ, a security with payoff X_τ at time τ is redundant. As explained in Section 6A, the absence of arbitrage implies that the price process V^τ of such a security is given in accordance with the equivalent martingale measure Q by

$$V_t^\tau = E_t^Q \left(\varphi_{t,\tau} X_\tau \right),$$

where $\varphi_{t,\tau} \equiv \exp \left(\int_t^\tau -r_s \, ds \right)$. Following the approach taken in Section 2I, consider the *rational exercise problem*

$$V_0^* = \sup_{\tau \in \mathcal{T}_{0,T}} V_0^\tau, \tag{10}$$

where $\mathcal{T}_{t,s}$ denotes the set of stopping times valued in $[t, s]$. This is the problem of maximizing the initial arbitrage-free value, over the set of candidate exercise policies.

We claim that if there is a stopping time τ^* solving (10), then the absence of arbitrage implies that the American security must sell initially for V_0^*. For example, if $V_0 < V_0^*$, then purchase of the American security for V_0, adoption of the rational exercise policy τ^*, and replication of the payoff $-X(\tau^*)$ at τ^* at an initial payoff of V_0^*, together generate a net initial profit of $V_0^* - V_0 > 0$ and no further cash flow. This is an arbitrage. Likewise, if $V_0 > V_0^*$, then sale of the American security and replication of the payoff X_τ chosen by the holder of the American security is possible for a net initial payoff of $V_0 - V_0^\tau \geq V_0 - V_0^* > 0$, an arbitrage. Indeed, then, the unique arbitrage-free American security price is given by (10). One should bear in mind that we have implicitly extended the definition of an arbitrage slightly in order to handle American securities. Moreover, the discussion of American security valuation given in Chapter 2 prompts some caution in applying this approach without literally complete markets.

There are two basic issues to broach, the existence of a rational exercise policy and the computation of V_0^*. Existence calls for certain technical regularity conditions.

American Regularity Conditions. *X is a non-negative continuous process and* $E(X_*^q) < \infty$ *for some* $q > 2$, *where* $X_* = \sup_{t \in [0,T]} X_t$. *The short-rate process r is bounded.*

The condition $E(X_*^q) < \infty$ is certainly satisfied for American put options, since their payoff is bounded by the strike price. In the original Black-Scholes setting, X is also continuous and r is bounded (in fact constant). The American regularity conditions are based on a source cited in the Notes, which includes a proof of the following result. The conditions in that source are somewhat different, but the same proof carries over once one shows that $E^Q(\sqrt{X_*}) < \infty$, which follows from the fact that $\sqrt{X_*}$ has finite variance under P and from the definition of Q as an equivalent martingale measure.

Proposition. *Under the American regularity conditions, there exists a rational exercise policy* τ^*, *that is, a stopping time solving (10). The optimal payoff* $X(\tau^*)$ *has a finite expectation under* Q.

Thus the American regularity conditions are also sufficient for V_0^* of (10) to be the arbitrage-free value of the American security. In the case of the Black-Scholes model, all of the American regularity conditions are satisfied for the American put with exercise price K, expiration at time T, constant short rate $\bar{r}$, constant stock volatility $\bar{\sigma}$, and initial stock price x. We can write the stock-price process S as the solution to

$$dS_t = \bar{r} S_t \, dt + \bar{\sigma} S_t \, dZ_t; \quad S_0 = x, \tag{11}$$

where Z is a standard Brownian motion under Q. The arbitrage-free put price is therefore

$$V_0^* = h(x, T) \equiv \max_{\tau \in \mathcal{T}_{0,T}} E^Q \left[e^{-\bar{r}\tau} (K - S_\tau)^+ \right]. \tag{12}$$

In Chapter 10 we review some numerical recipes for approximating this value.

By extending our arguments, we can handle an American security that promises a cumulative-dividend process H until exercised at a stopping time τ for a final payoff of X_τ. The absence of arbitrage implies that the price process V^* of the American security (H, X) is given by

$$V_t^* \equiv \sup_{\tau \in \mathcal{T}_{t,T}} E_t^Q \left(\int_t^\tau \varphi_{t,s} \, dH_s + \varphi_{t,\tau} X_\tau \right), \quad t < \tau, \tag{13}$$

whenever this problem for $t = 0$ is well defined and has a solution τ^*, the rational exercise policy.

F. Exercise and Continuation Regions for American Securities

Let's take the case of an American security X with $X_t = g(Y_t, t)$, where $g : \mathbb{R}^K \times [0, T] \to \mathbb{R}$ is continuous and Y is an Ito process in $\mathbb{R}^K$ satisfying the SDE (under the equivalent martingale measure Q):

$$dY_t = a(Y_t)\, dt + b(Y_t)\, d\hat{B}_t. \tag{14}$$

For simplicity, we take the interest-rate process r to be zero, and later show that this is without loss of generality. We adopt the American regularity conditions and again assume redundancy of the American security for any exercise policy. Starting at time t with initial condition $Y_t = y$ for (14), the arbitrage-free value is given by

$$h(y, t) \equiv \sup_{\tau \in \mathcal{T}_{t,T}} E_t^Q \left[g(Y_\tau, \tau) \right]. \tag{15}$$

By inspection, $h \geq g$. An optimal exercise policy is given by

$$\tau^* = \inf\{ t \in [0, T] : h(Y_t, t) = g(Y_t, t) \}. \tag{16}$$

In order to see this, let $\hat{\tau}$ be any optimal exercise policy (one of which exists by Proposition 7E), and let M be defined by

$$M_t = E_t^Q[X(\hat{\tau})], \quad t < \hat{\tau},$$

$$= X(\hat{\tau}), \quad t \geq \hat{\tau}.$$

We will use the fact that M is a martingale under Q. For $t < \hat{\tau}$, the definition of h implies that $M_t = h(Y_t, t)$. Since $h(Y_{\hat{\tau}}, \hat{\tau}) = g(Y_{\hat{\tau}}, \hat{\tau})$, we know that $\tau^* \leq \hat{\tau}$. Thus $E^Q[M(\tau^*)] = M_0 = h(Y_0, 0)$, implying that τ^* is indeed an optimal exercise policy.

By (16), $h(Y_t, t) > g(Y_t, t)$, $t < \tau^*$. Letting

$$\mathcal{E} = \{(y, t) \in \mathbb{R}^K \times [0, T] : h(y, t) = g(y, t)\},$$

we can write $\tau^* = \inf\{t : (Y_t, t) \in \mathcal{E}\}$, and safely call $\mathcal{E}$ the *exercise region* and its complement

$$\mathcal{C} = \{(y, t) \in \mathbb{R}^K \times [0, T) : h(y, t) > g(y, t)\}$$

the *continuation region*. In order to solve the optimal exercise problem, it is enough to break $\mathbb{R}^K \times [0, T]$ into these two sets. An optimal policy is then to exercise when in $\mathcal{E}$, and otherwise to wait. Typically, solving for the exercise region $\mathcal{E}$ is a formidable problem.

For a PDE characterization of the solution, suppose that h is sufficiently smooth for an application of Ito's Lemma. Letting $U_t = h(Y_t, t)$, we have $dU_t = \mathcal{D}h(Y_t, t)\, dt + h_y(Y_t, t)b(Y_t)\, d\hat{B}_t$, where

$$\mathcal{D}h(y, t) = h_t(y, t) + h_y(y, t)a(y) + \frac{1}{2}\text{tr}\left[h_{yy}(y, t)b(y)b(y)^\top\right].$$

For any initial conditions (y, t) and any stopping time $\tau \geq t$, we know from the definition of h that $E^Q[h(Y_\tau, \tau)] \leq h(y, t)$. From this, it is natural to conjecture that $\mathcal{D}h(y, t) \leq 0$ for all (y, t). Moreover, from the fact that M is a Q-martingale and $M_t = h(Y_t, t)$, $t < \tau^*$, it is easy to see that $\mathcal{D}h(y, t) = 0$ for all (y, t) in $\mathcal{C}$. We summarize these conjectured necessary conditions on h, supressing the arguments (y, t) everywhere for brevity. On $\mathbb{R}^K \times [0, T]$:

$$h \geq g, \quad \mathcal{D}h \leq 0, \quad (h - g)(\mathcal{D}h) = 0. \tag{17}$$

The last of these three conditions means that $\mathcal{D}h = 0$ wherever $h > g$, and conversely that $h = g$ wherever $\mathcal{D}h < 0$. Intuitively, this is a Bellman condition prescribing a policy of not exercising so long as the expected rate of change of the value function is not strictly negative. We also have the boundary condition

$$h(y, T) = g(y, T), \quad y \in \mathbb{R}^K. \tag{18}$$

Under strong technical assumptions from sources in the Notes that we will not review here, it turns out that these necessary conditions (17)–(18) are also sufficient for h to be the value function. This characterization (17)–(18) of the value function lends itself to a finite-difference algorithm for numerical solution of the value function h.

In order to incorporate nonzero interest rates, suppose that the short-rate process r can be written in the form $r_t = \alpha(Y_t)$ for some bounded measurable $\alpha : \mathbb{R}^K \to \mathbb{R}$. Letting $\beta_t = \int_0^t r_s\, ds$, we have $d\beta_t = \alpha(Y_t)\beta_t\, dt$, so all of the above goes through, replacing the orginal Ito process Y in $\mathbb{R}^K$ with the augmented Ito process $\hat{Y} = (Y, \beta)$ in $\mathbb{R}^{K+1}$, and replacing the original payoff function g with $\hat{g}$, where $\hat{g}[(Y_t, \beta_t), t] = g(Y_t, t)/\beta_t$. The variational inequality (17)–(18) for the value function h can then be written exactly as before, with the exception that $\mathcal{D}h(y, t)$ is replaced everywhere by

$\mathcal{D}h(y, t) - \alpha(y)h(y, t)$. Likewise, time dependence in the functions a, b, and α can be accommodated by augmenting $\hat{Y}$ with the trivial Ito process W given by elapsed time, that is, $W(t) = t$.

For the special case of the classic American put problem (12), a series of advances cited in the Notes has led to the following characterization of the solution. Since $Y = S$ is a non-negative process, the continuation region $\mathcal{C}$ can be treated as a subset of $\mathbb{R}_+ \times [0, T)$. It turns out that there is an increasing continuously differentiable function $S^* : [0, T) \to \mathbb{R}$, called the *optimal stopping boundary*, such that $\mathcal{C} = \{(x, t) : x > S_t^*\}$. Letting $S_T^* = K$, the optimal exercise policy τ^* is then to exercise when (and if) the stock price S "hits the boundary," that is, $\tau^* = \inf\{t : S_t = S_t^*\}$.

We can decompose the value function for the American put as the sum $h = p + e$, where p is the European put value function and e is the *early exercise premium*. These functions are defined as follows. For each initial condition (x, t) for the stock price, we have

$$p(x, t) = E^Q \left[e^{-\bar{r}(T-t)}(K - S_T)^+ \right]$$

and

$$e(x, t) = \int_t^T e^{-\bar{r}(u-t)} \bar{r}KQ(S_u < S_u^*) \, du. \tag{19}$$

The intuitive idea behind this decomposition is as follows. At time t, the option to exercise during a given "infinitesimal interval du" is worthless when S_u is above the critical value S_u^* for exercise, and is otherwise worth the present value at time t of the interest payment $\bar{r}K \, du$ that one gets at time u by investing the exercised price K at the short rate $\bar{r}$ during that "interval," rather than waiting until "$u + du$." Since $e^{-\bar{r}(u-t)}Q(S_u < S_u^*)$ is the value at time t of one unit of account paid at time u in the event that $S_u > S_u^*$, the market value at time t of that infinitesimally lived option is $e^{-\bar{r}(u-t)} \bar{r}KQ(S_u < S_u^*) \, du$. The total early exercise premium $e(x, t)$ is therefore the "sum over the intervals du" of these infinitesimal early exercise premiums, as indicated in (19).

Unfortunately, there is no explicit solution available for the optimal stopping boundary S^*. There are, however, numerical methods for estimating the value function h and exercise boundary S^*. One is the simple algorithm (3.23) for the "binomial" model, which, as we see in Chapter 10, can be taken as an approximation of the Black-Scholes model. The other is a direct finite-difference numerical solution of the associated partial differential inequality (17)–(18), which in this case can be written, with the change of variables from stock price x to its logarithm $y = \log(x)$: On $\mathbb{R} \times [0, T)$:

$$h(y, t) - (K - e^y)^+ \geq 0$$

$$\mathcal{D}h(y, t) - \bar{r}h(y, t) \leq 0 \tag{20}$$

$$[h(y, t) - (K - e^y)^+][\mathcal{D}h(y, t) - \bar{r}h(y, t)] = 0,$$

with boundary condition

$$h(y, T) = (K - e^y)^+, \quad y \in \mathbb{R}, \tag{21}$$

where

$$\mathcal{D}h(y, t) = h_t(y, t) + \left(\bar{r} - \frac{\bar{\sigma}^2}{2}\right) h_y(y, t) + \frac{\bar{\sigma}^2}{2} h_{yy}(y, t).$$

Not all of the indicated derivatives of h may exist, but it turns out, from sources cited in the Notes, that there is no essential difficulty in treating (20)–(21) as written for computational purposes.

G. One-Factor Term-Structure Models

The remainder of the chapter concerns models of the term structure of interest rates and associated derivative security prices. We begin with a class of *one-factor term-structure models*, by which we mean models of the short rate r given by an SDE of the form

$$dr_t = \mu(r_t, t)\, dt + \sigma(r_t, t)\, d\hat{B}_t, \tag{23}$$

where $\hat{B}$ is a standard Brownian motion under an equivalent martingale measure Q and where μ and σ are continuous functions satisfying technical conditions guaranteeing the existence of a solution to (23) for each $r_0 \geq 0$ such that, for all t and $T \geq t$,

$$\Lambda_{t,T} \equiv E_t^Q \left[\exp\left(-\int_t^T r_s\, ds\right)\right] < \infty. \tag{24}$$

As explained in Section 7A, $\Lambda_{t,T}$ is the price at time t of a unit zero-coupon riskless bond maturing at T. The Feynman-Kac approach to PDE solutions given in Appendix E implies, under technical conditions on μ and σ, that for all t and $T \geq t$,

$$\Lambda_{t,T} = f(r_t, t),$$

where $f \in C^{2,1}(\mathbb{R} \times [0, T))$ solves the PDE

$$\mathcal{D}f(x, t) - xf(x, t) = 0, \quad (x, t) \in \mathbb{R} \times [0, T), \tag{25}$$

with boundary condition

$$f(x, T) = 1, \quad x \in \mathbb{R}, \tag{26}$$

where

$$\mathcal{D}f(x, t) = f_t(x, t) + f_x(x, t)\mu(x, t) + \frac{1}{2}f_{xx}(x, t)\sigma(x, t)^2.$$

If μ and σ do not depend on t, then we can also view $f(r_0, t)$ as the bond price $\Lambda_{0,T-t}$, so that a single function f gives the entire initial term structure between 0 and T.

According to the results in Appendix E, in order for (23) through (26) to hold, it is enough that r is non-negative and that μ and σ satisfy Lipschitz conditions in x and have derivatives μ_x, σ_x, μ_{xx}, and σ_{xx} that are continuous and satisfy growth conditions in x. These technical conditions are unnecessarily strong, as we shall see from specific examples that violate them. One of the best known of these examples is the *Cox-Ingersoll-Ross* (CIR) model, for which

$$\mu(x, t) = A(\bar{x} - x); \qquad \sigma(x, t) = C\sqrt{x}, \quad x \geq 0, \tag{27}$$

for positive constants A, $\bar{x}$, and C. For this example, we assume that $r_0 \geq 0$, and we treat (23) through (26) by replacing the state space $\mathbb{R}$ with $[0, \infty)$. A source cited in the Notes implies the existence of a non-negative solution r to the corresponding SDE (23). Some of the properties of this solution are discussed in Section 9I, where the coefficients A, $\bar{x}$, and C are calculated in a general equilibrium setting in terms of the utility function and endowment of a representative agent. For the CIR model, it can be verified by direct computation of the derivatives that the solution for the term-structure PDE (25)–(26) is given by

$$f(x, t) = H_1(T - t) \exp\left[-H_2(T - t)x\right], \tag{28}$$

where

$$H_1(t) = \left[\frac{2\gamma e^{(\gamma+A)t/2}}{(\gamma + A)(e^{\gamma t} - 1) + 2\gamma}\right]^{2A\bar{x}/C^2}$$

$$H_2(t) = \frac{2(e^{\gamma t} - 1)}{(\gamma + A)(e^{\gamma t} - 1) + 2\gamma},$$

for $\gamma = (A^2 + 2C^2)^{1/2}$. The initial CIR term structure is thus $\Lambda_{0,t} = H_1(t) \exp[-H_2(t)r_0]$, for $t \in [0, T]$.

H. Term-Structure Derivatives

In applications, one is often interested in pricing a derivative security that has payoffs defined in terms of measurable real-valued functions h and g on $\mathbb{R} \times [0, T]$, specifying the dividend rate $h(r_t, t)$ at any time t in $[0, T]$, and the terminal payoff $g(r_\tau, \tau)$ at some particular time $\tau \le T$. By the definition of an equivalent martingale measure, the price at time t for such a security is

$$F(r_t, t) \equiv E_t^Q \left[\int_t^\tau \varphi_{t,s} h(r_s, s)\, ds + \varphi_{t,\tau} g(r_\tau, \tau) \right],$$

where $\varphi_{t,s} = \exp\left(-\int_t^s r_v\, dv\right)$. The Feynman-Kac PDE results of Appendix E give technical conditions on μ, σ, h, and g under which F solves the PDE

$$\mathcal{D}F(x, t) - xF(x, t) + h(x, t) = 0, \quad (x, t) \in \mathbb{R} \times [0, \tau), \tag{29}$$

with boundary condition

$$F(x, \tau) = g(x, \tau), \quad x \in \mathbb{R}, \tag{30}$$

where $\mathcal{D}F(x, t)$ is defined as in (25). Some examples follow, neglecting many variations that occur in practice.

(a) Consider a European option on a zero-coupon bond maturing at time T. The call option value, with exercise price K and expiration date $\tau < T$, is given by the solution F to (29)–(30), with $h = 0$ and $g(x, \tau) = [f(x, \tau) - K]^+$, where f solves (25)–(26).

(b) An *interest-rate swap* can be idealized as a contract paying the dividend rate $h(r_t, t) = r_t - r^*$, where r^* is a fixed interest rate agreed upon at time zero. In some cases there is a payment $g(r_\tau, \tau)$ (usually a constant) at the terminal swap date τ.

(c) A *cap* is a loan at a variable interest rate that is capped at some level $\bar{r}$. Per unit of the principal amount of the loan, the value of the cap is given by (29)–(30) with, in the idealized case, $h(r_t, t) = \min(r_t, \bar{r})$ and $g(r_\tau, \tau) = 1$.

(d) A *floor* is defined symmetrically with a cap, replacing the capped variable rate $\min(r_t, \bar{r})$ with a "floored" rate $h(r_t, t) = \max(r_t, \underline{r})$, for some floor rate $\underline{r}$. A loan with a capped and floored variable rate can also be valued in the obvious way.

(e) A *yield curve option* is defined by $h \equiv 0$ and, for the case of a call at strike K and expiration time τ, the terminal payoff $g(r_\tau, \tau) = [Y_n(r_\tau, \tau) - K]^+$, where $Y_n(r_\tau, \tau)$ is the yield at time τ on some particular n-period riskless bond that is an industry benchmark for the riskless term structure. (The *yield* on an n-period zero-coupon bond is that number y with the property that the bond's price is $(1 + y)^{-n}$.) Since a yield is not the price of anything in particular, this is not literally an option to buy anything, but rather is a derivative security that allows one to speculate or hedge based on the level of the yield in question. The notion of a yield curve option has been extended to that of a *slope-of-the-yield-curve option*, for which $g(r_\tau, \tau) = [S_{m,n}(r_\tau, \tau) - K]^+$, where

$$S_{m,n}(r_\tau, \tau) = \frac{Y_n(r_\tau, \tau) - Y_m(r_\tau, \tau)}{n - m}$$

defines the slope of the yield curve between two different times to maturity m and $n > m$.

In each of the above cases, practical considerations cause variations. For instance, the payments that we have modeled as a rate $h(r_t, t)$ are usually paid periodically (say monthly or quarterly) in lump-sum amounts. Such an instrument can be treated as a portfolio of different derivative securities, consisting of a security paying a lump sum $g_1(r_{\tau(1)})$ at the first dividend date $\tau(1)$, a security paying a lump sum $g_2(r_{\tau(2)})$ at the second dividend date $\tau(2)$, and so on. The value of a portfolio is of course the sum of the values of its constituent securities. A special case is a riskless coupon bond, for which g_i is constant for all i. Another practical consideration is that, for swaps, caps, floors, and other such securities, the relevant variable interest rate is often something other than the short rate r_t, such as the current yield y_t on some particular maturity of short-term riskless bonds. We can often write $y_t = Y(r_t, t)$ for some suitable function Y, in which case the same approach applies. There are typically lags between the dates at which payments are calculated, based on current interest rates, and the dates on which the payments are actually made. This can also be accommodated. In other cases, *path-dependent* derivative securities sometimes call for additional state variables, or for the more general non-Markovian approach considered elsewhere in this chapter. *Mortgage-backed securities* constitute an important class of path-dependent securities that is treated in sources cited in the Notes. Some interest-rate derivative securities are based on the yields of bonds that are subject to some risk of default, in which case the approach must be modified by accounting for default risk.

There are relatively few cases of practical interest for which the PDE (29)–(30) can be solved explicitly. Chapter 10 reviews a number of numerical solution techniques.

I. An Affine Class of Term-Structure Models

Rather than solving the term-structure PDE (25) for each of a number of cases of μ and σ, we will instead characterize the class of models with a bond-price function f solving (25)–(26) of the form

$$f(x, t) = \exp\left[a(T - t) + b(T - t)x\right], \tag{31}$$

where a and b are in $C^2([0, \infty))$. That is, we will deduce from (25) what functions μ and σ are consistent with (31). Since the yield $\log[f(x, t)]/(T-t)$ defined by (31) is affine in x for all t, we call (31) an *affine term-structure model.* (A function $H : \mathbb{R} \to \mathbb{R}$ is *affine* if there are constants α and β such that, for all x, $H(x) = \alpha + \beta x$.) For example, the CIR model (28) is an affine term-structure model with $a(t) = \log[H_1(t)]$ and $b(t) = -H_2(t)$. The general affine class (31) is based on a source cited in the Notes, and unifies a number of different parametric term-structure models in the literature.

Given the boundary condition (26), we must have $a(0) = b(0) = 0$. Relations (24) and (31) are both satisfied if and only if, for each $(x, t) \in \mathbb{R} \times [0, T)$,

$$b(T - t)\mu(x, t) = [1 + b'(T - t)]x + a'(T - t) - \frac{1}{2}b^2(T - t)\sigma^2(x, t), \quad (32)$$

Fixing a and b, there is a large family of pairs of functions of the form (μ, σ) satisfying (32). We assume that $b(t)$ is nonzero for all $t > 0$. Then, even if we fix the function σ arbitrarily, there is a unique solution μ to (32). Notably, for each t, the function $x \mapsto \mu(x, t)$ is affine if and only if $x \mapsto \sigma(x, t)^2$ is affine.

For the case in which μ and σ do not depend on t, (32) implies, for each τ, that

$$0 = -\mu_t(x, T - \tau)$$
$$= \frac{-b'(\tau)[1 + b'(\tau)]x}{b(\tau)^2} + \frac{b''(\tau)x}{b(\tau)} + \frac{a''(\tau)}{b(\tau)} - \frac{a'(\tau)b'(\tau)}{b(\tau)^2} - \frac{1}{2}b'(\tau)v(x),$$

where $v(x) = \sigma(x, t)^2$. Assuming that $b'(\tau)$ is nonzero, this implies that $v'(\cdot)$ is a constant, which in turn implies that v is affine. By our earlier reasoning, $x \mapsto \mu(x, t)$ is then also affine. In summary, if μ and σ are both time-independent and $b(\tau)$ and $b'(\tau)$ are nonzero for all $\tau > 0$, then (32) implies that both μ and σ^2 are affine functions of x. That is, we have some constants $\alpha_1, \alpha_2, \beta_1$, and β_2 such that

$$\mu(x, t) = \alpha_1 + \alpha_2 x; \qquad \sigma(x, t) = \sqrt{\beta_1 + \beta_2 x}. \tag{33}$$

This "affine class" of term-structure models includes the following examples from the literature:

(a) the Vasicek model, for which $\beta_2 = 0$;
(b) the Cox-Ingersoll-Ross model, for which $\beta_1 = 0$;
(c) the Gaussian path-independent model, for which $\alpha_2 = \beta_2 = 0$;
(d) the Pearson-Sun model, for which the coefficients are restricted so that $\alpha_1 - \alpha_2 \beta_1 / \beta_2 > 0$, in order to ensure existence of solutions on the state space $[-\beta_1/\beta_2, \infty)$.

For the Vasicek model, the distribution of r_t (under Q) is, for any time t, normal with a mean and variance that can be computed explicitly from the parameters α_1, α_2, and β_1. A special case is given by (c), which is called *path-independent* because $\alpha_2 = 0$ implies that we can write $r_t = R(t, \hat{B}_t)$ for some function $R : [0, \infty) \times \mathbb{R} \to \mathbb{R}$. That is, r_t depends only on t and $\hat{B}_t$, and not otherwise on the path $\{\hat{B}_s : 0 \le s \le t\}$. The general class of path-independent models has special computational advantages that can be seen in Exercises 3.12 (a discrete-time analogue) and 10.5 (the continuous-time limiting argument). The various models listed above are studied in detail in the literature cited in the Notes. The Pearson-Sun model (d) is also known as the *translated CIR model*.

Going the other way, given μ and σ from (33), we can derive differential equations for a and b from (31) by matching coefficients in x and τ respectively. These are

$$b'(\tau) = \alpha_2 b(\tau) - \beta_2 b^2(\tau) - 1; \quad b(0) = 0 \tag{34}$$

and, given the solution b to (34),

$$a'(\tau) = \alpha_1 b(\tau) - \beta_1 b^2(\tau); \quad a(0) = 0. \tag{35}$$

Finally, we consider the general affine case, in which

$$\mu(x, T - \tau) = \alpha_1(\tau) + \alpha_2(\tau)x; \qquad \sigma(x, T - \tau) = \sqrt{\beta_1(\tau) + \beta_2(\tau)x}, \tag{36}$$

for well-behaved functions $\alpha_1, \alpha_2, \beta_1$, and β_2. The corresponding solution f for bond prices is given by (31) where a and b solve (34)–(35), replacing the constant coefficients with these time-dependent coefficients. This idea is further pursued by sources cited in the Notes that extend the Vasicek, CIR, and Gaussian models to the case of time-dependent coefficients. For the Gaussian path-independent model (c) above, the extension to time-dependent α_1 and β_1 is sometimes called the *continuous-time Ho-Lee model*, and is also path-independent.

J. Green's Function and the Term Structure

Based on the results of Appendix E, under technical conditions we can also express the solution F of the PDE (29)–(30) for the value of a derivative term-structure security in the form

$$F(x, t) = \int_0^T \int_{y(1)}^{y(2)} G(x, t, y, s) h(y, s) \, dy \, ds \; + \int_{y(1)}^{y(2)} G(x, t, y, \tau) \, dy, \quad (37)$$

where G is the *fundamental solution* of the PDE (29). The relevant state space is shown as $[y(1), y(2)]$, which is typically $(0, \infty)$ or $(-\infty, +\infty)$. As explained in Appendix E, among its other properties, the fundamental solution G, sometimes called *Green's function*, is such that, for each (x, t) in $\mathbb{R} \times [0, T)$, there is a function $\psi \in C^{2,1}(\mathbb{R} \times (0, T])$, defined by $\psi(y, s) = G(x, t, y, s)$, that solves the *forward Kolmogorov equation*

$$\mathcal{D}^* \psi(y, s) - y \psi(y, s) = 0, \quad (38)$$

where

$$\mathcal{D}^* \psi(y, s) = -\psi_t(y, s) - \psi_x(y, s) \mu(y, s) + \frac{1}{2} \psi_{xx}(x, s) \sigma(y, s)^2.$$

The relevant boundary condition is that $\psi(\,\cdot\,, t)$ is the density at time t of a measure on $\mathbb{R}$ that converges (in a sense that we leave to sources cited in Appendix E) to a probability measure ν with $\nu(\{x\}) = 1$. Likewise, for any fixed (y, s) in $\mathbb{R} \times (0, T]$, there is a function $u \in C^{2,1}(\mathbb{R} \times [0, T))$, defined by $u(x, t) = G(x, t, y, s)$, solving the more familiar *backward Kolmogorov equation*

$$\mathcal{D}u(x, t) - xu(x, t) = 0, \quad (x, t) \in \mathbb{R} \times [0, s). \quad (39)$$

The boundary condition for u is symmetric to that for ψ.

For any times t and $s > t$, any short rate x, and any interval (y_1, y_2), we can think of $\int_{y_1}^{y_2} G(x, t, y, s) \, dy$ as the price at time t, given the current short rate $r_t = x$, of a security that pays one unit of account at time s in the event that r_s is in (y_1, y_2). In particular, the current price $\Lambda_{t,s}$ of the unit bond maturing at s is given by $\int_{-\infty}^{+\infty} G(r_t, t, y, s)\, dy$. Given G, the numerical solution of the derivative asset price function F is more easily treated by numerical integration of (37) than from a direct numerical attack on the PDE (29), say by finite-difference or Monte Carlo methods. Numerical methods for calculating F and G are pursued in Chapter 10.

A lengthy argument given by a source cited in the Notes shows that the fundamental solution G^* of the Cox-Ingersoll-Ross model (27) is given explicitly in terms of the parameters A, $\bar{x}$, and C by

$$G^*(x, 0, y, t) = \frac{\alpha(t) I_q \left[2\alpha(t)\sqrt{xye^{-\gamma t}} \right]}{\exp\left[\alpha(t)(y + xe^{-\gamma t}) - \eta(x + A\bar{x}t - y) \right]} \left(\frac{e^{\gamma t} y}{x} \right)^{q/2}, \quad (40)$$

where $\gamma = (A^2 + 2C^2)^{1/2}$, $\eta = (A - \gamma)/C^2$,

$$\alpha(t) = \frac{2\gamma}{C^2(1 - e^{-\gamma t})}, \qquad q = \frac{2A\bar{x}}{C^2} - 1,$$

and I_q is the modified Bessel function of the first kind of order q. The same source gives explicit solutions for the Green's functions of other models. For time-independent μ and σ, as with the CIR model, $G(x, t, y, s) = G(x, 0, y, s - t)$.

K. Other Term-Structure Models

This section has the simple purpose of listing some of the other types of term-structure models that have been studied in the literature. These include

(a) the Dothan model, with $\mu(x, t) = \alpha x$, $\sigma(x, t) = \beta x$;
(b) the Courtadon model, with $\mu(x, t) = \alpha_1 + \alpha_2 x$, $\sigma(x, t) = \beta x$;
(c) the log-normal model, with $\mu(x, t) = \alpha(t)x$, $\sigma(x, t) = \beta(t)x$;
(d) the generalized log-normal model, with $\mu(x, t) = \alpha_1(t)x + \alpha_2(t)x \log x$ and $\sigma(x, t) = \beta(t)x$;
(e) the Black-Derman-Toy model, for which μ and σ are such that $r_t = U(t)\exp[\beta(t)\hat{B}(t)]$, for some functions U and β in $C^1(\mathbb{R}_+)$.

In each case, the indicated parameters (such as α) are measurable real-valued functions on $[0, \infty)$ if they appear with the time argument (t), and are otherwise constants. An exercise calls for conditions on μ and σ under which the generalized log-normal model (d) specializes to the Black-Derman-Toy model (e), which is of the convenient path-independent class. The Black-Derman-Toy model was shown in a discrete-time version in Exercise 3.12. Exercise 10.5 shows convergence of the discrete-time model, with appropriate parameters, to this continous-time model.

The one-factor model (23) for the short rate is quite limiting. Even a casual review of the empirical properties of the term structure shows that it is valuable to allow a *multifactor term-structure model*, which we take to mean a model of the form $r_t = R(X_t, t)$, $t \leq 0$, where X is an Ito process in $\mathbb{R}^N$ solving a stochastic differential equation of the form

$$dX_t = \mu(X_t, t)\, dt + \sigma(X_t, t)\, d\hat{B}_t, \qquad (41)$$

where $\hat{B}$ is a standard Brownian motion in $\mathbb{R}^N$ under an equivalent martingale measure, while R, μ, and σ are functions on $\mathbb{R}^N \times [0, \infty)$ into $\mathbb{R}$, $\mathbb{R}^N$, and $\mathbb{R}^{N \times N}$, respectively, that satisfy enough technical regularity to guarantee that (41) has a unique solution and that (24) is satisfied. (Sufficient conditions are given in Appendix E.) In most examples, one of the component processes $X^1, \ldots, X^N$, say X^1, is itself the short-rate process r. In some examples, other component processes are explictly related to price levels, the yields of bonds, or the diffusion coefficient of the short-rate process. (The last of these are often called models with *stochastic volatility*.)

Derivative securities are, in the general case, given by some real-valued functions h and g on $\mathbb{R}^N \times [0, T]$. Extending (29), under technical conditions given in Appendix E, the associated arbitrage-free derivative security value is given by

$$\mathcal{D}F(x, t) - R(x, t)F(x, t) + h(x, t) = 0, \quad (x, t) \in \mathbb{R} \times [0, \tau), \qquad (42)$$

with boundary condition

$$F(x, \tau) = g(x, \tau), \quad x \in \mathbb{R}, \qquad (43)$$

where

$$\mathcal{D}F(x, t) = F_t(x, t) + F_x(x, t)\mu(x, t) + \frac{1}{2}\mathrm{tr}\left[\sigma(x, t)\sigma(x, t)^\top F_{xx}(x, t)\right].$$

Under technical conditions, we can also express the solution F as in (37) in terms of the fundamental solution G associated with (42), as discussed in Appendix E.

L. The Heath-Jarrow-Morton Model of Forward Rates

In modeling the term structure, we have so far taken as the primitive a model of the short-rate process under some equivalent martingale measure. A basic approach to constructing an equivalent martingale measure outlined in Chapter 6 is to take as given certain stochastic processes for some underlying "primitive" dividends and security prices, and then to apply Girsanov's Theorem. In modeling the term structure, it seems natural to take these primitive securities to be bonds. For example, we can take as given, at any time $t \geq 0$, the entire term structure $\{\Lambda_{t,T} : T \geq t\}$. It turns out to be convenient for some purposes to represent these bond prices in terms of their associated forward rates. For example, the forward price at time t for a zero-coupon unit bond for delivery at time $\tau \geq t$ with maturity at time $T \geq \tau$ is (in the absence of arbitrage) given by $\Lambda_{t,T}/\Lambda_{t,\tau}$. Proof of this is requested as an exercise. The associated forward rate is defined by

$$\Phi_{t,\tau,T} \equiv \frac{\log(\Lambda_{t,\tau}) - \log(\Lambda_{t,T})}{T - \tau}. \tag{44}$$

The *instantaneous forward rate*, when it exists, is defined for each time t and forward delivery date $\tau \geq t$, by

$$f(t, \tau) = \lim_{T \downarrow \tau} \Phi_{t,\tau,T}. \tag{45}$$

Of course, f exists if $\Lambda_{t,T}$ is differentiable with respect to T. Under technical conditions, we have $f(t, t) = r_t$ almost everywhere.

An issue studied in the literature is: "What stochastic behavior for the instantaneous forward rate model f is consistent with the absence of arbitrage?" In order to address this question, the *Heath-Jarrow-Morton (HJM) model* for the instantaneous forward rate process f takes B to be a standard Brownian motion in $\mathbb{R}^d$ under our original probability space $(\Omega, \mathcal{F}, P)$, with the standard filtration $\{\mathcal{F}_t : t \geq 0\}$ of tribes generated by B. The HJM model is given, for each fixed T, by

$$f(t, T) = f(0, T) + \int_0^t \mu(s, T) \, ds + \int_0^t \sigma(s, T) \, dB_s, \quad t \in [0, T], \tag{46}$$

where $\{\mu(t, T) : 0 \leq t \leq T\}$ and $\{\sigma(t, T) : 0 \leq t \leq T\}$ are adapted processes valued in $\mathbb{R}$ and $\mathbb{R}^d$ respectively such that (46) is well defined as an Ito process. Using (46) to derive bond-price processes as Ito processes whose drifts and diffusions are explicit in terms of μ and σ, an application of Girsanov's Theorem then provides sufficient conditions on μ and σ for the absence of arbitrage. This proceeds as follows. For each fixed T, suppose an $\mathbb{R}^d$-valued process a^T and a real-valued process b^T are well defined by

$$a_t^T = -\int_t^T \sigma(t, v) \, dv; \qquad b_t^T = \frac{\| a_t^T \|^2}{2} - \int_t^T \mu(t, v) \, dv, \quad t \in [0, T]. \tag{47}$$

With additional technical conditions, some calculations show that, for each fixed T,

$$\Lambda_{t,T} = \Lambda_{0,T} + \int_0^t \Lambda_{s,T}(r_s + b_s^T) \, ds + \int_0^t \Lambda_{s,T} \, a_s^T \, dB_s, \quad 0 \le t \le T. \tag{48}$$

Now, taking an arbitrary set $\{T(1), \dots, T(d)\}$ of d different maturities, we can consider the deflated bond-price processes $Z^1, \dots, Z^d$, defined by

$$Z_t^i = \exp\left(-\int_0^t r_s \, ds \right) \Lambda_{t,T(i)}, \quad t \in [0, T], \tag{49}$$

where $T = \min\{T(i) : 1 \le i \le d\}$. For the absence of arbitrage involving these d bonds until time T, Chapter 6 shows that it suffices, and in a sense is almost necessary, that there exists an equivalent martingale measure Q for $Z = (Z^1, \dots, Z^d)$. For this, it is sufficient that Z is L^2-reducible, in the sense of Section 6G. The question of L^2-reducibility hinges on the drift and diffusion processes of Z. Ito's Lemma implies that, for all i,

$$dZ_t^i = Z_t^i b_t^{T(i)} \, dt + Z_t^i a_t^{T(i)} \, dB_t, \quad t \in [0, T]. \tag{50}$$

For each $t \le T$, we let A_t be the $d \times d$ matrix whose (i, j)-element is the j-th element of the vector $a^{T(i)}{}_t$, and let λ_t be the vector in $\mathbb{R}^d$ whose i-th element is $b^{T(i)}{}_t$. We can then consider the system of linear equations

$$A_t \eta_t = \lambda_t, \quad t \in [0, T], \tag{51}$$

to be solved for an $\mathbb{R}^d$-valued process η in $\mathcal{L}^2$. Assuming such a solution η to (51) exists, and letting $\nu(Z) = \int_0^T \eta_t \cdot \eta_t \, dt/2$ and

$$\xi(Z) = \exp\left[\int_0^T -\eta_t \, dB_t - \nu(Z) \right],$$

Theorem 6G implies that μ and σ are consistent with the absence of arbitrage, and that there exists an equivalent martingale measure for Z that is denoted $Q(T)$, provided $\exp[\nu(Z)]$ has finite expectation and $\xi(Z)$ has finite variance. In this case, we can let

$$\frac{dQ(T)}{dP} = \xi(Z). \tag{52}$$

Provided A_t is nonsingular almost everywhere, $Q(T)$ is uniquely defined. Of course, T is arbitrary. A sufficient set of technical conditions for each of the above steps is cited in the Notes.

We say that the forward rate model f is *Gaussian* if $\mu(t, T)$ and $\sigma(t, T)$ are deterministic for each t and T. This, in particular, implies normally distributed forward rates and a normally distributed short rate. An exercise asks for a demonstration, under technical conditions, that a Gaussian forward rate model has bond prices $\{\Lambda_{t,T} : 0 \le t \le T\}$ that are log-normally distributed, and that these normality properties are also true under an equivalent martingale measure. The Gaussian forward rate model is extensively studied in a number of cited references. In particular, the prices of options on coupon bonds has been fairly explicitly and completely characterized.

Exercises

7.1 Show by use of Girsanov's Theorem that the futures-price process Φ defined by (8) is an Ito process (under the original measure P.)

7.2 Verify (9) with Ito's Lemma.

7.3 Show, as claimed in Section 7D, that if Φ is an Ito process and Y is bounded and bounded away from zero, then $\int Y \, d\Phi$ is a martingale if and only if Φ is a martingale. Hint: Use the unique decomposition property of Ito processes.

7.4 Show, for each $t < T$, that the value of the American put defined by (12) is differentiable in the level x of the stock price. Hint: Use the decomposition $h = p + e$, where p is the European put and e is the early exercise premium, defined by (19). Use an explicit formula for $Q(S_u < S_u^*)$, which depends on the initial condition (x, t) for the stock-price process S. Apply the Dominated Convergence Theorem.

7.5 Verify, for the CIR term-structure model specified by (27), that the bond price formula (28) satisfies the PDE (25)–(26).

7.6 Show restrictions on the coefficients of the generalized log-normal model (d) of Section 7K under which it can be viewed as the Black-Derman-Toy model (e).

7.7 Show, as claimed in Section 7L, that in the absence of arbitrage the forward price at time t for delivery at time τ of a zero-coupon unit bond maturing at time T is given by $\Lambda_{t,T}/\Lambda_{t,\tau}$. Show that if the short-rate process r is non-negative, then the forward interest rates defined by (44) and instantaneous forward rates defined by (45) are non-negative.

7.8 Let $\lambda_{t,\tau,T}$ denote the forward price at time t for delivery at time τ of one zero-coupon unit riskless bond maturing at time T. Now consider the forward price F_t at time t for delivery at time T of a security with price process S and deterministic dividend-rate process δ. Show, assuming integrability as needed, that the absence of arbitrage implies that

$$F_t = \frac{S_t}{\Lambda_{t,T}} - \int_t^T \lambda_{t,\tau,T}\delta_\tau \, d\tau.$$

Do not assume the existence of an equivalent martingale measure.

7.9 Verify (48) and (50), adding any technical integrability conditions needed.

7.10 (Gaussian Forward Rates) Consider the Gaussian forward rate model discussed at the end of Section 7L, in which the coefficients $\mu(t, T)$ and $\sigma(t, T)$ of (46) are deterministic and differentiable with respect to T. Let $d = 1$ for simplicity.

(A) Show that, under the equivalent martingale measure $Q(T)$ of (52), the short-rate process r is an Ito process with deterministic drift and diffusion processes μ_r and σ_r. Compute μ_r and σ_r explictly in terms of μ and σ. Compute $\Lambda_{t,T}$ explicitly for any t and T. Hint: Use the fact that an Ito process with deterministic drift and diffusion is a *Gaussian process*, meaning that its value at any time t is normally distributed.

(B) Calculate the arbitrage-free price at time t of a European call option on a unit zero-coupon riskless bond maturing at time T, with strike price K and expiration date τ, with $t < \tau < T$. To be specific, the option has payoff $(\Lambda_{\tau,T} - K)^+$ at time τ. Hint: Consider the deflator defined by normalizing prices relative to the price $\Lambda_{t,\tau}$ of the pure discount bond maturing at τ. With this deflation, compute an equivalent martingale measure $P(\tau)$ and the stochastic differential equation under $P(\tau)$ for the deflated bond-price process Z defined by $Z_t = \Lambda_{t,T}/\Lambda_{t,\tau}$, $t \leq \tau$ and $Z_t = \Lambda_{t,T}$, $t > \tau$. Show that Z_τ is log-normally distributed under $P(\tau)$. Using the fact that $\Lambda_{\tau,\tau} = 1$, show that the relevant option price is $\Lambda_{t,\tau}E^{P(\tau)}[(\Lambda_{\tau,T}-K)^+]$. An explicit solution is then obtained by using an explicit expression for $\Lambda_{t,T}$ from part (A) and the Black-Scholes option-pricing formula.

7.11   Suppose there are three traded securities. Security 1 has the price process X given by $X_t = x \exp(\alpha t + \beta \cdot B_t)$, where $\alpha \in \mathbb{R}$, $\beta \in \mathbb{R}^2$, and B is a standard Brownian motion in $\mathbb{R}^2$. Security 2 has the price process Y given by $Y_t = y \exp(a + b \cdot B_t)$, where $a \in \mathbb{R}$, $b \in \mathbb{R}^2$. Security 3 has the price process e^{rt}, where r is a constant. None of the securities pays dividends during $[0, T]$. Consider a contract paying, at some time $T > 0$, either k units of security 1 or 1 unit of security 2, whichever is preferred by the owner of the contract at that time. Calculate the arbitrage-free price of that contract.

Notes

The relationship between forwards and futures in Sections 7B, 7C, and 7D was developed by Cox, Ingersoll, and Ross (1981b). The derivation given here for the martingale property (8) of futures prices is original, although the formula itself is due to Cox, Ingersoll, and Ross (1981b), as is the subsequent replication strategy. For a Markov (PDE) approach, see Duffie and Stanton (1988). An explicit Gaussian example is given by Jamshidian (1990) and Jamshidian and Fein (1990). Grauer and Litzenberger (1979) give an example of the equilibrium determination of commodity forward prices. Duffie (1989) is a basic treatment of forward and futures markets.

Black (1976) showed how to extend the Black-Scholes option-pricing formula to the case of futures options. Carr (1987) and Hemler (1987) value the option to deliver various grades of the underlying asset against the futures contract. This problem is related to that of valuing compound options, and options on the maximum or minimum of several assets, which was solved (in the Black-Scholes setting) by Margrabe (1978), Geske (1979), Selby and Hodges (1987), and Johnson (1987).

McKean (1965), Merton (1973b), Harrison and Kreps (1979), and Bensoussan (1984) did important early work on American option pricing. Proposition 7E is from Karatzas (1988), although his technical conditions are slightly different. Karatzas defines the *fair price* of an American security, which turns out to be equal to the arbitrage-free price when both exist, and also extends Merton's analysis of *perpetual options*, those with no expiration. Jaillet, Lamberton, and Lapeyre (1988, 1990) review the treatment of the optimal stopping valuation problem as a variational inequality, which can be written in the form (20)–(21). The decomposition of the American option in terms of the early exercise premium (19) was derived in a sudden collection of papers by Jamshidian (1989c), Jacka (1991), Kim (1990), and Carr, Jarrow, and Myneni (1990), working from McKean's (1965) formulation of the free boundary problem. Van Moerbeke (1976) was the first to demonstrate, among other results, that the optimal stopping boundary S^* is continuously differentiable. Myneni (1992) surveys this and other literature on American put option pricing in the Black-Scholes setting. Approximate solutions to the American option price are given by Geske and Johnson (1984) and by Barone-Adesi and Elliott (1991) (who cite related literature).

The term-structure model of Cox, Ingersoll, and Ross (1985a) was developed in a general equilibrium setting, as explained in Chapter 9. It was also developed as a primitive arbitrage-based term-structure model by Richard (1978). The associated CIR short-rate process exists based on the results of Yamada and Watanabe (1971) reviewed in Appendix E. In order to apply their results, we can let $\sigma(x) = 0$ for $x < 0$. The non-negativity of solutions is then implied by the fact that zero is a natural boundary, in the sense of Gihman and Skorohod (1972). Feller (1951) solved for the Laplace transform of the distribution of r_t. The associated density was calculated by Yao, according to a footnote of Richard (1978). Further characterization is given in Cox, Ingersoll, and Ross (1985a). The pricing of mortgage-backed securities based on the CIR model is pursued by Stanton (1990), who also reviews some of the related literature. On pricing path-dependent securities, see Kishimoto (1989). Brown and Schaefer (1991) originated the idea of characterizing the family of short-rate prices consistent with an affine term structure model. The calculations given in Section 7I are based on Brown and Schaefer (1991) and Hull and White (1990a). The examples of the affine class listed in Section 7I are based on Vasicek (1977), Cox, Ingersoll, and Ross (1985a), Jamshidian (1989a, 1989b, 1989d, 1991), Pearson and Sun (1989), Dybvig (1988), and Carverhill (1988).

Study of the term structure in terms of the Green's function associated with the short-rate process is developed by Dash (1989), Beaglehole (1990), Beaglehole and Tenney (1990), and Jamshidian (1991). Other term-structure models appearing in this chapter are from Dothan (1978), Courtadon (1982), and Black, Derman, and Toy (1990). Examples of multifactor term-structure models are due to Brennan and Schwartz (1979), Langetieg (1980), Cox, Ingersoll, and Ross (1985a), Heston (1988b), and Longstaff and Schwartz (1990). The idea of using the instantaneous forward rate process appears in Richard (1978). The forward rate model of Heath, Jarrow, and Morton (1987) has been extensively treated in the case of Gaussian instantaneous forward rates by Jamshidian (1989a, 1989c, 1990), El Karoui and Rochet (1989), El Karoui, Lepage, Myneni, Roseau, and Viswanathan (1991), and Geman, El Karoui, and Rochet (1991). An example from these papers is given in Exercise 7.10 on bond-option pricing in the Gaussian forward rate setting. The HJM model is extended by Miltersen (1991). See also Babbs (1991).

Apelfeld and Conze (1990) study the term structure under imperfect information using filtering theory. Cox, Ingersoll, and Ross (1981a) and Cheng (1991) show what can go wrong if one begins with a model for the stochastic behavior of bond prices without first verifying conditions for the absence of arbitrage. See also Campbell (1986). Further reading on arbitrage-free models of the term structure is found in Bossaerts (1990), Carverhill (1990, 1991), Artzner and Delbaen (1990), Pederson, Shiu, and Thorlacius (1989), Constantinides (1990b), Heston (1988a, 1989), and Back (1991b).

Some derivative assets are path-dependent, in that their payoff depends on the entire sample path of the underlying asset's price. Among these are the option to buy at the low price and sell at the high price, valued by Goldman, Sosin, and Gatto (1979), and the *asian option*, based on an arithmetic average of the underlying price process, analyzed by Yor (1991). (The distribution of the maximum of a Brownian motion path between two dates, and related results, can be found in Harrison [1985].) In each of these path-dependent cases, the analysis is simplified by first reverting to an equivalent martingale measure.

Option pricing with stochastic volatility has been formulated by Heston (1990b).

8

Optimal Portfolio and Consumption Choice

THIS CHAPTER PRESENTS basic results on optimal portfolio and consumption choice, first using dynamic programming, then by general martingale and utility gradient methods. We begin with a review of the Hamilton-Jacobi-Bellman equation for stochastic control, and then apply it to Merton's problem of optimal consumption and portfolio choice in finite and infinite horizon settings. Then, exploiting the properties of equivalent martingale measures from Chapter 6, Merton's problem is solved once again in a non-Markovian setting. Finally, we turn to the general utility gradient approach from Chapter 2, and show that it coincides with the approach of equivalent martingale measures.

A. Stochastic Control

Dynamic programming in continuous time is often called *stochastic control*, and it uses the same basic ideas applied in the discrete-time setting of Chapter 3. The existence of well-behaved solutions in this setting is a delicate matter, however, and we shall focus mainly on necessary conditions. This helps us to conjecture a solution that, if correct, can often be easily validated.

Given is a standard Brownian motion $B = (B^1, \ldots, B^d)$ in $\mathbb{R}^d$ on a probability space $(\Omega, \mathcal{F}, P)$. We fix the standard filtration $\mathbb{F} = \{\mathcal{F}_t : t \geq 0\}$ of B and begin with the time horizon $[0, T]$ for some finite $T > 0$. The primitive objects of a stochastic control problem are:

- a set $A \subset \mathbb{R}^m$ of *actions*;
- a set $\mathcal{Y} \subset \mathbb{R}^K$ of *states*;
- a set $\mathcal{C}$ of A-valued adapted processes, called *controls*;
- a *controlled drift function* $g : A \times \mathcal{Y} \to \mathbb{R}^K$;

- a *controlled diffusion function* $h : A \times \mathcal{Y} \to \mathbb{R}^{K \times d}$;
- a *running reward function* $f : A \times \mathcal{Y} \times [0, T] \to \mathbb{R}$;
- a *terminal reward function* $F : \mathcal{Y} \to \mathbb{R}$.

The set $\mathcal{Y}$ of states of the problem is not to be confused with the underlying set Ω of "states of the world." A control c in $\mathcal{C}$ is *admissible* given an initial state y in $\mathcal{Y}$ if there is a unique Ito process Y^c valued in $\mathcal{Y}$ with

$$dY_t^c = g(c_t, Y_t^c) \, dt + h(c_t, Y_t^c) \, dB_t; \quad Y_0^c = y. \tag{1}$$

Let $\mathcal{C}_a(y)$ denote the set of admissible controls given initial state y. We assume that the primitives $(A, Y, \mathcal{C}, g, h, f, F)$ are such that, given any initial state $y \in \mathcal{Y}$, the utility of any admissible control c is well defined as

$$V^c(y) = E \left[\int_0^T f(c_t, Y_t^c, t) \, dt + F(Y_T^c) \right],$$

which we allow to take the values $-\infty$ or $+\infty$. The value of an initial state y in $\mathcal{Y}$ is then

$$V(y) = \sup_{c \in \mathcal{C}_a(y)} V^c(y), \tag{2}$$

with $V(y) = -\infty$ if there is no admissible control given initial state y. If $V^c(y) = V(y)$, then c is an *optimal control* at y.

One usually proceeds by conjecturing that $V(y) = J(y, 0)$ for some J in $C^{2,1}(\mathcal{Y} \times [0, T])$ that solves the Bellman equation:

$$\sup_{a \in A} \mathcal{D}^a J(y, t) + f(a, y, t) = 0, \quad (y, t) \in (\mathcal{Y}, [0, T)), \tag{3}$$

where

$$\mathcal{D}^a J(y, t) = J_y(y, t) g(a, y) + J_t(y, t) + \frac{1}{2} \operatorname{tr} \left[h(a, y) h(a, y)^\top J_{yy}(y, t) \right],$$

with boundary condition

$$J(y, T) = F(y), \quad y \in \mathcal{Y}. \tag{4}$$

An intuitive justification of (3) is obtained from an analogous discrete-time, discrete-state, discrete-action setting, in which the Bellman equation would be something like

$$J(y, t) = \sup_{a \in A} f(a, y, t) + E \left[J(Y_{t+1}^c, t+1) \mid Y_t^c = y, c_t = a \right],$$

where $f(a, y, t)$ is the running reward per unit of time. (The reader is invited to liberally apply imagination here. A complete development and rigorous justification of this analogy goes well beyond the goal of illustrating the idea.) For any given control process c, this discrete-time Bellman equation implies that

$$E_t \left[J(Y_{t+1}^c, t+1) - J(Y_t^c, t) \right] \geq -f(c_t, Y_t^c, t),$$

which for a model with intervals of length Δt may be rewritten

$$E_t \left[J(Y_{t+\Delta t}^c, t + \Delta t) - J(Y_t^c, t) \right] \geq -f(c_t, Y_t^c, t)\Delta t.$$

Now, returning to the continuous-time setting, dividing the last equation by Δt, and taking limits as $\Delta t \to 0$ leaves, under technical conditions described in Chapter 5,

$$\frac{d}{ds} E_t \left[J(Y_s^c, s) \right] \Big|_{s=t} = \mathcal{D}J(Y_t^c, t) \geq -f(c_t, Y_t^c, t),$$

with equality if c_t attains the supremum in the Bellman equation. This leads, again only by this incomplete heuristic argument, to the Bellman equation (3).

The continuous-time Bellman equation (3) is often called the *Hamilton-Jacobi-Bellman* equation. One should think of $J(y, t)$ as the optimal utility remaining at time t in state y. Given a solution J to (3)–(4), suppose that $C : \mathcal{Y} \times [0, T] \to A$ is defined so that $C(y, t)$ solves (3) given (y, t). The intuitive idea is that, if the time is t and the state is y, then the optimal action is $C(y, t)$. Properly speaking, we need to turn this feedback form of control policy function C into a control in the formal sense of problem (2). For this, suppose that there is a $\mathcal{Y}$-valued solution Y^* to the stochastic differential equation

$$dY_t^* = g[C(Y_t^*, t), Y_t^*] \, dt + h[C(Y_t^*, t), Y_t^*] \, dB_t; \quad Y_0^* = y.$$

Conditions on the primitives of the problem sufficient for the existence of a solution Y^* are difficult to formulate since C depends on J, which is usually an unknown function. Sources indicated in the Notes address this existence issue. Given Y^*, we can define an admissible control c^* by $c_t^* = C(Y_t^*, t)$. We conjecture that c^* is an optimal control, and attempt to verify this conjecture as follows. Let $c \in \mathcal{C}_a(y)$ be arbitrary. By (3),

$$\mathcal{D}^{c(t)} J(Y_t^c, t) + f(c_t, Y_t^c, t) \leq 0, \quad t \in [0, T]. \tag{5}$$

By Ito's Lemma,

$$J(Y_T^c, T) = J(y, 0) + \int_0^T \mathcal{D}^{c(t)} J(Y_t^c, t) \, dt + \int_0^T \beta_t \, dB_t, \tag{6}$$

where $\beta_t = J_x(Y_t^c, t) h(c_t, Y_t^c)$, $t \in [0, T]$. Assuming that β is in $\mathcal{H}^1$ (which is usually verified on a problem-by-problem basis), $E(\int_0^T \beta_t \, dB_t) = 0$ by Proposition 5B. We can then take the expectation of each side of (6) and use the boundary condition (4) and inequality (5) to see that

$$J(y, 0) \geq E \left[\int_0^T f(c_t, Y_t^c, t) \, dt + F(Y_T^c) \right] = V^c(y). \tag{7}$$

The same calculation applies with $c = c^*$, except that "$\leq$" may be replaced everywhere with "$=$," implying that

$$J(y, 0) = V^{c^*}(y). \tag{8}$$

Then (7) and (8) imply that $V(y) = J(y, 0)$ and that c^* is indeed optimal.

This is only a sketch of the general approach, with several assumptions made along the way. These assumptions can be replaced by strong technical regularity conditions on the primitives $(A, \mathcal{Y}, \mathcal{C}, g, h, f, F)$, but the known conditions are too restrictive for most applications in finance. Instead, one typically uses the Bellman equation (3)–(4) as a means of guessing an explicit solution that, if correct, can often be validated by the above procedure. In some cases, the Bellman equation can also be used as the basis for a finite-difference numerical solution.

B. Merton's Problem

Suppose $S = (S^1, \ldots, S^N)$ is an Ito process in $\mathbb{R}^N$ for the prices of N securities such that, for each i,

$$dS_t^i = \mu_i S_t^i \, dt + S_t^i \sigma^i \, dB_t; \quad S_0 > 0, \tag{9}$$

where σ^i is the i-th row of a matrix σ in $\mathbb{R}^{N \times d}$ with linearly independent rows, and where μ_i is a constant. Given a constant short rate r, the bond-price process β is defined by

$$d\beta_t = r\beta_t \, dt; \quad \beta_0 > 0. \tag{10}$$

This defines the price process $X = (\beta, S^1, \ldots, S^N)$. We assume, naturally, that $\mu_i > r$ for all i.

Utility is defined over the space D of *consumption-wealth* pairs (c, Z), where c is an adapted non-negative process with $E(\int_0^T c_t^2 \, dt) < \infty$ and Z is an $\mathcal{F}_T$-measurable non-negative random variable with $E(Z^2) < \infty$. Specifically, $U : D \to \mathbb{R}$ is defined by

$$U(c, Z) = E \left[\int_0^T u(c_t, t) \, dt + F(Z) \right],$$ (11)

where:

- F is increasing and concave;
- $u : \mathbb{R}_+ \times [0, T] \to \mathbb{R}$ is continuous and, for each t in $[0, T]$, $u(\cdot, t) : \mathbb{R}_+ \to \mathbb{R}$ is increasing and concave;
- F is strictly concave or, for each t in $[0, T]$, $u(\cdot, t)$ is strictly concave, or both.

A trading strategy is a process $\theta = (\theta^0, \ldots, \theta^N)$ in $\mathcal{H}^2(X)$. Given an initial wealth $w > 0$, a trading strategy θ *finances* a given (c, Z) in D if

$$\theta_t \cdot X_t = w + \int_0^t \theta_s \, dX_s - \int_0^t c_s \, ds \geq 0, \quad t \in [0, T],$$ (12)

and

$$\theta_T \cdot X_T = Z.$$ (13)

We will now restrict the set of trading strategies somewhat for technical reasons. Let $\mathcal{L}^\infty$ denote the space of bounded adapted processes. Finally, let

$$\Lambda(w) = \{(c, Z, \theta) : (c, Z) \in D; \ \theta \text{ finances } (c, Z); \ \varphi^n \in \mathcal{L}^\infty, \ 0 \leq n \leq N\},$$

where φ^n denotes the "fraction" of wealth held in the n-th security by θ, in the sense that

$$\varphi_t^n = \frac{\theta_t^n X_t^n}{\theta_t \cdot X_t}, \quad \theta_t \cdot X_t \neq 0,$$ (14)

with $\varphi_t^n = 0$ if $\theta_t \cdot X_t = 0$. The restriction of φ^n to $\mathcal{L}^\infty$ is purely technical.

This leaves the problem, for each initial wealth w,

$$\sup_{(c,Z,\theta)\in\Lambda(w)} U(c, Z). \tag{15}$$

Problem (15) is converted into a standard control problem of the variety in Section 8A by defining the primitives $(A, \mathcal{Y}, \mathcal{C}, g, h, f, F)$ as follows:

- $A = \mathbb{R}_+ \times \mathbb{R}^N$, with typical element $(\overline{c}, \overline{\varphi})$ representing the current consumption rate $\overline{c}$ and the fractions $\overline{\varphi}_1, \ldots, \overline{\varphi}_N$ of current wealth invested in the securites with respective price processes $S^1, \ldots, S^N$;
- $\mathcal{Y} = \mathbb{R}_+$, with typical element w representing current wealth;
- $\mathcal{C}$ is the space of processes of the form (c, φ), where c is an adapted "consumption" process with $E(\int_0^T c_t^2 \, dt) < \infty$, and $\varphi = (\varphi^1, \ldots, \varphi^N)$ is a process of "portfolio fractions" with $\varphi^n \in \mathcal{L}^\infty$, $1 \le n \le N$;
- $g[(\overline{c}, \overline{\varphi}), w] = w\overline{\varphi} \cdot \lambda + rw - \overline{c}$, where $\lambda \in \mathbb{R}^N$ is defined by $\lambda_i = \mu_i - r$, the "excess expected rate of return" on security i;
- $h[(\overline{c}, \overline{\varphi}), w] = w\overline{\varphi} \cdot \sigma$;
- $f[(\overline{c}, \overline{\varphi}), w, t] = u(\overline{c}, t)$, where u is as given by (11);
- $F(w)$ is as given by (11).

The wealth process W generated by an admissible control (c, φ) is defined by

$$dW_t = g[(c_t, \varphi_t), W_t] \, dt + h[(c_t, \varphi_t), W_t] \, dB_t; \quad W_0 = w. \tag{16}$$

If we let $\tau = \inf\{t : W_t = 0\}$, the non-negativity of W implies that (almost everywhere) $W_t = c_t = 0$, $t > \tau$.

The control problem $(A, \mathcal{Y}, \mathcal{C}, g, h, f, F)$ is equivalent to the original problem (15). One shows this fact by verifying that (c, Z, θ) is in $\Lambda(w)$ if and only if $(c, \varphi) \in \mathcal{C}$ determines the wealth process $\{W_t = \theta_t \cdot X_t : t \in [0, T]\}$ satisfying (16) and $W_T = Z$, where φ is defined from θ by (14).

The formulation of trading strategies defined in terms of portfolio "fractions" is useful since this clarifies that the current level of wealth W_t is a sufficient state-variable for the control problem. Working directly in terms of trading strategies would have called for feedback policies in terms of wealth and security prices, unnecessarily increasing the dimension of the state space. Later in the chapter, other techniques are used to formulate the problem directly in terms of trading strategies. Although the formulation there is slightly different, the solutions of the two formulations coincide. Still other formulations are given in sources cited in the Notes.

C. Solution to Merton's Problem

The Bellman equation (3) for Merton's problem is

$$\sup_{(\bar{c}, \bar{\varphi}) \in A} \mathcal{D}^{\bar{c}, \bar{\varphi}} J(w, t) + u(\bar{c}, t) = 0, \quad w > 0, \tag{17}$$

where

$$\mathcal{D}^{\bar{c}, \bar{\varphi}} J(w, t) = J_w(w, t)(w\bar{\varphi} \cdot \lambda + rw - \bar{c}) + J_t(w, t) + \frac{w^2}{2} \bar{\varphi}^\top \sigma \sigma^\top \bar{\varphi} J_{ww}(w, t),$$

with the boundary condition

$$J(w, T) = F(w), \quad w \geq 0. \tag{18}$$

We note that

$$J(0, t) = \int_t^T u(0, s) \, ds + F(0), \quad t \in [0, T], \tag{19}$$

from our remark regarding the non-negativity of solutions to (16).

Assuming that, for each t, $u(\cdot, t)$ is strictly concave and twice continuously differentiable on $(0, \infty)$, the first order condition for optimal choice of $\bar{c}$ in (17) implies that

$$\bar{c} = C(w, t) \equiv I[J_w(w, t), t], \tag{20}$$

where $I = 0$ if $u = 0$, and otherwise $I(\cdot, t)$ inverts $u_c(\cdot, t)$, meaning that $I[u_c(x, t), t] = x$ for all x and t. Assuming that the indirect utility function $J(\cdot, t)$ for wealth is strictly concave, the first order condition for optimal choice of $\bar{\varphi}$ in (17) implies that

$$\bar{\varphi} = \Phi(w, t) \equiv \frac{-J_w(w, t)}{w J_{ww}(w, t)} (\sigma \sigma^\top)^{-1} \lambda. \tag{21}$$

We remark that the optimal portfolio fractions are given by a fixed vector $(\sigma \sigma^\top)^{-1} \lambda$ multiplied by the Arrow-Pratt measure of relative risk tolerance (reciprocal of relative risk aversion) of $J(\cdot, t)$.

We focus for now on the special case $u = 0$ and $F(w) = w^\alpha / \alpha$, $\alpha < 1$, $\alpha \neq 0$. A natural conjecture is that $J(w, t) = k(t) w^\alpha / \alpha$, for some differentiable function $k : [0, T] \to \mathbb{R}$. Solving (21) leaves

$$\bar{\varphi} = \frac{(\sigma \sigma^\top)^{-1} \lambda}{1 - \alpha}, \tag{22}$$

or fixed portfolio fractions. Since $u = 0$,

$$\bar{c} = C(w, t) \equiv 0. \tag{23}$$

Based on the Bellman equation (17), we can substitute (22)–(23) into $\mathcal{D}^{\bar{c}, \bar{\varphi}} J(w, t) + u(\bar{c}, t) = 0$ and get the ordinary differential equation

$$k'(t) = -\epsilon k(t), \tag{24}$$

where

$$\epsilon = \frac{\alpha \lambda^\top (\sigma \sigma^\top)^{-1} \lambda}{2(1 - \alpha)} + r\alpha, \tag{25}$$

with the boundary condition from (18):

$$k(T) = 1. \tag{26}$$

Solving (24)–(26), we have

$$k(t) = e^{\epsilon(T-t)}, \quad t \in [0, T]. \tag{27}$$

We have found that the function J defined by $J(w, t) = e^{\epsilon(T-t)} w^\alpha / \alpha$ solves the Bellman equation (17) and boundary condition (18), so J is a logical candidate for the value function.

   We now verify this candidate for the value function, and also that the conjectured optimal control (c^*, φ^*), which is given by $c_t^* = 0$ and $\varphi_t^* = (\sigma\sigma^\top)^{-1}\lambda/(1 - \alpha)$ is indeed optimal. Let (c, φ) be an arbitrary admissible control for initial wealth w, and let W be the associated wealth process solving (16). From the Bellman equation (17) and the boundary condition (18),

$$J(w, 0) \geq F(W_T) - \int_0^T \beta_t \, dB_t, \tag{28}$$

where $\beta_t = J_w(W_t, t)\varphi_t W_t \sigma$. Since, for each n, φ^n is in $\mathcal{L}^\infty$, and since $J_w(W_t, t)W_t = e^{\epsilon(T-t)} W_t^\alpha$, it can be shown that β is in $\mathcal{H}^1$, so the stochastic integral in (28) has zero expectation. Taking expectations through (28), we have $V^{c,\varphi}(w) \leq J(w, 0)$. Like calculations for (c^*, φ^*) give $V^{c^*, \varphi^*}(w) = J(w, 0)$, implying the optimality of (c^*, φ^*) and confirming that the problem has optimal initial utility $J(w, 0) = e^{\epsilon T} w^\alpha / \alpha$.

D. The Infinite-Horizon Case

The primitives $(A, \mathcal{Y}, \mathcal{C}, g, h, f)$ of an infinite-horizon control problem are just as described in Section 8A, dropping the terminal reward F. The running reward function $f : A \times \mathcal{Y} \times [0, \infty) \to \mathbb{R}$ is usually defined, given a *discount rate* $\rho \in (0, \infty)$, by $f(a, y, t) = e^{-\rho t} v(a, y)$, for some $v : A \times \mathcal{Y} \to \mathbb{R}$. Given an initial state y in $\mathcal{Y}$, the value of an admissible control c in $\mathcal{C}$ is

$$V^c(y) = E \left[\int_0^\infty e^{-\rho t} v(c_t, Y_t^c) \, dt \right], \tag{29}$$

assuming that the expectation exists, where Y^c is given by (1). The supremum value $V(y)$ is as defined by (2). The finite-horizon Bellman equation (3) is replaced with

$$\sup_{a \in A} \mathcal{D}^a J(y) - \rho J(y) + v(a, y) = 0, \quad y \in \mathcal{Y}, \tag{30}$$

for J in $C^2(\mathcal{Y})$, where

$$\mathcal{D}^a J(y) = J_y(y) g(a, y) + \frac{1}{2} \text{tr} \left[h(a, y) h(a, y)^\top J_{yy}(y) \right].$$

Rather than the boundary condition (4), one can add technical conditions yielding the so-called *transversality condition*

$$\lim_{T \to \infty} E \left(e^{-\rho T} |J(Y_T^c)| \right) = 0, \tag{31}$$

for any given initial state $Y_0^c = y$ in $\mathcal{Y}$ and any admissible control c. With this, the same arguments and technical assumptions applied in Section 8A imply that a solution J to the Bellman equation (30) defines the value $J(y) = V(y)$ of the problem. The essential difference is the replacement of (7) with

$$J(y) \geq E \left[\int_0^T e^{-\rho t} v(c_t, Y_t^c) \, dt + e^{-\rho T} J(Y_T^c) \right],$$

from which $J(y) \geq V^c(y)$ for an arbitrary admissible control c by taking the limit of the right-hand side as $T \to \infty$, using (31). Similarly, a candidate optimal control is defined in feedback form by a function $C : \mathcal{Y} \to A$ with the property that, for each y, the action $C(y)$ solves the Bellman equation (30). Once again, technical conditions on the primitives guarantee the existence of an optimal control, but such conditions are often too restrictive in practice, and the Bellman equation is frequently used more as an aid in conjecturing a solution.

In Merton's problem, for example, with $v(\bar{c}, w) = \bar{c}^\alpha/\alpha$, $\alpha \in (0, 1)$, it is natural to conjecture that $J(w) = kw^\alpha/\alpha$ for some constant k. With some calculations, the Bellman equation (30) for this candidate value function J leads to $k = \gamma^{1/(\alpha-1)}$, where

$$\gamma = \frac{\rho - r\alpha}{1 - \alpha} - \frac{\alpha\lambda^\top(\sigma\sigma^\top)^{-1}\lambda}{2(1 - \alpha)^2}. \tag{32}$$

The associated portfolio and consumption policy (c^*, φ^*) is given by $\varphi_t^* = (\sigma\sigma^\top)^{-1}\lambda/(1-\alpha)$ and $c_t^* = \gamma W_t^*$, where W^* is the wealth process generated by (c^*, φ^*). In order to confirm the optimality of this policy, the transversality condition (31) must be checked, and is satisfied provided $\gamma(1-\alpha) > 0$. This verification is left as an exercise.

E. The Martingale Formulation

The objective now is to use the martingale results of Chapter 6 as the basis of a new method for solving Merton's problem (15). We take the somewhat simpler formulation

$$\sup_{(c, Z, \theta) \in \Gamma} U(c, Z), \tag{33}$$

where

$$\Gamma = \left\{ (c, Z, \theta) : (c, Z) \in D, \quad \theta \in \mathcal{H}^2(X), \quad \theta \text{ finances } (c, Z) \right\}.$$

Problems (33) and (15) differ only in their technical restrictions on the trading strategy θ. Their solutions generally coincide.

Given the security-price process X of Section 8B, consider the deflated price process $\hat{X}$ defined by $\hat{X}_t = X_t/\beta_t$. We take the finite-horizon setting of Section 8B.

Lemma. *Given an initial wealth $w \geq 0$, there exists some θ in $\mathcal{H}^2(X)$ financing a given (c, Z) in D if and only if there exists some $\hat{\theta}$ in $\mathcal{H}^2(\hat{X})$ such that*

$$\hat{\theta}_t \cdot \hat{X}_t = w + \int_0^t \hat{\theta}_s \, d\hat{X}_s, \quad t \in [0, T], \tag{34}$$

and

$$\hat{\theta}_T \cdot \hat{X}_T = e^{-rT}Z + \int_0^T e^{-rt}c_t \, dt. \tag{35}$$

Proof: The proof is in two steps. First, one shows that θ finances (c, Z) if and only if there exists $\hat{\theta}$ in $\mathcal{H}^2(X)$ such that

$$\hat{\theta}_t \cdot X_t = w + \int_0^t \hat{\theta}_s \, dX_s, \quad t \in [0, T], \tag{36}$$

and

$$\hat{\theta}_T \cdot X_T = Z + \int_0^T e^{r(T-t)} c_t \, dt. \tag{37}$$

Given (12)–(13), this is done by letting $\eta = (\eta^0, \dots, \eta^N)$ be the trading strategy defined by $\eta^j = 0, j \geq 1$, and

$$\eta_t^0 = \frac{1}{\beta_t} \int_0^t e^{r(t-s)} c_s \, ds, \quad t \in [0, T].$$

Then the strategy $\hat{\theta} = \theta + \eta$ is in $\mathcal{H}^2(X)$ and satisfies (36)–(37). Conversely, given $\hat{\theta}$ and c satisfying (36)–(37), the strategy $\theta = \hat{\theta} - \eta$ satisfies (12) and (13).

The second step, the equivalence of (36)–(37) and (34)–(35), follows from the Numeraire Invariance Theorem of Section 6B, or alternatively can be verified by direct calculation using Ito's Lemma. ∎

Thus Merton's problem (33) can be reformulated as

$$V(w) = \sup_{(c, Z, \theta) \in \hat{\Lambda}(w)} U(c, Z), \tag{38}$$

where

$$\hat{\Lambda}(w) = \{(c, W, \hat{\theta}) : (c, Z) \in D; \ \hat{\theta} \in \mathcal{H}^2(\hat{X}); \ \hat{\theta} \text{ satisfies } (34)–(35)\}.$$

For simplicity, we take the case $N = d$. By Girsanov's Theorem (Appendix E), there is an equivalent martingale measure for $\hat{X}$, that is, a probability measure Q equivalent to P under which $\hat{X}$ is a martingale. The measure Q can be defined by

$$E^Q(Z) = E^P(Z\xi_T), \tag{39}$$

for any random variable Z with $E^Q(|Z|) < \infty$, where

$$\xi_t = \exp\left(\nu^\top B_t - \frac{t}{2}\nu^\top \nu\right), \quad t \in [0, T], \tag{40}$$

and where

$$\nu = \sigma^{-1}\lambda. \tag{41}$$

(The invertibility of σ is implied by our earlier assumption that the rows of σ are linearly independent.)

Proposition. *Given initial wealth* w *and any* (c, Z) *in* D, *there exists some* θ *in* $\mathcal{H}^2(X)$ *financing* (c, Z) *if and only if*

$$E^Q \left(e^{-rT} W + \int_0^T e^{-rt} c_t \, dt \right) = w. \tag{42}$$

Proof: Suppose θ in $\mathcal{H}^2(X)$ finances (c, Z) in D. By the previous lemma, there is some $\hat{\theta}$ in $\mathcal{H}^2(\hat{X})$ such that

$$w + \int_0^T \hat{\theta}_t \, d\hat{X}_t = e^{-rT} W + \int_0^T e^{-rt} c_t \, dt. \tag{43}$$

The right-hand side of (43) has finite variance under P, as does ξ_T. By the same argument given in the proof Theorem 6F, $\int \hat{\theta} \, d\hat{X}$ is a Q-martingale, so $E^Q(\int_0^T \hat{\theta}_t \, d\hat{X}_t) = 0$. Taking expectations under Q through (43) therefore leaves (42).

Conversely, suppose (c, Z) in D satisfies (42), and let M be the Q-martingale defined by

$$M_t = E_t^Q \left(e^{-rT} W + \int_0^T e^{-rt} c_t \, dt \right), \quad t \in [0, T].$$

By the Martingale Representation Theorem (Appendix E), there is some $\eta = (\eta^1, \ldots, \eta^d)$ with components in $\mathcal{L}^2$ such that

$$M_t = w + \int_0^t \eta_s \, d\hat{B}_s, \quad t \in [0, T],$$

where $\hat{B}_t = B_t - \nu t$ defines the standard Brownian motion in $\mathbb{R}^d$ under Q, as in Girsanov's Theorem. Also by Girsanov's Theorem,

$$d\hat{X}_t^i = \hat{X}_t^i \sigma^i \, d\hat{B}_t, \quad 1 \leq i \leq N.$$

Since σ is invertible and $\hat{X}$ is strictly positive with continuous sample paths, we can choose $(\theta^1, \ldots, \theta^N)$ with components in $\mathcal{L}^2$ such that

$$(\theta_t^1 \hat{X}_t^1, \ldots, \theta_t^N \hat{X}_t^N)\sigma = \eta_t^\top, \quad t \in [0, T].$$

Letting $\theta_t^0 = M_t - \sum_{i=1}^N \theta_t^i \hat{X}_t^i$, it follows that $\theta = (\theta^0, \ldots, \theta^N)$ finances (c, Z). Since $E(M_T^2) < \infty$ by the definition of D, Proposition 5B implies that $\theta \in \mathcal{H}^2(X)$. ∎

From this proposition and strict monotonicity, problem (33) is equivalent to

$$\sup_{(c,Z)\in D} U(c, Z), \tag{44}$$

subject to

$$E^Q \left(e^{-rT} W + \int_0^T e^{-rt} c_t \, dt \right) \le w. \tag{45}$$

F. Martingale Solution

By the Saddle Point Theorem (which can be found in Appendix B) and strict monotonicity, (c^*, W^*) solves (44)-(45) if and only if there is a scalar Lagrange multiplier $\gamma > 0$ such that (c^*, W^*) solves the unconstrained problem

$$\sup_{(c,Z)\in D} U(c, Z) - \gamma E^Q \left(e^{-rT} W + \int_0^T e^{-rt} c_t \, dt - w \right), \tag{46}$$

with

$$E^Q \left(e^{-rT} W^* + \int_0^T e^{-rt} c_t^* \, dt - w \right) = 0. \tag{47}$$

Problem (46) is easier to analyze by writing out $U(c, Z)$ explicitly and by using the fact that $E^Q(Z) = E(\xi_T Z)$ for any Z with $E^Q(|Z|) < \infty$. In order to state the resulting form of Merton's problem, let π denote the process defined by $\pi_t = e^{-rt}\xi_t$. As shown in Section 6J, and as shown again in the present context by the following result, π may be treated as a state-price deflator.

Proposition. *There is a trading strategy θ^* such that (c^*, W^*, θ^*) solves Merton's problem (38) if and only if*

$$E \left(\int_0^T \pi_t c_t^* \, dt + \pi_T W^* \right) = w \tag{48}$$

and there is a constant $\gamma^* > 0$ such that (c^*, W^*) solves

$$\sup_{(c,Z)\in D} \mathcal{L}(c, Z; \gamma^*),$$

where

$$\mathcal{L}(c, Z; \gamma) = E \left(\int_0^T [u(c_t, t) - \gamma \pi_t c_t] \, dt + F(Z) - \gamma \pi_T Z \right).$$

Proof: We need only show that (45) (with equality) and (48) are equivalent. Then the result follows from Proposition 8E, the Saddle Point Theorem (Appendix B), and the strict monotonicity of either or both of F and $\{u(\,\cdot\,,t) : t \in [0,T]\}$. By Fubini's Theorem, the fact that c is an adapted process, the law of iterated expectations, and the fact that ξ is a martingale,

$$
\begin{aligned}
E^Q\left(e^{-rT}Z + \int_0^T e^{-rt}c_t\,dt\right) &= E\left[\xi_T\left(e^{-rT}Z + \int_0^T e^{-rt}c_t\,dt\right)\right] \\
&= E\left(\xi_T e^{-rT}Z + \int_0^T \xi_T e^{-rt}c_t\,dt\right) \\
&= E\left[\xi_T e^{-rT}Z + \int_0^T E_t(\xi_T e^{-rt}c_t)\,dt\right] \\
&= E\left[\xi_T e^{-rT}Z + \int_0^T e^{-rt}c_t E_t(\xi_T)\,dt\right] \\
&= E\left(\xi_T e^{-rT}W + \int_0^T e^{-rt}c_t\xi_t\,dt\right).
\end{aligned}
$$

This completes the result. ∎

In order to solve intuitively the problem characterized by this proposition, it is best to begin by thinking of "E" and "$\int$" as finite sums, in which case the first order conditions for optimality of $(c^*, Z^*) \gg 0$ for the problem $\sup_{(c,Z)} \mathcal{L}(c, Z; \gamma)$, assuming differentiability, are

$$u_c(c_t^*, t) - \gamma\pi_t = 0, \quad t \in [0, T], \tag{49}$$

and

$$F'(Z^*) - \gamma\pi_T = 0. \tag{50}$$

Solving,

$$c_t^* = I(\gamma\pi_t, t), \quad t \in [0, T], \tag{51}$$

and

$$W^* = I_F(\gamma\pi_T), \tag{52}$$

where $I_F = 0$ if $F = 0$ and otherwise I_F inverts F'. We'll confirm these conjectured solutions in the proof of the next theorem.

Under strict concavity, the inversions $I(\,\cdot\,,t)$ and I_F are continuous and strictly decreasing. A decreasing function $\hat{w} : (0,\infty) \to \mathbb{R}$ is therefore defined by

$$\hat{w}(\gamma) = E\left[\int_0^T \pi_t I(\gamma\pi_t, t)\,dt + \pi_T I_F(\gamma\pi_T)\right]. \tag{53}$$

(The expectation may be $+\infty$.) All of this implies that (c^*, W^*) of (51)–(52) solves (46) provided the required initial investment $\hat{w}(\gamma)$ is equal to the endowed initial wealth w. This leaves an equation $\hat{w}(\gamma) = w$ to solve for the "correct" Lagrange multiplier γ^*, and with that an explicit solution (51)–(52) to the optimal consumption policy for Merton's problem with $\gamma = \gamma^*$.

We can be a little more systematic about the properties of u and F in order to guarantee that $\hat{w}(\gamma) = w$ can be solved for a unique $\gamma^* > 0$. A strictly concave increasing function $F : \mathbb{R}_+ \to \mathbb{R}$ that is differentiable on $(0, \infty)$ satisfies *Inada conditions* if $\inf_x F'(x) = 0$ and $\sup_x F'(x) = +\infty$. If F satisfies these Inada conditions, then the inverse I_F of F' is well defined as a strictly decreasing continuous function on $(0, \infty)$ whose image is $(0, \infty)$.

Condition A. *Either F is zero or F is strictly concave satisfying Inada conditions. Either u is zero or, for all t, $u(\cdot, t)$ is strictly concave satisfying Inada conditions. At least one of u and F is nonzero. For each $\gamma > 0$, $\hat{w}(\gamma)$ is finite.*

Theorem. *Under Condition A, for any $w > 0$, Merton's problem (38) has a solution (c^*, Z^*, θ^*), where (c^*, Z^*) is given by (51)–(52) for a unique $\gamma \in (0, \infty)$.*

Proof: Under Condition A, the Dominated Convergence Theorem implies that $\hat{w}$ is continuous. Since one or both of $I(\cdot, t)$ and I_F have $(0, \infty)$ as their image and are strictly decreasing, $\hat{w}$ inherits these two properties. From this, given any initial wealth $w > 0$, there is a unique γ^* with $\hat{w}(\gamma^*) = w$. Let (θ, c, Z) be any budget-feasible choice. Let (c^*, Z^*) be defined by (51)–(52), replacing γ with γ^*. Let θ^* be a trading strategy financing (c^*, Z^*), which exists by Proposition 8E. By Proposition 8E, (c, Z) satisfies (42), which is equivalent to (48). The first order conditions (49) and (50) imply that, for all t,

$$u(c_t^*, t) - \gamma^* \pi_t c_t^* \geq u(c_t, t) - \gamma^* \pi_t c_t$$

and that

$$F(W^*) - \gamma^* \pi_T Z^* \geq F(Z) - \gamma^* \pi_T Z.$$

Integrating these two inequalities and applying (48) to both (c, Z) and (c^*, Z^*) leaves $U(c^*, Z^*) \geq U(c, Z)$, implying the optimality of (c^*, Z^*, θ^*). ∎

For a specific example, suppose that $u \equiv 0$ and $F(w) = w^\alpha / \alpha$. Then $c^* = 0$ and the calculations above imply that $\hat{w}(\gamma) = E\left[\pi_T(\gamma \pi_T)^{\alpha-1}\right]$. Solving $\hat{w}(\gamma^*) = w$ for γ^* leaves

$$\gamma^* = w^{1/(\alpha-1)} E\left(\pi_T^\alpha\right)^{1/(\alpha-1)}. \tag{54}$$

It is left as an exercise to check that (52) can be reduced explicitly to

$$W^* = I_F(\gamma^* \pi_T) = W_T,$$

where

$$dW_t = W_t(r + \overline{\varphi} \cdot \lambda)\, dt + W_t \overline{\varphi}^\top \sigma\, dB_t; \quad W_0 = w, \tag{55}$$

where $\overline{\varphi} = (\sigma\sigma^\top)^{-1}\lambda/(1-\alpha)$ is the vector of fixed optimal portfolio fractions found previously from the Bellman equation.

G. A Generalization

We generalize the security-price process $X = (\beta, S^1, \ldots, S^N)$ to be of the form

$$
\begin{aligned}
d\beta_t &= r_t \beta_t\, dt; \quad \beta_0 > 0, \\
dS_t^i &= \mu_t^i S_t^i\, dt + S_t^i \sigma_t^i\, dB_t; \quad S_0^i > 0, \quad 1 \le i \le N,
\end{aligned}
\tag{56}
$$

where r, $\mu = (\mu^1, \ldots, \mu^N)$, and σ^i, for all i, are bounded adapted processes valued in $\mathbb{R}$, $\mathbb{R}^N$, and $\mathbb{R}^d$ respectively. We assume for simplicity that $N = d$, that σ^i is the i-th row of a process σ valued in $\mathbb{R}^{d \times d}$ that is nonsingular almost everywhere. The excess expected returns of the securities are defined by an $\mathbb{R}^N$-valued process λ given by $\lambda_t^i = \mu_t^i - r_t$. We assume that λ is strictly positive, that the process ν defined by $\nu_t = \sigma_t^{-1}\lambda_t$ satisfies the Novikov condition

$$E\left[\exp\left(\frac{1}{2}\int_0^T \nu_t^\top \nu_t\, dt\right)\right] < \infty, \tag{57}$$

and that $\mathrm{var}(\xi_T) < \infty$, where

$$\xi_t = \exp\left(-\frac{1}{2}\int_0^T \nu_s^\top \nu_s\, ds - \int_0^t \nu_s\, dB_s\right), \quad t \in [0, T]. \tag{58}$$

A reading of Chapter 6 shows that these assumptions, aside from technical integrability conditions, are of the nature that (a) markets are complete, stemming from the invertibility of σ, and (b) there is no arbitrage, confirmed by the existence of an equivalent martingale measure Q for the deflated price processes, defined by $E^Q(Z) = E(\xi_T Z)$.

In this setting, the state-price deflator π is defined by

$$\pi_t = \exp\left(-\int_0^t r_s\, ds\right)\xi_t, \quad t \in [0, T]. \tag{59}$$

The reformulation of Merton's problem given by Proposition 8F and the form (51)–(52) of the solution (when it exists) still apply, substituting only the state-price process π of (59) for that given in the earlier special case of constant r, λ, and σ. Once again, the only serious difficulty to overcome is a solution γ^* to $\hat{w}(\gamma^*) = w$, where $\hat{w}$ is again defined by (53). This is guaranteed by Condition A of the previous section. The proof of Theorem 8F thus suffices for the following extension.

Proposition. *Suppose X is defined by (56). Under Condition A, for any $w > 0$, Merton's problem (38) has the optimal consumption policy given by (51)–(52) for a unique scalar γ.*

Although this approach generates an explicit solution for the optimal consumption policy, it does not say much about the form of the optimal trading strategy, beyond its existence. The Notes cite sources in which an optimal strategy is represented in terms of the *Malliavin calculus*. The original stochastic control approach, in a Markov setting, gives explicit solutions for the optimal trading strategy in terms of the derivatives of the value function. Although there are few examples in which these derivatives are known explicitly, they can be approximated by a numerical solution of the Hamilton-Jacobi-Bellman equation, by extending the finite-difference methods given in Chapter 10.

H. The Utility Gradient Approach

The martingale approach can be simplified, at least under technical conditions, by adopting the utility gradient approach of Chapter 2. Although conceptually easy, this theory has only been developed to the point of theorems under restrictive conditions and with complicated proofs beyond the scope of this book, so we shall merely sketch out the basic ideas and refer to the Notes for sources with proofs and more details.

Letting $L_+ = \{c \in \mathcal{H}^2 : c \geq 0\}$, we adopt a concave utility function $U : L_+ \to \mathbb{R}$. We fix the security price process X of Section 8G. Fixing the initial wealth w, we say that a consumption process c in L_+ is budget-feasible if there is some θ in $\mathcal{H}^2(X)$ such that

$$\theta_t \cdot X_t = w + \int_0^t \theta_s \, dX_s - \int_0^t c_s \, ds, \quad t \in [0, T], \tag{60}$$

with $\theta_T \cdot X_T = 0$. We have the problem

$$\sup_{c \in A} U(c), \tag{61}$$

where A is the set of budget-feasible consumption processes. If c^* is budget-feasible and the gradient $\nabla U(c^*)$ of U at c^* exists, the gradient approach to optimality reviewed in Appendix B leads to the first order condition for optimality,

$$\nabla U(c^*; c^* - c) \le 0, \quad c \in A. \tag{62}$$

This problem is a special case of problem (33) if U is of the form

$$U(c) = E \left[\int_0^T u(c_t, t) \, dt \right]. \tag{63}$$

Other utility functions, such as habit formation and recursive utility (reviewed, in discrete time, in Exercises 2.8 and 2.9) have been studied in continuous time, so we do not limit our study here to the additive-utility model.

Suppose c^* is budget-feasible and $\nabla U(c^*)$ exists, with a Riesz representation π in $\mathcal{H}^2$. That is,

$$\nabla U(c^*; c - c^*) = E \left[\int_0^T (c_t - c_t^*)\pi_t \, dt \right], \quad c \in A. \tag{64}$$

As shown in Appendix F, this is true for the additive model, under conditions, taking $\pi_t = u_c(c_t^*, t)$. Based on Proposition 2D and the results of Section 8G, it is natural to conjecture that c^* is optimal if and only if π is a state-price deflator. In order to explore this conjecture, we suppose that π is indeed a state-price deflator, meaning in this case that the deflated price process X^π is a martingale. The Numeraire Invariance Theorem (or direct calculation) implies that $c \in A$ if and only if there is some $\theta \in \mathcal{H}^2(X)$ with

$$\theta_t \cdot X_t^\pi = w\pi_0 + \int_0^t \theta_s \, dX_s^\pi - \int_0^t c_s \pi_s \, ds, \quad t \in [0, T], \tag{65}$$

and $\theta_T \cdot X_T^\pi = 0$. Assuming that any trading strategy θ is in $\mathcal{H}^1(X^\pi)$, relation (65) implies that, for any c in A, since $\int \theta \, dX^\pi$ is a martingale,

$$E \left(\int_0^T c_t \pi_t \, dt \right) = w\pi_0.$$

(This is consistent with [48].) Applying this in particular to c^*, we have

$$\nabla U(c^*; c - c^*) = E \left[\int_0^T \pi_t(c_t - c_t^*) \, dt \right] = 0, \quad c \in A. \tag{66}$$

Thus, assuming some technical conditions along the way, we have shown that the first order conditions for optimality are satisfied if X^π is a martingale. We would next like to be able to deduce what c^* must be if $\nabla U(c^*)$ is to have a Riesz representation π that is a state-price deflator.

Since any given deflator π is an Ito process, we can write

$$d\pi_t = \mu_\pi(t)\, dt + \sigma_\pi(t)\, dB_t, \tag{67}$$

for some $\mu_\pi \in \mathcal{L}^1$ and $\sigma_\pi \in \mathcal{L}(B)$. If X^π is a martingale, then β^π in particular is a martingale, and therefore has a zero drift process. By Ito's Lemma, this gives us

$$\beta_t r_t \pi_t + \mu_\pi(t)\beta_t = 0, \quad t \in [0, T],$$

which is equivalent to

$$\mu_\pi(t) = -\pi_t r_t, \quad t \in [0, T]. \tag{68}$$

Again using Ito's Lemma and the fact that S^π is also to be a martingale, we have, for all $j \in \{1, \ldots, N\}$,

$$\mu_t^j S_t^j \pi_t + \mu_\pi(t)\, S_t^j + S_t^j \sigma_t^j \cdot \sigma_\pi(t) = 0.$$

Combining this with (68) implies that $\sigma_\pi/\pi = \nu$, where ν solves

$$\sigma_t \nu_t = -\lambda_t, \quad t \in [0, T], \tag{69}$$

and where $\lambda_t^j = \mu_t^j - r_t$. Together, (68) and (69) yield

$$d\pi_t = -\pi_t\, r_t\, dt - \pi_t\, \nu_t\, dB_t,$$

which can be reduced, using Ito's Lemma to calculate $\log(\pi_t)$, to the expression

$$\pi_t = \pi_0 \exp\left(-\int_0^t r_s\, ds\right) \xi_t, \tag{70}$$

where ξ is given by (60). This is an explicit solution for π up to choice of π_0. It coincides, of course, with the relationship shown in Chapter 6 between state-price deflators and equivalent martingale measures.

It remains to recover a budget-feasible consumption process c^* with the property that $\nabla U(c^*)$ has a Riesz representation π of the form (70). In the additive case, we have $\pi_t = u_c(c_t^*, t)$, so that $c_t^* = I(\pi_t, t)$, where $I(\cdot, t)$ inverts $u_c(\cdot, t)$. Finally, we need to choose π_0 so that c^* is budget-feasible. It suffices by the same numeraire invariance argument made earlier that

$$\pi_0 \, w = E \left(\int_0^T c_t^* \pi_t \, dt \right) = E \left[\int_0^T I(\pi_t, t) \pi_t \, dt \right]. \tag{71}$$

Provided $I(\cdot, t)$ has range $(0, \infty)$ for all t, the arguments used in Section 8G can be applied for the existence of π_0 with this property. It is enough, for instance, that ν can be chosen to be bounded, and that I satisfies a uniform growth condition in its first argument. The Notes cite examples of a nonadditive utility function U with the property that, for each deflator π in a suitably general class, one can recover a unique consumption process c^* with the property that $\nabla U(c^*)$ has π as its Riesz representation. Subject to regularity conditions, the habit-formation and recursive-utility functions have this property.

For the case of incomplete markets (for which it is not true that rank$(\sigma) = d$ almost everywhere), all of the above steps can be carried out in the absence of arbitrage, except that there need not be a trading strategy θ^* that finances the proposed solution c^*. Papers cited in the Notes have taken the following approach to this issue. With incomplete markets, there is a family of different ν solving (69). The objective is to choose a solution ν^* with the property that c^* can be financed. This can be done under technical regularity conditions.

Exercises

8.1 Solve Merton's problem in the following cases. Add any regularity conditions that you feel are appropriate.

(A) Let T be finite, $F = 0$, and $u(c, t) = e^{-\rho t} c^\alpha / \alpha, \alpha \in (0, 1)$.

(B) Let T be finite and $u(c, t) = \log c$.

(C) Let $T = +\infty$ and $u(c, t) = e^{-\rho t} c^\alpha / \alpha, \, \alpha \in (0, 1)$. Verify the solution given by $c_t^* = \gamma W_t^*$ and $\varphi_t^* = (\sigma \sigma^\top)^{-1} \lambda / (1 - \alpha)$, where γ is given by (32). Verify the so-called transversality condition (31) with $\gamma(1 - \alpha) > 0$.

8.2 Extend the example in Section 8D, with $v(\bar{c}, w) = \bar{c}^\alpha / \alpha$, to the case without a riskless security. Add regularity conditions as appropriate.

8.3 The rate of growth of capital stock in a given production technology is determined by a "random shock" process Y solving the stochastic differential equation

$$dY_t = (b - \kappa Y_t)\, dt + k\sqrt{Y_t}\, dB_t; \quad Y_0 = y \in \mathbb{R}_+, \qquad t \geq 0,$$

where b, κ, and k are strictly positive scalars with $2b > k^2$, and where B is a standard Brownian motion. Let $\mathcal{C}$ be the space of non-negative adapted consumption processes satisfying $\int_0^T c_t\, dt < \infty$ almost surely for all $T \geq 0$. For each c in $\mathcal{C}$, a capital stock process K^c is defined by

$$dK_t^c = (K_t^c h Y_t - c_t)\, dt + K_t^c \epsilon \sqrt{Y_t}\, dB_t; \quad K_0^c = x > 0,$$

where h and ϵ are strictly positive scalars with $h > \epsilon^2$. Consider the control problem

$$V(x, y, 0) = \sup_{c \in \mathcal{C}}\ E\left[\int_0^T e^{-\rho t} \log(c_t)\, dt\right],$$

subject to $K_t^c \geq 0$ for all t in $[0, T]$.

(A) Let $C : \mathbb{R}_+ \times [0, T] \to \mathbb{R}_+$ be defined by

$$C(x, t) = \frac{\rho x}{1 - e^{-\rho(T-t)}},$$

and let K be the solution of the SDE

$$dK_t = [K_t h Y_t - C(K_t, t)]\, dt + K_t \epsilon \sqrt{Y_t}\, dB_t; \quad K_0 = x > 0.$$

Finally, let c^* be the consumption process defined by $c_t^* = C(K_t, t)$. Show that c^* is the unique optimal consumption control. Hint: Verify that the value function is of the form

$$V(x, y, t) = A_1(t) \log(x) + A_2(t)y + A_3(t), \quad (x, y, t) \in \mathbb{R}_+ \times \mathbb{R} \times [0, T),$$

where A_1, A_2, and A_3 are (deterministic) real-valued functions of time. State the function A_1 and differential equations for A_2 and A_3.

(B) Explicitly state the value function and the optimal consumption control for the infinite-horizon case. Add regularity conditions as appropriate.

8.4 An agent has the objective of maximizing $E[u(W_T)]$, where W_T denotes wealth at some future time T and $u : \mathbb{R} \to \mathbb{R}$ is increasing and strictly concave. The wealth W_T is the sum of the market value of a fixed portfolio of assets and the terminal value of the margin account of a futures trading strategy, as elaborated below. This problem is one of characterizing optimal futures hedging. The first component of wealth is the spot market value of a fixed portfolio $p \in \mathbb{R}^M$ of M different assets whose price processes $S^1, \ldots, S^M$ satisfy the respective stochastic differential equations

$$dS_t^m = \mu_m(t)\, dt + \sigma_m(t)\, dB_t; \quad t \geq 0; \quad S_0^m = 1, \quad m \in \{1, \ldots, M\},$$

where, for each m, $\mu_m : [0, T] \rightarrow \mathbb{R}$ and $\sigma_m : [0, T] \rightarrow \mathbb{R}^d$ are continuous. There are futures contracts for K assets with delivery at some date $\tau > T$, having futures-price processes $F^1, \ldots, F^k$ satisfying the stochastic differential equations:

$$dF_t^k = m_k(t)\, dt + v_k(t)\, dB_t; \quad t \in [0, T], \quad 1 \leq k \leq K,$$

where m_k and v_k are continuous on $[0, T]$ into $\mathbb{R}$ and $\mathbb{R}^d$ respectively. For simplicity, we assume that there is a constant short rate r for borrowing or lending. One takes a futures position merely by committing oneself to mark a margin account to market. Conceptually, that is, if one holds a long (positive) position of, say, ten futures contracts on a particular asset and the price of the futures contract goes up by a dollar, then one receives ten dollars from the short side of the contract. (In practice, the contracts are largely insured against default by the opposite side, and it is normal to treat the contracts as default-free for modeling purposes.) The margin account earns interest at the riskless rate (or, if the margin account balance is negative, one loses interest at the riskless rate). We ignore margin calls or borrowing limits. (Formally, as described in Section 7C, the futures-price process is actually the cumulative-dividend process of a futures contract; the true price process is zero.) Given any bounded adapted process $\theta = (\theta^1, \ldots, \theta^K)$ for the agent's futures-position process, the agent's wealth at time T is $p \cdot S_T + X_T$, where X is the Ito process for the agent's margin account value, defined by $X_0 = 0$ and $dX_t = rX_t\, dt + \theta_t\, dF_t$.

(A)   Set up the agent's dynamic hedging problem for choice of futures-position process θ in the framework of continuous-time stochastic control. State the Bellman equation and first order conditions. Derive an explicit expression for the optimal futures position θ_t involving the (unknown) value function. Make regularity assumptions such as differentiability and nonsingularity. Hint: Let $W_t = p \cdot S_t + X_t$, $t \in [0, T]$.

(B)   Solve for the optimal policy θ in the case $m \equiv 0$, meaning no expected futures-price changes. Add any regularity conditions needed.

(C)   Solve the problem explicitly for the case $u(w) = -e^{-\alpha w}$, where $\alpha > 0$ is a scalar risk aversion coefficient. Add any regularity conditions needed.

8.5   In the setting of Section 8B, consider the special case of the utility function

$$U(c, Z) = E\left[\int_0^T \log(c_t)\, dt + \sqrt{Z}\,\right].$$

Obtain a closed-form solution for Merton's problem (15). Hint: The mixture of logarithm and power function in the utility makes this a situation in which the martingale approach has an advantage over the Bellman approach, for which it might be difficult to conjecture a value function. Once the optimal consumption policy is found, do not forget to calculate the optimal portfolio trading strategy.

8.6   Suppose B is a standard Brownian motion and there are two securities with price processes S and β given by

$$dS_t = \mu_t S_t\, dt + \sigma_t S_t\, dB_t; \quad S_0 > 0$$

$$d\beta_t = r_t \beta_t\, dt; \quad \beta_0 > 0,$$

where μ, σ, and r are bounded adapted processes with $\mu_t > r_t$ for all t. We take the infinite horizon case, with utility function U defined by

$$U(c) = E\left(\int_0^\infty e^{-\rho t} c_t^\alpha\, dt\right),$$

where $\alpha \in (0, 1)$ and $\rho \in (0, \infty)$. Taking the approach of Section 8H, c^* is, in principle, an optimal choice if and only if

$$E\left(\int_0^\infty \pi_t c_t^*\, dt\right) = w,$$

where $\nabla U(c^*)$ has Riesz representation π, and where S^π and β^π are martingales. Assuming that the solution c^* is an Ito process with

$$dc_t^* = c_t^* \mu_t^*\, dt + c_t^* \sigma_t^*\, dB_t,$$

we can write

$$d\pi_t = \pi_t \mu_\pi(t)\, dt + \pi_t \sigma_\pi(t)\, dB_t$$

for processes μ_π and σ_π that can be solved explicitly in terms of μ^* and σ^* from Ito's Lemma and the fact that $\pi_t = e^{-\rho t} c_t^{\alpha-1}/\alpha$. Assuming that S^π and β^π are indeed martingales, solve for μ^* and σ^* explicitly.

Notes

Standard treatments of stochastic control in this setting are given by Fleming and Rishel (1975), Krylov (1980), Bensoussan (1983), and Lions (1981, 1983). Perhaps the first application of the Hamilton-Jacobi-Bellman equation in the field of investments is in Mirrlees (1974), which appeared in manuscript form in December 1965. Merton (1969, 1971) initiated the problem found in Section 8B and its solution in Sections 8C and 8D. Extensions and corrections are found in Lehoczky, Sethi, and Shreve (1983, 1985), Karatzas, Lehoczky, Sethi, and Shreve (1986), Sethi and Taksar (1988), Fleming and Zariphopoulou (1989), Fitzpatrick and Fleming (1990), Aase (1984), Richard (1975), Jacka (1984), Ocone and Karatzas (1991) (who apply the Malliavin calculus), and Merton (1990b).

The martingale approach in Section 8E has been developed in a series of papers. Principle among these are Cox and Huang (1989) and Karatzas, Lehoczky, and Shreve (1987). This literature includes Cox (1983), Pliska (1986), Cox and Huang (1985), Back (1986), Back and Pliska (1987), Pagès (1987), Jeanblanc-Picqué and Pontier (1990), Huang and Pagès (1991), and Richardson (1989). For the case of incomplete markets or other constraints, duality techniques have been applied by He and Pearson (1991a,b), and Karatzas, Lehoczky, Shreve, and Xu (1991), and extended by Cvitanić and Karatzas (1991). Other work involving hedging in incomplete markets can be found in Föllmer and Sondermann (1986), Duffie and Jackson (1990), Duffie and Richardson (1991), He and Pagès (1990), Svensson and Werner (1990), Adler and Detemple (1988), and Dybvig (1989).

For optimality under various nonadditive utility criteria, see Uzawa (1968), Ryder and Heal (1973), Sundaresan (1989), Svensson (1989), Duffie and Epstein (1992), Duffie and Skiadas (1990), Detemple and Zapatero (1990), and Hindy and Huang (1989a, b; 1990). For the underlying non-additive utility models, see Uzawa (1968), Ryder and Heal (1973), Hindy, Huang, and Kreps (1991), Duffie and Epstein (1989), and Duffie and Lions (1990).

The "utility gradient" approach of Section 8H is based on work by Harrison and Kreps (1979), Kreps (1981), Huang (1985a), Foldes (1978, 1979, 1991a, b, c), Back (1991a), and Duffie and Skiadas (1990), and is extended in these sources to an abstract setting with more general information and utility functions. For extensions of Merton's problem to the case of transactions costs, see Constantinides (1986), Davis and Norman (1990), Dumas and Luciano (1989), Fleming, Grossman, Vila, and Zariphopoulou (1989), Zariphopoulou (1989), Davis and Panas (1991), and Alvarez (1991). For problems with borrowing constraints, see Vila and Zariphopoulou (1991), Scheinkman and Weiss (1986), Back and Pliska (1986), He and Pagès (1990), and Hindy (1991). For problems in a Markov setting with incomplete information, usually requiring filtering of the state, see Dothan and Feldman (1986), Gennotte (1984), Detemple (1991), and J. Wang (1990). Karatzas (1989) surveys some of the topics in this chapter. Exercise 8.3 is from Cox, Ingersoll, and Ross (1985a).

9

Equilibrium

THIS CHAPTER REVIEWS security market equilibrium in the continuous-time setting and derives several implications for security prices and expected returns. These include Breeden's consumption-based capital asset pricing model (in both complete and incomplete market settings) as well as the Cox-Ingersoll-Ross model of the term structure.

A. The Primitives

As usual, we let $B = (B^1, \ldots, B^d)$ denote a standard Brownian motion in $\mathbb{R}^d$ on a probability space $(\Omega, \mathcal{F}, P)$, and let $\mathbb{F} = \{\mathcal{F}_t : t \geq 0\}$ denote the standard filtration of B. The consumption space is the set L of adapted processes satisfying the integrability constraint $E\left(\int_0^T c_t^2 \, dt\right) < \infty$ for some fixed-time horizon $T > 0$.

There are m agents. Agent i is defined by a nonzero consumption endowment process e^i in the set L_+ of non-negative processes in L, and by a strictly increasing utility function $U_i : L_+ \to \mathbb{R}$.

As in Section 6K, a cumulative-dividend process is a finite-variance process of the form $C = Z + V - W$, where $Z = \int \theta \, dB$ for some $\theta \in \mathcal{L}(B)$, and where V and W are increasing adapted right-continuous processes. For any time t, the jump $\Delta C_t \equiv C_t - C_{t-}$ represents the lump-sum payment at time t. For example, if the security is a unit zero-coupon bond that matures at time τ, then $C_t = 0$, $t < \tau$, and $C_t = 1$, $t \geq \tau$. By convention, any dividend process C satisfies $C_{0-} = C_0 = 0$. For example, a dividend-rate process δ in L defines the cumulative-dividend process $C = V - W$ with $V_t = \int_0^t \delta_s^+ \, ds$ and $W_t = \int_0^t \delta_s^- \, ds$. There are $N+1$ securities, numbered 0 through N, with security j defined by a cumulative-dividend process D^j.

Mainly for expositional reasons, we assume that the given dividend processes are measured in nominal units of account, and will shortly define the price process for consumption in terms of the same nominal units of account. We later normalize by the price of consumption in order to recover continuous-time versions of the utility-based asset pricing results of Chapter 2. Altogether, the set of primitives of the economy is:

$$\mathcal{E} = \left\{ (\Omega, \mathcal{F}, \mathbb{F}, P); \, B; \, (e^i, U_i), \, 1 \leq i \leq m; \, D^j, \, 0 \leq j \leq N \right\}. \tag{1}$$

B. Security-Spot Market Equilibrium

The dividend process $D = (D^0, \ldots, D^N)$ is assigned a price process $X = (X^0, \ldots, X^N)$ such that the gain process $G = D + X$ is an Ito process in $\mathbb{R}^{N+1}$. We treat X_t as the ex-dividend price at time t, that is, the price without including the current dividend jump ΔD_t. There is also a process p in L for the price of the single consumption commodity. A trading strategy is a process $\theta = (\theta^0, \ldots, \theta^N)$ in $\mathcal{H}^2(G)$. Given the consumption-price process p, a trading strategy θ *finances a consumption process c* if

$$\theta_t \cdot (X_t + \Delta D_t) = \int_0^t \theta_s \, dG_s - \int_0^t p_s c_s \, ds, \quad t \in [0, T], \tag{2}$$

and

$$\theta_T \cdot (X_T + \Delta D_T) = 0. \tag{3}$$

Given a security-price process X and a consumption-price process p, agent i faces the problem

$$\sup_{(c,\theta) \in \Lambda(i)} \, U_i(c), \tag{4}$$

where $\Lambda(i) = \{ (c, \theta) \in L_+ \times \mathcal{H}^2(G) : \theta \text{ finances } c - e^i \}$.

A *security–spot market equilibrium* for the economy $\mathcal{E}$ of (1) is a collection

$$\left\{ X; \, p; \, (c^i, \theta^i), \, 1 \leq i \leq m \right\} \tag{5}$$

such that, given the security-price process X and the consumption-price process p, for each agent i, (c^i, θ^i) solves (4), and markets clear: $\sum_{i=1}^m \theta^i = 0$ and $\sum_{i=1}^m c^i - e^i = 0$.

C. Arrow-Debreu Equilibrium

A related notion of equilibrium is one in which any consumption process c in L can be purchased at time zero for some price $\Pi(c)$ that is given by a nonzero linear *price function* $\Pi : L \to \mathbb{R}$. Paralleling the definitions given in Chapter 2, an allocation $(c^1, \ldots, c^m) \in (L_+)^m$ of consumption processes is feasible if $\sum_{i=1}^m c^i \le \sum_{i=1}^m e^i$. An Arrow-Debreu equilibrium is a collection $[\Pi, (c^1, \ldots, c^m)]$ consisting of a price function Π and a feasible allocation $(c^1, \ldots, c^m)$ such that, for each i, c^i solves

$$\sup_{c \in L_+} U_i(c) \quad \text{subject to} \quad \Pi(c) \le \Pi(e^i). \tag{6}$$

Conditions for the existence of an Arrow-Debreu equilibrium are given in Section 9G and in the Notes.

Lemma. *Suppose* $\Pi : L \to \mathbb{R}$ *is linear and strictly increasing. There is a unique* π *in* L *such that*

$$\Pi(c) = E\left(\int_0^T \pi_t c_t \, dt\right), \quad c \in L. \tag{7}$$

Moreover, π *is strictly positive.*

A proof of this continuous-time analogue of Lemma 2C is relegated to the Notes. Since U_i is strictly increasing by assumption, any Arrow-Debreu equilibrium price function Π is strictly increasing and therefore has a representation of the form (7) for a unique process $\pi \gg 0$, which is known as the Riesz representation of Π.

If feasible, an allocation $(c^1, \ldots, c^m)$ is Pareto optimal if there is no feasible allocation $(b^1, \ldots, b^m)$ such that $U_i(b^i) \ge U_i(c^i)$ for all i, with strict inequality for at least one i.

The First Welfare Theorem. *Any Arrow-Debreu equilibrium allocation is Pareto optimal.*

Proof: Let $[\Pi, (c^1, \ldots, c^m)]$ be an Arrow-Debreu equilibrium, and let π denote the Riesz representation of Π. Suppose $(b^1, \ldots, b^m)$ is a feasible allocation with $U_i(b^i) \ge U_i(c^i)$ for all i, with at least one strict inequality, say for agent j. We need a contradiction to complete the proof. Since $U_j(b^j) > U_j(c^j)$, we know that

$$\Pi(b^j) > \Pi(c^j). \tag{8}$$

If for some i, $\epsilon \equiv \Pi(c^i) - \Pi(b^i) > 0$, we could let

$$\hat{c}^i = b^i + \frac{\epsilon}{\Pi(\pi)}\pi, \tag{9}$$

from which $\Pi(\hat{c}^i) = \Pi(c^i)$. But then, since U_i is strictly increasing and $\pi > 0$, we would have $U_i(\hat{c}^i) > U_i(c^i)$, which is impossible by the definition of an equilibrium. Thus

$$\Pi(b^i) \geq \Pi(c^i), \quad 1 \leq i \leq m. \tag{10}$$

Combining (8), (10), and feasibility produces the contradiction

$$\Pi\left(\sum_{i=1}^m e^i\right) \geq \Pi\left(\sum_{i=1}^m b^i\right) > \Pi\left(\sum_{i=1}^m c^i\right) = \Pi\left(\sum_{i=1}^m e^i\right), \tag{11}$$

which proves the result. ∎

The following result is shown with the Separating Hyperplane Theorem in exactly the same manner as for Lemma 1E.

Proposition. *Suppose, for all i, that U_i is concave. Then $(c^1, \ldots, c^m)$ is a Pareto optimal allocation if and only if there is a nonzero vector λ in $\mathbb{R}_+^m$ such that $(c^1, \ldots, c^m)$ solves the problem*

$$\sup_{(\hat{c}^1, \ldots, \hat{c}^m)} \sum_{i=1}^m \lambda_i \, U_i(\hat{c}^i) \quad \text{subject to} \quad \hat{c}^1 + \cdots + \hat{c}^m \leq e^1 + \cdots + e^m. \tag{12}$$

D. Implementing Arrow-Debreu Equilibrium

In this section we fix an Arrow-Debreu equilibrium $[\Pi, (c^1, \ldots, c^m)]$ and examine spanning conditions on the cumulative-dividend process D under which there exists a security–spot market equilibrium with the same consumption allocation. We assume throughout the following that $D_t^0 = 0$, $t < T$, with $D_T^0 = 1$, meaning that D^0 is a (nominal) zero-coupon unit bond maturing at T. This assumption can be relaxed at a cost in notational complexity.

The Martingale Representation Theorem of Appendix E states that any martingale M has a martingale representation $M_t = M_0 + \int_0^t \eta_s \, dB_s$, $t \geq 0$, for some $\eta = (\eta^1, \ldots, \eta^d)$ in $\mathcal{L}(B)$. The following spanning condition on cumulative-dividend processes is unnecessarily restrictive (in a sense discussed in the Notes), but simplifies the following exposition.

Dynamic Spanning Condition. *D^0 is a nominal zero-coupon unit bond maturing at T. Let M denote the martingale in $\mathbb{R}^{N+1}$ defined by $M_t = E_t(D_T)$. Let $\{M_0 + \int_0^t \eta_s \, dB_s : t \in [0, T]\}$ denote the martingale representation of M. Then $\text{rank}(\eta) = d$ almost everywhere.*

Obviously, D^0 makes no contribution toward meeting the rank restriction on η of the dynamic spanning condition, which therefore implies that there are at least $d+1$ securities. It is sufficient for this rank condition that $D^j_T = \int_0^T \sigma^j_t \, dB_t$, where $\sigma^1, \ldots, \sigma^N$ are the rows of a matrix process σ that has rank d almost everywhere. This means that $d+1$ is also a sufficient number of securities.

Theorem. *Suppose that the cumulative-dividend process D satisifies the dynamic spanning condition. Let $\left[\Pi, (c^1, \ldots, c^m)\right]$ be an Arrow-Debreu equilibrium. Let p denote the Riesz representation of Π and let*

$$X_t = E_t(D_T - D_t), \quad t \in [0, T]. \tag{13}$$

If p is bounded, then $\{X; p; (c^i, \theta^i), 1 \le i \le m\}$ is a security–spot market equilibrium for some $(\theta^1, \ldots, \theta^m)$.

Proof: Pick an arbitrary agent i and let Y be the martingale defined by

$$Y_t = E_t\left[\int_0^T (c^i_s - e^i_s) \, p_s \, ds\right], \quad t \in [0, T]. \tag{14}$$

Since $\Pi(c^i - e^i) = 0$ and p is the Riesz representation of Π, we know that $Y_0 = 0$. The Martingale Representation Theorem implies that there is some φ in $\mathcal{L}(B)$ with

$$Y_t = \int_0^t \varphi_s \, dB_s, \quad t \in [0, T]. \tag{15}$$

Likewise, the gain process $G = X + D$ is a martingale since $G_t = X_t + D_t = E_t(D_T)$ for all t. Thus G can be written

$$G_t = G_0 + \int_0^t \eta_s \, dB_s, \quad t \in [0, T], \tag{16}$$

with $\text{rank}(\eta) = d$ almost everywhere from the dynamic spanning condition. Because of this, there is a trading strategy $\theta = (\theta^0, \ldots, \theta^N)$ solving

$$\theta_t \eta_t = \varphi_t, \quad t \in [0, T]. \tag{17}$$

Since p is bounded and c^i and e^i are in L, $E(Y_T^2) < \infty$. Thus $\theta \in \mathcal{H}^2(G)$ by Proposition 5B. Since $G^0 \equiv 1$, $\int \theta \, dG$ is unaffected by redefining θ^0 so that

$$\theta^0_t = \sum_{j=1}^N \left[\int_0^t \theta^j_s \, dG^j_s - \theta^j_t(X^j_t + \Delta D^j_t)\right] - \int_0^t p_s(c^i_s - e^i_s) \, ds. \tag{18}$$

Simple algebra and (14)–(18) imply that $\theta_T \cdot (X_T + \Delta D_T) = 0$ and that

$$\theta_t \cdot (X_t + \Delta D_t) = \int_0^t \theta_s \, dG_s - \int_0^t (c_s^i - e_s^i) \, p_s \, ds, \quad t \in [0, T]. \qquad (19)$$

That is, θ finances $c^i - e^i$.

If, for some agent i, $\hat{\theta}$ is a trading strategy financing $\hat{c} - e^i$ for some consumption process $\hat{c}$, we claim that $U_i(\hat{c}) \leq U_i(c^i)$. If, on the contrary, $U_i(\hat{c}) > U_i(c^i)$, then we have $\Pi(\hat{c}) > \Pi(c^i) = \Pi(e^i)$ by the properties of an Arrow-Debreu equilibrium, so $E\left[\int_0^T (\hat{c}_t - e_t^i) \, p_t \, dt\right] > 0$. This, however, is inconsistent with the requirement of the financing condition that

$$0 = \theta_T \cdot (X_T + \Delta D_T) = \int_0^T \hat{\theta}_t \, dG_t - \int_0^T (\hat{c}_t - e_t^i) \, p_t \, dt, \qquad (20)$$

as can be seen by taking expectations through (20) and using the fact that $E\left(\int_0^T \hat{\theta}_t \, dG_t\right) = 0$. Thus (c^i, θ) solves agent i's problem (4).

Let θ^i be chosen in this fashion for each agent $i > 1$, and let $\theta^1 = -\sum_{i=2}^m \theta^i$. It can be checked from the linearity of stochastic integration that θ^1 finances $c^1 - e^1$, so (c^1, θ^1) is a solution to problem (4) for agent 1. By construction, $\sum_{i=1}^m \theta^i = 0$. By the feasibility of $(c^1, \ldots, c^m)$, we conclude that $\{X; \, p; \, (c^i, \theta^i), \; 1 \leq i \leq m\}$ is an equilibrium. ∎

E. Real Security Prices

The equilibrium $\{X; \, p; \, (c^i, \theta^i), \, 1 \leq i \leq m\}$ shown in the last theorem has a nominal security-price process X that is "risk-neutral," in the sense of (13). Relative to the price of the consumption commodity, or in *real* terms, security prices are not generally risk-neutral. For example, consider a particular security paying the nominal cumulative-dividend process C defined by $C_t = \int_0^t \delta_s \, ds$, for some dividend-rate process δ in L. We let Y denote the nominal price process of this security. By (13), $Y_t = E_t(\int_t^T \delta_s \, ds)$. The *real* price process $\hat{Y}$, defined by $\hat{Y}_t = Y_t/p_t$, and real dividend-rate process $\hat{\delta}$, defined by $\hat{\delta}_t = \delta_t/p_t$, are therefore related by

$$\hat{Y}_t = \frac{1}{p_t} E_t \left(\int_t^T p_s \hat{\delta}_s \, ds \right), \quad t \in [0, T]. \qquad (21)$$

A more general type of cumulative-dividend process is of the form $C = V - W$, where V and W are adapted increasing right-continuous processes.

Since the real dividend process $\hat{C}$ corresponding to C is given by $\hat{C}_t = \int_0^t p_s^{-1} \, dC_s$ (assuming the integral exists), the real price process $\hat{Y}$ for a security promising the real cumulative-dividend process $\hat{C}$ is given from (13) by

$$\hat{Y}_t = \frac{1}{p_t} E_t \left(\int_t^T p_s \, d\hat{C}_s \right), \quad t \in [0, T]. \tag{22}$$

A simple example is a real zero-coupon unit bond maturing at some time τ in $[0, T]$ (possibly a stopping time). We have $\hat{C}_t = 0$, $t < \tau$, and $\hat{C}_t = 1$, $t \geq \tau$. The real bond-price process is then given from (22) by

$$\Lambda_{t,\tau} \equiv \frac{1}{p_t} E_t(p_\tau), \quad t < \tau, \tag{23}$$

with $\Lambda_{t,\tau} = 0$, $t \geq \tau$. This defines the term structure of interest rates. Although we will have no need for it, the extension of (22) for a cumulative-dividend process $\hat{C}$ that is an Ito process may be calculated from the general formula given in Chapter 6 for the deflation of Ito dividend processes.

The central issue, to which we now turn, is the characterization of the consumption price process p. After the normalization to real prices that we have carried out above, it is apparent that p is a state-price deflator in the sense of Chapter 6.

F. Optimality with Additive Separable Utility

For most of the remainder of the chapter we will be exploiting the properties of *smooth-additive* utility functions, defined as follows.

Definition. *A utility function $U : L_+ \to \mathbb{R}$ is smooth-additive (u) if*

$$U(c) = E \left[\int_0^T u(c_t, t) \, dt \right], \tag{24}$$

where $u : \mathbb{R}_+ \times [0, T] \to \mathbb{R}$ is smooth on $(0, \infty) \times [0, T]$ and, for each t in $[0, T]$, $u(\cdot, t) : \mathbb{R}_+ \to \mathbb{R}$ is increasing, strictly concave, with an unbounded derivative $u_c(\cdot, t)$ on $(0, \infty)$.

For the purposes of this definition, we call a function "smooth" if it can be extended to an open set with continuous derivatives of any order. (In our applications, the order required will sometimes be as high as three.) A special case of a utility function U that is smooth-additive (u) is that given by $u(c, t) = e^{-\rho t} c^\alpha / \alpha$, with $\alpha < 1$ and $\alpha \neq 0$. The Inada condition of unbounded u_c guarantees that, given the opportunity, consumption will be strictly positive.

Consider the choice problem in an Arrow-Debreu equilibrium with smooth-additive utility:

$$\sup_{c \in L_+} E\left[\int_0^T u(c_t, t)\, dt\right] \quad \text{subject to} \quad E\left(\int_0^T p_t c_t\, dt\right) \le w, \quad (25)$$

where p is the Riesz representation of the equilibrium price function Π and $w > 0$ is the market value $\Pi(\hat{e})$ of the agent's endowment $\hat{e}$. Given the strict monotonicity and concavity of utility, the Saddle Point Theorem implies that a necessary and sufficient condition for c^* to solve (25) is the existence of a Lagrange multiplier $\gamma > 0$ such that c^* solves the unconstrained problem

$$\sup_{c \in L_+} E\left(\int_0^T [u(c_t, t) - \gamma p_t c_t]\, dt\right), \quad (26)$$

along with $E(\int_0^T p_t c_t^*\, dt) = w$. This is argued in Section 8F.

Naturally, one can do no better than to maximize $u(c_t, t) - \gamma p_t c_t$ separately for each t and each state of the world. Since $u_c(\,\cdot\,, t)$ is unbounded, this implies, for optimal c^*, that $c^* \gg 0$ and that

$$u_c(c_t^*, t) = \gamma p_t, \quad t \in [0, T]. \quad (27)$$

In fact, this leads directly to a method for solving (25) that is described in Section 8G, but that is not needed here. Relation (27) gives us our first characterization of the state-price deflator p in the security–spot market equilibrium studied in Sections 9D and 9E. We know, for some $\gamma > 0$, that

$$p_t = \frac{1}{\gamma} u_c(c_t^*, t), \quad t \in [0, T],$$

assuming that one of the agents has the optimal consumption process c^* and a utility function that is smooth-additive (u). The fact that the Lagrange multiplier γ is unknown is of no consequence, since $\{\gamma p_t : t \in [0, T]\}$ is also a state-price deflator for any constant $\gamma > 0$. This characterization of the state-price deflator is in terms of an individual agent's consumption process. Now we work toward a like characterization of p in terms of aggregate consumption.

G. Equilibrium with Smooth-Additive Utility

This section further characterizes state-price deflators under the assumption of smooth-additive utility. A proof of the following theorem is cited in the Notes.

Theorem. *Suppose that the aggregate endowment process e is bounded away from zero and that, for each i, U_i is smooth-additive (u_i). Then there is an Arrow-Debreu equilibrium $[\Pi, (c^1, \ldots, c^m)]$ for which Π has a bounded Riesz representation p, and such that, for all i, c^i is bounded away from zero.*

Coupling this result with Theorem 9D, we have conditions for the existence of a security-spot market equilibrium under smooth-additive utility.

Corollary. *Suppose, in addition, that D satisfies the dynamic spanning condition. Let X be given by (12). Then there are trading strategies $(\theta^1, \ldots, \theta^m)$ such that $[X; p; (c^i, \theta^i), 1 \leq i \leq m]$ is a security–spot market equilibrium.*

We fix the equilibrium consumption allocation $(c^1, \ldots, c^m)$ and consumption-price process p of this result for the remainder of this section and the next. By Theorem 9C, $(c^1, \ldots, c^m)$ is a Pareto optimal allocation. By Proposition 9C, there exists a nonzero "weight" vector $\lambda \in \mathbb{R}^m_+$ such that $(c^1, \ldots, c^m)$ solves the problem

$$\sup_{(b^1,\ldots,b^m)} \sum_{i=1}^m \lambda_i E\left[\int_0^T u_i(b^i_t, t)\, dt\right] \quad \text{subject to} \quad b^1 + \cdots + b^m \leq e. \quad (28)$$

Because of the additive nature of utility, one can solve this problem separately for each time t in $[0, T]$ and state ω in Ω. In order to see this, let $u_\lambda : \mathbb{R}_+ \times [0, T] \to \mathbb{R}$ be defined by

$$u_\lambda(y, t) = \sup_{x \in \mathbb{R}^m} \sum_{i=1}^m \lambda_i\, u_i(x_i, t) \quad \text{subject to} \quad x_1 + \cdots + x_m \leq y. \quad (29)$$

Since $(c^1, \ldots, c^m)$ solves (28), it follows that $[c^1(\omega, t), \ldots, c^m(\omega, t)]$ solves problem (29) for $y = e(\omega, t)$, except perhaps for (ω, t) in a null subset. (A set $A \subset \Omega \times [0, T]$ is *null* if $E(\int_0^T 1_A(t)\, dt) = 0$, where $1_A(t)$ is the random variable whose outcome is 1 if (ω, t) is in A, and is zero otherwise.) This is shown as follows. Suppose not, and let $(b^1, \ldots, b^m)$ be a feasible allocation and A a non-null subset of $\Omega \times [0, T]$ such that, for all (ω, t) in A,

$$\sum_{i=1}^m \lambda_i\, u_i\left[b^i(\omega, t), t\right] > \sum_{i=1}^m \lambda_i\, u_i\left[c^i(\omega, t), t\right].$$

Let $(a^1, \ldots, a^m)$ be the feasible allocation defined by

$$a^i(\omega, t) = b^i(\omega, t), \qquad (\omega, t) \in A,$$

$$= c^i(\omega, t), \qquad \text{otherwise.}$$

Then

$$\sum_{i=1}^{m} \lambda_i U_i(a^i) > \sum_{i=1}^{m} \lambda_i U_i(c^i),$$

contradicting the fact that $(c^1, \ldots, c^m)$ solves (28).

An exercise in applying the implicit function theorem shows that the utility function $U_\lambda : L_+ \to \mathbb{R}$, defined by

$$U_\lambda(c) = E \left[\int_0^T u_\lambda(c_t, t) \, dt \right], \tag{30}$$

is smooth-additive (u_λ). With $y > 0$, the first order conditions for optimality of x^* in (29) imply that

$$\lambda_i \, u_{ic}(x_i^*, t) = u_{\lambda c}(y, t), \quad i \in \{1, \ldots, m\}, \tag{31}$$

where subscripts indicate derivatives in the customary way. This implies that, almost everywhere and for all i,

$$\lambda_i u_{ic}(c_t^i, t) = u_{\lambda c}(e_t, t). \tag{32}$$

Joining (32) with the first order condition (27) for individual optimality implies that the Riesz representation p of Π is given by

$$k p_t = u_{\lambda c}(e_t, t), \quad t \in [0, T], \tag{33}$$

for a constant $k > 0$ that can be taken to be 1 by rescaling p.

We have thus characterized a state-price deflator p in terms of the "marginal utility of a representative agent." It should be kept in mind that the weights $\lambda_1, \ldots, \lambda_m$ generally depend on the original endowment $(e^1, \ldots, e^m)$, and indeed on the particular equilibrium if there is more than one. (Uniqueness of equilibrium is implied by a gross substitutes condition cited in the Notes.) Despite these limitations, (33) is a useful representation of state prices on intuitive grounds, and the smoothness of u_λ is also important for future applications of Ito's Lemma.

Returning to the security–spot market equilibrium of Theorem 9D, we can rewrite the security valuation equation (22) in the form

$$\hat{Y}_t = \frac{1}{u_{\lambda c}(e_t, t)} E_t \left[\int_t^T u_{\lambda c}(e_s, s) \, d\hat{C}_s \right], \quad t \in [0, T], \tag{34}$$

which should strike a familiar note from a reading of Chapter 2.

H. The Consumption-Based CAPM

Section 9G showed that a state-price deflator p is given by $p_t = u_{\lambda c}(e_t, t)$, where u_λ is defined by (29) for some fixed utility weight vector $\lambda \in \mathbb{R}_+^m$. We henceforth assume that e is an Ito process of the form $de_t = \mu_e(t) \, dt + \sigma_e(t) \, dB_t$, which implies by Ito's Lemma and the smoothness of u_λ that p is also an Ito process with

$$dp_t = \mu_p(t) \, dt + \sigma_p(t) \, dB_t, \tag{35}$$

where $\sigma_p(t) = u_{\lambda cc}(e_t, t)\sigma_e(t)$ and

$$\mu_p(t) = u_{\lambda cc}(e_t, t)\mu_e(t) + u_{\lambda ct}(e_t, t) + \frac{1}{2}u_{\lambda ccc}(e_t, t)\sigma_e(t) \cdot \sigma_e(t). \tag{36}$$

Based on a review of Section 6D, the fact that p is a state-price deflator implies that the real short-rate process r must be given by $r_t = -\mu_p(t)/p_t$. We can thus think of the short rate r_t at time t as the expected exponential rate of decline of the representative agent's "marginal utility," which is $p_t = u_{\lambda c}(e_t, t)$. Also from Section 6D, if the cumulative return of a given security is given by an Ito process R, then the fact that p is a state-price deflator implies that

$$\mu_R(t) - r_t = -\frac{1}{p_t}\sigma_R(t) \cdot \sigma_p(t) = \gamma_t \sigma_R(t) \cdot \sigma_e(t), \tag{37}$$

where $\gamma_t \equiv -u_{\lambda cc}(e_t, t)/u_{\lambda c}(e_t, t)$ is the *Arrow-Pratt measure* of risk aversion of $u_\lambda(\cdot, t)$ at e_t. In other words, excess expected returns are increasing in "instantaneous covariance" of returns with aggregate consumption changes, and increasing in "representative risk aversion." Moreover, these relationships are linear. Under stronger technical conditions, Section 9J extends this *consumption-based capital asset pricing model* (CCAPM) to incomplete markets. Within the restrictive setting of smooth-additive utility, the CCAPM is thus quite general. Without going into details, however, there is currently only weak empirical evidence in its support.

We can also view the CCAPM from a traditional "beta" perspective. The required calculations are shown in Section 6E. Since $\sigma_p(\omega, t)$ and $\sigma_e(\omega, t)$ are co-linear vectors for all (ω, t), the beta calculations in Section 6E apply equivalently to both e and p. These calculations lead to the "beta" formula

$$\mu_R(t) - r_t = \beta_R(t)(\mu_t^* - r_t), \tag{38}$$

where

$$\beta_R(t) = \frac{\sigma_R(t) \cdot \sigma_t^*}{\sigma_t^* \cdot \sigma_t^*} \tag{39}$$

is the instantaneous analogue to the beta coefficient of the CAPM, and where μ^* and σ^* are the drift and diffusion of a return process R^* with the property that $\sigma_t^* = k_t \, \sigma_e(t)$ for some strictly positive real-valued process k. In the sense of Section 6E, R^* is a return process with perfect instantaneous correlation with the aggregate consumption process e.

I. The CIR Term Structure

We will work out an equilibrium justification of the Cox-Ingersoll-Ross (CIR) model of the term structure that was assumed in Chapter 7. Our starting point is the solution to Exercise 8.3 involving the optimal consumption process δ from a technology with a capital stock process K. For a given "discount rate" $\rho \in (0, \infty)$, let

$$U(c) \equiv E\left[\int_0^T e^{-\rho t} \log(c_t) \, dt\right], \quad c \in L_+. \tag{40}$$

The single agent in the economy has the utility function $U : L_+ \to \overline{\mathbb{R}}$ defined by (40).

For simplicity, we take the Brownian motion B to be one-dimensional. Repeating the solution to Exercise 8.3, the optimal capital-stock process K is the Ito process defined by

$$dK_t = (K_t h Y_t - \delta_t) \, dt + K_t \epsilon \sqrt{Y_t} \, dB_t; \quad K_0 > 0, \tag{41}$$

where

$$\delta_t = \frac{\rho K_t}{1 - e^{-\rho(T-t)}}, \quad t \in [0, T], \tag{42}$$

and where Y solves the SDE

$$dY_t = (b - \kappa Y_t) \, dt + k\sqrt{Y_t} \, dB_t; \quad Y_0 > 0, \tag{43}$$

for strictly positive scalars κ, b, k, h, and ϵ such that $2b > k^2$ and $h > \epsilon^2$. We can think of Y as a "shock" process that affects the productivity of capital. The existence and non-negativity of the process Y is treated in the Notes of Chapter 7. The existence of the process K defined by (41)–(42) follows by expressing K_t in terms of Y, which can be done by expanding $\log(K_t)$ with the aid of Ito's Lemma.

We will start by assuming that the single agent's endowment process e is the optimal "drawdown" rate δ on the capital stock defined by (42). From this point, despite some slight differences in technical assumptions, we can reproduce the asset pricing results developed earlier in the chapter. An exercise asks for a demonstration that this drawdown rate and consumption process can be decentralized in a production-exchange equilibrium in which a firm selects δ to maximize its stock-market value.

In equilibrium, the real price process S of any security promising an increasing right-continuous real cumulative-dividend process $\hat{C}$ is given by (22), where p is the state-price deflator defined by

$$p_t = u_{\lambda c}(e_t, t) = \frac{e^{-\rho t}}{\delta_t}, \quad t \in [0, T]. \tag{44}$$

With the aid of Ito's Lemma,

$$dp_t = (\epsilon^2 - h) Y_t p_t \, dt + p_t \epsilon \sqrt{Y_t} \, dB_t. \tag{45}$$

The short-rate process r is given as in Section 9H by

$$r_t = \frac{-\mu_p(t)}{p_t} = (h - \epsilon^2) Y_t. \tag{46}$$

Since $dr_t = (h - \epsilon^2) \, dY_t$, we calculate

$$dr_t = \kappa(r^* - r_t) \, dt + \sigma_r \sqrt{r_t} \, dB_t, \tag{47}$$

where $r^* = b(h - \epsilon^2)/\kappa$ and $\sigma_r = k\sqrt{h - \epsilon^2}$. This is the form of the short rate assumed in the CIR model of the term structure studied in Section 7G in a "risk-neutral" setting. It is a convenient fact, to be shown shortly, that for the equilibrium state-price deflator p of (45), the associated "risk-neutral" version of the short-rate process is of the same square-root mean-reverting form, although with different coefficients.

For $r_t > r^*$, the drift of r is negative; for $r_t < r^*$, the drift of r is positive. We can therefore view r as a *mean-reverting* process, reverting toward r^*. We can be more precise about this, as follows. It has been shown, as indicated in the Notes, that $\bar{r}_t \equiv E(r_t)$ is finite and continuous in t. It follows from Fubini's Theorem (Appendix C) that $E(\int_0^T r_t \, dt) < \infty$, and therefore, by Proposition 5B, that the stochastic integral $\int_0^T \sigma_r \sqrt{r_t} \, dB_t$ has zero expectation. Thus

$$\bar{r}_\tau = r_0 + E\left[\int_0^\tau \kappa(r^* - r_t) \, dt \right].$$

Applying Fubini's Theorem again, $\bar{r}_\tau = r_0 + \int_0^\tau \kappa(r^* - \bar{r}_t) \, dt$, which is equivalent to the ordinary differential equation

$$\frac{d\bar{r}_t}{dt} = \kappa(r^* - \bar{r}_t); \quad \bar{r}_0 = r_0,$$

with solution $\bar{r}_t = r^* + (r_0 - r^*)e^{-\kappa t}$. Thus, $E(r_t) \to r^*$ exponentially as $t \to \infty$, and r^* is the "long-run mean" of the short-rate process. By using Fubini's Theorem for conditional expectations, we can show likewise that, for any times t and $s \geq t$,

$$E_t(r_s) = r^* + (r_t - r^*)e^{-\kappa(s-t)} \quad \text{almost surely.}$$

As we know from Chapter 7, in order to price term-structure instruments, it is enough to be able to represent the short-rate process r under an equivalent martingale measure. We can apply Ito's Lemma to represent p in the form

$$p_t = p_0 \exp\left(\frac{h}{\epsilon^2 - h} \int_0^t r_s \, ds + \frac{\epsilon}{\sqrt{h - \epsilon^2}} \int_0^t \sqrt{r_s} \, dB_s \right). \tag{48}$$

Based on equation (6.15), the density process ξ of an equivalent martingale measure is given by

$$\xi_t = \exp\left(\int_0^t r_s \, ds \right) \frac{p_t}{p_0}$$

$$= \exp\left(\frac{\epsilon^2}{\epsilon^2 - h} \int_0^t r_s \, ds + \frac{\epsilon}{\sqrt{h - \epsilon^2}} \int_0^t \sqrt{r_s} \, dB_s \right). \tag{49}$$

From Girsanov's Theorem of Appendix D, a standard Brownian motion $\hat{B}$ under the equivalent martingale measure Q is defined by

$$d\hat{B}_t = dB_t - \frac{\epsilon}{\sqrt{h - \epsilon^2}} \sqrt{r_t} \, dt. \tag{50}$$

Thus, under the equivalent martingale measure Q, we can represent the short-rate process r in the same square-root mean-reverting form

$$dr_t = \kappa(r^* - r_t)\,dt + \sigma_r\sqrt{r_t}\left(d\hat{B}_t - \frac{\epsilon}{\sqrt{h - \epsilon^2}}\sqrt{r_t}\,dt\right)$$

$$= [b(h - \epsilon^2) - (\kappa + k\epsilon)r_t]\,dt + \sigma_r\sqrt{r_t}\,d\hat{B}_t.$$

In particular, $\Lambda_{t,s} = E_t^Q\left[\exp\left(\int_t^s -r_u\,du\right)\right]$, which is solved explicitly in Section 7G. Sections 7G, 7H, and 7I give extensions, applications to derivative term-structure pricing, and an explicit solution for the "Green's function," or fundamental solution, of the PDE associated with r.

J. The CCAPM without Dynamic Spanning

We can recover a version of the CCAPM without assuming complete markets, although more demanding technical assumptions are required and there is as yet no set of conditions that is sufficient for the existence of equilibrium except in trivial or simple parametric examples. We will pass over most of the technical details, which are handled in papers cited in the Notes, and take as an assumption the first order conditions for individual optimality.

Section 8H shows that, in principle, if the gradient $\nabla U_i(c^i)$ of the utility of agent i at an optimal consumption process c^i exists and has a Riesz representation given by a deflator π^i, then π^i is a state-price deflator. The discrete-time analogue of this result is Proposition 2D. As shown in Appendix F, the gradient of a utility function U that is smooth-additive (u), at a consumption process c that is bounded away from zero, has a Riesz representation π given by $\pi_t = u_c(c_t, t)$.

Let us assume that, for each agent i, the utility function U_i is smooth-additive (u_i) and that the equilibrium consumption process c^i is an Ito process bounded away from zero, so that

$$dc_t^i = \mu_c^i(t)\,dt + \sigma_c^i(t)\,dB_t,$$

for appropriate processes μ_c^i and σ_c^i. The Riesz representation π^i of $\nabla U_i(c^i)$ exists and is given by $\pi_t^i = u_{ic}(c_t^i, t)$. This implies that π^i is an Ito process, with $d\pi_t^i = \mu_\pi^i(t)\,dt + \sigma_\pi^i(t)\,dB_t$, where

$$\mu_\pi^i(t) = u_{icc}(c_t^i, t)\mu_c^i(t) + u_{ict}(e_t, t) + \frac{1}{2}u_{iccc}(e_t, t)\sigma_c^i(t)\cdot\sigma_c^i(t)$$

and $\sigma_\pi^i(t) = u_{icc}(c_t^i, t)\sigma_c^i(t)$.

From this point, the calculations in Section 9H for the representative agent can be repeated for agent i. This replaces (37) with

$$\mu_R(t) - r_t = \gamma_t^i \sigma_R(t) \cdot \sigma_c^i(t), \tag{51}$$

where $r_t = -\mu_\pi^i(t)/\pi_t^i$, and where $\gamma_t^i = -u_{icc}(c_t^i, t)/u_{ic}(c_t^i, t)$ is the "risk aversion" of agent i at time t. If there exists a return process R with $\sigma_R = 0$, then r is the short-rate process. In any case, r_t is the expected return on any trading strategy whose return process R has $\sigma_R(t) \cdot \sigma_c^i(t) = 0$.

Assuming that there is indeed a short-rate process r, we can divide each side of (51) by γ_t^i and then sum the resulting expression over the m agents. Since $\sigma_e(t) = \sigma_c^1(t) + \cdots + \sigma_c^m(t)$, we get

$$\mu_R(t) - r_t = \Gamma_t \sigma_R(t) \cdot \sigma_e(t), \tag{52}$$

where

$$\Gamma_t \equiv \left(\frac{1}{\gamma_t^1} + \cdots + \frac{1}{\gamma_t^m} \right)^{-1}$$

is referred to as the *market risk aversion*. Thus, (52) extends (37), showing that excess expected rates of return on all securites are proportional to "instantaneous covariance" of returns with aggregate consumption increments, with a "market-risk-aversion" constant of proportionality. A "beta" form of the CCAPM can now be derived, as shown in Section 6E.

Exercises

9.1   Prove Proposition 9C.

9.2   Show the calculations verifying relations (44) through (50).

9.3   Let $\tilde{r} = \{\tilde{r}_t : 0 \le t \le T\}$ be an arbitrary non-negative bounded adapted process. This question allows you to prove the existence of a continuous-time security–spot market equilibrium with classical preferences in which the short-rate process is $\tilde{r}$.

First, for the model of preferences, suppose there is a single agent with a utility function that is smooth-additive (u), where $u(x, t) = e^{-\rho t} x^\alpha$, for $\alpha \in (0, 1)$. Next, suppose that the consumption endowment process e is defined by $e_t = \exp(Z_t)$, where

$$Z_t = Z_0 + \int_0^t (a + b\tilde{r}_s) \, ds + \int_0^t \sqrt{\tilde{r}_s} \sigma \, dB_s, \tag{53}$$

where a and b are constants, and where σ is a constant vector in $\mathbb{R}^d$.

(A)   Choose the constants a and b so that the equilibrium short-rate process is $\tilde{r}$.

(B)   Suppose there are heterogeneous agents with utility functions defined, for $i \in \{1, \ldots, m\}$, by

$$U_i(c) = E\left(\int_0^T \exp\left[-\int_0^t \rho_i(s)\, ds\right] c_t^\alpha\, dt\right),$$

where ρ_i is a bounded adapted process. The endowment for agent i is a process e^i such that $e = \sum_{i=1}^m e^i$ is the process defined above in terms of $\tilde{r}$. Assume the existence of an equilibrium with dynamic spanning. Calculate the short-rate process r in terms of the vector $\lambda \in \mathbb{R}_+^m$ (of "weights" on the I agents' utility functions) that defines the representative agent.

(C)   Repeat part (B) in the special case that $\rho_i = \bar{\rho}$ for all i, where $\bar{\rho}$ is a constant. Do not assume complete markets (dynamic spanning). That is, calculate the short-rate process once again. Can you choose a and b so that the short-rate process is $\tilde{r}$? Support your answer. Hint: Take note of the possibility that the vector λ depends on the equilibrium consumption allocation. Show that, in fact, it does not.

9.4   This is an alternative to the CIR model of the term structure found in Section 9I. In the CIR model, the equilibrium interest rate has an attractive mean-reverting property. Here we derive a less-attractive term structure because of a cruder model for adjustment of the capital stock. Although one must make some minor technical assumptions, there is only one natural closed-form solution.

The capital stock K solves the stochastic integral equation

$$K_t = K_0 + \int_0^t (hK_s - \delta_s)\, ds + \int_0^t \epsilon K_s\, dB_s, \quad t \geq 0,$$

where h and ϵ are strictly positive scalar, B is a standard Brownian motion in $\mathbb{R}$, and $\delta = \{\delta_t : t \geq 0\}$ is a non-negative dividend process. As in Exercise 8.3, the single firm in question depletes its capital stock K_t at the rate δ_t. We take an infinite-horizon setting and assume that the firm depletes its stock so as to maximize the agent's utility $U(\delta)$, with

$$U(\delta) = E\left(\int_0^\infty e^{-\rho t} \delta_t^\alpha\, dt\right),$$

where $\rho > 0$ is a scalar discount rate and $\alpha \in (0, 1)$.

(A)   Solve the firm's dividend control problem.

The consumer ignores what the firm is trying to do, and merely takes it that the firm's common share sells for $S(K_t)$, $t \geq 0$, where S is a C^2 strictly increasing function, and that each share pays the dividend process δ that the firm determines. The consumer is free to purchase any number of these shares (or to short-sell them), and is also able to borrow or lend at a short-rate process r given by $r_t = h(K_t)$, for some function h of the current capital stock. These are the only two securities available. The consumer has one share of the firm's stock as an initial endowment. Let W_t denote the consumer's total wealth at any time t in stock and bond. The consumer must choose at any time t the fraction z_t of wealth to hold in the firm's share (with the remainder reinvested continually at the short rate) and must also decide at what rate to consume. (Consumption is the numeraire.)

(B)   Briefly formulate the consumer's portfolio-consumption control problem. Derive the Bellman equation and first order conditions, assuming differentiability and interior optima.

Choose a stock-pricing function S and an interest-rate function h at which the consumer optimally holds none of the bond and one share of the firm. In other words:

(C)   State an equilibrium security-price process and an interest-rate process, both as functions of the current capital stock K_t.

(D)   Calculate the initial equilibrium market value of a zero-net-supply bond paying one unit of real wealth at a given time $\tau > 0$. Supply also the equilibrium market value of a *consol*, a pure income bond paying consumption perpetually at a fixed rate of one unit of consumption per unit of time.

(E)   State a differential equation for the equilibrium market value of a security paying dividends at a rate given by a bounded C^2 function f (with bounded derivative) of the current capital stock. Include a boundary condition.

9.5   Consider the following continuous-time analogue to the Markov single-agent asset pricing model of Chapter 4. Let X be the Ito process in $\mathbb{R}^N$ solving the stochastic differential equation

$$dX_t = \nu(X_t)\, dt + \eta(X_t)\, dB_t; \quad X_0 = x \in R^K, \qquad (54)$$

where $\nu : \mathbb{R}^N \to \mathbb{R}^N$ and $\eta : \mathbb{R}^N \to \mathbb{R}^{N \times d}$ are sufficiently well-behaved for existence. There are N securities in total supply of one each, paying dividends according to a bounded measurable function $f : \mathbb{R}^N \to \mathbb{R}_+^N$. That is, security n pays dividends at the rate $f(X_t)_n$ at time t. The security-price process is an Ito process S in $\mathbb{R}^N$. The single agent chooses a non-negative real-valued bounded adapted consumption process c and a bounded trading strategy $\theta = (\theta^1, \ldots, \theta^k)$. The wealth process $W^{c\theta}$ of an agent initially endowed with all of the securities and adopting the consumption-portfolio strategy (c, θ) is thus given by

$$W_T^{c\theta} = \mathbf{1} \cdot S_0 + \int_0^T [\theta_t f(X_t) - c_t] \, dt + \int_0^T \theta_t \, dS_t, \quad T \geq 0,$$

where $\mathbf{1} = (1, 1, \ldots, 1)^\top \in \mathbb{R}^K$. The agent's utility function U is defined by

$$U(c) = E\left[\int_0^\infty e^{-\rho t} u(c_t) \, dt \right],$$

where $\rho \in (0, \infty)$ and $u : \mathbb{R}_+ \to \mathbb{R}$ is increasing and strictly concave. An equilibrium for this economy is a security-price process S such that the problem $\max_{c,\theta} U(c)$ has a solution (c, θ) with $c_t = \mathbf{1} \cdot f(X_t)$ and $\theta_t = \mathbf{1}$ for all $t \in [0, \infty)$.

(A) Suppose the security-price process S is given by $S_t = \mathcal{S}(X_t)$ for all t, for some twice continuously differentiable function $\mathcal{S} : \mathbb{R}^K \to \mathbb{R}^K$. Provide the Bellman equation for the agent's stochastic control problem.

(B) Based on your understanding of the relationship between this model and the discrete-time Markov analogue, give an expression for the term structure of interest rates. That is, provide an expression for the market value at time t of a T-period pure discount bond, which is a zero-net-supply contract to pay one unit of the consumption numeraire at time $t + T$. No proof or explanation is required here. The expression should involve only the primitives of the model, ν, η, d, u, ρ, the initial state $x \in \mathbb{R}^N$, and future states, $X_t, t \geq 0$.

(C) Provide a PDE for the market value of any security as a necessary condition for an equilibrium, under stated regularity conditions, using the following infinite-horizon version of the Feynman-Kac formula. (We drop the argument $x \in \mathbb{R}^N$ from all functions for simplicity.) We do not supply the "strong regularity conditions" referred to in the result; there is a range of possible assumptions that are cumbersome and purely of mathematical interest.

A Version of the Feynman-Kac Formula. *Suppose* $R : \mathbb{R}^N \to \mathbb{R}$ *and* $h : \mathbb{R}^N \to \mathbb{R}$ *are measurable, and that* (ν, η, h, R) *satisfies the strong regularity conditions. Suppose* $F \in C^2(\mathbb{R}^N)$ *satisfies a growth condition. Then F satisfies the partial differential equation* $\mathcal{D}F - RF + h = 0$ *if and only if*

$$F(x) = E\left(\int_0^\infty \exp\left[-\int_0^t R(X_s)\,ds\right] h(X_t)\,dt\right), \quad x \in \mathbb{R}^N,$$

where $\mathcal{D}F = F_x \nu + \frac{1}{2}\mathrm{tr}(\eta^\top F_{xx}\eta)$.

(D)   Solve for the term structure of interest rates in the special case of $N = 1$ and:

$$u(y) = \frac{y^{(\alpha+1)} - 1}{\alpha + 1}, \quad \alpha \in (-1, 0),$$

$$\nu(x) = Ax, \qquad A \in \mathbb{R}$$

$$\eta(x) = D, \qquad D \in \mathbb{R}^d$$

$$f(x) = e^{bx}, \qquad b \in \mathbb{R}.$$

Also, solve for the current equilibrium short-rate process r in this economy.

(E)   For this last part, a further extension of the Black-Scholes model, we do not take the parametric assumptions of part (D). Suppose the short-rate process is given by $r_t = R(X_t)$ for all t, where $R : \mathbb{R}^N \to \mathbb{R}$, and that the security-price process is given by $S_t = S(X_t)$ for all t, for some twice continuously differentiable function $S : \mathbb{R}^N \to \mathbb{R}^N$. Give a PDE for the arbitrage-free value of an additional security defined by a dividend process $\{h(X_t) : t \geq 0\}$, where $h : \mathbb{R}^N \to \mathbb{R}$ is bounded and measurable. In particular, state regularity conditions implying redundancy of this additional security. Finally, give a solution to the PDE you suggest, in the form of an expectation, and provide the corresponding regularity conditions.

9.6   This exercise is to verify that the CIR model of the term structure given in Section 9J can be embedded in a stock-market equilibrium with decentralized production decisions. The objective is to construct an equilibrium $[(S, \pi), \delta, (c, \theta)]$ of the following form:

(a) δ is the optimal real output rate process of a firm controlling the capital stock production process and maximizing its share price;

(b) π is a state-price deflator;

(c) S is the real stock-price process of the firm that is taken as given by the agent, and is equal to the share-price process generated as the market value of the firm's solution to the problem of maximizing its real market value, given the state-price deflator π;

(d) $(c_t, \theta_t) = (\delta_t, 1)$ solves the agent's optimal consumption and trading strategy problem, given (S, δ) as the price process and real dividend-rate process of the firm.

(A)   Formally define a stochastic equilibrium consistent with the loose description just given. In particular, state precisely the agent's problem and the firm's problem.

(B)   In the setting of Exercise 8.4, show that the (real) stock-price process $S = K$, the capital-stock process of (41), and the dividend rate δ given by (42) are consistent with equilibrium, in terms of first order conditions for optimality in the appropriate Bellman equations for both the firm and the agent. Add any technical regularity conditions that you find appropriate. Hint: Be careful about real versus nominal values.

9.7   Given the Markov shock process X of (54) and an equilibrium characterized by Theorem 9G and its corollary, suppose that the aggregate endowment process e is defined by $e_t = g(X_t, t)$, where $g \in C^{2,1}(\mathbb{R}^N \times [0, T])$. Express a state-price deflator p and the short rate r in the form $p_t = \varphi(X_t, t)$ and $r_t = R(X_t, t)$, for measurable functions g and R on $\mathbb{R}^N \times [0, T]$. Show that, under technical conditions, the density process ξ of an equivalent martingale measure Q for real security prices is defined by $\xi_t = \exp(\int_0^t r_s \, ds) p_t$. Show that $d\xi_t = -\xi_t \Theta(X_t, t) \, dB_t$ for some $\mathbb{R}^d$-valued function Θ on $\mathbb{R}^N \times [0, T]$. Show that there is a standard Brownian motion $\hat{B}$ in $\mathbb{R}^d$ under Q such that X solves an SDE of the form

$$dX_t = \alpha(X_t, t) \, dt + \eta(X_t, t) \, d\hat{B}_t,$$

and state the function α. Show that, under technical regularity conditions, the price of a security promising a real dividend-rate process of the form $\{h(X_t, t) : t \in [0, T]\}$ is given as the solution to a PDE of the Cauchy type examined in Appendix E. State the PDE.

Notes

The basic framework of this section is standard. Existence of Arrow-Debreu equilibria in infinite-dimensional settings similar to the one treated in this chapter was first shown by Bewley (1972). The first result that applies directly to the case of square-integrable functions, treated here, is due to Mas-Colell (1986a). Recent developments are surveyed by Mas-Colell and

Zame (1990). On Pareto optimality in infinite-dimensional economies, see Mas-Colell (1986b).

Lemma 9C is proved as follows. First, L is a Banach lattice under the norm

$$c \mapsto \left[E \left(\int_0^T c_t^2 \, dt \right) \right]^{1/2}$$

Any increasing linear function $\Pi : L \to \mathbb{R}$ on a Banach lattice L is continuous, as shown, for example, by Aliprantis and Burkinshaw (1985). Under the given norm, L is a Hilbert space with inner product $(p, c) \mapsto E(\int_0^T p_t c_t \, dt)$. Since Π is continuous, there is a unique π in L such that Π has the representation $\Pi(c) = E(\int_0^T \pi_t c_t \, dt)$, based on the same reasoning used in Exercise 1.17. Since Π is strictly increasing, π is strictly positive.

The seminal continuous-time equilibrium asset pricing model is due to Merton (1973a). Section 9C is standard in general equilibrium theory. Section 9D is based on Duffie and Huang (1985) and Duffie (1986). Theorem 9G is from Duffie and Zame (1989). Other proofs of essentially the same result are given by Araujo and Monteiro (1989), Karatzas, Lakner, Lehoczky, and Shreve (1990), Dana and Pontier (1990), and Dana (1990), who studies the uniqueness of equilibria. An extension showing existence with recursive utility is given in an appendix of Duffie and Skiadas (1990). A sense in which this formulation is extremely restrictive is given in Araujo and Monteiro (1987). The dynamic spanning condition and the assumption that securities are defined in nominal terms can be weakened, as explained by Duffie and Zame (1989). The remainder of Section 9G is based on Huang (1987). Section 9H presents Breeden's (1979) consumption-based capital asset pricing model, whose discrete-time antecedent is Rubinstein (1976). The line of proof shown here, however, is from Duffie and Zame (1989). Section 9I is condensed from Cox, Ingersoll, and Ross (1985a).

Karatzas, Lehoczky, and Shreve (1992) show the existence of equilibrium with *singular price* behavior, meaning that the state-price deflator is not an Ito process. This implies, for example, that there is no short-rate process. Asset pricing examples with nonadditive utility models are given by Sundaresan (1989) and Constantinides (1990a), who studied habit-formation utility, and by Duffie and Epstein (1992) and Ma (1991b), who give examples with recursive utility. See also Campbell (1990).

Section 9J contains Breeden's consumption-based CAPM once again, this time without complete markets. The general line of proof is from Grossman and Shiller (1982) and Back (1991a); the latter has a more general information filtration. For further development of this model, see Cornell (1981) and Madan (1988). Breeden's original proof is based on the assumed existence of smooth solutions to each agent's value function for stochastic control in a Markov setting. Breeden follows Merton (1973a) in this regard. The impact of transactions costs on the consumption-based CAPM is studied by Grossman and Laroque (1989). Related results are found in Black (1990) and Heston (1990a). For an empirical analysis of the consumption-based CAPM, see Breeden, Gibbons, and Litzenberger (1989). For empirical analysis of the Cox, Ingersoll, and Ross term-structure model, see Gibbons and Ramaswamy (1986) and Pearson and Sun (1989). A discrete-time analogue of the Cox, Ingersoll, and Ross term-structure model is due to Gibbons and Sun (1986). For further analysis in a Markov setting, see Cox, Ingersoll, and Ross (1985a) and Breeden (1986).

Related models with incomplete or asymmetric information are provided by Dothan and Feldman (1986), Gennotte (1984), and J. Wang (1989).

Dumas (1989) works out an explicit two-agent equilibrium model with additive utility. Chamberlain (1988) gives sufficient conditions for the Capital Asset Pricing Model, based on the market portfolio. Duffie and Epstein (1992) show that homothetic recursive utility generates a family of two-factor asset pricing models, one factor being the market portfolio, the other being aggregate consumption.

Exercise 9.3 is based partly on Heston (1988b). Part (D) of Exercise 9.5 is from Hansen and Singleton (1986). Exercise 9.7 is based on Cox, Ingersoll, and Ross (1985b), Huang (1987), and Duffie and Zame (1989).

10

Numerical Methods

THIS CHAPTER REVIEWS three numerical approaches to pricing securities in a continuous-time setting: "binomial" approximation, Monte Carlo simulation, and finite-difference solution of the associated partial differential equation.

A. Central Limit Theorems

It is well known that a normal random variable can be represented as the limit of normalized sums of $i.i.d.$ binomial random variables. This idea, a version of the Central Limit Theorem, leads to the characterization given in this section of the Black-Scholes option-pricing formula (equation [5.11]) as the limit of the binomial option pricing formula (equation [2.16]), letting the number of trading periods per unit of time go to infinity. Aside from making an interesting connection between the discrete- and continuous-time settings, this also suggests a numerical recipe for calculating continuous-time arbitrage-free derivative security prices.

A sequence $\{X_n\}$ of random variables *converges in distribution* to a random variable X, denoted $X_n \Rightarrow X$, if, for any bounded continuous function $f : \mathbb{R} \to \mathbb{R}$, we have $E[f(X_n)] \to E[f(X)]$. We could take X and each of $X_1, X_2, \ldots$ to be defined on different probability spaces. A standard version of the Central Limit Theorem reads along the following lines. A random variable is *standard normal* if it has the standard normal cumulative distribution function.

Central Limit Theorem. *Suppose $Y_1, Y_2, \ldots$ is a sequence of independent and identically distributed random variables on a probability space, each with expected value*

μ and finite variance $\sigma^2 > 0$. For each n, let $Z_n = Y_1 + \cdots + Y_n$. Then, for any standard normal random variable X,

$$\frac{Z_n - n\mu}{\sigma\sqrt{n}} \Rightarrow X.$$

A proof can be found in any good book on probability; several are cited in the Notes. This version of the Central Limit Theorem is not general enough to handle convergence of the binomial option-pricing formula of Exercise 2.1 to the Black-Scholes formula. In order to set up the required extension, we say that a collection

$$Y = \{Y_1^n, Y_2^n, \ldots, Y_{k(n)}^n : n \in \{1, 2, \ldots\}\},$$

with $k(n) \to \infty$, is a *triangular array* if, for each n, $Y_1^n, \ldots, Y_{k(n)}^n$ are independently distributed random variables on some probability space. The following version of the Central Limit Theorem is sufficient for our purposes here, and can be proved as an easy corollary of the Lindeberg-Feller Central Limit Theorem given in Appendix C.

Proposition. *Suppose Y is a triangular array of random variables such that $Y_1^n, \ldots,$ $Y_{k(n)}^n$ are bounded in absolute value by a constant y_n, with $y_n \to 0$. Let $Z_n = Y_1^n + \cdots + Y_{k(n)}^n$. If $E(Z_n) \to \mu$ and $\mathrm{var}(Z_n) \to \sigma^2 > 0$, then Z_n converges in distribution to a normally distributed random variable with mean μ and variance σ^2.*

B. Convergence from Binomial to Black-Scholes

Recall the setup from Section 5E of the Black-Scholes model for pricing a European put option:

- a probability space on which there is a standard Brownian motion B;
- a stock-price process S defined by $S_t = x \exp(\alpha t + \sigma B_t)$ and a bond-price process β defined by $\beta_t = \beta_0 e^{rt}$, for constants α, σ, and r;
- the put-option payoff $(K - S_T)^+$, defined by the expiration time T and exercise price K.

The solution (5.26) of the arbitrage-free put price is

$$P(x, 0) = E\left[e^{-rT}\left(K - xe^{X_T}\right)^+\right], \tag{1}$$

where $X_T = (r - \sigma^2/2)T + \sigma B_T$. We can treat X_t as the cumulative continuously compounding return on the stock up to time t, after "risk-neutralizing" the probability measure. This is formalized in Chapter 6, but is apparent in the Feynman-Kac approach.

In the binomial setting of Exercise 2.1, the stock has a binomial return in each period with outcomes D and $U > D$. The riskless bond has a return $R \in \{D, U\}$ in each period. The risk-neutralized probabilistic representation of the put price is given, as with the call-price formula (2.16), by

$$P_0^T = E\left[R^{-T}(K - xe^\rho)^+\right], \tag{2}$$

where $\rho = Y_1 + \cdots + Y_T$, and where $Y_1, \ldots, Y_T$ are *i.i.d.* binomial random variables having outcomes $u = \log(U)$ and $d = \log(D)$ with respective risk-neutral probabilities $p = (R - D)/(U - D)$ and $1 - p$. We can calibrate the binomial stock returns U and D, as well as the bond return R, to our model of the continuous-time stock- and bond-price processes as follows. Obviously, we set the bond return at $R = e^r$. The stock returns U and D require more thought. To maintain some probabilistic similarity between the continuous-time and binomial models, we will explictly model an exogenously given probability q of an up-return U, and choose U and D so that the mean and standard deviation of the continuously compounding stock returns are the same in the two settings. The probability q should not be confused with the "risk-neutralized" probability p constructed from the returns. Let us arbitrarily choose $q = 0.50$, and then select $u = \mu + \sigma$ and $d = \mu - \sigma$. With this, the continuously compounding stock returns in both models have mean μ and variance σ^2 per unit of time. Many other combinations of q, u, and d would work.

Let "Model n" refer to the binomial model with n trading periods per unit of time and with returns U_n, D_n, and R_n per trading period. We will allow n to approach infinity, always calibrating, as above, the binomial returns to the continuous-time returns. In order to maintain the mean and variance of total returns per unit of time at the continuously compounding levels μ and σ^2 respectively, we reset the per-trading-period continuously compounding returns $u_n = \log(U_n)$ and $d_n = \log(D_n)$ to $u_n = \mu/n + \sigma/\sqrt{n}$ and $d_n = \mu/n - \sigma/\sqrt{n}$. We leave q_n fixed at 0.50. With *i.i.d.* returns, the per-unit-of-time mean and variance of the continuously compounding returns are then, respectively,

$$n\left[q_n u_n + (1 - q_n)d_n\right] = \mu$$

and

$$nq_n(1 - q_n)(u_n - d_n)^2 = \sigma^2,$$

precisely as required. The per-trading-period return on the bond is $R_n = e^{r/n}$. The number of trading periods required for passage of T units of calendar time is Tn. We rewrite the put-price formula (2) for Model n as

$$P(n) = E\left(e^{-rT}\left[K - xe^{\rho(n)}\right]^+\right), \tag{3}$$

where $\rho(n) = Y_1^n + \cdots + Y_{Tn}^n$ and where $Y_1^n, \ldots, Y_{Tn}^n$ are *i.i.d.* binomial with outcomes u_n and d_n at respective risk-neutralized probabilities of p_n and $1 - p_n$, where

$$p_n = \frac{R_n - D_n}{U_n - D_n}. \tag{4}$$

The per-unit-of-time risk-neutralized mean and variance of returns are, respectively,

$$M_n = n\left[p_n u_n + (1 - p_n)d_n\right]$$

and

$$V_n = np_n(1 - p_n)(u_n - d_n)^2.$$

An exercise shows that $M_n \to r - \sigma^2/2$ and $V_n \to \sigma^2$. Thus, in risk-neutral terms, $E[\rho(nT)] \to (r - \sigma^2/2)T$ and $\text{var}[\rho(nT)] \to \sigma^2 T$. Because u_n and d_n each converge to zero, the version of the Central Limit Theorem given by Proposition 10A implies that $\rho(n) \Rightarrow X_T$. Since the function $h : \mathbb{R} \to \mathbb{R}$ defined by $h(y) = (K - xe^y)^+$ is bounded and continuous, the binomial put price $P(n)$ converges to the Black-Scholes put price $P(x, 0)$ given in equation (1) as the number n of trading intervals per unit of time goes to infinity.

The only properties of the put payoff function h used above are its continuity and its boundedness. The same arguments therefore allow one to conclude that, for any bounded continuous g, the arbitrage-free price of a claim to $g(S_{Tn})$ in the binomial setting with n trading periods per unit of time converges to the corresponding continuous-time arbitrage-free price $E[e^{-rT}g(Z_T)]$ obtained from the Feynman-Kac formula, where $Z_T = x\exp[(r - \sigma^2/2)T + \sigma B_T]$.

By put-call parity, the binomial call-pricing formula converges to the Black-Scholes call-pricing formula in the same sense. That is, put-call parity implies both that

$$C_n = x + P_n - e^{-rT}K$$

and that

$$C(x, 0) = x + P(x, 0) - e^{-rT}K.$$

Since $P_n \to P(x, 0)$, we have $C_n \to C(x, 0)$.

C. Binomial Convergence for Unbounded Derivative Payoffs

It may now be apparent why we began with the case of put options and only then treated calls by put-call parity. The call payoff function $x \mapsto (e^x - K)^+$ is not bounded! By a slightly more tedious argument, we could have shown convergence for the call-price formula directly, without applying put-call parity, by using the following results. This section is not essential and can be skipped on a first reading. Uniformly integrable random variables are defined in Appendix C.

Continuous Mapping Theorem. *Suppose* $X_n \Rightarrow X$ *and* g *is a continuous function. Then* $g(X_n) \Rightarrow g(X)$.

Proposition. *Suppose* $X_n \Rightarrow X$. *If* $\{X_n\}$ *is uniformly integrable, then* $E(X_n) \to E(X)$. *Conversely, if* $X, X_1, X_2, \ldots$ *are non-negative and have finite expectations with* $E(X_n) \to E(X)$, *then* $\{X_n\}$ *is uniformly integrable.*

It can be shown as an exercise that, for $\rho(n)$ as defined in the previous section, the sequence of call payoffs $\{[xe^{\rho(n)} - K]^+\}$ is uniformly integrable, from which the above two results directly imply convergence of the binomial call-price formula to the Black-Scholes formula.

More generally, consider any derivative security with payoff function g such that $\{V_n\}$ is uniformly integrable when defined by $V_n = g[xe^{\rho(n)}]$. Suppose, moreover, that g is continuous and satisfies a polynomial growth condition, as defined in Appendix E, so that the Feynman-Kac pricing formula (5.26) applies. We then have convergence of the binomial price $E(e^{-rT}V_n)$ to the continuous-time price $E[e^{-rT}g(Z_T)]$, where $Z_T = x \exp[(r - \sigma^2/2)T + \sigma B_T]$.

D. Discretization of Asset Price Processes

The Feynman-Kac solution (5.40) for derivative asset prices is typically difficult to calculate explicitly. This section and the following two address the numerical solution of (5.40) by Monte Carlo simulation of a discrete-time approximation of the stochastic differential equation (5.41).

We begin with a probability space on which is defined a standard Brownian motion B in $\mathbb{R}^d$, along with its standard filtration. The SDE to be approximated is assumed to be of the form

$$dX_t = a(X_t, t)\, dt + b(X_t, t)\, dB_t; \quad X_0 = x \in \mathbb{R}^N, \tag{6}$$

where $a : \mathbb{R}^N \times [0, \infty) \to \mathbb{R}^N$ and $b : \mathbb{R}^N \times [0, \infty) \to \mathbb{R}^{N \times d}$ have, for any k, bounded k-th derivatives. Referring to Appendix D, this is more than

enough to ensure the existence of a unique Ito process X in $\mathbb{R}^N$ satisfying (6).
A natural scheme for approximating (6) is the *Euler approximation*: For n
periods per unit of time, let $\hat{X}^n$ be the discrete-time $\mathbb{R}^N$-valued process
defined on some (possibly different) probability space $(\Omega, \mathcal{F}, P)$ by

$$\hat{X}^n_{k+1} - \hat{X}^n_k = \frac{1}{n} a\left(\hat{X}^n_k, \frac{k}{n}\right) + \frac{1}{\sqrt{n}} b\left(\hat{X}^n_k, \frac{k}{n}\right) \epsilon_{k+1}; \quad \hat{X}^n_0 = x, \quad (7)$$

where $\epsilon_1, \epsilon_2, \ldots$ is an *i.i.d.* sequence of standard normal vectors valued in
$\mathbb{R}^d$. This is known as the Euler approximation of (6).

Our objective is to approximate an expression of the form $E[f(X_T)]$,
where T is a fixed time, X is the solution of (6), and $f : \mathbb{R}^N \to \mathbb{R}$ satisfies a
polynomial growth condition (defined in Appendix E) and has derivatives
of any order. Our tentative approximation is $f_n = E[f(\hat{X}^n_{Tn})]$. The issue
is: How good is this approximation? Let $e_n = E[f(X_T)] - f_n$ denote the
approximation error. It can be shown that $e_n \to 0$. Even better, we can
given an *order of convergence*. A sequence $\{y_n\}$ has *order-k convergence* if $y_n n^k$ is
bounded in n. The Euler approximation is said to be a *first order scheme* in that
e_n has order-1 convergence. More precisely, there is a constant C such that
$e_n + C/n$ has order-2 convergence. The error coefficient C may be positive
or negative, and gives a notion of bias in the approximation. Although C
is usually unknown, it turns out that C can itself be approximated to first
order by $C_n = 2(f_n - f_{2n})$.

The Notes give a source for these properties of the Euler approximation
as well as references to more complicated schemes with order-2 error. For
instance, with $N = 1$ and under technical conditions, an order-2 scheme is
given by the *Milshtein approximation*. Given μ and σ in $C^2(\mathbb{R})$ such that, for
all t, we have $a(x, t) = \mu(x)$ and $b(x, t) = \sigma(x)$, the Milshtein approximation
is given by

$$\begin{aligned}
\hat{X}^n_{k+1} - \hat{X}^n_k &= \frac{1}{n}\left[\mu\left(\hat{X}^n_k\right) - \frac{1}{2}\sigma\left(\hat{X}^n_k\right)\sigma'\left(\hat{X}^n_k\right)\right] \\
&\quad + \frac{1}{\sqrt{n}}\sigma\left(\hat{X}^n_k\right)\epsilon_{k+1} + \frac{1}{2n}\sigma\left(\hat{X}^n_k\right)\sigma'\left(\hat{X}^n_k\right)\epsilon^2_{k+1} \qquad (8) \\
&\quad + \frac{1}{n^{3/2}}\nu\left(\hat{X}^n_k\right)\epsilon_{k+1} + \frac{1}{n^2}\eta\left(\hat{X}^n_k\right),
\end{aligned}$$

where

$$\nu(x) = \frac{1}{2}\mu(x)\sigma'(x) + \frac{1}{2}\mu'(x)\sigma(x) + \frac{1}{4}\sigma(x)^2\sigma''(x)$$

and

$$\eta(x) = \frac{1}{2}\mu(x)\mu'(x) + \frac{1}{4}\mu''(x)\sigma(x)^2.$$

E. Large Deviations of Monte Carlo Asset Price Simulations

Of course, we do not generally know even the approximation $E[f(\hat{X}^n_{Tn})]$, but we can in turn estimate this quantity by Monte Carlo simulation. We will use the law of large numbers: If $Y_1, Y_2, \ldots$ is an *i.i.d.* sequence of random variables of finite expectations, then $(Y_1 + \cdots + Y_k)/k \to E(Y_1)$ almost surely. The rate of convergence can be checked from the following result based on the *moment-generating function* φ of Y_i, defined by $\varphi(\theta) = E[\exp(\theta Y_i)]$.

Large Deviations Theorem. *Suppose $\theta > 0$ is such that $\varphi(\theta) < \infty$. Then*

$$p_k \equiv P\left[\frac{Y_1 + \cdots + Y_k}{k} - E(Y_1) \geq \delta\right] \leq e^{-k\gamma(\theta)},$$

where $\gamma(\theta) = \delta\theta - \log[\varphi(\theta)]$. Moreover, θ can be chosen so that $\gamma(\theta) > 0$, implying that p_k converges exponentially to 0.

In order to apply this result to the estimation of $E[f(\hat{X}^n_{Tn})]$, let $Y_1 = f(\hat{X}^n_{Tn})$ be defined as above. This is the first simulation of the random variable whose mean is to be computed. Let Y_2 be defined in the same manner, with the exception that, for each j, we substitute ϵ_{j+Tn} for ϵ_j. Let Y_3 be defined likewise, substituting ϵ_{j+2Tn} everywhere for ϵ_j, and so on. Since $\epsilon_1, \epsilon_2, \ldots$ is *i.i.d.*, the sequence $Y_1, Y_2, \ldots$ qualifies for an application of the law of large numbers, leaving

$$f(n, k) \equiv \frac{Y_1 + \cdots + Y_k}{k} \to E\left[f\left(\hat{X}^n_{Tn}\right)\right] \quad a.s. \tag{9}$$

In practice, one often substitutes *pseudo-random* numbers for $\{\epsilon_j\}$, using some deterministic scheme. There are a number of methods, called *variance reduction techniques*, that can improve the convergence properties of Monte Carlo simulation. For example, our first approach above was to simulate Y_i with the disturbance sequence

$$D_i \equiv \left(\epsilon_{1+Tn(i-1)}, \epsilon_{2+Tn(i-1)}, \epsilon_{3+Tn(i-1)}, \ldots, \epsilon_{Tni}\right).$$

Instead, one can typically improve the convergence properties of the simulation by substituting, for even-numbered i, the disturbance sequence $-D_{i-1}$.

F. Computation Time and Error Size

At this point, (9) gives us an approximation $f(n, k)$ of $E[f(X_T)]$ based on a discrete-time approximation $\hat{X}^n$ of the Ito process X with n periods per unit of time, and with k simulations of the process $\hat{X}^n$. The number of additions required to compute $f(n, k)$ is roughly proportional to $N^2 Tnk$. Since N and T are presumably fixed for a given problem, we are concerned about the size of nk, given limited computation time. We are also concerned with the error size $e(n, k) = |f(n, k) - E[f(X_T)]|$. Suppose that our objective is to have an error of size δ or larger with probability no greater than p. That is, we want to choose n and k so that $P[e(n, k) > \delta] \leq p$. Assume that we are given an SDE approximation with error of order m and that the moment-generating function φ_n of $f(\hat{X}^n_{Tn})$ has some $\theta > 0$ with $\varphi_n(\theta) < \infty$. Then, for some $\bar{n}$ and for any $n \geq \bar{n}$, the Large Deviations Theorem implies that

$$P[e(n, k) > \delta] \leq P\left(|f(n, k) - f_n| + |f_n - E[f(X_T)]| > \delta\right)$$

$$\leq P\left[|f(n, k) - f_n| + \frac{C}{n^m} > \delta\right] \tag{10}$$

$$\leq e^{-k\Gamma(\theta, n)},$$

where k is a constant depending on the SDE approximation and

$$\Gamma(\theta, n) = \left(\delta - \frac{C}{n^m}\right)\theta - \log \varphi_n(\theta).$$

This upper bound on the error probability can be sharpened by maximizing $\Gamma(\theta, n)$ with respect to θ. For rough calculation purposes, if we are willing to replace φ_n with the moment-generating function φ of $f(X_T)$ and are willing to make some technical regularity assumptions, the first order condition for this maximization is

$$\text{cov}[\exp(\theta Y^*), Y^*] = \delta - \frac{C}{n^m},$$

where $Y^* = f(X_T)$.

Relation (10) clarifies the tradeoff between simulation size k and the number n of time steps per unit of time in discretizing the SDE. In order to keep the upper bound $\exp[-k\Gamma(\theta, n)]$ under the maximum allowable probability p of an error of at least δ, one would have to choose a simulation size of at least

$$k^*(n) = \frac{-\log p}{(\delta - K/n^m)\theta - \log \varphi_n(\theta)}. \tag{11}$$

Since the number of computations was judged to be proportional to nk, one could even go on to minimize $nk^*(n)$ with respect to n, solve for n^*, and consider choosing $n = n^*$ and $k = k^*(n^*)$. Again assuming for rough calculation purposes that one can get a good approximation by replacing φ_n with φ, the first order condition for n^* (treated as a real number) is easy to calculate. The Notes cite an alternative approach to dealing with this tradeoff between finer time discretization and more simulation.

G. Estimation of the Feynman-Kac Pricing Solution

Consider the solution given by (5.40) for the price $C(x,0)$ of a derivative asset paying $g(S_T)$ at time T, where S is defined by (5.34) and where the short rate at time t is given by $r(S_t, t)$. To repeat, we have

$$C(x,0) = E[Y_T g(Z_T)], \qquad (12)$$

where $Y_t = \exp[\int_0^t -r(Z_s, s) \, ds]$ and where

$$dZ_t = r(Z_t, t) Z_t \, dt + \sigma(Z_t, t) \, dB_t; \quad Z_0 = x.$$

Since $dY_t = -r(Z_t, t) Y_t \, dt$, the $\mathbb{R}^{N+1}$-valued process X defined by $X_t = (Y_t, Z_t)$ solves an SDE of the same form as (6). We assume that the associated coefficient functions a and b satisfy the technical regularity conditions imposed with (6) of Section 10D. This calls for r to be bounded with bounded derivatives of every order and for σ to have bounded derivatives of every order. The Feynman-Kac solution (12) can be written in the form $E[f(X_T)]$, where $f : \mathbb{R}^{N+1} \to \mathbb{R}$ is defined by $f(y, z_1, \ldots, z_N) = yg(z_1, \ldots, z_N)$. If g has derivatives of every order and satisfies a polynomial growth condition, then the derivative asset price $C(x,0)$ can be approximated as suggested in the previous section.

The case of options requires special handling. The payoff function g of a call, defined by $g(x) = (x - K)^+$, is not even once differentiable. The "kink" at K is the only issue to overcome. The function g can be satisfactorily approximated by g_α, where, for any $\alpha > 0$,

$$g_\alpha(x) = \frac{x - K + \sqrt{(x - K)^2 + \alpha}}{2}. \qquad (13)$$

Indeed, g_α has continuous derivatives of any order, satisfies a growth condition, and converges uniformly and monotonically from above to g as $\alpha \to 0$. The Dominated Convergence Theorem therefore implies that the associated Feynman-Kac solution also converges to $C(x,0)$ as $\alpha \to 0$.

H. Finite-Difference Methods

This section reviews a simple finite-difference method for the PDE associated
with asset prices. After reviewing the basic idea, we will work out an example
based on the Cox-Ingersoll-Ross model of the term structure.

We will treat the *Cauchy problem*: Given real-valued functions r, g, h, μ,
and σ on $\mathbb{R} \times [0, T]$, find a function f in $C^{2,1}(\mathbb{R} \times [0, T))$ solving

$$\mathcal{D}f(x, t) - r(x, t)f(x, t) + h(x, t) = 0, \quad (x, t) \in \mathbb{R} \times [0, T), \qquad (14)$$

with boundary condition

$$f(x, T) = g(x, T), \quad x \in \mathbb{R}, \qquad (15)$$

where

$$\mathcal{D}f(x, t) = f_t(x, t) + f_x(x, t)\mu(x, t) + \frac{1}{2}\sigma(x, t)^2 f_{xx}(x, t).$$

As we have seen in Chapter 5, we can interpret the solution f to (14)–(15) as
the arbitrage-free market value of a security that promises the dividend rate
$h(x, t)$ at time t when the state is x, assuming that the security has a terminal
value of $g(x, T)$ at time T when the state is x. The short rate is $r(x, t)$ at time
t when the state is x, and the "primitive" securities have prices and dividends
determining the functions μ and σ in the manner described in Chapter 5.
Alternatively, μ and σ could be determined directly from the equilibrium
approach shown in Chapter 9 (see Exercise 9.7). Regularity conditions
that ensure the existence and uniqueness of solutions are treated in Appendix E, where probabilistic Feynman-Kac solutions are also treated.

The basic idea of the finite-difference method for solving (14)–(15) is
to choose a *grid*

$$\{(x_i, t_j) : i \in \{1, \ldots, N\}, \ j \in \{1, \ldots, M\}\} \subset \mathbb{R} \times [0, T],$$

and to find an approximate solution of (14)–(15) in the form of an $N \times M$
matrix F whose (i, j)-element F_{ij} is to be an approximation of $f(x_i, t_j)$. We
always take $t_1 = 0$ and $t_M = T$. We take constants Δx and Δt to define the
mesh sizes of the grid, so that $x_i - x_{i-1} = \Delta x$ for all $i > 1$ and $t_j - t_{j-1} = \Delta t$
for all $j > 1$, as depicted in Figure 10.1. In principle, increasing the number
N of space points or $M = T/\Delta t$ of time points increases the accuracy of the
approximation, although the convergence and stability properties of finite-
difference methods can be a delicate issue. Various finite-difference methods could be suitable for the Cauchy problem, depending on the properties
of μ, σ, and r. We will merely describe one of these, sometimes known as the

Crank-Nicholson method, which has reasonable properties. We leave a characterization of the accuracy and stability of this and other finite-difference schemes to sources cited in the Notes.

The basis of the Crank-Nicholson method is the following approximation of the derivatives of f given F:

$$f_t(x_i, t_j) \sim \frac{F_{i,j+1} - F_{ij}}{\Delta t}$$

$$f_x(x_i, t_j) \sim \frac{F_{i+1,j+1} - F_{i-1,j+1} + F_{i+1,j} - F_{i-1,j}}{4\Delta x}$$

$$f_{xx}(x_i, t_j) \sim \frac{F_{i+1,j+1} - 2F_{i,j+1} + F_{i-1,j+1} + F_{i+1,j} - 2F_{ij} + F_{i-1,j}}{2(\Delta x)^2}.$$

Substituting these approximations, (14) is replaced at (x_i, t_j), for $1 < i < N$, by

$$a_{ij}F_{i-1,j} + b_{ij}F_{ij} + c_{ij}F_{i+1,j} = -a_{ij}F_{i-1,j+1} + \beta_{ij}F_{i,j+1} - c_{ij}F_{i+1,j+1} + e_{ij}, \quad (16)$$

where

$$a_{ij} = -\frac{\mu(x_i, t_j)}{4\Delta x} + \frac{\sigma(x_i, t_j)^2}{4(\Delta x)^2}$$

$$b_{ij} = -r(x_i, t_j) - \frac{1}{\Delta t} - \frac{\sigma(x_i, t_j)^2}{2(\Delta x)^2}$$

$$c_{ij} = \frac{\mu(x_i, t_j)}{4\Delta x} + \frac{\sigma(x_i, t_j)^2}{4(\Delta x)^2}$$

$$\beta_{ij} = -\frac{1}{\Delta t} + \frac{\sigma(x_i, t_j)^2}{2(\Delta x)^2}$$

$$e_{ij} = -h(x_i, t_j).$$

Of course, (16) is not defined at $i = 1$ or $i = N$, for which we substitute with equations of the form

$$b_{1j}F_{1j} + c_{1j}F_{2j} = d_{1j}; \qquad a_{Nj}F_{N-1,j} + b_{Nj}F_{Nj} = d_{Nj}, \quad (17)$$

for suitable coefficients b_{1j}, c_{1j}, d_{1j}, a_{Nj}, b_{Nj}, and d_{Nj} that may depend on the particular problem at hand.

We can combine (16) and (17) to obtain a backward difference equation for the columns $F_1, F_2, \ldots, F_M$ of F, given by

$$A_j F_j = d_j, \quad (18)$$

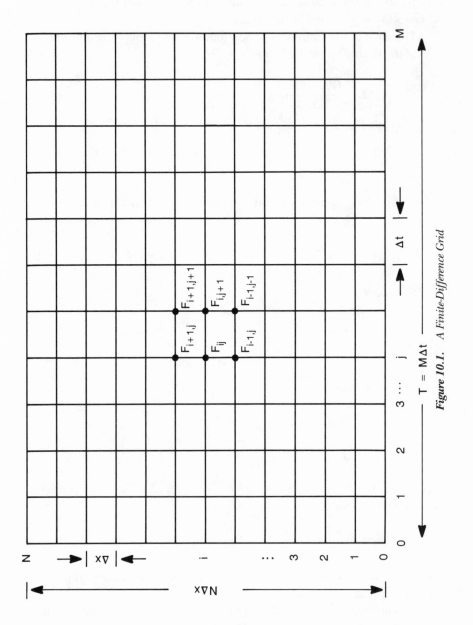

Figure 10.1. A Finite-Difference Grid

with terminal boundary condition

$$F_{iM} = g(x_i, T), \quad i \in \{1, \ldots, N\}, \tag{19}$$

where A_j is the *tridiagonal matrix* given by

$$A_j = \begin{pmatrix} b_{1j} & c_{1j} & 0 & 0 & 0 & \cdots & 0 \\ a_{2j} & b_{2j} & c_{2j} & 0 & 0 & \cdots & 0 \\ 0 & a_{3j} & b_{3j} & c_{3j} & 0 & \cdots & 0 \\ 0 & 0 & a_{4j} & b_{4j} & c_{4j} & \cdots & 0 \\ \vdots & & & & \ddots & & \vdots \\ 0 & \cdots & 0 & 0 & a_{N-1,j} & b_{N-1,j} & c_{N-1,j} \\ 0 & \cdots & 0 & 0 & 0 & a_{Nj} & b_{Nj} \end{pmatrix} \tag{20}$$

and where $d_j \in \mathbb{R}^N$ is the vector with i-th element

$$d_{ij} = -a_{ij}F_{i-1,j+1} + \beta_{ij}F_{i,j+1} - c_{ij}F_{i+1,j+1} + e_{ij}, \quad 1 < i < N. \tag{21}$$

Standard algorithms for solving linear equations of the tridiagonal form (18) can be found in off-the-shelf software packages. (One such package is indicated in the Notes.) Such algorithms exploit the special structure of A_j, avoiding a "brute-force" calculation of its inverse.

To summarize, the basic finite-difference algorithm (18)–(19) begins by fixing F_M according to the terminal boundary condition (19). Then d_{M-1} is computed from F_M by (21). Then F_{M-1} is computed by solving the tridiagonal equation (18) with $j = M - 1$. Next d_{M-2} is computed from F_{M-1}, (18) is solved for F_{M-2}, and so on, until F_1 is solved. If the functions μ, σ, and r do not depend on the time parameter, then the matrix A_j does not depend on j, and can be computed once before the backward difference solution is propagated. The boundary equations given by (17) usually call for special treatment.

Sources indicated in the Notes treat finite-difference methods for more than one state variable. The number of computations grows exponentially with the number of state variables, as opposed to the linear growth of computations with the Monte Carlo approach. The finite-difference approach can also be more difficult to implement, and its convergence is a more delicate issue. For problems with one or two state variables, however, it is typically the case that the finite-difference approach requires fewer computations in total than the Monte Carlo approach in order to obtain similar accuracy.

I. A Finite-Difference Term-Structure Example

Consider a model for the short rate r given by the stochastic differential equation

$$dr_t = \mu(r_t, t)\, dt + \sigma(r_t, t)\, d\hat{B}_t; \quad r_0 \geq 0, \tag{22}$$

where $\hat{B}$ is a standard Brownian motion under an equivalent martingale measure and where μ and σ satisfy regularity conditions.

Consider the problem of solving for the term structure. For a given time T and any $t < T$, we would like to solve for the price $f(x, t)$ of a security paying one unit of account at time T, when the current time is t and the current short rate is x. Since the short rate is itself the state variable x, and since there are no intermediate dividends to consider, the PDE (14) specializes to

$$\mathcal{D}f(x, t) - xf(x, t) = 0, \tag{23}$$

with boundary condition

$$f(x, T) = 1, \quad x \in \mathbb{R}. \tag{24}$$

If the functions μ and σ do not depend on t, we can also view $f(x, t)$ as the price at time zero for a unit bond maturing at $T - t$, so the solution of (23)–(24) characterizes the entire term structure up to maturity T.

It would be easy to implement the finite-difference algorithm (18)–(19) directly, although practical considerations often suggest a change of state variables. For example, suppose that μ and σ are continuous and that, for all t, we have $\mu(0, t) \geq 0$ and $\sigma(0, t) = 0$. Then the solution of (22) is non-negative, as indicated in the Notes to Chapter 7. In that case, we can treat the original state space as $[0, \infty)$, and consider a change of state variables, which has been used in the literature cited in the Notes, given by a function Y, with

$$Y(x) = \frac{1}{1 + \gamma x}, \quad x \in [0, \infty) \tag{25}$$

for some $\gamma > 0$. In other words, the short rate x corresponds to a new state $y = Y(x)$. The new state space is $(0, 1]$, which makes for natural boundary conditions, as follows. We can extend the range of Y to $[0, 1]$ by treating $Y(+\infty)$ as 0. A grid

$$\left\{ (y_i, t_j) : i \in \{1, \ldots, N\},\ j \in \{1, \ldots, M\} \right\} \subset [0, 1] \times [0, T],$$

with fixed mesh size Δy in the new state variable generates a solution with varying mesh size in the old short-rate state variable x, and with greater grid point concentration at lower interest-rate levels, in a fashion dictated by the coefficient γ. This is a desirable feature of this change of variables. We take $y_1 = 0$ and $y_N = 1$.

Inverting (25), we can write the short rate as a function of the new state variable given by

$$X(y) = \frac{1-y}{\gamma y}, \quad y \in (0, 1].$$

If we let $\hat{f}(y, t) = f[X(y), t]$ for all y and t, the PDE (23)–(24) may be written

$$\hat{\mathcal{D}}\hat{f}(y, t) - X(y)\hat{f}(y, t) = 0; \qquad \hat{f}(y, T) = 1, \tag{26}$$

where

$$\hat{\mathcal{D}}\hat{f}(y, t) = \hat{f}_y(y, t)\hat{\mu}(y, t) + \hat{f}_t(y, t) + \frac{1}{2}\hat{\sigma}(y, t)^2 \hat{f}_{yy}(y, t),$$

and where, using Ito's Lemma,

$$\hat{\mu}(y, t) = Y'[X(y)]\mu[X(y, t)] + \frac{1}{2}Y''[X(y)]\sigma[X(y), t]^2$$

$$\hat{\sigma}(y, t) = Y'[X(y)]\sigma[X(y), t].$$

The value equation (26) also applies for other well-behaved changes of variables given by some C^2 function Y with an inverse X. The Notes cite a source proposing a special change of variables with the property that $\hat{\sigma} \equiv 1$, which has computational advantages.

Solving for an approximation F_{ij} to the bond price $f[X(y_i), t_j]$ is now easily accomplished by the Crank-Nicholson solution (18)–(19) corresponding to (26). Throughout, we take $F_{1j} = 0$, corresponding to a zero bond price at an "infinite" interest rate. This determines the boundary equation of (17) for $i = 1$. For $i = N$, we use the fact that $\sigma(0, t) = 0$ and evaluate (26) at $y = 1$ ($x = 0$), leaving

$$\hat{f}_y(1, t)\hat{\mu}(1, t) + \hat{f}_t(1, t) = 0.$$

Replacing the usual Crank-Nicholson approximation for $\hat{f}_y(y_N, t_j)$ with the nonsymmetric approximation

$$\hat{f}_y(y_N, t_j) \sim \frac{F_{N,j} - F_{N-1,j}}{\Delta y},$$

the boundary equations (17) are then specified by the coefficients $b_{1j} = 1$, $c_{1j} = 0$, $d_{1j} = 0$, and

$$a_{Nj} = -\frac{\hat{\mu}(1)}{\Delta y}; \qquad b_{Nj} = -\frac{1}{\Delta t} + \frac{\hat{\mu}(1)}{\Delta y}; \qquad d_{Nj} = -\frac{1}{\Delta t}F_{N,j+1}. \tag{27}$$

Table 10.1. *Convergence of Finite-Difference Solution*

	Ten-Year Discount: Grid Density[a] n					Exact[b]
r_0	40	80	160	320	640	∞
0.05	41.45	41.19	41.06	40.99	40.96	40.93
0.10	33.45	33.16	33.03	32.96	32.92	32.89
0.15	27.00	26.71	26.57	26.50	26.46	26.43

[a]Crank-Nicholson method; n space points, n time points.
[b]Explicit solution.

For a coupon bond, or any other security promising lump-sum payments during $[0, T]$, the finite-difference equation (18) should be replaced by

$$F_j = F_{j+} + D_j; \qquad A_j F_{j+} = d_j, \tag{18'}$$

where D_j is the vector in $\mathbb{R}^N$ whose i-th element is the lump-sum dividend paid at time t_j if the state is between $x_i - \Delta x/2$ and $x_i + \Delta x/2$, so that we can treat F_{j+} as the ex-dividend approximation and F_j as the cum-dividend approximation. Linear approximations could be made in the obvious fashion if the lump-sum payments do not occur exactly as suggested in terms of the grid points.

Table 1 shows a computed finite-difference solution for the CIR example

$$\mu(x, t) = A(\bar{x} - x); \qquad \sigma(x, t) = C\sqrt{x}, \tag{28}$$

where A, $\bar{x}$, and C are positive constants. Computer code for this solution is given in Appendix G. For this numerical example, we took values of A, $\bar{x}$, and C that were estimated from U.S. Treasury bond price data in research cited in the Notes.

J. Finite-Difference Algorithms with Early Exercise Options

Suppose the security whose value is to be determined has an early exercise feature, so that at any time t the security can be exercised at a payoff of $g(x, t)$ if the state is x. For example, if the state x represents a primitive security price and the derivative security in question is an American put option at strike K, then $g(x, t) = (K - x)^+$ for all x and t, as discussed in Sections 7E and 7F. With an early exercise feature, it is natural to conjecture that the finite-difference algorithm given in the previous section can be adjusted merely by replacing the backward difference step (18) with

$$F_{ij} = \max \left[\hat{F}_{ij}, g(x_i, t_j) \right], \quad i \in \{1, \ldots, N\}, \tag{29}$$

where $\hat{F}_j$ is the vector in $\mathbb{R}^N$ solving $A_j \hat{F}_j = d_j$. In other words, at each step, the value of the American security is taken to be the larger of its exercised value and its unexercised value, in line with the anlaysis of Section 3G. Computer code for bond-option prices, based on this algorithm, is shown in Appendix G.

A largely unstudied issue is the convergence of this modified algorithm (29) to the solution of the associated continuous-time optimal stopping problem that is shown in Section 7E to characterize the American security's true arbitrage-free value. Some of the literature dealing with this issue is cited in the Notes.

K. The Numerical Solution of State Prices

Returning to the setting of the PDE (14)–(15) for security valuation, suppose there are many different securities to be valued, all based on the same functions r, μ, and σ. Only the functions h and g differ from security to security. In this case, given a grid $\{(x_i, t_j)\}$ defined by mesh sizes Δx and Δt, it makes sense to find an approximation Ψ_{ij} of the market value at time 0 of a security that pays $1/\Delta x$ units of account at time t_j in the event that the state is between $x_i + \Delta x/2$ and $x_i - \Delta x/2$. With this, it is reasonable to approximate the market value at time 0 of the security with payoff functions h for dividend rate and g for terminal value by

$$V(h, g) \equiv \Delta t \Delta x \sum_{j=1}^{M} \left[\sum_{i=1}^{N} \Psi_{ij} h(x_i, t_j) \right] + \Delta x \sum_{i=1}^{N} \Psi_{iM} g(x_i, T). \tag{30}$$

We will show how the same finite-difference approach used to calculate F in Section H can be modified to calculate the "approximate state prices" specified by Ψ. This is based on the fundamental solution, or "Green's function," of the PDE (14), reviewed in Appendix E. Under technical conditions, for each initial state x^* in $\mathbb{R}$, there is a function $\psi \in C^{2,1}(\mathbb{R} \times (0, T])$ with the following essentially equivalent properties:

(a) ψ satisfies

$$\mathcal{D}^*\psi(x, t) - r(x, t)\psi(x, t) = 0, \quad (x, t) \in \mathbb{R} \times (0, T], \qquad (31)$$

where

$$\mathcal{D}^*\psi(x, t) = -\psi_t(x, t) - \psi_x(x, t)\mu(x, t) + \frac{1}{2}\sigma(x, t)^2\psi_{xx}(x, t),$$

with an initial boundary condition requiring essentially that $\psi(\,\cdot\,, t)$ is the density of a measure that converges as $t \to 0$ to a probability measure ν with $\nu(\{x^*\}) = 1$; and

(b) for any (g, h) satisfying technical conditions, the solution f of the PDE (14)–(15) satisfies

$$f(x^*, 0) = \int_0^T \int_{-\infty}^{+\infty} \psi(x, t)h(x, t)\,dx\,dt + \int_{-\infty}^{+\infty} \psi(x, T)g(x, T)\,dx,$$
$$(32)$$

which is the integral analogous to the sum given by (30).

The PDE (31) is sometimes called the *Fokker-Planck equation,* or the forward Kolmogorov equation, to distinguish it from the backward Kolmogorov equation (15). For the case $r \equiv 0$, one can literally treat $\psi(\,\cdot\,, t)$ as the probability density of X_t, where X solves the underlying stochastic differential equation $dX_t = \mu(X_t, t)\,dt + \sigma(X_t, t)\,dB_t$, with $X_0 = x^*$. Much more can be said on this point, as indicated in sources cited in the Notes. The initial boundary condition for (31) stated above corresponds naturally to this interpretation of ψ. An explicit solution for ψ for the Cox-Ingersoll-Ross model (28) is given in Section 7I.

Now, given (32) and the equivalence between (a) and (b), in order to solve for $f(x^*, 0)$ we would like to approximate ψ with a finite-difference solution Ψ of the PDE (31). The same Crank-Nicholson approach can be applied, generating the forward difference equation for the columns $\Psi_1, \Psi_2, \ldots, \Psi_M$ of Ψ given by

$$A_j^*\Psi_j = d_j^*, \qquad (33)$$

with boundary condition for a given initial state $x_k = x^*$ of

$$\Psi_{k1} = \frac{1}{\Delta x}; \qquad \Psi_{i1} = 0, \quad i \neq k, \qquad (34)$$

where the tridiagonal matrix A_j^* and the vector d_j^* can be calculated for each j in the same manner as for the backward difference equation, using the Crank-Nicholson approximations for the derivatives of ψ in terms of Ψ. Specifically, we have

$$d_{ij}^* = -a_{ij}^* \Psi_{i-1,j-1} + \beta_{ij}^* \Psi_{i,j-1} - c_{ij}^* \Psi_{i+1,j-1} \tag{35}$$

and

$$A_j^* = \begin{pmatrix} b_{1j}^* & c_{1j}^* & 0 & 0 & 0 & \cdots & 0 \\ a_{2j}^* & b_{2j}^* & c_{2j}^* & 0 & 0 & \cdots & 0 \\ 0 & a_{3j}^* & b_{3j}^* & c_{3j}^* & 0 & \cdots & 0 \\ 0 & 0 & a_{4j}^* & b_{4j}^* & c_{4j}^* & \cdots & 0 \\ \vdots & & & & \ddots & & \vdots \\ 0 & \cdots & 0 & 0 & a_{N-1,j}^* & b_{N-1,j}^* & c_{N-1,j}^* \\ 0 & \cdots & 0 & 0 & 0 & a_{Nj}^* & b_{Nj}^* \end{pmatrix}, \tag{36}$$

where

$$a_{ij}^* = \frac{\mu(x_i, t_j)}{4\Delta x} + \frac{\sigma(x_i, t_j)^2}{4(\Delta x)^2}$$

$$b_{ij}^* = -\frac{1}{\Delta t} - \frac{\sigma(x_i, t_j)^2}{2(\Delta x)^2}$$

$$c_{ij}^* = -\frac{\mu(x_i, t_j)}{4\Delta x} + \frac{\sigma(x_i, t_j)^2}{4(\Delta x)^2}$$

$$\beta_{ij}^* = r(x_i, t_j) - \frac{1}{\Delta t} + \frac{\sigma(x_i, t_j)^2}{2(\Delta x)^2}.$$

The cases of $i = 1$ and $i = N$ again require special consideration.

One begins with the initial condition (34) for Ψ_1, and then propagates the solution forward, calculating Ψ_j at each stage by (33), given d_j^* in terms of Ψ_{j-1}.

Given Ψ, the approximate value of any security with dividend rate h and terminal value g is given by (30). If there is but a single security to value, equation (30) involves an extra set of computations that is not required with the backward approach. With many securities to value, however, the "forward approach" can involve significant savings in computations.

The astute reader will notice that we could have avoided the scaling factors Δx and $1/\Delta x$ in (30) and (34), respectively, in which case Ψ would not be an approximation for ψ, but rather for $\Delta x \psi$.

L. Numerical Solution of the Pricing Semi-Group

In the tridiagonal system (33)–(35), we have $d_j^* = C_j^* \Psi_{j-1}$ for the tridiagonal matrix

$$
C_j^* = \begin{pmatrix}
\beta_{1j}^* & -c_{1j}^* & 0 & 0 & 0 & \cdots & 0 \\
-a_{2j}^* & \beta_{2j}^* & -c_{2j}^* & 0 & 0 & \cdots & 0 \\
0 & -a_{3j}^* & \beta_{3j}^* & -c_{3j}^* & 0 & \cdots & 0 \\
0 & 0 & -a_{4j}^* & \beta_{4j}^* & -c_{4j}^* & \cdots & 0 \\
\vdots & & & & & \ddots & \vdots \\
0 & \cdots & 0 & 0 & -a_{N-1,j}^* & \beta_{N-1,j}^* & -c_{N-1,j}^* \\
0 & \cdots & 0 & 0 & 0 & -a_{Nj}^* & \beta_{Nj}^*
\end{pmatrix}.
$$

Thus (33) can be re-expressed in the recursive form

$$
\Psi_j = \Pi_j \Psi_{j-1}, \tag{37}
$$

where $\Pi_j = (A_j^*)^{-1} C_j^*$. (In practice, A_j^* can be usually inverted with an LU decomposition algorithm.) It follows that, for any j and $k \geq j$,

$$
\Psi_k = \Pi_{jk} \Psi_j, \tag{38}
$$

where

$$
\Pi_{jk} = \Pi_{j+1} \Pi_{j+2} \cdots \Pi_k, \tag{39}
$$

and where Π_{jj} denotes the identity matrix. The collection $\Pi = \{\Pi_{jk} : 1 \leq j \leq k \leq M\}$ of $N \times N$ matrices is a semi-group since it has the property: Whenever $j \leq k \leq m$, we have $\Pi_{jm} = \Pi_{jk} \Pi_{km}$. We will describe some of the useful properties of the semi-group Π.

First, for any initial state x_k in the grid, the associated approximate state-price matrix Ψ is given by

$$
\Psi_j = \Pi_{1j} \Psi_1, \tag{40}
$$

where Ψ_1 is given by (34). This means that, given the semi-group Π, the state prices associated with any given initial state can be obtained without repeated solution of the tridiagonal equations (37).

Second, given any payoff functions h and g, the $N \times M$ matrix F^* approximating the solution f to (14)–(15) is easily characterized as follows. For any j and $k \geq j$, we have

$$
F_j^* = \Pi_{jk} F_k^* + \sum_{m=j+1}^{k} \Pi_{jm} H_m, \tag{41}
$$

where H_j is the vector in $\mathbb{R}^N$ with $h(x_i, t_j)\Delta t$ as its i-th element. In particular, (41) applies with $k = M$ and the boundary condition $F_{iM}^* = g(x_i, T)$.

Although solving for the semi-group Π can be computationally intensive, there are obvious compensations. For the case in which μ, σ, and r do not depend on t, the matrices A_j^* and C_j^* do not depend on j, so there is but a single matrix $\overline{\Pi}$ to compute, with $\Pi_j = \overline{\Pi}$ for all j.

The close parallel between (41) and the Markov chain valuation equation (3.17) is not an accident. One can indeed approximate the solution X to the SDE $dX_t = \mu(X_t, t)\,dt + \sigma(X_t, t)\,dB_t$ with that of an N-state Markov chain having transition matrix $q^{(j)}$ at period $j \in \{1, \ldots, M\}$ given by

$$q_{ik}^{(j)} = [1 + r(x_i, t_j)\Delta t]\Pi_{ik}. \tag{42}$$

A source given in the Notes gives the sense of this approximation and further details on this connection between continuous and discrete pricing.

The parallel with the discrete-time case extends to the pricing of American securities. Using the semi-group approach, one can replace the backward difference equation (22) for the American security described in Section 10I with the backward equation

$$F_j^* = \max \left[\Pi_{j+1}(F_{j+1} + H_{j+1}), G_j \right], \tag{43}$$

where the maximum is taken element-wise and where G_j is the vector in $\mathbb{R}^N$ whose i-th element is $g(x_i, t_j)$. Equation (3.21) gives the exact discrete-time version of this American valuation algorithm. Since (43) is simpler than (29), computation of the semi-group Π may be worth the effort if one wishes to price many different American securities.

M. Numerically Fitting the Initial Term Structure

In the context of the term-structure model (22), there are many practical applications in which the initial term structure is given from market data in the form of vector p in $\mathbb{R}^N$, with p_j denoting the price at time 0 of a unit pure discount bond maturing at t_j. (In practice, p is often obtained from the prices of coupon bonds by spline methods that we do not describe here.) Since a model rarely coincides with reality, the functions μ and σ determining the risk-neutral behavior of the short rate will not, in general, generate a term structure consistent with the market data p. Suppose, however, that for each t, the functions $\mu(\,\cdot\,, t)$ and $\sigma(\,\cdot\,, t)$ depend on a free parameter $\lambda(t)$. One can imagine choosing the function λ in order to match the solution of the term structure to that given by p. For example, one could extend the CIR model (28) by replacing the constant $\bar{x}$ with $\lambda(t)$, and then choose $\lambda(t_1), \lambda(t_2), \ldots, \lambda(t_M)$ so that the solution given in Section I for the term structure is consistent with p.

One can imagine a number of different numerical approaches to this term-structure matching procedure. One that has been suggested by a source cited in the Notes is based on the numerical solution Ψ for state prices. Using the fact that $\sum_{i=1}^{N} \Psi_{ij}$ approximates p_j, the proposed algorithm for λ is given by the following steps.

(a) Let $j = 2$.
(b) Search for that number $\lambda(t_j)$ such that, given Ψ_{j-1}, we have

$$\hat{p}_j[\lambda(t_j), \Psi_{j-1}] = p_j, \tag{44}$$

where $\hat{p}_j[\lambda(t_j), \Psi_{j-1}] = \sum_{i=1}^{N} \Psi_j$ is notation indicating the dependence of the solution Ψ_j of (33) on Ψ_{j-1} and $\lambda(t_j)$ given by (35) and (36). This one-dimensional search could be conducted by a Newton-Raphson iterative method.

(c) Let j be increased by 1, and return to step (b) if $j \leq M$. Otherwise, stop.

In order for the numerical search for $\lambda(t_j)$ in step (44) to succeed, and for the solution to be uniquely defined, the model should be such that $\hat{p}_j(\cdot, \Psi_{j-1})$ is a strictly monotonic continuous function with range $(0, 1)$. This is true for the CIR example given above, in which $\bar{x}$ is replaced in (28) with $\lambda(t)$.

One could match additional parameters to market data on the prices of derivative securities, such as options. The idea is to obtain better "calibration" with the market in order, in principle, to obtain higher accuracy in the pricing of derivative securities. For example, one can extend by taking λ to be an $\mathbb{R}^2$-valued function specifying 2 free parameters, to be matched against the initial term structure of bond prices as well as the initial "volatility structure" implicit in bond-option prices, an approach taken in papers cited in the Notes.

Of course, with the passage of time, the "matched" model will fall out of calibration, implying that the free parameter vector λ was in fact inappropriate. In typical practice, a new set of free parameters is chosen, and valuation proceeds again. This process of routine reparameterization is theoretically inconsistent (and, to the author's knowledge, has been applied with relatively little econometric sophistication), but seems to some degree unavoidable. The "name of the game" is apparently to specify an accurate term-structure model that is both tractable and relatively stable over time.

Exercises

10.1 Show, as claimed in Section 10B, that the per-unit-of-time risk-neutralized mean M_n and variance V_n converge to $r - \sigma^2/2$ and σ^2 respectively.

10.2 Show that the sequence $\{[xe^{\rho(n)} - K]^+\}$ of "binomial" call-option payoffs constructed in Section C is uniformly integrable. Hint: Use the converse part of Theorem 10C.

10.3 Verify the Crank-Nicholson equation (16) from (14) and the Crank-Nicholson derivative approximations.

10.4 Verify the version of the Central Limit Theorem given in Proposition 10A. Hint: Use the Lindeberg-Feller Theorem of Appendix C.

10.5 (Binomial Approximation of Black-Derman-Toy Term-Structure Model) The continuous-time version of the Black-Derman-Toy model shown in Section 7K has the short-rate process r given by

$$r_t^c = U(t) \exp\left[\beta(t)\hat{B}(t)\right],$$

where $\hat{B}$ is a standard Brownian motion under an equivalent martingale measure and where $U : [0, \infty) \to \mathbb{R}_{++}$ and $\beta : [0, \infty) \to \mathbb{R}_{++}$ are continuously differentiable. The discrete-time version of the Black-Derman-Toy model given in Exercise 3.12 has the short-rate process r given by $r_t^d = a_t \exp(b_t X_t)$, where, for each time $t \in \{0, 1, \ldots\}$, a_t and b_t are strictly positive constants, and X_t is a shock process with the property that, under an equivalent martingale measure Q, we have, for all t,

$$Q\left(X_{t+1} - X_t = 1 \mid X_0, \ldots, X_t\right) = Q\left(X_{t+1} - X_t = 0 \mid X_0, \ldots, X_t\right) = \frac{1}{2}.$$

This exercise calls for the construction, at each t, of sequences $\{a_t^n\}$ and $\{b_t^n\}$ of coefficients for the discrete-time Black-Derman-Toy model with the property that, for each $t \in \{1, 2, \ldots\}$,

$$r_t^n \equiv a_t^n \exp(b_t^n X_{tn}) \Rightarrow r_t^c,$$

or convergence in distribution of the discrete-time model with n time periods per unit of calendar time to the continuous-time model. Hint: Use the Continuous Mapping Theorem, and the fact that $z \mapsto U(t) \exp\left(\beta(t)z\right)$ defines a continuous function on $\mathbb{R}$ into $\mathbb{R}$. We can write

$$r_t^n = U(t) \exp\left[\beta_t \left(X_{tn} b_t^n - \log\left[\frac{a_t^n}{U(t)}\right]\right)\right].$$

Show that it is therefore enough to choose $\{a_t^n\}$ and $\{b_t^n\}$ so that

$$X_{tn}\, b_t^n - \log\left[\frac{a_t^n}{U(t)}\right] \Rightarrow Z,$$

where Z is normally distributed with mean zero and variance t. Make use of the Central Limit Theorem to design $\{a_t^n\}$ and $\{b_t^n\}$ accordingly.

Notes

Standard references on probability theory include Chung (1974), Chow and Teicher (1978), Billingsley (1986), and Durrett (1991), all of which include the law of large numbers and the Central Limit Theorem. The convergence of the binomial option-pricing formula to the Black-Scholes formula is due to Cox, Ross, and Rubinstein (1979). Extensions of this approach can be found in Duffie (1988b), Nelson and Ramaswamy (1989), Madan, Milne, and Shefrin (1989), Duffie and Protter (1988), Lee (1991), Cutland, Kopp, and Willinger (1990), He (1990), Lamberton and Pagès (1990), Willinger and Tacqu (1991), and Eberlein (1991), among many other papers.

Section 10D is based on Talay and Tubaro (1990). Milshtein (1974, 1978) introduced second-order schemes such as (8). Talay (1984, 1986, 1990) provides more complicated second-order schemes for discretization of stochastic differential equations in $\mathbb{R}^n$. See also Newton (1990) in this regard. The large deviation results of Section 10E are standard; the version here is from Durrett (1991). Section 10F is apparently original. An alternative approach is to appear in joint research involving the author. The smooth approximation g_α in Section 10G of the call payoff function appears in Duffie (1988b), and was related to the author by Stephen Smale. Various applications of the Monte Carlo estimation of derivative asset prices are given by Jones and Jacobs (1986) and Boyle (1977, 1988, 1990). See also Boyle, Evnine, and Gibbs (1989).

Mitchell and Griffiths (1980) and Smith (1985) are basic treatments of the finite-difference solution of PDEs. An example of a more advanced finite-difference approach is given by Lawson and Morris (1978). Schwartz (1977) has one of the earliest applications of finite-difference methods in finance. The term-structure example of Section 10I is based on Courtadon (1982) and Stanton (1990). Jamshidian (1991) gives an alternate change of variables under which the diffusion is a constant. The literature in finance is reviewed and summarized by Clelow (1990). The Crank-Nicholson approximation is known as an *implicit* method. Hull and White (1990b) show how the range of the simpler *explicit* methods can be extended. Hull (1989) reviews some of the simpler implicit and explicit methods. Justification of the valuation algorithm (29) for securities with early exercise options is a delicate issue that is treated by Jaillet, Lamberton, and Lapeyre (1988, 1990). An early variation of this algorithm for the Black-Scholes (log-normal) put option problem is found in Brennan and Schwartz (1977). The methods of Chernoff and Petkau (1984) also give a practical accurate numerical approximation to the American put value.

The valuation of securities in terms of state prices also appears in the literature under such labels as *path integrals,* as in Dash (1989), or Green's function, as in Beaglehole (1990) and Beaglehole and Tenney (1990), who calculate the fundamental solution G explicitly for the Cox-Ingersoll-Ross model (28), or Jamshidian (1990, 1991). The idea of using pricing semigroups goes back at least to Garman (1985).

The issue of matching parameters to the initial term structure apparently originated with Ho and Lee (1986) in their "binomial" model of the term structure. Subsequent work in this vein can be found in Black, Derman, and Toy (1990), Dybvig (1988), Heath, Jarrow, and Morton (1987, 1990), Hull and White (1990a), and Jamshidian (1991). Further references are given in the Notes to Chapter 7. The Newton-Raphson search, and other numerical optimization techniques, can be found in Luenberger (1984).

Computer code for the solution of tridiagonal systems of equations such as (18), and for Newton-Raphson searches, is given by Press, Flannery, Teukolsky, and Vetterling (1988). Nelson and Ramaswamy (1989) treat finite-difference methods that are based on replacing the underlying stochastic differential equation with a Markov chain that has binomial transitions, extending the range of application of the binomial approach. Kishimoto (1989), Stanton (1990), and Barles, Daher, and Romano (1990) numerically solve "path-dependent" security prices, such as mortgage-backed securities.

An important topic that we have not treated is numerical solution of dynamic programming problems. Examples in the literature include Tauchen and Hussey (1991), Judd (1989), and Gagnon and Taylor (1986), who treat discrete-time models. Fitzpatrick and Fleming (1990) and Prigent (1991) treat convergence of optimal policies from discrete to continuous time.

Appendixes

A

Probability — The Finite-State Case

SUPPOSE Ω is a finite set. A *tribe* on Ω is a collection $\mathcal{F}$ of subsets of Ω that includes the empty set $\emptyset$ and that satisfies the two conditions:

   (a) if B is in $\mathcal{F}$, then its *complement* $\{\omega \in \Omega : \omega \notin B\}$ is also in $\mathcal{F}$;

   (b) if A and B are in $\mathcal{F}$, their union $A \cup B$ is in $\mathcal{F}$.

A tribe $\mathcal{F}$ is also known as an *algebra* or *field*, among other terms. When Ω is to be thought of as the states of the world, the elements of $\mathcal{F}$ are called *events*. Conditions (a) and (b) allow for simple logical rules regarding the probabilities of events. Specifically, a *probability measure* is a function $P : \mathcal{F} \to [0, 1]$ satisfying $P(\emptyset) = 0$, $P(\Omega) = 1$, and, for any disjoint events A and B,

$$P(A \cup B) = P(A) + P(B).$$

Under P, an event B has *probability* $P(B)$. A pair $(\Omega, \mathcal{F})$ consisting of a finite set Ω and a tribe $\mathcal{F}$ on Ω is called a measurable space. With the addition of a probability measure P on $\mathcal{F}$, the triple $(\Omega, \mathcal{F}, P)$ is a called a *probability space*.

Fixing a measurable space $(\Omega, \mathcal{F})$, a *random variable* is a function $X : \Omega \to \mathbb{R}$ with the property: For any $x \in \mathbb{R}$, the set $\{\omega \in \Omega : X(\omega) = x\}$ is in $\mathcal{F}$. Intuitively, X is a random variable if, for any possible outcome x, we will know whether X has this outcome from knowing the outcomes (true or false) of the events in $\mathcal{F}$. If X is a random variable with respect to $(\Omega, \mathcal{F})$, we also say that X is *$\mathcal{F}$-measurable*.

Since Ω is finite, for any random variable X there are events $B_1, \ldots, B_n$ and some α in $\mathbb{R}^n$ such that $X = \alpha_1 1_{B_1} + \cdots + \alpha_n 1_{B_n}$, where the *indicator function* 1_B for an event B is defined by $1_B(\omega) = 1$ for ω in B, and $1_B(\omega) = 0$

otherwise. Given a probability measure P, the *expectation* of X is then defined by

$$E(X) = \alpha_1 P(B_1) + \cdots + \alpha_n P(B_n), \qquad (A.1)$$

merely the probability-weighted average of the outcomes.

For a probability space $(\Omega, \mathcal{F}, P)$ with Ω finite, if $\mathcal{G}$ is a tribe on Ω that is contained by $\mathcal{F}$, then $\mathcal{G}$ represents in some sense "less information," and is known as a *sub-tribe* of $\mathcal{F}$. For any $\mathcal{F}$-measurable random variable X, the *conditional expectation* of X given a sub-tribe $\mathcal{G}$ of $\mathcal{F}$ is defined as any $\mathcal{G}$-measurable random variable Y with the property $E(XZ) = E(YZ)$ for any $\mathcal{G}$-measurable random variable Z. The *law of iterated expectations* states that if $\mathcal{G}$ is a sub-tribe of another sub-tribe $\mathcal{H}$, then for any random variable X, $E[E(X|\mathcal{H})|\mathcal{G}] = E(X|\mathcal{G})$.

If Y is a non-negative random variable with $E(Y) = 1$, then we can create a new probability measure Q from the old probability measure P by defining $Q(B) = E(1_B Y)$ for any event B. In this case, we write $\frac{dQ}{dP} = Y$, and call Y the *Radon-Nikodym derivative* of Q with respect to P. It also follows that, for any random variable X,

$$E^Q(X) = E^P(YX),$$

where E^Q denotes expectation under Q, and likewise for E^P. If $Q(B) > 0$ whenever $P(B) > 0$, and vice versa, then P and Q are said to be *equivalent measures*; they have the same events of probability zero.

If $\mathcal{G}$ is a sub-tribe of $\mathcal{F}$ and Q is equivalent to P, then

$$E^Q(Z|\mathcal{G}) = \frac{1}{E^P(\xi|\mathcal{G})} E^P(\xi Z|\mathcal{G}), \qquad (A.2)$$

where $\xi = \frac{dQ}{dP}$.

The tribe *generated* by a set Z of random variables is the smallest sub-tribe, often denoted $\sigma(Z)$, with respect to which each random variable in Z is measurable. It is enough to think of $\sigma(Z)$ as the set of events that can be ascertained as true or false by observing the outcomes of all of the random variables in Z.

Suppose there are multiple periods given by a set T of times such as $\{0, 1, \ldots, T\}$ or $\{0, 1, \ldots\}$. A *filtration* $\mathbb{F} = \{\mathcal{F}_t : t \in T\}$ of sub-tribes of $\mathcal{F}$ is usually given, as described in Section 2A. We always assume that $\mathcal{F}_t \subset \mathcal{F}_s$ whenever $t \leq s$. Given $\mathbb{F}$, a *stopping time* is a random variable taking values in $T \cup \{+\infty\}$ such that, for any time t in T, the event $\{\omega \in \Omega : \tau(\omega) \leq t\}$ is in $\mathcal{F}_t$. The event $\tau = +\infty$ is allowed for convenience. For example, if two processes X and Y are not the same, then the stopping time $\tau = \inf\{t : X_t \neq Y_t\}$ has a strictly positive probability of being finite-valued, but may also have a strictly positive probability of being $+\infty$. (We follow the usual convention that the infimum of the empty set is $+\infty$.) A stopping time τ is nontrivial if $P(\tau = +\infty) < 1$. A martingale can be defined as in Section 2A, or alternatively as any $\mathbb{F}$-adapted process X such that, for any finite-valued stopping time τ, we have $E(X_\tau) = E(X_1)$.

B

Separating Hyperplanes and Optimality

THIS APPENDIX REVIEWS some applications of the following basic well-known result. Good basic references are Rockafellar (1970) and Luenberger (1984).

Separating Hyperplane Theorem. *Suppose that A and B are convex disjoint subsets of* $\mathbb{R}^n$*. There is some nonzero linear functional F such that* $F(x) \le F(y)$ *for each x in A and y in B. Moreover, if x is in the interior of A or y is in the interior of B, then* $F(x) < F(y)$*.*

Our first application of the Separating Hyperplane Theorem is a special case for separation of cones that is applied in Theorem 1A.

Linear Separation of Cones. *Suppose M and K are closed convex cones in* $\mathbb{R}^n$ *that intersect precisely at zero. If K is not a linear subspace, then there is a nonzero linear functional F such that* $F(x) < F(y)$ *for each x in M and each nonzero y in K.*

Proof: Let $\epsilon = \inf\{\| x - y \|: x \in M, y \in K, \| y \| = 1\}$. Since both M and K are closed, $\epsilon > 0$. We next let $J = \{y + \| y \| z : y \in K, y \ne 0, \| z \| < \epsilon\}$, and note that M and J are disjoint convex sets, with J open and $K \subset J$. By the Separating Hyperplane Theorem, the result follows. ∎

Our next application of the Separating Hyperplane Theorem is the Saddle Point Theorem for optimality. A *concave program* is a triple (U, X, g) of the form

$$\sup_{x \in X} U(x) \quad \text{subject to} \quad g(x) \le 0, \tag{B.1}$$

where X is a convex subset of some vector space, $U : X \to \mathbb{R}$ is concave, and $g : X \to \mathbb{R}^m$ is convex for some integer m. The *Lagrangian* for (U, X, g)

227

is the function $\mathcal{L} : X \times \mathbb{R}_+^m \to \mathbb{R}$ defined by $\mathcal{L}(x, \lambda) = U(x) - \lambda \cdot g(x)$. A pair (x_0, λ_0) in $X \times \mathbb{R}_+^m$ is a *saddle point* of $\mathcal{L}$ if, for all (x, λ) in $X \times \mathbb{R}_+^m$, we have $\mathcal{L}(x, \lambda_0) \leq \mathcal{L}(x_0, \lambda_0) \leq \mathcal{L}(x_0, \lambda)$. If (x_0, λ_0) is a saddle point, we often term λ_0 a *Lagrange multiplier* for problem (B.1). The following version of the conditions for optimality is proved with the Separating Hyperplane Theorem. The existence of some $\underline{x}$ in X with $g(\underline{x}) \ll 0$ is known as the *Slater condition*.

Saddle Point Theorem. *Let (U, X, g) be a concave program.*

    I. *(Necessity) Suppose the Slater condition is satisfied. If x_0 solves (B.1), then there exists $\lambda_0 \in \mathbb{R}_+^m$ such that (x_0, λ_0) is a saddle point of the Lagrangian $\mathcal{L}$. Moreover, $\lambda_0 \cdot g(x_0) = 0$, which is called the complimentary slackness condition.*

    II. *(Sufficiency) If (x_0, λ_0) is a saddle point of $\mathcal{L}$, then x_0 solves (B.1).*

Proof: For the first part of the result, let $L = \mathbb{R} \times \mathbb{R}^m$, with subsets

$$A = \{(r, z) : \exists x \in X; r \leq U(x), z \geq g(x)\}$$

and

$$B = \{(r, z) : r > U(x_0), z \ll 0\},$$

which are both convex. By the fact that x_0 solves (B.1), the sets A and B are disjoint. By the Separating Hyperplane Theorem, there is a linear functional $F : L \to \mathbb{R}$ such that $F(v) < F(w)$ for each v in A and w in B. It follows, for any v in A and w in the closure of B, that $F(v) \leq F(w)$. There is some scalar α and λ in $\mathbb{R}^m$ such that, for any (r, z) in L, we have $F(r, z) = \alpha r + \lambda \cdot z$. Using the Slater condition, we can check that $\alpha < 0$ and $\lambda \geq 0$. Let $\lambda_0 = -\lambda/\alpha$. It follows, using the fact that $[U(x_0), 0]$ is in both A and the closure of B, that (x_0, λ_0) is a saddle point, and that complementary slackness holds.

    The second part of the result is easy to show. ∎

    Now we turn to first order conditions for optimality. Consider

$$\sup_{x \in X} U(x), \tag{B.2}$$

where X is a convex subset of a vector space L and $U : X \to \mathbb{R}$ is some function. We are interested in necessary and sufficient conditions for x^* to solve (B.2). For $x \in X$, let

$$F(x) = \{y \in L : \exists \epsilon \in (0, 1), \quad x + \alpha y \in X, \quad \alpha \in [0, \epsilon]\},$$

the set of *feasible directions* from x. The derivative of U at some x in X in the direction $y \in F(x)$, if it exists, is defined as the limit

$$\delta U(x; y) \equiv \lim_{\alpha \downarrow 0} \frac{U(x + \alpha y) - U(x)}{\alpha}. \tag{B.3}$$

This is sometimes known as the *directional* or *Gateaux* derivative. If $y \mapsto \delta U(x; y)$ defines a linear function on $F(x)$, this function is called the *gradient* of U at x, and is denoted $\nabla U(x)$. In that case, we write $\nabla U(x; y) = \delta U(x; y)$ for the value of $\nabla U(x)$ at y. For example, if $U : \mathbb{R}^n \to \mathbb{R}$ is a differentiable function, then the gradient $\nabla U(x)$ exists at any x and $\nabla U(x; y) = \partial U(x) \cdot y$, where $\partial U(x)$ is the vector of partial derivatives of U at x.

Suppose x^* solves (B.2) and $\nabla U(x^*)$ exists. Then $\nabla U(x^*; y) \leq 0$ for all y in $F(x^*)$, for if not, there is some feasible direction y with $\nabla U(x^*; y) > 0$, in which case there is some $\alpha > 0$ with $U(x + \alpha y) - U(x) > 0$, which contradicts the optimality of x^*. If $F(x^*)$ is the entire vector space L, it follows that $\nabla U(x^*) \equiv 0$ is necessary for the optimality of x^*, for if $\nabla U(x^*; y) < 0$, then $-y$ is a feasible direction of strict improvement.

If U is concave, $\nabla U(x^*)$ exists, and $F(x^*) = L$, then it is both necessary and sufficient for the optimality of x^* that $\nabla U(x^*) \equiv 0$. Necessity has been shown. For sufficiency, concavity of U implies that, for any x and $y \in X$,

$$U(y) - U(x) \leq \nabla U(x; y - x). \tag{B.4}$$

Taking $x = x^*$, we have $U(y) \leq U(x^*)$ for all y. There are extensions of these results to the case of nondifferentiable U.

C

Probability — The General Case

THIS APPENDIX EXTENDS the definitions of Appendix A to handle probability spaces with possibly infinitely many distinct events. We also add some useful general results, such as the Dominated Convergence Theorem, the Central Limit Theorem, and Fubini's Theorem. Standard references are Billingsley (1986) and Chung (1974).

Given a set Ω of states, a *tribe* on Ω is a collection $\mathcal{F}$ of subsets of Ω that includes the empty set $\emptyset$ and that satisfies the two conditions:

(a) if B is in $\mathcal{F}$, then its *complement* $\{\omega \in \Omega : \omega \notin B\}$ is also in $\mathcal{F}$;

(b) for any sequence $\{B_1, B_2, \ldots\}$ in $\mathcal{F}$, the union $B_1 \cup B_2 \cup \cdots$ is in $\mathcal{F}$.

A tribe is also known in this general context as a *σ-algebra* or *σ-field*. For any collection $\mathcal{A}$ of subsets of Ω, the tribe *generated* by $\mathcal{A}$ is the intersection of all tribes containing $\mathcal{A}$. An important example is to take $\Omega = \mathbb{R}^n$ and to let $\mathcal{F}$ be the tribe generated by the open sets of $\mathbb{R}^n$. In this case, $\mathcal{F}$ is known as the *Borel* tribe on $\mathbb{R}^n$, and is denoted $\mathcal{B}(\mathbb{R}^n)$.

Suppose Ω is a set with tribe $\mathcal{F}$. A *random variable* is a function $X : \Omega \to \mathbb{R}$ with the property: For any set A in the Borel tribe $\mathcal{B}(\mathbb{R})$, the set $\{\omega \in \Omega : X(\omega) \in A\}$ is in $\mathcal{F}$. A *probability measure* is a function $P : \mathcal{F} \to [0, 1]$ satisfying $P(\emptyset) = 0$, $P(\Omega) = 1$, and, for any sequence $B_1, B_2, \ldots$ of disjoint events,

$$P(B_1 \cup B_2 \cup \cdots) = \sum_{n=1}^{\infty} P(B_n).$$

The triple $(\Omega, \mathcal{F}, P)$ is a probability space.

An event B is said to be *almost sure* if $P(B) = 1$. For example, "$X = Y$ *almost surely*" means, in formal notation, that $P(\{\omega \in \Omega : X(\omega) = Y(\omega)\}) = 1$. We sometimes write instead, more informally, that "$P(X = Y) = 1$." It is our practice throughout to take "$X = Y$" to mean merely that $X = Y$ almost surely, but the phrase "almost surely" is sometimes added for emphasis.

Given a probability space $(\Omega, \mathcal{F}, P)$, a *null set* is a subset of an event of zero probability. In order to assign zero probability to null sets, the probability space can be *completed*, which means that we can replace $\mathcal{F}$ with the tribe $\mathcal{F}^\sim$ generated by the union of $\mathcal{F}$ and the set of all null sets. The probability measure P then extends uniquely to a probability measure $P^\sim$ on $(\Omega, \mathcal{F}^\sim)$ with the property that $P^\sim(A) = P(A)$ for all A in $\mathcal{F}$ and $P^\sim(A) = 0$ for any null set A. The space $(\Omega, \mathcal{F}^\sim, P^\sim)$ is called the *completion* of $(\Omega, \mathcal{F}, P)$.

Suppose X is a random variable that can be written as a linear combination, $X = \alpha_1 1_{B_1} + \cdots + \alpha_n 1_{B_n}$, of indicator functions. In this case, X is called *simple*. As in the finite-state case, the *expectation* of X given a probability measure P on $(\Omega, \mathcal{F})$ is defined by

$$E(X) = \alpha_1 P(B_1) + \cdots + \alpha_n P(B_n),$$

merely the probability-weighted average of the outcomes. If X is not necessarily simple, but is a non-negative random variable, then the expectation of X is defined as

$$E(X) \equiv \sup_{Y \in \mathcal{S}} E(Y) \quad \text{subject to} \quad Y \le X, \tag{C.1}$$

where $\mathcal{S}$ is the set of simple random variables. More generally, any random variable X may be written as $X = X^+ - X^-$, where $X^+ \equiv \max(X, 0)$ and $X^- \equiv \max(-X, 0)$; that is, X is the difference between its positive and negative parts. If both $E(X^+)$ and $E(X^-)$ are finite, then X is said to be *integrable*, and its expectation is defined by

$$E(X) \equiv E(X^+) - E(X^-), \tag{C.2}$$

which coincides with the definition for simple random variables when X is itself simple. If X^+ is integrable and X^- is not, we define $E(X) = -\infty$, and symmetrically define $E(X) = +\infty$ when X^- is integrable and X^+ is not.

Fixing a probability space $(\Omega, \mathcal{F}, P)$, a sequence $\{X_n\}$ of random variables *converges in distribution* to a random variable X if, for any bounded continuous $f : \mathbb{R} \to \mathbb{R}$, we have $E[f(X_n)] \to E[f(X)]$. The sequence $\{X_n\}$ *converges in probability* to X if, for all $\epsilon > 0$, $P(|X_n - X| \ge \epsilon) \to 0$. The sequence $\{X_n\}$ converges almost surely to X if there is an event B of probability 1 such that $X_n(\omega) \to X(\omega)$ for all ω in B. The definition of convergence in distribution extends as given to the case of X_n defined on a (possibly different) probability space $(\Omega_n, \mathcal{F}_n, P_n)$ for each n.

Dominated Convergence Theorem. *Suppose $\{X_n\}$ is a sequence of random variables on a probability space with $|X_n| \le Y$ for all n, where Y is a random variable with*

$E(|Y|) < \infty$. *Suppose, almost surely, or in probability, or in distribution, that X_n converges to X. Then $E(X_n) \to E(X)$.*

Convergence almost surely implies convergence in probability, which in turn implies convergence in distribution, so we could have stated the Dominated Convergence Theorem just for convergence in distribution and had the same result.

A sequence $\{X_n\}$ of random variables on a given probability space is *independently distributed* if, for any finite subset $\{X_1, \ldots, X_k\}$ and any bounded measurable functions $f_i : \mathbb{R} \to \mathbb{R}$, $1 \le i \le k$, we have

$$E[f_1(X_1)f_2(X_2) \cdots f_k(X_k)] = E[f_1(X_1)]E[f_2(X_2)] \cdots E[f_k(X_k)].$$

A sequence $\{X_n\}$ of random variables on a given probability space is *uniformly integrable* if

$$\lim_{\alpha \to \infty} \sup_n E(Y_{\alpha n}) = 0,$$

where $Y_{\alpha n}(\omega) = |X_n(\omega)|$ if $|X_n(\omega)| \ge \alpha$ and otherwise $Y_{\alpha n}(\omega) = 0$.

We next describe a version of the Central Limit Theorem. For this, we define

$$Y = \left\{ Y_1^n, Y_2^n, \ldots, Y_{k(n)}^n : n \in \{1, 2, \ldots\} \right\},$$

with $k(n) \to \infty$, to be a *triangular array* if, for each n, $Y_1^n, \ldots, Y_{k(n)}^n$ are independently distributed random variables on some probability space. For any constant $\epsilon > 0$, let $U(\epsilon)$ denote the "ϵ-truncated" triangular array defined by $U_j^n(\epsilon) = 0$ for $|Y_j^n| \le \epsilon$ and $U_j^n(\epsilon) = Y_j^n$ for $|Y_j^n| > \epsilon$. The array Y satisfies the *Lindeberg-Feller condition* if, for any $\epsilon > 0$,

$$\lim_{n \to \infty} \operatorname{var}\left[U_1^n(\epsilon) + \cdots + U_{k(n)}^n(\epsilon) \right] = 0.$$

The Lindeberg-Feller Central Limit Theorem. *Suppose Y is a triangular array of random variables, all with zero expectations, satisfying the Lindeberg-Feller condition. For each n, let $Z_n = Y_1^n + \cdots + Y_{k(n)}^n$ and let $s_n^2 = \operatorname{var}(Z_n)$. If $s_n^2 \to \sigma^2 > 0$, then Z_n converges in distribution to a Normal random variable with mean zero and variance σ^2.*

For any integrable random variable X, the *conditional expectation* of X given a sub-tribe $\mathcal{G}$ of $\mathcal{F}$ is defined as any $\mathcal{G}$-measurable random variable Y with the property $E(XZ) = E(YZ)$ for any $\mathcal{G}$-measurable random variable Z such that XZ is integrable. The existence of this conditional expectation is assured, but we do not show that here. The *law of iterated expectations* applies as in the finite-state case.

As in the finite-state setting, Q and P are equivalent probability measures on $(\Omega, \mathcal{F})$ if, for any event A, $P(A) = 0$ if and only if $Q(A) = 0$. In this case, there is always a strictly positive random variable ξ called the *Radon-Nikodym* derivative of Q with respect to P, with the property: If Z is such that $E^Q(|Z|) < \infty$, then $E^Q(Z) = E^P(\xi Z)$. Under the same assumptions, if $\mathcal{G}$ is a sub-tribe of $\mathcal{F}$, then

$$E^Q(Z|\mathcal{G}) = \frac{1}{E^P(\xi|\mathcal{G})} E^P(\xi Z|\mathcal{G}). \qquad (C.3)$$

It is common to denote ξ by $\frac{dQ}{dP}$.

If there are multiple periods, we fix a set of times denoted $\mathcal{T}$, usually with $\mathcal{T} = \{0, 1, \ldots, T\}$, or $\mathcal{T} = \{0, 1, \ldots\}$, or $\mathcal{T} = [0, T]$, or $\mathcal{T} = [0, \infty)$. A filtration $\mathbb{F} = \{\mathcal{F}_t : t \in \mathcal{T}\}$ of sub-tribes of $\mathcal{F}$ is usually given, as in the finite-state case. We always assume that $\mathcal{F}_t \subset \mathcal{F}_s$ whenever $t \leq s$. In this case, a *martingale* is an adapted process X that is *integrable*, in the sense that X_t is integrable for each t, and such that $E(X_t|\mathcal{F}_s) = X_s$ whenever $t \geq s$. As in the finite-state case, a martingale can also be defined as an adapted integrable process such that, for any bounded stopping time τ, we have $E(X_\tau) = E(X_0)$.

For the case $\mathcal{T} = [0, T]$ or $[0, \infty)$, we often require a family $X = \{X_t : t \in \mathcal{T}\}$ of random variables to be measurable when treated as a function $X : \Omega \times \mathcal{T} \to \mathbb{R}$. "Measurable" here means *product measurable*, sometimes called *jointly measurable*, that is, measurable with respect to the smallest tribe on $\Omega \times \mathcal{T}$ containing all sets of the form $A \times B$, where $A \in \mathcal{F}$ and B is in the Borel tribe on $\mathcal{T}$. In fact, we always take it as a matter of definition, given at the beginning of Chapter 5, that a *process* $X : \Omega \times \mathcal{T} \to \mathbb{R}$ is product measurable so as to avoid continually referring to product measurability.

Fubini's Theorem states the following. Suppose $(\Omega, \mathcal{F}, P)$ is a probability space and $X : \Omega \times [0, T] \to \mathbb{R}$ is product measurable. If

$$E\left(\int_0^T |X_t| \, dt\right) < \infty,$$

then $E\left(\int_0^T X_t \, dt\right) = \int_0^T E(X_t) \, dt$. That is, we can reverse the order of the expectation and the time integral. More generally, if $\mathcal{G}$ is a sub-tribe of $\mathcal{F}$, then the conditions above for Fubini's Theorem imply that

$$E\left(\int_0^T X_t \, dt \,\middle|\, \mathcal{G}\right) = \int_0^T E(X_t|\mathcal{G}) \, dt \quad \text{almost surely.} \qquad (C.4)$$

Fubini's Theorem also applies as stated with $T = +\infty$. This version can be found in Ethier and Kurtz (1986: 74).

Stochastic Integration

THIS APPENDIX SUMMARIZES the definition of the stochastic integral and reviews two useful related results, Girsanov's Theorem and the Martingale Representation Theorem. Standard references are Chung and Williams (1990), Karatzas and Shreve (1988), and Revuz and Yor (1991). For the case of a general information filtration, see Protter (1990).

We fix a standard Brownian motion $B = (B^1, \ldots, B^d)$ in $\mathbb{R}^d$ on a complete probability space $(\Omega, \mathcal{F}, P)$, as well as the standard filtration $\mathbb{F} = \{\mathcal{F}_t : t \geq 0\}$ of B, as defined in Section 5I. We remind the reader that a "process" has been defined for the purposes of this book as a jointly measurable function on $\Omega \times [0, \infty)$ into some Euclidean space. We also recall that B is defined by the fact that it is an $\mathbb{R}^d$-valued process with continuous sample paths such that

(a) $P(B_0 = 0) = 1$;

(b) for any times t and $s > t$, $B_s - B_t$ is normally distributed in $\mathbb{R}^d$ with mean zero and covariance matrix $(s - t)I$;

(c) for any times $t_0, \ldots, t_n$ with $0 < t_0 < t_1 < \cdots < t_n < \infty$, the random variables $B(t_0), B(t_1) - B(t_0), \ldots, B(t_n) - B(t_{n-1})$ are independently distributed.

Finally, recall that $\mathcal{F}_t$ is the tribe (often called the σ-algebra) generated by the union of the tribe $\sigma(B_s : 0 \leq s \leq t)$ and the null sets of $\mathcal{F}$.

In order to define the stochastic integral, we fix a time interval $[0, T]$ and take M to be one of the processes $B^1, \ldots, B^d$, say B^i. An adapted process $\theta : \Omega \times [0, T] \to$ is *simple* if there is a partition of $[0, T]$ given by times $0 = t_0 < t_1 < \cdots < t_N = T$ such that, for all $n > 0$,

$$\theta(t) = \theta(t_n), \quad t \in (t_{n-1}, t_n].$$

For a simple process θ, it is natural to define the stochastic integral $\int \theta \, dM$, at any time $t \in [t_n, t_{n+1})$, for any n, by

$$\int_0^t \theta_s \, dM_s \equiv \sum_{i=0}^{n-1} \theta(t_i) \left[M(t_{i+1}) - M(t_i) \right] + \theta(t_n) \left[M(t) - M(t_n) \right].$$

An important fact that we shall not prove here is that, for any $\theta \in \mathcal{H}^2$ (the space of square-integrable adapted processes defined in Section 5B), there is a sequence $\{\theta_n\}$ of adapted simple processes approximating θ in the sense that

$$E \left(\int_0^T [\theta_n(t) - \theta(t)]^2 \, dt \right) \to 0.$$

It also turns out that, for each θ in $\mathcal{H}^2$, there is a unique random variable Y_θ with the property that, for any such approximating sequence $\{\theta_n\}$ of θ,

$$E \left(\left[Y_\theta - \int_0^T \theta_n(t) \, dM_t \right]^2 \right) \to 0.$$

(To be more precise, Y_θ is uniquely defined in the sense that, if another random variable Y has the same property, then $Y = Y_\theta$ almost surely.) This random variable Y_θ is denoted $\int_0^T \theta_t \, dM_t$. Since T and $M = B^i$ are arbitrary, we have defined the stochastic integral $\int_0^T \theta_t \, dB_t$ for any θ in $\mathcal{H}^2(B)$ and any T. The fact that this definition of the stochastic integral is possible, and the fact that the process $\int \theta \, dB$ satisfies the properties laid out in Chapter 5, are both shown, for example, in Karatzas and Shreve (1988: Sec. 3.2). In particular, this stochastic integral is defined so that every sample path is continuous. Karatzas and Shreve have taken special care to extend the usual definition of $\int \theta \, dB$ for "progressively measurable" θ in $\mathcal{H}^2(B)$ to allow any θ in $\mathcal{H}^2(B)$. Then, by a "localization" argument, they further extend the definition of $\int \theta \, dB$ to allow any θ in $\mathcal{L}(B)$.

Bick and Willinger (1991) point out that, for some of the applications treated in this book such as the Black-Scholes option-pricing formula, the stochastic integral simplifies to the usual Stieltjes integral. The remainder of this appendix is devoted to some key additional properties of stochastic integration.

The Martingale Representation Theorem. *If M is a martingale, then there exists θ in $\mathcal{L}(B)$ such that*

$$M_t = M_0 + \int_0^t \theta_s \, dB_s, \quad t \geq 0. \tag{D.1}$$

The following result is closely related, as can be seen from the sketch of its proof.

Dudley's Theorem. *Fix $T > 0$ and let X be any $\mathcal{F}_T$-measurable random variable. Suppose $d = 1$ or $E(|X|) < \infty$. Then there exists a constant x and some θ in $\mathcal{L}(B)$ such that*

$$X = x + \int_0^T \theta_t \, dB_t \quad a.s. \tag{D.2}$$

We can give the proof for $E(|X|) < \infty$. In that case $\{M_t = E_t(X), \ t \geq 0\}$ is a martingale with $M_0 = x \equiv E(X)$ and $M_T = X$. Then (D.2) follows from (D.1). The proof for $d = 1$, as well as that of the Martingale Representation Theorem, are standard and can be found, for example, in Karatzas and Shreve (1988).

We move now to Girsanov's Theorem. We restrict ourselves for the remainder of the appendix to a fixed time horizon $T < \infty$. In particular, the probability space is $(\Omega, \mathcal{F}_T, P)$ and the standard filtration $\mathbb{F} = \{\mathcal{F}_t : 0 \leq t \leq T\}$ of $B = \{B_t : 0 \leq t \leq T\}$ are as previously defined, with all defining conditions restricted to $[0, T]$. A vector $\theta = (\theta^1, \ldots, \theta^d)$ of processes in $\mathcal{L}^2$ satisfies *Novikov's condition* if

$$E\left[\exp\left(\frac{1}{2} \int_0^T \theta_s \cdot \theta_s \, ds\right)\right] < \infty. \tag{D.3}$$

Girsanov's Theorem. *Let X be an Ito process in $\mathbb{R}^N$ of the form*

$$X_t = x + \int_0^t \mu_s \, ds + \int_0^t \sigma_s \, dB_s, \quad 0 \leq t \leq T. \tag{D.4}$$

Suppose $\nu = (\nu^1, \ldots, \nu^N)$ is a vector of processes in $\mathcal{L}^1$ such that there exists some θ satisfying Novikov's condition with

$$\sigma_t \theta_t = \mu_t - \nu_t, \quad 0 \leq t \leq T. \tag{D.5}$$

Then there exists a probability measure Q equivalent to P such that

$$\hat{B}_t = B_t + \int_0^t \theta_s \, ds, \quad 0 \leq t \leq T, \tag{D.6}$$

defines a standard Brownian motion $\hat{B}$ in $\mathbb{R}^d$ on $(\Omega, \mathcal{F}, Q)$ that has the same standard filtration $\mathbb{F}$. The process X defined by (D.4) is also an Ito process with respect to $(\Omega, \mathcal{F}, \mathbb{F}, Q)$, and

$$X_t = x + \int_0^t \nu_s \, ds + \int_0^t \sigma_s \, d\hat{B}_s, \quad 0 \leq t \leq T. \tag{D.7}$$

Finally, for any random variable W such that $E^Q(|W|) < \infty$,

$$E^Q(W) = E^P(W\xi_T),\qquad\qquad\text{(D.8)}$$

where

$$\xi_t = \exp\left(-\int_0^t \theta_s\,dB_s - \frac{1}{2}\int_0^t \theta_s\cdot\theta_s\,ds\right),\quad t\in[0,T].\qquad\text{(D.9)}$$

In short, Girsanov's Theorem is a way to adjust probability assessments so that a given Ito process can be rewritten as an Ito process with almost arbitrary drift.

The following invariance of the diffusion process σ under a change of measure is a useful implication of Girsanov's Theorem.

Diffusion Invariance Principle. *Let X be an Ito process X, with $dX_t = \mu_t\,dt + \sigma_t\,dB_t$. If X is a martingale with respect to an equivalent probability measure Q, then there is a standard Brownian motion $\hat{B}$ in $\mathbb{R}^d$ under Q such that $dX_t = \sigma_t\,d\hat{B}_t,\ t\in[0,T]$.*

E

SDEs, PDEs, and the Feynman-Kac Formula

THIS APPENDIX TREATS the existence of solutions to stochastic differential equations (SDEs) and shows how SDEs can be used to represent solutions to partial differential equations (PDEs) of the parabolic type. Standard references include Karatzas and Shreve (1988) and Chung and Williams (1990).

As usual, a standard Brownian motion B in $\mathbb{R}^d$ is given on some probability space $(\Omega, \mathcal{F}, P)$, along with the standard filtration $\mathbb{F}$ of B, as defined in Appendix D. An SDE is an expression of the form

$$dX_t = \mu(X_t, t)\, dt + \sigma(X_t, t)\, dB_t, \qquad (\text{E.1})$$

where $\mu : \mathbb{R}^N \times [0, \infty) \to \mathbb{R}^N$ and $\sigma : \mathbb{R}^N \times [0, \infty) \to \mathbb{R}^{N \times d}$ are given functions. We are interested in conditions on μ and σ under which, for each x in $\mathbb{R}^N$, there is a unique Ito process X satisfying (E.1) with $X_0 = x$. In this case, we say that X solves (E.1) with initial condition x. A process such as X is often called a *diffusion*, although there is no generally accepted definition for "diffusion." By saying "unique," we mean as usual that any other Ito process with the same properties is equal to X almost everywhere. A unique solution in this sense is sometimes called a *strong solution*. We will have no need for what is known as a *weak solution*.

Sufficient conditions for a solution to (E.1) are *Lipschitz* and *growth* conditions on μ and σ. In order to explain these, we first define a norm on matrices by letting $\|A\| = [\text{tr}(AA^\top)]^{1/2}$ for any matrix A. (This coincides with the usual Euclidean norm when A has one row or column.) We then say that σ satisfies a Lipschitz condition in x if there is a constant k such that, for any x and y in $\mathbb{R}^N$ and any time t,

$$\|\sigma(x, t) - \sigma(y, t)\| \leq k\|x - y\|. \tag{E.2}$$

Similarly, σ satisfies a growth condition in x if there is a constant k such that, for any x in $\mathbb{R}^N$ and any time t,

$$\|\sigma(x, t)\|^2 \leq k(1 + \|x\|^2). \tag{E.3}$$

Note that these conditions apply *uniformly in* t, in that the constants apply for all t simultaneously. The same conditions (E.2) and (E.3), substituting μ for σ, define Lipschitz and growth conditions, respectively, on μ.

SDE Proposition. *Suppose μ and σ are measurable and satisfy Lipschitz and growth conditions in x. Then, for each x in $\mathbb{R}^N$, there is a unique Ito process X in $\mathbb{R}^N$ satisfying the SDE (E.1) with initial condition x. Moreover, X is a Markov process, and for each time T there is a constant C such that*

$$E\left(\|X_t\|^2\right) \leq Ce^{Ct}\left(1 + \|x\|^2\right). \tag{E.4}$$

One can weaken somewhat the Lipschitz conditions for solutions to (E.1). We say that σ is *locally Lipschitz* in x if, for each positive constant K, there is a constant k such that (E.2) is satisfied for all t and for all x and y bounded in norm by K. The conclusion that X is a Markov process can be strengthened to the conclusion that X is a strong Markov process, a property that we do not define here.

SDE Theorem. *Suppose μ and σ are measurable, satisfy growth conditions in x, and are locally Lipschitz in x. Then, for each x in $\mathbb{R}^N$, there is a unique Ito process X in $\mathbb{R}^N$ satisfying the SDE (E.1) with initial condition x. Moreover, X is a Markov process. If, in addition, μ and σ are continuous functions, then X is a finite-variance process.*

Even these weaker conditions do not cover the case of "square root" diffusions, of the sort used in the Cox-Ingersoll-Ross model in Chapters 7 and 9. For this special case, we can rely on the following result for the one-dimensional case ($N = d = 1$) due to Yamada and Watanabe (1971), reported in Karatzas and Shreve (1988: 291). It is enough that μ is continuous and satisfies a Lipschitz condition in X, and that σ is continuous with the property that

$$|\sigma(x, t) - \sigma(y, t)| \leq \rho(|x - y|),$$

for all x and y and all t, where $\rho : [0, \infty) \to [0, \infty)$ is a strictly increasing function with $\rho(0) = 0$ such that, for any $\epsilon > 0$,

$$\int_{(0,\epsilon)} \rho^{-2}(x)\, dx = +\infty.$$

It is enough to take $\rho(x) = \sqrt{x}$, which covers the CIR model (taking $\sigma(x) = 0, x < 0$). While even these weak conditions are further weakened by Yamada and Watanabe (1971), it should be noted that there are counterexamples to the uniqueness of solutions for the case $\sigma(x) = |x|^\alpha$ for $\alpha < 1/2$.

These SDE existence results can be gleaned from such sources as Ikeda and Watanabe (1981), Karatzas and Shreve (1988), Chung and Williams (1990), Revuz and Yor (1991), or Friedman (1975). The conditions of these results also imply that, for any given time τ and any x in $\mathbb{R}^N$, there is a unique Ito process X satisfying (E.1) for $t \geq \tau$ with $X_t = x$, $t \leq \tau$. In this case, we say that X solves (E.1) with initial condition x at time τ.

We next consider the *Cauchy problem*, for given $T > 0$: Find $f \in C^{2,1}(\mathbb{R}^N \times [0, T))$ solving

$$\mathcal{D}f(x, t) - r(x, t)f(x, t) + h(x, t) = 0, \quad (x, t) \in \mathbb{R}^N \times [0, T), \qquad \text{(E.5)}$$

with the boundary condition

$$f(x, T) = g(x), \quad x \in \mathbb{R}^N, \qquad \text{(E.6)}$$

where

$$\mathcal{D}f(x, t) = f_t(x, t) + f_x(x, t)\mu(x, t) + \frac{1}{2}\operatorname{tr}\left[\sigma(x, t)\sigma(x, t)^\top f_{xx}(x, t)\right], \qquad \text{(E.7)}$$

and where $r : \mathbb{R}^N \times [0, T] \to \mathbb{R}$, $h : \mathbb{R}^N \times [0, T] \to \mathbb{R}$, $g : \mathbb{R}^N \to \mathbb{R}$, $\mu : \mathbb{R}^N \times [0, T] \to \mathbb{R}^N$, and $\sigma : \mathbb{R}^N \times [0, T] \to \mathbb{R}^{N \times d}$.

The Feynman-Kac solution to (E.5)–(E.6), should it exist, is given by

$$f(x, t) = E^{x,t}\left[\int_t^T \varphi_{t,s}\, h(X_s, s)\, ds + \varphi_{t,T}\, g(X_T)\right], \qquad \text{(E.8)}$$

where

$$\varphi_{t,s} = \exp\left[-\int_t^s r(X_\tau, \tau)\, d\tau\right],$$

and where $E^{x,t}$ indicates that X is assumed to solve the SDE (E.1) with initial condition x at time t. The term "Feynman-Kac" is widely considered a misnomer in that it originally refers to the probabilistic representation of the solution to a narrower class of parabolic equations than the Cauchy problem. Typically, (E.8) would be called a *probabilistic solution* of the PDE (E.5)–(E.6).

Momentarily putting aside the delicate issue of existence of solutions to the Cauchy problem, the Feynman-Kac representation of a given solution is itself not difficult to verify under technical assumptions. In order to see this, suppose that X solves (E.1) and that f is a solution to the Cauchy problem. For an arbitrary (x, t) in $\mathbb{R}^N \times [0, T]$, let Y be the Ito process defined by $Y_s = f(x, t)$, $s < t$, and

$$Y_s = f(X_s, s)\varphi_{t,s}, \quad s \in [t, T],$$

where X solves (E.1) with initial condition x at time t. By Ito's Lemma,

$$Y_T = f(x, t) + \int_t^T \varphi_{t,s} \left[\mathcal{D}f(X_s, s) - r(X_s, s)f(X_s, s) \right] \, ds$$

$$+ \int_t^T \varphi_{t,s} f_x(X_s, s)\sigma(X_s, s) \, dB_s.$$

Taking expectations through each side, rearranging, and assuming enough technical conditions for integrability and (from Proposition 5B) for the integral with respect to B to be a martingale, we have

$$f(x, t) = E^{x,t} \left(\varphi_{t,T} f(X_T, T) - \int_t^T \varphi_{t,s} \left[\mathcal{D}f(X_s, s) - r(X_s, s)f(X_s, s) \right] \, ds \right),$$

from which (E.8) follows with substitution of (E.5) and (E.6). Sufficient technical conditions are:

(a) all of r, g, h, μ, σ, and f are continuous;

(b) the solution f satisfies a *polynomial growth condition* in x, meaning that, for some positive constants M and ν,

$$|f(x, t)| \leq M \left(1 + \|x\|^\nu \right), \quad (x, t) \in \mathbb{R}^N \times [0, T];$$

(c) g and h are each either non-negative or satisfy a polynomial growth condition in x;

(d) r is non-negative; and

(e) μ and σ satisfy Lipschitz and growth conditions in x.

We state this more formally:

Proposition. *Suppose conditions (a)–(e) above are satisfied and that f solves* (E.5)– (E.6). *Then* (E.5)–(E.6) *is solved by* (E.8). *There is no other solution to* (E.5)– (E.6) *that satisfies a polynomial growth condition.*

A proof is found in Karatzas and Shreve (1988: 366). Reducing the PDE solution to an expectation in this fashion can sometimes ease the computation of the solution, as is the case for the Black-Scholes formula. The expectation can also can be used as the basis for a numerical solution by Monte Carlo methods, a topic considered in Chapter 10. The Feynman-Kac approach can also be applied to other types of parabolic and elliptic PDEs.

The previous proposition does not resolve whether or not a solution to the PDE actually exists. For this, stronger technical conditions are typically imposed. Different sets of conditions are available in the literature; we will give some of these from different sources. A function $F : \mathbb{R}^N \to \mathbb{R}^K$ is *Hölder continuous* if there is some $\alpha \in (0, 1]$ such that

$$\sup_{x,y, \, x \neq y} \frac{\|F(x) - F(y)\|}{\|x - y\|^\alpha} < \infty.$$

A function has a property (such as Hölder continuity) *locally* if it has the property when restricted to any compact subset of its domain.

Condition 1. *The functions μ, σ, g, h, and r are all continuous and:*

(a) *μ and σ are bounded and locally Lipschitz in (x, t);*

(b) *σ is Hölder continuous in x, uniformly in t;*

(c) *r is bounded and, locally: r is Hölder continuous in x uniformly in t;*

(d) *h is Hölder continuous in x, uniformly in t, and satisfies a polynomial growth condition in x;*

(e) *$\sigma\sigma^\top$ is uniformly parabolic, in that there is some scalar $\epsilon > 0$ such that the eigenvalues of $\sigma(x, t)\sigma(x, t)^\top$ are larger than ϵ for all $(x, t) \in \mathbb{R}^N \times [0, T]$; and*

(f) *g satisfies a polynomial growth condition.*

We can substitute strong smoothness conditions for some of the stringent bounding and uniform ellipticity properties of Condition 1.

Condition 2. *All of μ, σ, g, r, and h satisfy a Lipschitz condition in x, and r is non-negative. All of μ, σ, g, r, h, μ_x, σ_x, g_x, r_x, h_x, μ_{xx}, σ_{xx}, g_{xx}, r_{xx}, and h_{xx} exist, are continuous, and satisfy a growth condition in x.*

Theorem. *Under Condition 1 or Condition 2, there is a unique solution of* (E.5)–(E.6) *that satisfies a polynomial growth condition in x, and this solution is given by* (E.8).

Condition 1 is from Friedman (1975), while Condition 2 is a special case from Krylov (1980). Unfortunately, neither Condition 1 nor Condition 2 includes the exact case of the Black-Scholes option-pricing formula, so we offer the following special conditions for that case.

Condition 3. *The functions μ, σ, and r are constant. The function h is continuous and uniformly Hölder continuous in x. The function g is continuous. For some positive constants a and A, g and h satisfy the exponential growth conditions*

$$|h(x, t)| \leq A \exp\left(a \|x\|^2\right), \quad (x, t) \in \mathbb{R}^N \times [0, T]$$

$$|g(x)| \leq A \exp\left(a \|x\|^2\right), \quad x \in \mathbb{R}^N.$$

Special Theorem. *Under Condition 3, there is a unique solution f of* (E.5)–(E.6) *that satisfies the exponential growth condition*

$$|f(x, t)| \leq A' \exp\left(a' \|x\|^2\right), \quad (x, t) \in \mathbb{R}^N \times [0, T],$$

for some positive constants a' and A'. This solution is given by (E.8).

This result is an easy consequence of the approach in Friedman (1975: 139–49). The point to note is that the transition density, Γ^* in Friedman's notation, of the Ito process X with constant coefficients is well known to be the "fundamental solution" (described below) to the corresponding backward Kolmogorov equation, this solution being given by the Normal density with a particular mean vector and covariance matrix. Condition 3 applies to the Black-Scholes setting by taking $h = 0$ and by a change of variables from x to $y = e^x$. (I am grateful to Ravi Myneni for sorting out this special treatment of the constant-coefficients model.)

Under technical conditions on μ, σ, and r, there is a function G : $\mathbb{R}^N \times [0, T] \times \mathbb{R}^N \times [0, T] \to \mathbb{R}$, called the *fundamental solution* of (E.5)–(E.6), or sometimes the *Green's function*, that has the following useful properties.

(a) For any $(x_0, t_0) \in \mathbb{R}^N \times [0, T)$, the function ψ defined by $\psi(x, t) = G(x_0, t_0, x, t)$ is in $C^{2,1}(\mathbb{R}^N \times (t_0, T])$ and solves the PDE

$$\mathcal{D}^*\psi(x, t) - r(x, t)\psi(x, t) = 0, \quad (x, t) \in \mathbb{R}^N \times (t_0, T], \qquad \text{(E.9)}$$

where

$$\mathcal{D}^*\psi(x, t) = -\psi_t(x, t) - \psi_x(x, t)\mu(x, t) + \frac{1}{2}\text{tr}\left[\sigma(x, t)\sigma(x, t)^\top \psi_{xx}(x, t)\right].$$

The PDE (E.9) is sometimes called the *Fokker-Planck equation,* or the *forward Kolmogorov equation,* distinguishing it from the *backward Kolmogorov equation* (E.5)–(E.6).

(b) Under technical conditions on g and h, the solution to (E.5)–(E.6) is given by

$$f(x_0, t_0) = \int_{t_0}^T \int_{\mathbb{R}^N} G(x_0, t_0, x, t)h(x, t)\,dx\,dt \qquad \text{(E.10)}$$
$$+ \int_{\mathbb{R}^N} G(x_0, t_0, x, T)g(x)\,dx.$$

A sufficient set of technical conditions, as well as boundary conditions for (E.9), are given by Friedman (1964, 1975). Knowledge of the fundamental solution G is valuable since particular solutions of the PDE (E.5)–(E.6) can be computed from (E.10) for each of a number of different cases for g and h. In the case of $N = 1$, numerical solution of G is treated by a finite-difference approach given in Chapter 10.

Further work on probabilistic solutions of PDEs has been done by Freidlin (1985).

F

Calculation of Utility Gradients

THIS APPENDIX GIVES an example of the calculation of a utility gradient in a continuous-time setting. Further examples are found in Duffie and Skiadas (1990).

First recall the Mean Value Theorem: If $f : [a, b] \to \mathbb{R}$ is continuous on the interval $[a, b]$ and has a derivative on (a, b), then there is some $c \in (a, b)$ such that $f(b) - f(a) = f'(c)(b - a)$.

We fix a probability space and the time interval $[0, T]$. A process $c : \Omega \times [0, T] \to \mathbb{R}$ is *square-integrable* if $E\left(\int_0^T c_t^2 \, dt\right) < \infty$. Let L denote the space of square-integrable processes and L_+ the space of non-negative processes in L. We recall from Appendix B that the gradient of a function $U : L_+ \to \mathbb{R}$, when well defined at $c \in L_+$, is given by

$$\nabla U(c; h) = \lim_{\alpha \to 0} \frac{U(c + \alpha h) - U(c)}{\alpha}, \quad h \in F(c),$$

where $F(c)$ is the set of feasible directions at c.

Consider the additive-utility function U defined by

$$U(c) = E\left[\int_0^T u(c_t, t) \, dt\right],$$

where u is continuous and, for each t, $u(\cdot, t)$ is continuously differentiable on $(0, \infty)$ with a derivative $u_c(\cdot, t)$ satisfying a growth condition $|u_c(y, t)| \leq k + ky$, for some constant k independent of t. Let $c \in L_+$ and $h \in F(c)$. Let $\{\alpha_n\}$ be any sequence of strictly positive scalars smaller than 1 and converging to zero. For each n, ω, and t, let $\zeta_{n,t}(\omega)$ be chosen, by the Mean Value Theorem, so that

$$u_c\left[c_t(\omega) + \zeta_{n,t}(\omega), t\right] \alpha_n h_t(\omega) = u\left[c_t(\omega) + \alpha_n h_t(\omega), t\right] - u\left[c_t(\omega), t\right].$$

In fact, this can be done so that ζ_n is a process in L_+. It follows that, for all n,

$$\left| \frac{u(c_t + \alpha_n h_t, t) - u(c_t, t)}{\alpha_n} \right| = |u_c(c_t + \zeta_{n,t}, t) h_t|$$

$$\leq (k + k|c_t + \zeta_{n,t}|)|h_t|$$

$$\leq (k + k|c_t| + k\alpha_n|h_t|)|h_t|$$

$$\leq y_t \equiv (k + k|c_t| + |h_t|)|h_t|.$$

Moreover, $E\left(\int_0^T |y_t|\, dt \right) < \infty$ by the Cauchy-Schwartz inequality since both c and h are in L. The Dominated Convergence Theorem implies that

$$\lim_{n \to \infty} \frac{U(c + \alpha_n h) - U(c)}{\alpha} = E\left[\int_0^T \lim_n u_c(c_t + \zeta_{n,t}, t) h_t\, dt \right]$$

$$= E\left[\int_0^T u_c(c_t, t) h_t\, dt \right],$$

since $\zeta_{n,t}(\omega)$ converges with n to 0 for all (ω, t). Thus, for any $h \in F(c)$,

$$\nabla U(c; h) = E\left(\int_0^T \pi_t h_t\, dt \right),$$

where $\pi_t = u_c(c_t, t)$. This implies that the gradient of U at c exists and has the Riesz representation π.

Suppose, for any $\epsilon > 0$, that u_c satisfies the growth condition given above restricted to $(\epsilon, \infty) \times [0, T]$, but not necessarily on the whole domain $[0, \infty) \times [0, T]$. This is important, for example, in dealing with Inada conditions, as in the example $u(x, t) = e^{-\rho t} x^\alpha$. In that case, the above calculations extend to obtain the same solution for utility gradients so long as the given consumption process c is bounded away from zero. That is, suppose for some $\epsilon > 0$ that $c_t \geq \epsilon$ for all t. In order to be a feasible direction, $c + \delta h \geq 0$ for some $\delta \in (0, 1)$, so $c + \alpha h$ must be bounded away from zero for all $\alpha \in (0, \delta/2)$, and all of the above calculations carry through to this case. This situation covers the equilibrium described by Theorem 9G, in which the consumption process c^i of an arbitrary agent i is indeed bounded away from zero.

G

Finite Difference Computer Code

THIS APPENDIX GIVES computer code written in C by Ravi Myneni, at the author's direction, for the numerical solution of coupon-bond and coupon-bond option prices for the Cox-Ingersoll-Ross model of the term structure, using the Crank-Nicholson finite-difference algorithm given in Chapter 10. Zero-coupon bond prices, of course, are also given directly in terms of the explicit solution shown in Chapter 7, from which coupon-bond prices can be computed by treating a coupon bond as a portfolio of zero-coupon bonds of different maturities. This code is merely for the pedagogic purposes of Chapter 10, and is not intended for commerical or other uses. Although this code has been successfully applied by the author to various examples, neither the author nor Ravi Myneni accept any liability for any losses related to its use, or misuse, for any purpose.

The code should be linked with the following copyrighted subroutines from *Numerical Recipes in C,* by Press, Flannery, Teukolsky, and Vetterling (1988).

(a) tridag( ),
(b) ivector( ),
(c) dvector( ),
(d) free_ivector( ),
(e) free_dvector( ).

These subroutines are also supplied on a diskette normally sold with copies of *Numerical Recipes in C.* Neither the author of this book nor Ravi Myneni accept any liability for the use or misuse of these subroutines.

The code requires the use of so-called "include" files. Because such files vary from system to system, they are not included here.

```
#define MAX(a,b) (a,b, a > b ? a : b)
  fdi_bond_option(number_space_points,number_time_points,parameters,
                  coupon,par,bond_maturity,option_maturity,call_put,
                  american_european,strike,spot_rates,bond_prices,
                  accrued_interest,option_prices)
  /****************************************************************************
fdi_bond_option() is an implicit finite difference algorithm
        for valuing bond options in the CIR model with constant speed
        of adjustment, long term mean and volatility parameters.
  ------------------------------------------------------------------------
int    number_time_points  = number of time points
               (Note: actual number of temporal steps is one less.)
int    number_space_points = number of space points
               (Note: actual number of spatial steps is one less.)
        double *parameters        = model parameters vector:
                                      0 <-> speed of adjustment
                                      1 <-> long term mean
                                      2 <-> volatility parameter
        double coupon             = coupon rate (annual % par)
        double par                = bond's par value (%)
double bond_maturity      = bond time to maturity (in years)
double option_maturity    = option time to maturity (in years)
        char    call_put          = call ('C') or put ('P')
        char    american_european = american ('A') or european ('E')
        double strike             = option strike on flat price
        double *spot_rates        = vector of spot rates
        double *bond_prices       = vector of flat bond prices
        double *accrued_interest  = accrued interest on bond
        double *option_prices     = vector of option prices
  ------------------------------------------------------------------------
  ****************************************************************************/
  int number_space_points,number_time_points;
  double *parameters,coupon,par,bond_maturity,option_maturity,strike;
  char call_put,american_european;
  double *spot_rates,*bond_prices,*accrued_interest,*option_prices;
  {
   int error;
   int i,j,k,option_expiration_period,*coupon_flows,*ivector();
   double r,s,t,semi_annual_coupon,accrued,*mu,*sigma,gamma;
   double *a,*b,*c,*y_bond,*y_option,*dvector();
   double time_delta,space_delta;
   void free_ivector(),free_dvector();
   /**** Some useful checks ****/
   if (number_space_points < 10 || number_space_points > 3000)
     { printf("! number_space_points out of bounds\n"); return(1); }
   if (number_time_points < 10 || number_time_points > 5000)
     { printf("! number_time_points out of bounds\n"); return(2); }
   if (bond_maturity < 2.0/365.0 || bond_maturity > 50.0)
     { printf("! bond_maturity invalid\n"); return(3); }
   if (option_maturity < 1.0/365.0 || option_maturity > 50.0)
     { printf("! option_maturity invalid\n"); return(4); }
   if (option_maturity >= bond_maturity)
     { printf("! option_maturity exceeds bond_maturity\n"); return(5); }
   if (strike < 0.0)
     { printf("! strike is negative\n"); return(6); }
   /**** Initialization of parameters ****/
   space_delta= 1.0 / (double)(number_space_points-1);
   time_delta= bond_maturity / (double)(number_time_points-1);
   if (time_delta >= 0.5)
     { printf("! number_space_points too small\n"); error= 7; goto fre; }
   gamma= 12.5;
   /**** Calculation of semi-annual coupon ****/
   semi_annual_coupon= coupon * par / 200.0;
   /**** Calculation of option expiration node ****/
   option_expiration_period= (int)((option_maturity / time_delta) + 0.5);
   if (option_expiration_period == 0 || option_expiration_period ==
```

```
number_time_points-1)
  { printf("! option_maturity out of bounds\n"); error= 8; goto fre; }
/**** Allocation of memory ****/
a= dvector(0,number_space_points-1);
b= dvector(0,number_space_points-1);
c= dvector(0,number_space_points-1);
y_bond= dvector(0,number_space_points-1);
y_option= dvector(0,number_space_points-1);
mu= dvector(0,number_space_points-1);
sigma= dvector(0,number_space_points-1);
coupon_flows= ivector(0,number_time_points-1);
/**** Calculation of semi-annual coupon nodes ****/
for (j=number_time_points-1,i=0 ; j >= 0 ; j--)
  {
    k= (int)(((double)(i)*0.5 / time_delta) + 0.5);
    if (j == number_time_points-k-1)
      { coupon_flows[j]= 1; i++; }
    else
      { coupon_flows[j]= 0; }
  }
/**** Initialization of terminal bond price ****/
for (i=0 ; i < number_space_points ; i++)
  { bond_prices[i]= par; }
/**** Calculation of pde parameters ****/
for (i=1 ; i < number_space_points ; i++)
  {
    error= fdi_sdv(i,gamma,space_delta,parameters,&spot_rates[i],&mu[i],
    &sigma[i]);
    if (error)
      { printf("! error %d occurred in fdi_sdv()\n",error); error= 9; goto fre;

  }
/**** Main valuation loop until option expiration ****/
for (j=number_time_points-1 ; j > option_expiration_period ; j--)
  {
    /**** Addition of semi-annual coupon ****/
    if (coupon_flows[j])
      {
        for (i=0 ; i < number_space_points ; i++)
  { bond_prices[i] += semi_annual_coupon; }
      }
    /**** Highest spot rate case is treated differently ****/
    spot_rates[0]= 1.0e+12;
    a[0]= 0.0;
    b[0]= 1.0;
    c[0]= 0.0;
    if (j == number_time_points-1)
      { y_bond[0]= bond_prices[0] / time_delta; }
    else
      { y_bond[0]= 0.0; }
    /**** Lowest spot rate case is also treated differently ****/
    a[number_space_points-1]= -mu[number_space_points-1] / space_delta;
    b[number_space_points-1]= mu[number_space_points-1] / space_delta
                            - 1.0 / time_delta;
    c[number_space_points-1]= 0.0;
    y_bond[number_space_points-1]= -bond_prices[number_space_points-1] /
                                    time_delta;
    /**** Now do the intermediate points ****/
    for (i=1 ; i < number_space_points-1 ; i++)
      {
        r= mu[i] / (4.0 * space_delta);
        s= sigma[i] / (2.0 * pow(space_delta,2.0));
        a[i]= (s - r);
        b[i]= -((1.0 / time_delta) + (2.0 * s) + spot_rates[i]);
        c[i]= (s + r);
        y_bond[i]= (r - s) * bond_prices[i-1] + ((2.0 * s) -
```

```
                (1.0 / time_delta))
                        * bond_prices[i] - (r + s) * bond_prices[i+1];
        }
    /**** Solution of tridiagonal system ****/
    tridag(a,b,c,bond_prices,y_bond,number_space_points);
    }
/**** Initialization of terminal value of option ****/
if (coupon_flows[option_expiration_period])
  { accrued= 0.0; }
else
  {
    for (i=option_expiration_period ; !coupon_flows[i] ; i++) {;}
    accrued= (1.0 - ((double)(i - option_expiration_period)
            * time_delta / 0.5)) * semi_annual_coupon;
  }
for (i=0 ; i < number_space_points ; i++)
    {
      if (call_put == 'C' || call_put == 'c')
        { option_prices[i]= MAX(bond_prices[i]-accrued-strike,0.0); }
      else
        { option_prices[i]= MAX(strike-bond_prices[i]+accrued,0.0); }
    }
/**** Main valuation loop until initial period ****/
for (j=option_expiration_period ; j > 0 ; j--)
    {
    /**** Addition of semi-annual coupon ****/
    if (coupon_flows[j])
        {
          for (i=0 ; i < number_space_points ; i++)
    { bond_prices[i] += semi_annual_coupon; }
        }
    /**** Highest spot rate case is treated differently ****/
    spot_rates[0]= 1.0e+12;
    a[0]= 0.0;
    b[0]= 1.0;
    c[0]= 0.0;
    if (j == number_time_points-1)
        {
          y_bond[0]= bond_prices[0] / time_delta;
          y_option[0]= option_prices[0] / time_delta;
        }
    else
        {
          y_bond[0]= 0.0;
          y_option[0]= 0.0;
        }
    /**** Lowest spot rate case is also treated separately ****/
    a[number_space_points-1]= -mu[number_space_points-1] / space_delta;
    b[number_space_points-1]= mu[number_space_points-1] / space_delta
                        - 1.0 / time_delta;
    c[number_space_points-1]= 0.0;
    y_bond[number_space_points-1]= -bond_prices[number_space_points-1] /
                            time_delta;
    y_option[number_space_points-1]= -option_prices[number_space_points-1] /
                            time_delta;
    /**** Now do the intermediate points ****/
    for (i=1 ; i < number_space_points-1 ; i++)
        {
          r= mu[i] / (4.0 * space_delta);
          s= sigma[i] / (2.0 * pow(space_delta,2.0));
          a[i]= (s - r);
          b[i]= -((1.0 / time_delta) + (2.0 * s) + spot_rates[i]);
          c[i]= (s + r);
          y_bond[i]= (r - s) * bond_prices[i-1] + ((2.0 * s) -
          (1.0 / time_delta))
                        * bond_prices[i] - (r + s) * bond_prices[i+1];
```

```
                    y_option[i]= (r - s) * option_prices[i-1] + ((2.0 * s) -
                    (1.0 / time_delta))
                               * option_prices[i] - (r + s) * option_prices[i+1];
                 }
          /**** Solution of tridiagonal system ****/
          tridag(a,b,c,bond_prices,y_bond,number_space_points);
          tridag(a,b,c,option_prices,y_option,number_space_points);
          /**** American feature is handled by the Wald-Bellman equation ****/
          if (american_european == 'A' || american_european == 'a')
             {
                if (coupon_flows[j-1])
                  { accrued= 0.0; }
                else
                  {
                     for (i=j-1 ; !coupon_flows[i] ; i++) {;}
                     accrued= (1.0 - ((double)(i - j + 1)
                              * time_delta / 0.5)) * semi_annual_coupon;
                  }
                for (i=0 ; i < number_space_points ; i++)
                   {
                      if (call_put == 'C' || call_put == 'c')
                        { option_prices[i]= MAX(option_prices[i],bond_prices[i]-accrued-
strike); }
                      else
                        { option_prices[i]= MAX(option_prices[i],strike-bond_prices[i]+
                        accrued); }
                   }
             }
        }
    if (coupon_flows[0])
      { *accrued_interest= 0.0; }
    else
      {
         *accrued_interest= (1.0 - ((double)(coupon_flows[0]) * time_delta
                            / 0.5)) * semi_annual_coupon;
         for (i=0 ; i < number_space_points ; i++)
    { bond_prices[i] -= *accrued_interest; }
      }
    /**** Cleanup ****/
    error= 0;
 fre:
    free_dvector(a,0,number_space_points-1);
    free_dvector(b,0,number_space_points-1);
    free_dvector(c,0,number_space_points-1);
    free_dvector(y_bond,0,number_space_points-1);
    free_dvector(y_option,0,number_space_points-1);
    free_dvector(mu,0,number_space_points-1);
    free_dvector(sigma,0,number_space_points-1);
    free_ivector(coupon_flows,0,number_time_points-1);
    return(error);
 }
fdi_sdv(position,gamma,space_delta,parameters,spot_rate,mu,sigma)
 /*************************************************************************
fdi_sdv() computes the coefficients for fdi_bond_option().
 ----------------------------------------------------------------------
long    position    = position along the space axis.
        double gamma      = scaling factor (usually 12.5).
        double space_delta = one interval of space axis.
        double *parameters    = model parameters vector:
                                0 <-> speed of adjustment
                                1 <-> long term mean
                                2 <-> volatility parameter
        double *spot_rate = spot rate (in decimal).
        double *mu        = drift rate modified by gamma (in decimal).
        double *sigma     = variance modified by gamma (in decimal).
 ----------------------------------------------------------------------
```

```
    ***********************************************************************/
int position;
double gamma,space_delta,*parameters,*spot_rate,*mu,*sigma;
{
  int error;
  int i,j,k;
  double r,s,y;
      /**** Some useful checks ****/
      if (position < 0)
        { printf("! position invalid\n"); return(1); }
      if (gamma < 1.0 || gamma > 100.0)
        { printf("! gamma out of bounds\n"); return(2); }
      if (space_delta <= 0)
        { printf("! space_delta invalid\n"); return(3); }
      /**** Compute spot rate ****/
      y= (double)(position) * space_delta;
      *spot_rate= (1.0 - y)/ (gamma * y);
      /**** Useful calculation ****/
      s= *spot_rate * pow(parameters[2],2.0);
      /**** Compute drift ****/
      r= parameters[0] * (parameters[1] - *spot_rate);
      r *= -gamma * pow(y,2.0);
      r += pow(gamma,2.0) * pow(y,3.0) * s;
      *mu= r;
      /**** Compute variance/2.0 ****/
      r= 0.5 * pow(gamma,2.0) * pow(y,4.0) * s;
      *sigma= r;
  return(0);
}
```

Bibliography

Aase, K. 1984. "Optimum Portfolio Diversification in a General Continuous Time Model." *Stochastic Processes and Their Application* 18: 81–98.

Abel, A. 1986. "Stock Prices under Time-Varying Dividend Risk: An Exact Solution in an Infinite-Horizon General Equilibrium Model." Unpublished, Wharton School, University of Pennsylvania.

Adler, M., and J. Detemple. 1988. "On the Optimal Hedge of a Non-Traded Cash Position." *Journal of Finance* 43: 143–153.

Aiyagari, S., and M. Gertler. 1990. "Asset Returns with Transactions Costs and Uninsured Individual Risk: A Stage III Exercise." Working Paper, 454, Federal Reserve Bank of Minneapolis.

Aliprantis, C., and O. Burkinshaw. 1985. *Positive Operators.* Orlando: Academic Press.

Alvarez, O. 1991. "Gestion de portefeuille avec coût de transaction." Unpublished, École Polytechnique.

Ansel, J.-P., and C. Stricker. 1991. "Lois de Martingale, Densités et Décompositions de Föllmer Schweizer." Unpublished, Université de Franche-Comté.

Apelfeld, R., and A. Conze. 1990. "The Term Structure of Interest Rates: The Case of Imperfect Information." Unpublished, Department of Economics, University of Chicago.

Araujo, A., and P. Monteiro. 1989. "Equilibrium without Uniform Conditions." *Journal of Economic Theory* 48: 416–427.

———. 1987. "Generic Non-Existence of Equilibria in Finance Models." *Journal of Mathematical Economics* 20: 489–501.

Arnold, L. 1974. *Stochastic Differential Equations: Theory and Applications.* New York: Wiley.

Arrow, K. 1951. "An Extension of the Basic Theorems of Classical Welfare Economics." In J. Neyman, *Proceedings of the Second Berkeley Symposium on Mathematical Statistics and Probability*, pp. 507–32. Berkeley: University of California Press.

———. 1953. "Le Rôle des valeurs boursières pour la repartition la meilure des risques." *Econometrie*. Colloq. Internat. Centre National de la Recherche Scientifique 40 (Paris 1952), pp. 41–47; discussion, pp. 47–48, C.N.R.S. (Paris 1953) English translation in *Review of Economic Studies* 31 (1964): 91–96.

———. 1970. *Essays in the Theory of Risk Bearing*. London: North-Holland.

Arrow, K., and G. Debreu. 1954. "Existence of an Equilibrium for a Competitive Economy." *Econometrica* 22: 265–290.

Artzner, P., and F. Delbaen. 1990. "Term Structure of Interest Rates: The Martingale Approach." Unpublished, I.R.M.A., Strasbourg. Forthcoming in *Advances in Applied Mathematics*.

Artzner, P., and D. Heath. 1990. "Completeness and Non-Unique Pricing." Unpublished, Cornell University.

Babbs, S. 1991. "A Family of Ito Process Models for the Term Structure of Interest Rates." Financial Options Research Centre, University of Warwick.

Bachelier, L. 1900. "Théorie de la speculation." *Annales scientifiques de l'école normale supérieure* 3d ser., 17: 21–88, Translation in *The Random Character of Stock Market Prices*, ed. Paul Cootner, pp. 17–79. Cambridge, Mass.: MIT Press, 1964.

Back, K. 1986. "Securities Market Equilibrium without Bankruptcy: Contingent Claim Valuation and the Martingale Property." Research Paper 683, Center for Mathematical Studies in Economics and Management Science, Northwestern University.

———. 1991a. "Asset Pricing for General Processes." *Journal of Mathematical Economics* 20: 371–396.

———. 1991b. "Term Structure Notes." Washington University, St. Louis.

Back, K., and S. Pliska. 1986. "Discrete versus Continuous Trading in Securities Markets with Net Worth Constraints." Working Paper, 700, Center for Mathematical Studies in Economics and Management Science, Northwestern University.

———. 1987. "The Shadow Price of Information in Continuous Time Decision Problems." *Stochastics* 22: 151–186.

———. 1991. "On the Fundamental Theorem of Asset Pricing with an Infinite State Space." *Journal of Mathematical Economics* 20: 1–18.

Balasko, Y. 1989. *Foundations of the Theory of General Equilibrium*. New York: Academic Press.

Balasko, Y., and D. Cass. 1986. "The Structure of Financial Equilibrium with Exogenous Yields: The Case of Incomplete Markets." *Econometrica* 57: 135–162.

Balasko, Y., D. Cass, and P. Siconolfi. 1990. "The Structure of Financial Equilibrium with Exogenous Yields: The Case of Restricted Participation." *Journal of Mathematical Economics* 19: 195–216.

Barles, G., C. Daher, and M. Romano. 1990. "Evaluation of Assets with Path-Dependent Cash Flows." Unpublished, Caisse Autonome de Refinancement, Paris.

Barone-Adesi, G., and R. Elliott. 1991. "Approximations for the Values of American Options." *Stochastic Analysis and Applications* 9: 115–131.

Bartle, R. 1976. *The Elements of Real Analysis* (2d ed.). New York: Wiley.

Beaglehole, D. 1990. "Tax Clienteles and Stochastic Processes in the Gilt Market." Unpublished, Graduate School of Business, University of Chicago.

Beaglehole, D., and M. Tenney. 1990. "General Solutions of Some Interest Rate Contingent Claim Pricing Equations." Unpublished, Graduate School of Business, University of Chicago. Forthcoming in *Journal of Fixed Income.*

Bellman, R. 1957. *Dynamic Programming.* Princeton, N.J.: Princeton University Press.

Bensoussan, A. 1983. "Lectures on Stochastic Control." In S. Mitter and A. Moro, *Nonlinear Filtering and Stochastic Control,* Lecture Notes in Mathematics 972, pp. 1–62. New York: Springer-Verlag.

———. 1984. "On the Theory of Option Pricing." *Acta Applicandae Mathematicae* 2: 139–158.

Benveniste, L., and J. Scheinkman. 1979. "On the Differentiability of the Value Function in Dynamic Models of Economics." *Econometrica* 47: 727–732.

Bergman, Y. 1985. "Time Preference and Capital Asset Pricing Models." *Journal of Financial Economics* 14: 145–159.

———. 1991. "Option Pricing with Divergent Borrowing and Lending Rates." Unpublished, Department of Economics, Brown University.

Bertsekas, D. 1976. *Dynamic Programming and Stochastic Control.* New York: Academic Press.

Bertsekas, D., and S. Shreve. 1978. *Stochastic Optimal Control, The Discrete Time Case.* New York: Academic Press.

Bewley, T. 1972. "Existence of Equilibria in Economies with Infinitely Many Commodities." *Journal of Economic Theory* 4: 514–540.

———. 1982. "Thoughts on Volatility Tests of the Intertemporal Asset Pricing Model." Unpublished, Department of Economics, Northwestern University.

Bick, A. 1986. "On Viable Diffusion Price Processes." Unpublished, Graduate School of Business, New York University.

Bick, A., and W. Willinger. 1991. "Dynamic Spanning without Probabilities." Faculty of Business Administration, Simon Fraser University. Forthcoming in *Mathematical Finance.*

Billingsley, P. 1986. *Probability and Measure* (2d ed.). New York: Wiley.

Black, F. 1972. "Capital Market Equilibrium with Restricted Borrowing." *Journal of Business* 45: 444–454.

———. 1976. "The Pricing of Commodity Contracts." *Journal of Financial Economics* 3: 167–179.

———. 1990. "Mean Reversion and Consumption Smoothing." *Review of Financial Studies* 3: 107–114.

Black, F., E. Derman, and W. Toy. 1990. "A One-Factor Model of Interest Rates and Its Application to Treasury Bond Options." *Financial Analysts Journal*: 33–39.

Black, F., and M. Scholes. 1973. "The Pricing of Options and Corporate Liabilities." *Journal of Political Economy* 81: 637–654.

Blackwell, D. 1965. "Discounted Dynamic Programming." *Annals of Mathematical Statistics* 36: 226–235.

Blume, L., D. Easley, and M. O'Hara. 1982. "Characterization of Optimal Plans for Stochastic Dynamic Programs." *Journal of Economic Theory* 28: 221–234.

Bossaerts, P. 1990. "Modern Term Structure Theory." Unpublished, California Institute of Technology.

Bottazzi, J.-M. 1991. "Note on the Algebraic Dimension of Critical Prices in Incomplete Markets." Unpublished, Laboratoire d'Econométrie de l'école Polytechnique, Paris.

Boyle, P. 1977. "Options: A Monte Carlo Approach." *Journal of Financial Economics* 4: 323–338.

———. 1988. "A Lattice Framework for Option Pricing with Two State Variables." *Journal of Financial and Quantitative Analysis* 23: 1–12.

———. 1990. "Valuation of Derivative Securities Involving Several Assets Using Discrete Time Methods." Unpublished, Accounting Group, University of Waterloo.

Boyle, P., J. Evnine, and S. Gibbs. 1989. "Numerical Evaluation of Multivariate Contingent Claims." *Review of Financial Studies* 2: 241–250.

Breeden, D. 1979. "An Intertemporal Asset Pricing Model with Stochastic Consumption and Investment Opportunities." *Journal of Financial Economics* 7: 265–296.

———. 1986. "Consumption, Production, Inflation and Interest Rates." *Journal of Financial Economics* 16: 3–39.

Breeden, D., M. Gibbons, and R. Litzenberger. 1989. "Empirical Tests of the Consumption Oriented CAPM." *Journal of Finance* 44: 231–262.

Breeden, D., and R. Litzenberger. 1978. "Prices of State-Contingent Claims Implicit in Option Prices." *Journal of Business* 51: 621–651.

Brennan, M., and E. Schwartz. 1977. "The Valuation of American Put Options." *Journal of Finance* 32: 449–462.

———. 1979. "A Continuous Time Approach to the Pricing of Bonds." *Journal of Banking and Finance* 3: 133–155.

Brock, W. 1979. "An Integration of Stochastic Growth Theory and the Theory of Finance, Part I: The Growth Model." In J. Green and J. Scheinkman, *General Equilibrium, Growth, and Trade*, pp. 165–92. New York: Academic Press.

———. 1982. "Asset Prices in a Production Economy." In J. McCall, *The Economics of Information and Uncertainty*, pp. 1–46. Chicago: University of Chicago Press.

Brown, D., and M. Gibbons. 1985. "A Simple Econometric Approach for Utility-Based Asset Pricing Models." *Journal of Finance* 40: 359–81.

Brown, R., and S. Schaefer. 1991. "Interest Rate Volatility and the Term Structure." Unpublished, London Business School.

Campbell, J. 1984. "Bond and Stock Returns in a Simple Exchange Model." Unpublished, Department of Economics, Princeton University.

———. 1986. "A Defense of Traditional Hypotheses about the Term Structure of Interest Rates." *Journal of Finance* 41: 183–93.

———. 1990. "Intertemporal Asset Pricing without Consumption." Unpublished, Department of Economics, Princeton University.

Carr, P. 1987. "Treasury Bond Futures and the Quality Option." Unpublished, Graduate School of Management, University of California, Los Angeles.

Carr, P., and R. Jarrow. 1990. "The Stop-Loss Start-Gain Paradox and Option Valuation: A New Decomposition into Intrinsic and Time Value." *Review of Financial Studies* 3: 469–92.

Carr, P., R. Jarrow, and R. Myneni. 1990. "Alternative Characterizations of American Put Options." Unpublished, Johnson School of Management, Cornell University.

Cass, D. 1984. "Competitive Equilibria in Incomplete Financial Markets." Working Paper, 84–09, Center for Analytic Research in Economics and the Social Sciences, University of Pennsylvania.

———. 1989. "Sunspots and Incomplete Financial Markets: The Leading Example." In G. Feiwel, *The Economics of Imperfect Competition and Employment: Joan Robinson and Beyond*, pp. 677–93. London: Macmillan.

———. 1991. "Incomplete Financial Markets and Indeterminacy of Financial Equilibrium." In J.-J. Laffont, *Advances in Economic Theory* Cambridge: Cambridge University Press.

Carverhill, A. 1988. "The Ho and Lee Term Structure Theory: A Continuous Time Version." Working Paper, 88-5, Financial Options Research Centre, University of Warwick.

———. 1990. "A Survey of Elementary Techniques for Pricing Options on Bonds and Interest Rates." Working Paper, 90-9, Financial Options Research Centre, University of Warwick.

———. 1991. "The Term Structure of Interest Rates and Associated Options; Equilibrium versus Evolutionary Models." Working Paper, 91-21, Financial Options Research Centre, University of Warwick.

Chae, S. 1988. "Existence of Equilibria in Incomplete Markets." *Journal of Economic Theory* 44: 9-18.

Chamberlain, G. 1988. "Asset Pricing in Multiperiod Securities Markets." *Econometrica* 56: 1283–1300.

Chernoff, H., and A. Petkau. 1984. "Numerical Methods for Bayes Sequential Decisions Problems." Technical Report 34, Statistics Center, Massachusetts Institute of Technology.

Cheng, S. 1991. "On the Feasibility of Arbitrage-Based Option Pricing When Stochastic Bond Price Processes Are Involved." *Journal of Economic Theory* 53: 185–198.

Chew, S. 1983. "A Generalization of the Quasilinear Mean with Applications to the Measurement of Income Inequality and Decision Theory Resolving the Allais Paradox." *Econometrica* 51: 1065–92.

———. 1989. "Axiomatic Utility Theories with the Betweenness Property." *Annals of Operations Research* 19: 273–298.

Chew, S.-H., and L. Epstein. 1991. "Recursive Utility under Uncertainty." In A. Khan and N. Yannelis, *Equilibrium Theory with an Infinite Number of Commodities*. New York: Springer-Verlag.

Chow, Y., and H. Teicher. 1978. *Probability Theory: Independence Interchangeability Martingales*. New York: Springer-Verlag.

Christensen, B. J. 1991. "Statistics for Arbitrage-Free Asset Pricing." Unpublished, Department of Finance, New York University.

Christensen, P. 1987. "An Intuitive Approach to the Harrison and Kreps Concept of Arbitrage Pricing for Continuous Time Diffusions." Unpublished, Department of Management, Odense University, Denmark.

Chung, K.L. 1974. *A Course in Probability Theory* (2d ed.). New York: Academic Press.

Chung, K.L., and R. Williams. 1990. *An Introduction to Stochastic Integration* 2d ed. Boston: Birkhäuser.

Clark, S. 1990. "The Valuation Problem in Arbitrage Price Theory." Unpublished, Department of Statistics, University of Kentucky. Forthcoming in *Journal of Mathematical Economics*.

Clelow, L. 1990. "Finite Difference Techniques for One and Two Dimension Option Valuation Problems." Unpublished, Financial Options Research Center, University of Warwick.

Constantinides, G. 1982. "Intertemporal Asset Pricing with Heterogeneous Consumers and without Demand Aggregation." *Journal of Business* 55: 253–267.

———. 1986. "Capital Market Equilibrium with Transactions Costs." *Journal of Political Economy* 94: 842–62.

———. 1989. "Theory of Valuation: Overview and Recent Developments." In S. Bhattacharya and G. Constantinides, *Theory of Valuation, Frontiers of Modern Financial Theory*, pp. 1–23. Totowa, New Jersey: Rowman and Littlefield.

———. 1990a. "Habit Formation: A Resolution of the Equity Premium Puzzle." *Journal of Political Economy* 98: 519–543.

———. 1990b. "Theory of the Term Structure of Interest Rates: The Squared Autoregressive Instruments Nominal Term Structure (SAINTS) Model." Unpublished, Graduate School of Business, University of Chicago.

Constantinides, G., and D. Duffie. 1991. "Asset Pricing with Heterogeneous Consumers." Unpublished, Graduate School of Business, Stanford University.

Conze, A., and R. Viswanathan. 1991. "Probability Measures and Numeraires." Unpublished, CEREMADE, Université de Paris.

Cornell, B. 1981. "The Consumption Based Asset Pricing Model." *Journal of Financial Economics* 9: 103–8.

Courtadon, G. 1982. "The Pricing of Options on Default-Free Bonds." *Journal of Financial and Quantitative Analysis* 17: 75–100.

Cox, J. 1983. "Optimal Consumption and Portfolio Rules When Assets Follow a Diffusion Process." Working Paper, 658, Graduate School of Business, Stanford University.

Cox, J., and C.-F. Huang. 1991. "A Variational Problem Arising in Financial Economics with an Application to a Portfolio Turnpike Theorem." *Journal of Mathematical Economics* 20: 465–88.

———. 1989. "Optimal Consumption and Portfolio Policies When Asset Prices Follow a Diffusion Process." *Journal of Economic Theory* 49: 33–83.

Cox, J., J. Ingersoll, and S. Ross. 1981a. "A Re-examination of Traditional Hypotheses about the Term Structure of Interest Rates." *Journal of Finance* 36: 769–799.

———. 1981b. "The Relation between Forward Prices and Futures Prices." *Journal of Financial Economics* 9: 321–346.

———. 1985a. "A Theory of the Term Structure of Interest Rates." *Econometrica* 53: 385–408.

———. 1985b. "An Intertemporal General Equilibrium Model of Asset Prices." *Econometrica* 53: 363–384.

Cox, J., and S. Ross. 1976. "The Valuation of Options for Alternative Stochastic Processes." *Journal of Financial Economics* 3: 145–166.

Cox, J., S. Ross, and M. Rubinstein. 1979. "Option Pricing: A Simplified Approach." *Journal of Financial Economics* 7: 229–263.

Cox, J., and M. Rubinstein. 1985. *Options Markets.* Englewood Cliffs, N.J.: Prentice-Hall.

Cutland, N., P. Kopp, and W. Willinger. 1990. "A Nonstandard Approach to Option Pricing." *Mathematical Finance* 1/4: 1–38.

Cvitanič, J., and I. Karatzas. 1991. "Convex Duality in Constrained Portfolio Optimization." Unpublished, Department of Statistics, Columbia University.

Dana, R.-A. 1990. "Existence, Uniqueness and Determinacy of Arrow-Debreu Equilibria in Finance Models." Unpublished, University of Paris.

Dana, R.-A., and M. Pontier. 1990. "On the Existence of a Stochastic Equilibrium." Unpublished, University of Paris. Forthcoming in *Mathematics of Operations Research.*

Dash, J. 1989. "Path Integrals and Options — I." Financial Strategies Group, Merrill Lynch Capital Markets.

Davis, M., and A. Norman. 1990. "Portfolio Selection with Transaction Costs." *Mathematics of Operations Research* 15: 676–713.

Davis, M., and V. Panas. 1991. "European Option Pricing with Transaction Costs." Proceedings of the Thirtieth IEEE Conference on Decision and Control, Brighton, December.

Debreu, G. 1953. "Une Economie de l'incertain." Unpublished, Electricité de France.

———. 1954. "Valuation Equilibrium and Pareto Optimum." *Proceedings of the National Academy of Sciences* 40: 588–592.

———. 1959. *Theory of Value.* Cowles Foundation Monograph 17. New Haven, Conn.: Yale University Press.

———. 1972. "Smooth Preferences." *Econometrica* 40: 603–15; Corrigendum 44 (1976): 831–32.

———. 1982. "Existence of Competitive Equilibrium." In K. Arrow and M. Intriligator, *Handbook of Mathematical Economics, Volume II*, pp. 697–743 Amsterdam: North-Holland.

Dekel, E. 1987. "Asset Demands without the Independence Axiom." Unpublished, Department of Economics, University of California, Berkeley.

Delbaen, F. 1991. "Representing Martingale Measures When Asset Prices Are Continuous and Bounded." Unpublished, Department of Mathematics, Vrije Universiteit Brussel.

Detemple, J. 1991. "Further Results on Asset Pricing with Incomplete Information." *Journal of Economic Dynamics and Control* 15: 425–454.

Detemple, J., and F. Zapatero. 1990. "Asset Prices in an Exchange Economy with Habit Formation." Unpublished, Graduate School of Business, Columbia University.

Donaldson, J., T. Johnson, and R. Mehra. 1987. "The Behavior of the Term Structure of Interest Rates in a Real Business Cycle Model." Unpublished, Graduate School of Business, Columbia University.

Donaldson, J., and R. Mehra. 1984. "Comparative Dynamics of an Equilibrium Intertemporal Asset Pricing Model." *Review of Economic Studies* 51: 491–508.

Dothan, M. 1978. "On the Term Structure of Interest Rates." *Journal of Financial Economics* 7: 229–264.

———. 1990. *Prices in Financial Markets.* New York: Oxford University Press.

Dothan, M., and D. Feldman. 1986. "Equilibrium Interest Rates and Multiperiod Bonds in a Partially Observable Economy." *Journal of Finance* 41: 369–382.

Duffie, D. 1986. "Stochastic Equilibria: Existence, Spanning Number, and the 'No Expected Financial Gain from Trade' Hypothesis." *Econometrica* 54: 1161–84.

———. 1987. "Stochastic Equilibria with Incomplete Financial Markets." *Journal of Economic Theory* 41: 405–16, Corrigendum 49 (1989): 384.

———. 1988a. "An Extension of the Black-Scholes Model of Security Valuation." *Journal of Economic Theory* 46: 194–204.

———. 1988b. *Security Markets: Stochastic Models.* Boston: Academic Press.

———. 1989. *Futures Markets.* Englewood Cliffs, N.J.: Prentice-Hall.

———. 1991. "The Nature of Incomplete Markets." In J.-J. Laffont, *Advances in Economic Theory.* Cambridge: Cambridge University Press, forthcoming.

Duffie, D., and L. Epstein. 1992. "Stochastic Differential Utility." *Econometrica* 60: 353–394.

———. 1991. "Asset Pricing with Stochastic Differential Utility." Research Paper 1155, Graduate School of Business, Stanford University. Forthcoming in *The Review of Financial Studies.*

Duffie, D., and M. Garman. 1985. "Intertemporal Arbitrage and the Markov Valuation of Securities." Working Paper, 975, Graduate School of Business, Stanford University. Forthcoming in *Cuadernos Economicos de ICE*.

Duffie, D., J. Geanakoplos, A. Mas-Colell, and A. McLennan. 1988. "Stationary Markov Equilibria." Unpublished, Graduate School of Business, Stanford University.

Duffie, D., and C.-F. Huang. 1985. "Implementing Arrow-Debreu Equilibria by Continuous Trading of Few Long-Lived Securities." *Econometrica* 53: 1337–56.

———. 1986. "Multiperiod Security Markets with Differential Information: Martingales and Resolution Times." *Journal of Mathematical Economics* 15: 283–303.

Duffie, D., and M. Jackson. 1990. "Optimal Hedging and Equilibrium in a Dynamic Futures Market." *Journal of Economic Dynamics and Control* 14: 21–33.

Duffie, D., and P.-L. Lions. 1990. "PDE Solutions of Stochastic Differential Utility." Research Paper 1095, Graduate School of Business, Stanford University. Forthcoming in *Journal of Mathematical Economics*.

Duffie, D., and P. Protter. 1988. "From Discrete to Continuous Time Finance: Weak Convergence of the Financial Gain Process." Research Paper 1097, Graduate School of Business, Stanford University. Forthcoming in *Mathematical Finance*.

Duffie, D., and H. Richardson. 1991. "Mean-Variance Hedging in Continuous Time." *Annals of Applied Probability* 1: 1–15.

Duffie, D., and W. Shafer. 1986. "Equilibrium in Incomplete Markets II: Generic Existence in Stochastic Economies." *Journal of Mathematical Economics* 15: 199–216.

Duffie, D., and K. Singleton. 1989. "Simulated Moments Estimation of Markov Models of Asset Prices." Research Paper 1083, Graduate School of Business, Stanford University.

Duffie, D., and C. Skiadas. 1990. "Continuous-Time Security Pricing: A Utility Gradient Approach." Research Paper 1096, Graduate School of Business, Stanford University.

Duffie, D., and R. Stanton. 1988. "Pricing Continuously Resettled Contingent Claims." Unpublished, Graduate School of Business, Stanford University. Forthcoming in *Journal of Economic Dynamics and Control*.

Duffie, D., and W. Zame. 1989. "The Consumption-Based Capital Asset Pricing Model." *Econometrica* 57: 1279–97.

Dumas, B. 1989. "Two-Person Dynamic Equilibrium in the Capital Market." *Review of Financial Studies* 2: 157–188.

Dumas, B., and E. Luciano. 1989. "An Exact Solution to a Dynamic Portfolio Choice Problem under Transactions Costs." Unpublished, Wharton School of the University of Pennsylvania.

Dunn, K., and K. Singleton. 1986. "Modeling the Term Structure of Interest Rates under Nonseparable Utility and Durability of Goods." *Journal of Financial Economics* 17: 27–55.

Durrett, R. 1991. *Probability: Theory and Examples.* Belmont, Calif.: Wadsworth Publishing Co.

Dybvig, P. 1988. "Bond and Bond Option Pricing Based on the Current Term Structure." Unpublished, School of Business, Washington University, St. Louis.

———. 1989. "Hedging Nontraded Wealth." Unpublished, School of Business, Washington University, St. Louis.

Dybvig, P., and C.-F. Huang. 1988. "Nonnegative Wealth, Absence of Arbitrage, and Feasible Consumption Plans." *Review of Financial Studies* 1: 377–401.

Dynkin, E., and A. Yushkevich. 1979. *Controlled Markov Processes.* Berlin, New York: Springer-Verlag.

Eberlein, E. 1991. "On Modelling Questions in Security Valuation." Unpublished, Institut für Mathematische Stochastik, Universität Freiburg.

El Karoui, M. Jeanblanc-Picqué, and R. Viswanathan. 1991. "On the Robustness of the Black-Scholes Equation." Unpublished, LAMM, École Normale Supérieure de Cachan, France.

El Karoui, N., C. Lepage, R. Myneni, N. Roseau, and R. Viswanathan. 1991. "The Valuation and Hedging of Contingent Claims with Gaussian Markov Interest Rates." Unpublished, University of Paris.

El Karoui, N., and H. Quenez. 1991. "Evaluation dans les marchés incomplets et programmation dynamique." Unpublished, University of Paris.

El Karoui, N., and J.-C. Rochet. 1989. "A Pricing Formula for Options on Coupon Bonds." Unpublished, University of Paris.

Elliott, R. 1982. *Stochastic Calculus and Applications.* New York: Springer-Verlag.

Epstein, L. 1988. "Risk Aversion and Asset Prices." *Journal of Monetary Economics* 22: 179–192.

———. 1991. "Behavior under Risk: Recent Developments in Theory and Application." In J.-J. Laffont, *Advances in Economic Theory* Cambridge: Cambridge University Press, forthcoming.

Epstein, L., and S. Zin. 1989. "Substitution, Risk Aversion and the Temporal Behavior of Consumption and Asset Returns I: A Theoretical Framework." *Econometrica* 57: 937–69.

———. 1991. "The Independence Axiom and Asset Returns." Unpublished, Department of Economics, University of Toronto.

Ethier, S., and T. Kurtz. 1986. *Markov Processes: Characterization and Convergence.* New York: Wiley.

Feller, W. 1951. "Two Singular Diffusion Problems." *Annals of Mathematics* 54: 173–182.

Fitzpatrick, B., and W. Fleming. 1990. "Numerical Methods for Optimal Investment—Consumption Models." Proceedings of the Twenty-Ninth IEEE Conference on Decision and Control.

Fleming, W., S. Grossman, J.-L. Vila, and T. Zariphopoulou. 1989. "Optimal Portfolio Rebalancing with Transaction Costs." Unpublished, Department of Applied Mathematics, Brown University.

Fleming, W., and R. Rishel. 1975. *Deterministic and Stochastic Optimal Control.* Berlin: Springer-Verlag.

Fleming, W., and T. Zariphopoulou. 1989. "An Optimal Investment/Consumption Model with Borrowing." Unpublished, LCDC/CCS No. 89–15, Department of Applied Mathematics, Brown University.

Foldes, L. 1978. "Martingale Conditions for Optimal Saving—Discrete Time." *Journal of Mathematical Economics* 5: 83–96.

———. 1979. "Optimal Saving and Risk in Continuous Time." *Review of Economic Studies* 46: 39–65.

———. 1991a. "Certainty Equivalence in the Continuous-Time Portfolio-cum-Saving Model." In M.H.A. Davis and R. Elliott, *Applied Stochastic Analysis.* London: Gordon and Breach.

———. 1991b. "Existence and Uniqueness of an Optimum in the Infinite-Horizon Portfolio-cum-Saving Model with Semimartingale Investments." L.S.E. Financial Markets Group Discussion Paper 109, London School of Economics.

———. 1991c. "Optimal Sure Portfolio Plans." *Mathematical Finance* 1: 15–55.

Föllmer, H., and D. Sondermann. 1986. "Hedging of Non-Redundant Contingent Claims." In A. Mas-Colell and W. Hildenbrand, *Contributions to Mathematical Economics,* pp. 205–223. Amsterdam: North-Holland.

Freedman, D. 1983. *Markov Chains.* New York: Springer-Verlag.

Freidlin, M. 1985. *Functional Integration and Partial Differential Equations.* Princeton, N.J.: Princeton University Press.

Friedman, A. 1964. *Partial Differential Equations of the Parabolic Type.* Englewood Cliffs, N.J.: Prentice-Hall.

———. 1975. *Stochastic Differential Equations and Applications, Vol. I.* New York: Academic Press.

Gabay, D. 1982. "Stochastic Processes in Models of Financial Markets." Proceedings of the IFIP Conference on Control of Distributed Systems, Toulouse.

Gagnon, J., and J. Taylor. 1986. "Solving and Estimating Stochastic Equilibrium Models with the Extended Path Method." Unpublished, Department of Economics, Stanford University.

Gale, David. 1960. *The Theory of Linear Economic Models.* New York: McGraw-Hill.

Gallant, R., and H. White. 1988. *A Unified Theory of Estimation and Inference for Nonlinear Dynamic Models.* New York: Basil Blackwell.

Garman, M. 1985. "Towards a Semigroup Pricing Theory." *Journal of Finance* 40: 847–861.

Geanakoplos, J. 1990. "An Introduction to General Equilibrium with Incomplete Asset Markets." *Journal of Mathematical Economics* 19: 1–38.

Geanakoplos, J., and A. Mas-Colell. 1989. "Real Indeterminacy with Financial Assets." *Journal of Economic Theory* 47: 22–38.

Geanakoplos, J., and H. Polemarchakis. 1986. "Existence, Regularity, and Constrained Suboptimality of Competitive Allocations When the Asset Market Is Incomplete." In W. Heller and D. Starrett, *Essays in Honor of Kenneth J. Arrow, Volume III*, pp. 65–96. Cambridge: Cambridge University Press.

Geman, H., N. El Karoui, and J.-C. Rochet. 1991. "Probability Changes and Option Pricing." Unpublished, University of Paris.

Gennotte, G. 1984. "Continuous-Time Production Economies under Incomplete Information I: A Separation Theorem." Working Paper, 1612–84, Sloan School, Massachusetts Institute of Technology.

Geske, R. 1979. "The Valuation of Compound Options." *Journal of Financial Economics* 7: 63–81.

Geske, R., and H. Johnson. 1984. "The American Put Option Valued Analytically." *Journal of Finance* 39: 1511–1524.

Gibbons, M., and K. Ramaswamy. 1986. "The Term Structure of Interest Rates: Empirical Evidence." Unpublished, Graduate School of Business, Stanford University.

Gibbons, M., and T. Sun. 1986. "The Term Structure of Interest Rates: A Simple Exposition of the Cox, Ingersoll, and Ross Model." Unpublished, Graduate School of Business, Stanford University.

Gihman, I., and A. Skorohod. 1972. *Stochastic Differential Equations.* Berlin: Springer-Verlag.

Giovannini, A., and P. Weil. 1989. "Risk Aversion and Intertemporal Substitution in the Capital Asset Pricing Model." National Bureau of Economic Research.

Goldman, B., H. Sosin, and M. Gatto. 1979. "Path Dependent Options: 'Buy at the Low, Sell at the High'." *Journal of Finance* 34: 1111–27.

Gorman, W. 1953. "Community Preference Fields." *Econometrica* 21: 63–80.

Grauer, F., and R. Litzenberger. 1979. "The Pricing of Commodity Futures Contracts, Nominal Bonds, and Other Risky Assets under Commodity Price Uncertainty." *Journal of Finance* 44: 69–84.

Grodal, B., and K. Vind. 1988. "Equilibrium with Arbitrary Market Structure." Unpublished, Department of Economics, University of Copenhagen.

Grossman, S., and G. Laroque. 1989. "Asset Pricing and Optimal Portfolio Choice in the Presence of Illiquid Durable Consumption Goods." *Econometrica* 58: 25–52.

Grossman, S., and R. Shiller. 1982. "Consumption Correlatedness and Risk Measurement in Economies with Non-Traded Assets and Heterogeneous Information." *Journal of Financial Economics* 10: 195–210.

Hakansson, N. 1970. "Optimal Investment and Consumption Strategies under Risk for a Class of Utility Functions." *Econometrica* 38: 587–607.

Hansen, L. 1982. "Large Sample Properties of Generalized Method of Moments Estimators." *Econometrica* 50: 1029–54.

Hansen, L., and R. Jaganathan. 1990. "Implications of Security Market Data for Models of Dynamic Economies." *Journal of Political Economy* 99: 225–262.

Hansen, L., and S. Richard. 1987. "The Role of Conditioning Information in Deducing Testable Restrictions Implied by Dynamic Asset Pricing Models." *Econometrica* 55: 587–614.

Hansen, L., and K. Singleton. 1982. "Generalized Instrumental Variables Estimation of Nonlinear Rational Expectations Models." *Econometrica* 50: 1269–86.

———. 1983. "Stochastic Consumption, Risk Aversion, and the Temporal Behavior of Asset Returns." *Journal of Political Economy* 91: 249–65.

———. 1986. "Efficient Estimation of Linear Asset Pricing Models with Moving Average Errors." Unpublished, Department of Economics, University of Chicago.

Harris, M. 1987. *Dynamic Economic Analysis.* New York: Oxford University Press.

Harrison, J.M. 1982. "Stochastic Calculus and Its Applications." Lecture Notes, Graduate School of Business, Stanford University.

———. 1985. *Brownian Motion and Stochastic Flow Systems.* New York: Wiley.

Harrison, J.M., and D. Kreps. 1979. "Martingales and Arbitrage in Multiperiod Securities Markets." *Journal of Economic Theory* 20: 381–408.

Harrison, J.M., and S. Pliska. 1981. "Martingales and Stochastic Integrals in the Theory of Continuous Trading." *Stochastic Processes and Their Applications* 11: 215–260.

Hart, O. 1975. "On the Optimality of Equilibrium When the Market Structure Is Incomplete." *Journal of Economic Theory* 11: 418–43.

He, H. 1990. "Convergence from Discrete- to Continuous-Time Contingent Claims Prices." *Review of Financial Studies* 3: 523–46.

He, H., and H. Pagès. 1990. "Consumption and Portfolio Decisions with Labor Income and Borrowing Constraints." Working Paper, August Research Program in Finance, University of California, Berkeley.

He, H., and N. Pearson. 1991a. "Consumption and Portfolio Policies with Incomplete Markets: The Infinite-Dimensional Case." *Journal of Economic Theory* 54: 259–305.

———. 1991b. "Consumption and Portfolio Policies with Incomplete Markets: The Finite-Dimensional Case." *Mathematical Finance* 1:1–10.

Heath, D., R. Jarrow, and A. Morton. 1987. "Bond Pricing and the Term Structure of Interest Rates: A New Methodology." Unpublished, Cornell University. Forthcoming in *Econometrica*.

———. 1990. "Bond Pricing and the Term Structure of Interest Rates: A Discrete Time Approximation." *Journal of Financial and Quantitative Analysis* 25: 419–440.

Heaton, J. 1988. "The Interaction between Time-Nonseparable Preferences and Time Aggregation." Unpublished, Sloan School of Management, Massachusetts Institute of Technology.

Heaton, J., and D. Lucas. 1991. "Asset Pricing with Uninsurable Risks and Trading Costs." Unpublished, Northwestern University.

Hellwig, M. 1991. "Rational Expectations Equilibria in Sequence Economies with Symmetric Information: The Two Period Case." Unpublished, University of Basel.

Hemler, M. 1987. "The Quality Delivery Option in Treasury Bond Futures Contracts." Unpublished, Graduate School of Business, University of Chicago.

Henrotte, P. 1991. "Transactions Costs and Duplication Strategies." Unpublished, Graduate School of Business, Stanford University.

Heston, S. 1988a. "Generalized Interest Rate Processes for the Goldman, Sachs, and Company Mortgage Valuation Model." Unpublished, Graduate School of Industrial Administration, Carnegie-Mellon University.

———. 1988b. "Testing Continuous Time Models of the Term Structure of Interest Rates." Unpublished, Graduate School of Industrial Administration, Carnegie-Mellon University.

———. 1989. "Discrete Time Versions of Continuous Time Interest Rate Models." Unpublished, Graduate School of Industrial Administration, Carnegie-Mellon University.

———. 1990a. "Sticky Consumption, Optimal Investment, and Equilibrium Asset Prices." Unpublished, Yale School of Organization and Management.

———. 1990b. "A Closed-Form Solution for Options with Stochastic Volatility." Unpublished, Yale School of Organization and Management.

Hildenbrand, W., and P. Kirman. 1989. *Introduction to Equilibrium Analysis*, 2d ed. Amsterdam: North-Holland Elsevier.

Hindy, A. 1991. "Viable Prices in Financial Markets with Solvency Constraints." Unpublished, Graduate School of Business, Stanford University. Forthcoming in *Econometrica*.

Hindy, A., and C.-F. Huang. 1989a. "On Intertemporal Preferences for Uncertain Consumption: A Continuous Time Approach." Research Paper 1139, Graduate School of Business, Stanford University.

———. 1989b. "On Intertemporal Preferences with a Continuous Time Dimension II: The Case of Uncertainty." Unpublished, Sloan School of Management, Massachusetts Institute of Technology. Forthcoming in *Journal of Mathematical Economics*.

———. 1990. "Optimal Consumption and Portfolio Rules with Local Substitution." Research Paper 1120, Graduate School of Business, Stanford University.

Hindy, A., C.-F. Huang, and D. Kreps. 1991. "On Intertemporal Preferences with a Continuous Time Dimension: The Case of Certainty." Unpublished, Sloan School of Management, Massachusetts Institute of Technology.

Ho, T., and S. Lee. 1986. "Term Structure Movements and Pricing Interest Rate Contingent Claims." *Journal of Finance* 41: 1011–29.

Huang, C.-F. 1985a. "Information Structures and Viable Price Systems." *Journal of Mathematical Economics* 14: 215–40.

———. 1985b. "Information Structures and Equilibrium Asset Prices." *Journal of Economic Theory* 31: 33–71.

———. 1987. "An Intertemporal General Equilibrium Asset Pricing Model: The Case of Diffusion Information." *Econometrica* 55: 117–42.

Huang, C.-F., and R. Litzenberger. 1988. *Foundations for Financial Economics*. Amsterdam: North-Holland.

Huang, C.-F., and H. Pagès. 1991. "Optimal Consumption and Portfolio Policies with an Infinite Horizon: Existence and Convergence." *Annals of Applied Probability* 2: 36–64.

Hull, J. 1989. *Options, Futures, and Other Derivative Securities*. Englewood Cliffs, N.J.: Prentice-Hall.

Hull, J., and A. White. 1990a. "Pricing Interest Rate Derivative Securities." *Review of Financial Studies* 3: 573–92.

———. 1990b. "Valuing Derivative Securities Using the Explicit Finite Difference Method." *Journal of Financial and Quantitative Analysis* 25: 87–100.

Ikeda, N., and S. Watanabe. 1981. *Stochastic Differential Equations and Diffusion Processes*. Amsterdam: North-Holland.

Ingersoll, J. 1987. *Theory of Financial Decision Making.* Totowa, N.J.: Rowman and Littlefield.

Jacka, S. 1984. "Optimal Consumption of an Investment." *Stochastics* 13: 45–60.

———. 1991. "Optimal Stopping and the American Put." *Mathematical Finance* 1: 1–14.

Jaillet, P., D. Lamberton, and B. Lapeyre. 1988. "Inéquations variationelles et théorie des options." *Comtes rendus de l'Academie de Sciences de Paris* 307: 961–965.

———. 1990. "Variational Inequalities and the Pricing of American Options." CERMA-ENPC La Courtine.

Jamshidian, F. 1989a. "An Exact Bond Option Formula." *Journal of Finance* 44: 205–9.

———. 1989b. "Closed-Form Solution for American Options on Coupon Bonds in the General Gaussian Interest Rate Model." Unpublished, Financial Strategies Group, Merrill Lynch Capital Markets.

———. 1989c. "Free Boundary Formulas for American Options." Unpublished, Financial Strategies Group, Merrill Lynch Capital Markets.

———. 1989d. "The Multifactor Gaussian Interest Rate Model and Implementation." Unpublished, Financial Strategies Group, Merrill Lynch Capital Markets.

———. 1990. "Commodity Option Evaluation in the Gaussian Futures Term Structure Model." Unpublished, Financial Strategies Group, Merrill Lynch Capital Markets.

———. 1991. "Forward Induction and Construction of Yield Curve Diffusion Models." *Journal of Fixed Income* 1: 62–74.

Jamshidian, F., and M. Fein. 1990. "Closed Form Solutions for Oil Futures and European Options in the Gibson-Schwartz Model: A Comment." Unpublished, Financial Strategies Group, Merrill Lynch Capital Markets.

Jarrow, R. 1988. *Finance Theory.* Englewood Cliffs, N.J.: Prentice-Hall.

Jarrow, R., and D. Madan. 1991. "A Characterization of Complete Security Markets on a Brownian Filtration." Unpublished, *Mathematical Finance* 1: 31–44.

Jeanblanc-Picqué, M., and M. Pontier. 1990. "Optimal Portfolio for a Small Investor in a Market Model with Discontinuous Prices." *Applied Mathematics and Optimization* 22: 287–310.

Johnson, H. 1987. "Options on the Maximum or the Minimum of Several Assets." *Journal of Financial and Quantitative Analysis* 22: 277–283.

Johnson, H., and D. Shanno. 1987. "Option Pricing When the Variance Is Changing." *Journal of Financial and Quantitative Analysis* 22: 143–151.

Jones, R., and R. Jacobs. 1986. "History Dependent Financial Claims: Monte Carlo Valuation." Unpublished, Simon Fraser University.

Jouini, E., and H. Kallal. 1991. "Martingales, Arbitrage, and Equilibrium in Security Markets with Transactions Costs." Unpublished, Department of Economics, University of Chicago.

Judd, K. 1989. "Minimum Weighted Residual Methods for Solving Dynamic Economic Models." Unpublished, Hoover Institution.

Kakutani, S. 1941. "A Generalization of Brouwer's Fixed-Point Theorem." *Duke Mathematical Journal* 8: 451–59.

Kan, R. 1991. "Structure of Pareto Optima When Agents Have Stochastic Recursive Preferences." Unpublished, Graduate School of Business, Stanford University.

Kandori, M. 1988. "Equivalent Equilibria." *International Economic Review* 29: 401–417.

Karatzas, I. 1987. "Applications of Stochastic Calculus in Financial Economics." Unpublished, Graduate School of Business, Columbia University.

———. 1988. "On the Pricing of American Options." *Applied Mathematics and Optimization* 17: 37–60.

———. 1989. "Optimization Problems in the Theory of Continuous Trading." *SIAM Journal of Control and Optimization* 27: 1221–59.

Karatzas, I., P. Lakner, J. Lehoczky, and S. Shreve. 1990. "Equilibrium in a Simplified Dynamic, Stochastic Economy with Heterogeneous Agents." Department of Mathematics, Carnegie-Mellon University.

Karatzas, I., J. Lehoczky, S. Sethi, and S. Shreve. 1986. "Explicit Solution of a General Consumption/Investment Problem." *Mathematics of Operations Research* 11: 261–94.

Karatzas, I., J. Lehoczky, and S. Shreve. 1987. "Optimal Portfolio and Consumption Decisions for a 'Small Investor' on a Finite Horizon." *SIAM Journal of Control and Optimization* 25: 1157–86.

———. 1991. "Equilibrium Models with Singular Asset Prices." *Mathematical Finance* 1/3: 11–30.

Karatzas, I., J. Lehoczky, S. Shreve, and G.-L. Xu. 1991. "Martingale and Duality Methods for Utility Maximization in Incomplete Markets." *SIAM Journal of Control and Optimization* 29: 702–30.

Karatzas, I., and S. Shreve. 1988. *Brownian Motion and Stochastic Calculus.* New York: Springer-Verlag.

Kim, I. 1990. "The Analytic Valuation of American Options." *Review of Financial Studies* 3: 547–72.

Kishimoto, N. 1989. "A Simplified Approach to Pricing Path Dependent Securities." Unpublished, Fuqua School of Business, Duke University.

Kocherlakota, N. 1990. "On the Discount Factor in 'Growth' Economies." *Journal of Monetary Economics* 25: 43–47.

Koopmans, T. 1960. "Stationary Ordinary Utility and Impatience." *Econometrica* 28: 287–309.

Kopp, P. 1984. *Martingales and Stochastic Integrals*. Cambridge: Cambridge University Press.

Krasa, S., and Werner, J. 1991. "Equilibria with Options: Existence and Indeterminacy." *Journal of Economic Theory* 54: 305–20.

Kraus, A., and R. Litzenberger. 1975. "Market Equilibrium in a Multiperiod State Preference Model with Logarithmic Utility." *Journal of Finance* 30: 1213–27.

Kreps, D. 1979. "Three Essays on Capital Markets." Technical Report 298, Institute for Mathematical Studies in the Social Sciences, Stanford University.

———. 1981. "Arbitrage and Equilibrium in Economies with Infinitely Many Commodities." *Journal of Mathematical Economics* 8: 15–35.

———. 1982. "Multiperiod Securities and the Efficient Allocation of Risk: A Comment on the Black-Scholes Option Pricing Model." In J. McCall, *The Economics of Uncertainty and Information*, pp. 203–232. Chicago: University of Chicago Press.

———. 1988. *Notes on the Theory of Choice*. Boulder and London: Westview Press.

———. 1990. *A Course in Microeconomic Theory*. Princeton, N.J.: Princeton University Press.

Kreps, D., and E. Porteus. 1978. "Temporal Resolution of Uncertainty and Dynamic Choice." *Econometrica* 46: 185–200.

Krylov, N. 1980. *Controlled Diffusion Processes*. New York: Springer-Verlag.

Lamberton, D., and G. Pagès. 1990. "Sur l'approximation des réduites." *Annales de l'Institut Henri Poincaré* 26: 331–55.

Langetieg, T. 1980. "A Multivariate Model of the Term Structure." *Journal of Finance* 35: 71–97.

Lawson, J., and J. Morris. 1978. "The Extrapolation of First Order Methods for Parabolic Partial Differential Equations I." *SIAM Journal of Numerical Analysis* 15: 1212–24.

Lee, J.-J. 1991. "A Note on Binomial Approximation for Contingent Securities." Graduate School of Business, Stanford University.

Lehoczky, J., S. Sethi, and S. Shreve. 1983. "Optimal Consumption and Investment Policies Allowing Consumption Constraints and Bankruptcy." *Mathematics of Operations Research* 8: 613–636.

———. 1985. "A Martingale Formulation for Optimal Consumption/Investment Decision Making." In G. Feichtinger, *Optimal Control and Economic Analysis 2*, pp. 135–53. Amsterdam: North-Holland.

Lehoczky, J.P., and S. Shreve. 1986. "Explicit Equilibrium Solutions for a Multi-Agent Consumption/Investment Problem." Technical Report 384, Department of Statistics, Carnegie-Mellon University.

Leland, H. 1985. "Option Pricing and Replication with Transactions Costs." *Journal of Finance* 40: 1283–1301.

LeRoy, S. 1973. "Risk Aversion and the Martingale Property of Asset Prices." *International Economic Review* 14: 436–446.

Levhari, D., and T. Srinivasan. 1969. "Optimal Savings under Uncertainty." *Review of Economic Studies* 59: 153–165.

Levine, D. 1985. "Infinite Horizon Equilibria with Incomplete Markets." Working Paper, 418, Economics Department, University of California, Los Angeles.

Lintner, J. 1965. "The Valuation of Risky Assets and the Selection of Risky Investment in Stock Portfolios and Capital Budgets." *Review of Economics and Statistics* 47: 13–37.

Lions, P.-L. 1981. "Control of Diffusion Processes in R^N." *Communications in Pure and Applied Mathematics* 34: 121–47.

———. 1983. "Optimal Control of Diffusion Processes." Unpublished, Université de Paris IX, Dauphine.

Longstaff, F., and E. Schwartz. 1990. "Interest Rate Volatility and the Term Structure: A Two-Factor General Equilibrium Model." Working Paper, 29–90, Graduate School of Management, U.C.L.A.

Lucas, D. 1991. "Asset Pricing with Undiversifiable Income Risk and Short Sales Constraints: Deepening the Equity Premium Puzzle." Kellogg School of Management, Northwestern University.

Lucas, R. 1978. "Asset Prices in an Exchange Economy." *Econometrica* 46: 1429–45.

Luenberger, D. 1969. *Optimization by Vector Space Methods.* New York: Wiley.

———. 1984. *Introduction to Linear and Nonlinear Programming* 2d ed. Reading, Massachusetts: Addison-Wesley.

Ma, C. 1991a. "Market Equilibrium with Heterogeneous Recursive-Utility-Maximizing Agents." Unpublished, Department of Economics, University of Toronto.

———. 1991b. "Valuation of Derivative Securities with Mixed Poisson-Brownian Information and with Recursive Utility." Unpublished, Department of Economics, University of Toronto.

Machina, M. 1982. "'Expected Utility' Analysis without the Independence Axiom." *Econometrica* 50: 277–323.

McKean, H. 1965. "Appendix: Free Boundary Problem for the Heat Equation Arising from a Problem in Mathematical Economics." *Industrial Management Review* 6: 32–39.

McKenzie, L. 1954. "On Equilibrium in Graham's Model of World Trade and Other Competitive Systems." *Econometrica* 22: 147–161.

McManus, D. 1984. "Incomplete Markets: Generic Existence of Equilibrium and Optimality Properties in an Economy with Futures Markets." Unpublished, Department of Economics, University of Pennsylvania.

Madan, D. 1988. "Risk Measurement in Semimartingale Models with Multiple Consumption Goods." *Journal of Economic Theory* 44: 398–412.

Madan, D., F. Milne, and H. Shefrin. 1989. "The Multinomial Option Pricing Model and Its Brownian and Poisson Limits." *Review of Financial Studies* 2: 251–66.

Magill, M.J.P., and W. Shafer. 1985. "Equilibrium and Efficiency in a Canonical Asset Trading Model." *May* Department of Economics, University of Southern California.

———. 1990. "Characterization of Generically Complete Real Asset Structures." Working Paper, University of Southern California.

Malliaris, A. 1982. *Stochastic Methods in Economics and Finance.* Amsterdam: North-Holland.

Mankiw, G. 1986. "The Equity Premium and the Concentration of Aggregate Shocks." *Journal of Financial Economics* 17: 211–19.

Marcet, A., and K. Singleton. 1991. "Optimal Consumption and Savings Decisions and Equilibrium Asset Prices in a Model with Heterogeneous Agents Subject to Portfolio Constraints." Carnegie-Mellon University and Graduate School of Business, Stanford University.

Margrabe, W. 1978. "The Value of an Option to Exchange One Asset for Another." *Journal of Finance* 33: 177–86.

Marimon, R. 1987. "Kreps' 'Three Essays on Capital Markets' Almost Ten Years Later." Unpublished, Department of Economics, University of Minnesota. Forthcoming in *Revista Espanola de Economia.*

Mas-Colell, A. 1985. *The Theory of General Economic Equilibrium—A Differentiable Approach.* Cambridge: Cambridge University Press.

———. 1986a. "The Price Equilibrium Existence Problem in Topological Vector Lattices." *Econometrica* 54: 1039–1054.

———. 1986b. "Valuation Equilibrium and Pareto Optimum Revisited." In W. Hildenbrand and A. Mas-Colell, *Contributions to Mathematical Economics,* pp. 317–32. Amsterdam: North-Holland.

———. 1987. "An Observation on Geanakoplos and Polemarchakis." Unpublished, Department of Economics, Harvard University.

———. 1991. "Indeterminacy in Incomplete Market Economies." *Economic Theory* 1: 45–62.

Mas-Colell, A., and P. Monteiro. 1991. "Self-Fulfilling Equilibria: An Existence Theorem for a General State Space." Department of Economics, Paper 2, Harvard University, Economic Theory Discussion.

Mas-Colell, A., and W. Zame. 1990. "Equilibrium Theory in Infinite Dimensional Spaces." In W. Hildenbrand and H. Sonnenschein, *Handbook of Mathematical Economonics, Vol. 4*, pp. 1835–98. Amsterdam: North-Holland.

Mehra, R., and E. Prescott. 1985. "The Equity Premium: A Puzzle." *Journal of Monetary Economics* 15: 145–61.

Mehrling, P. 1990. "Heterogeneity, Incomplete Markets, and the Equity Premium." Working Paper, Barnard College and Columbia University.

Merton, R. 1969. "Lifetime Portfolio Selection under Uncertainty: The Continuous Time Case." *Review of Economics and Statistics* 51: 247–57.

———. 1971. "Optimum Consumption and Portfolio Rules in a Continuous Time Model." *Journal of Economic Theory* 3: 373–413; Erratum 6 (1973); 213–14.

———. 1973a. "An Intertemporal Capital Asset Pricing Model." *Econometrica* 41: 867–88.

———. 1973b. "The Theory of Rational Option Pricing." *Bell Journal of Economics and Management Science* 4: 141–83.

———. 1974. "On The Pricing of Corporate Debt: The Risk Structure of Interest Rates." *Journal of Finance* 29: 449–470.

———. 1976. "Option Pricing When the Underlying Stock Returns Are Discontinuous." *Journal of Financial Economics* 5: 125–44.

———. 1977. "On the Pricing of Contingent Claims and the Modigliani-Miller Theorem." *Journal of Financial Economics* 5: 241–50.

———. 1990a. "Capital Market Theory and the Pricing of Financial Securities." In B. Friedman and F. Hahn, *Handbook of Monetary Economics*, pp. 497–581. Amsterdam: North-Holland.

———. 1990b. *Continuous-Time Finance*. Oxford: Basil Blackwell.

Milshtein, G. 1974. "Approximate Integration of Stochastic Differential Equations." *Theory of Probability and Its Applications* 3: 557–62.

———. 1978. "A Method of Second-Order Accuracy Integration of Stochastic Differential Equations." *Theory of Probability and its Applications* 23: 396–401.

Miltersen, K. 1991. "The Term Structure of Interest Rates and the Pricing of Contingent Claims Written on Interest Rate Sensitive Assets." Unpublished, Department of Management, Odense University.

Mirrlees, J. 1974. "Optimal Accumulation under Uncertainty: The Case of Stationary Returns to Investment." In J. Drèze, *Allocation under Uncertainty: Equilibrium and Optimality*, pp. 36–50. New York: Wiley.

Mitchell, A., and D. Griffiths. 1980. *The Finite Difference Method in Partial Differential Equations*. New York: John Wiley.

Modigliani, F., and M. Miller. 1958. "The Cost of Capital, Corporation Finance, and the Theory of Investment." *American Economic Review* 48: 261–97.

Monteiro, P. 1991. "A New Proof of the Existence of Equilibrium in Incomplete Markets Economies." Universidade Federal do Rio de Janeiro, Harvard University.

Müller, S. 1985. *Arbitrage Pricing of Contingent Claims.* Lecture Notes in Economics and Mathematical Systems, vol. 254. New York: Springer-Verlag.

Myneni, R. 1992. "The Pricing of American Options." *Annals of Applied Probability* 2: 1–23.

Negishi, T. 1960. "Welfare Economics and Existence of an Equilibrium for a Competitive Economy." *Metroeconometrica* 12: 92–97.

Nelson, D., and K. Ramaswamy. 1989. "Simple Binomial Processes as Diffusion Approximations in Financial Models." *Review of Financial Studies* 3: 393–430.

Newton, N. 1990. "Asymptotically Efficient Runge-Kutta Methods for a Class of Ito and Stratonovich Equations." Unpublished, Department of Electrical Engineering, University of Essex.

Nielsen, L.T. 1990a. "Equilibrium in CAPM without a Riskless Asset." *Review of Economic Studies* 57: 315–24.

———. 1990b. "Existence of Equilibrium in CAPM." *Journal of Economic Theory* 52: 223–31.

Ocone, D., and I. Karatzas. 1991. "A Generalized Clark Representation Formula, with Application to Optimal Portfolios." *Stochastics and Stochastics Reports* 34: 187–220.

Ohashi, K. 1991. "A Note on the Terminal Date Security Prices in a Continuous Time Trading Model with Dividends." *Journal of Mathematical Economics* 20: 219–24.

Oksendal, B. 1985. *Stochastic Differential Equations.* Berlin: Springer-Verlag.

O'Nan, M. 1976. *Linear Algebra*, 2d ed. New York: Harcourt Brace Jovanovich.

Pagès, H. 1987. "Optimal Consumption and Portfolio Policies When Markets Are Incomplete." Unpublished, Department of Economics, Massachusetts Institute of Technology.

Pearson, N., and T.-S. Sun. 1989. "A Test of the Cox, Ingersoll, Ross Model of the Term Structure of Interest Rates Using the Method of Moments." Sloan School of Management, Massachusetts Institute of Technology.

Pedersen, H., E. Shiu, and A. Thorlacius. 1989. "Arbitrage-Free Pricing of Interest Rate Contingent Claims." *Transactions of the Society of Actuaries* 41: 231–65.

Pliska, S. 1986. "A Stochastic Calculus Model of Continuous Trading: Optimal Portfolios." *Mathematics of Operations Research* 11: 371–82.

Polemarchakis, H., and P. Siconolfi. 1991. "Competitive Equilibria without Free Disposal or Nonsatiation." Research Paper 9115, CORE, Université Catholique de Louvain.

Pollard, D. 1984. *Convergence of Stochastic Processes.* New York: Springer-Verlag.

Prescott, E., and R. Mehra. 1980. "Recursive Competitive Equilibrium: The Case of Homogeneous Households." *Econometrica* 48: 1365–79.

Press, W., B. Flannery, S. Teukolsky, and W. Vetterling. 1988. *Numerical Recipes in C: The Art of Scientific Computing.* Cambridge: Cambridge University Press.

Prigent, J.-L. 1991. "From Discrete to Continuous Time Finance: Weak Convergence of the Optimal Financial Trading Strategies." Institute of Mathematical Research of Rennes, University of Rennes.

Prisman, E. 1985. "Valuation of Risky Assets in Arbitrage Free Economies with Frictions." Unpublished, University of Arizona.

Protter, P. 1990. *Stochastic Integration and Differential Equations.* New York: Springer-Verlag.

Radner, R. 1967. "Equilibre des marchés a terme et au comptant en cas d'incertitude." *Cahiers d'Econométrie* 4: 35–52.

——. 1972. "Existence of Equilibrium of Plans, Prices and Price Expectations in a Sequence of Markets." *Econometrica* 40: 289–303.

Reisman, H. 1986. "Option Pricing for Stocks with a Generalized Log-Normal Price Distribution." Unpublished, Department of Finance, University of Minnesota.

Repullo, R. 1986. "On the Generic Existence of Radner Equilibria When There Are as Many Securities as States of Nature." *Economics Letters* 21: 101–5.

Revuz, D. 1975. *Markov Chains.* Amsterdam: North-Holland.

Revuz, D., and M. Yor. 1991. *Continuous Martingales and Brownian Motion.* New York: Springer-Verlag.

Richard, S. 1975. "Optimal Consumption, Portfolio, and Life Insurance Rules for an Uncertain Lived Individual in a Continuous Time Model." *Journal of Financial Economics* 2: 187–203.

——. 1978. "An Arbitrage Model of the Term Structure of Interest Rates." *Journal of Financial Economics* 6: 33–57.

Richardson, H. 1989. "A Minimum Variance Result in Continuous Trading Portfolio Optimization." *Management Science* 35: 1045–55.

Rockafellar, R.T. 1970. *Convex Analysis.* Princeton, N.J.: Princeton University Press.

Rogers, C., and D. Williams. 1987. *Diffusions, Markov Processes, and Martingales: Ito Calculus.* New York: Wiley.

Ross, S. 1976. "The Arbitrage Theory of Capital Asset Pricing." *Journal of Economic Theory* 13: 341–60.

——. 1978. "A Simple Approach to the Valuation of Risky Streams." *Journal of Business* 51: 453–75.

——. 1987. "Arbitrage and Martingales with Taxation." *Journal of Political Economy* 95: 371–93.

——. 1989. "Information and Volatility: The No-Arbitrage Martingale Approach to Timing and Resolution Irrelevancy." *Journal of Finance* 64: 1–17.

Rothschild, M. 1986. "Asset Pricing Theories." In W. Heller and D. Starrett, *Uncertainty, Information and Communication—Essays in Honor of Kenneth J. Arrow*, vol. 3, pp. 97–128. Cambridge: Cambridge University Press.

Royden, H. 1968. *Real Analysis* 2d ed. New York: Macmillan.

Rubinstein, M. 1974a. "A Discrete-Time Synthesis of Financial Theory." Working Paper, 20, School of Business, University of California, Berkeley.

——. 1974b. "An Aggregation Theorem for Securities Markets." *Journal of Financial Economics* 1: 225–44.

——. 1976. "The Valuation of Uncertain Income Streams and the Pricing of Options." *Bell Journal of Economics* 7: 407–25.

——. 1987. "Derivative Assets Analysis." *Economics Perspectives* 1: 73–93.

Rudin, W. 1973. *Functional Analysis.* New York: McGraw-Hill.

Ryder, H., and G. Heal. 1973. "Optimal Growth with Intertemporally Dependent Preferences." *Review of Economic Studies* 40: 1–31.

Samuelson, P. 1969. "Lifetime Portfolio Selection by Dynamic Stochastic Programming." *Review of Economics and Statistics* 51: 239–46.

Scarsini, M. 1986. "Comparison of Random Cash Flows." *IMA Journal of Mathematics in Management* 1: 25–32.

Scheinkman, J. 1989. "Market Incompleteness and the Equilibrium Valuation of Assets." In S. Bhattacharya and G. Constantinides, *Theory of Valuation, Frontiers of Financial Theory*, pp. 45–51. Totowa, N.J.: Rowman and Littlefield.

Scheinkman, J., and L. Weiss. 1986. "Borrowing Constraints and Aggregate Economic Activity." *Econometrica* 54: 23–45.

Schwartz, E. 1977. "The Valuation of Warrants: Implementing a New Approach." *Journal of Financial Economics* 4: 79–94.

Selby, M., and S. Hodges. 1987. "On the Evaluation of Compound Options." *Management Science* 33: 347–55.

Selden, L. 1978. "A New Representation of Preference over 'Certain x Uncertain' Consumption Pairs: The 'Ordinal Certainty Equivalent' Hypothesis." *Econometrica* 46: 1045–60.

Sethi, S., and M. Taksar. 1988. "A Note on Merton's 'Optimum Consumption and Portfolio Rules in a Continuous-Time Model'." *Journal of Economic Theory* 46: 395–401.

Sharpe, W. 1964. "Capital Asset Prices: A Theory of Market Equilibrium under Conditions of Risk." *Journal of Finance* 19: 425–42.

———. 1985. *Investments*, 3d ed. Englewood Cliffs, N.J.: Prentice-Hall.

Shreve, S., and G.-L. Xu. 1990. "A Duality Approach to Stochastic Portfolio/Consumption Decision in Continuous Time Markets with Short Selling Restrictions." Research Paper 90–70, Department of Statistics, Carnegie-Mellon University.

Singleton, K. 1987. "Specification and Estimation of Intertemporal Asset Pricing Models." In B. Friedman and F. Hahn, *Handbook of Monetary Economics*, vol. 1, pp. 583–626. Amsterdam: North-Holland.

Skiadas, C. 1991. "Time-Consistent Choice and Preferences for Information." Unpublished, Operations Research Department, Stanford University.

Smith, G. 1985. *Numerical Solution of Partial Differential Equations: Finite Difference Methods* 3d ed. Oxford: Clarendon Press.

Stanton, R. 1990. "Rational Prepayment and the Valuation of Mortgage-Backed Securities." Graduate School of Business, Stanford University.

Stapleton, R., and M. Subrahmanyam. 1978. "A Multiperiod Equilibrium Asset Pricing Model." *Econometrica* 46: 1077–93.

Stokey, N., and R. Lucas, with E. Prescott. 1989. *Recursive Methods in Economic Dynamics*. Cambridge, Mass.: Harvard University Press.

Streufert, P. 1991a. "Existence and Characterization Results for Stochastic Dynamic Programming." Research Paper 91–09, Department of Economics, University of California, San Diego.

———. 1991b. "Nonnegative Stochastic Dynamic Preferences." Research Paper 91–10, Department of Economics, University of California, San Diego.

———. 1991c. "Ordinal Dynamic Programming." Research Paper 9104, Department of Economics, University of Wisconsin, Madison.

Stricker, C. 1984. "Integral Representation in the Theory of Continuous Trading." *Stochastics and Stochastic Reports* 13: 249–65.

———. 1990. "Arbitrage et lois de martingale." *Annales de l'Institut Henri Poincaré* 26: 451–60.

Stroock, D., and S.R.S. Varadhan. 1979. *Multidimensional Diffusion Processes*. New York: Springer-Verlag.

Stulz, R. 1982. "Options on the Minimum or the Maximum of Two Risky Assets: Analysis and Applications." *Journal of Financial Economics* 10: 161–85.

Sundaresan, S. 1989. "Intertemporally Dependent Preferences in the Theories of Consumption, Portfolio Choice and Equilibrium Asset Pricing." *Review of Financial Studies* 2: 73–89.

Svensson, L.E.O. 1989. "Portfolio Choice with Non-Expected Utility in Continuous Time." *Economic Letters* 30: 313–17.

Svensson, L.E.O., and I. Werner. 1990. "Portfolio Choice and Asset Pricing with Non-Traded Assets." Research Paper 2005, Graduate School of Business, Stanford University.

Talay, D. 1984. "Efficient Numerical Schemes for the Approximation of Expectations of Functionals of S.D.E." In H. Korezlioglu, G. Mazziotto, and J. Szpirglas, *Filtering and Control of Random Processes*. Lecture Notes in Control and Information Sciences 61.

———. 1986. "Discrétiation d'une equation différentielle stochastique et calcul approché d'espérances de fonctionelles de la solution." *Mathematical Modeling and Numerical Analysis* 20: 141–79.

———. 1990. "Second Order Discretization Schemes of Stochastic Differential Systems for the Computation of the Invariant Law." Research Paper, Institut National de Recherche en Informatique et en Automatique, Sophia Antipolis, France.

Talay, D., and L. Tubaro. 1990. "Expansion of the Global Error for Numerical Schemes Solving Stochastic Differential Equations." Research Paper 1069, Institut National de Recherche en Informatique et en Automatique, Sophia Antipolis, France.

Tauchen, G., and R. Hussey. 1991. "Quadrature-Based Methods for Obtaining Approximate Solutions to the Integral Equations of Nonlinear Rational Expectations Models." *Econometrica* 59: 371–96.

Telmer, C. 1990. "Asset Pricing and Incomplete Markets." Unpublished, Department of Economics, Queen's University.

Uzawa, H. 1968. "Time Preference, the Consumption Function and Optimal Asset Holdings." In J. Wolfe, *Value, Capital and Growth: Papers in Honor of Sir John Hicks*, 485–504. Chicago: Aldine.

van Moerbeke, P. 1976. "On Optimal Stopping and Free Boundary Problems." *Archive for Rational Mechanics and Analysis* 60: 101–148.

Varian, H. 1984. *Microeconomic Analysis*, 2d ed. New York: Norton.

Vasicek, O. 1977. "An Equilibrium Characterization of the Term Structure." *Journal of Financial Economics* 5: 177–88.

Vila, J.-L., and T. Zariphopoulou. 1991. "Optimal Consumption and Portfolio Choice with Borrowing Constraints." Unpublished, Sloan School of Management, Massachusetts Institute of Technology.

Walras, L. 1874–77. *Eléments d'économie politique pure* 4d ed. Lausanne: L. Corbaz, English translation of the definitive edition by W. Jaffé, *Elements of Pure Economics* (London: Allen and Unwin, 1954).

Wang, J. 1989. "Asset Prices, Stock Returns, Price Volatility, Risk Premium, and Trading Strategies under Asymmetric Information." Unpublished, Finance Department, the Wharton School, University of Pennsylvania.

Wang, S. 1989. "The Integrability Problem of Asset Prices." Unpublished, Department of Economics, University of Toronto.

———. 1991a. "Is Kreps-Porteus Utility Distinguishable from Intertemporal Expected Utility." Unpublished, Department of Economics, University of Toronto.

———. 1991b. "The Local Recoverability of Risk Aversion and Intertemporal Substitution." Unpublished, Department of Economics, University of Toronto.

Weil, P. 1990. "Equilibrium Asset Prices with Undiversifiable Labor Income Risk." Unpublished, Department of Economics, Harvard University.

Werner, J. 1985. "Equilibrium in Economies with Incomplete Financial Markets." *Journal of Economic Theory* 36: 110–19.

———. 1991. "On Constrained Optimal Allocations with Incomplete Markets." *Economic Theory* 1: 205–9.

Willinger, W., and M. Tacqu. 1991. "Toward a Convergence Theory for Continuous Stochastic Securities Market Models." *Mathematical Finance* 1: 55–100.

Yamada, T., and S. Watanabe. 1971. "On the Uniqueness of Solutions of Stochastic Differential Equations." *Journal of Mathematics of Kyoto University* 11: 155–67.

Yamazaki, A. 1991. "Equilibrium in Economies with Incomplete Markets and Outside Money: Transactions Costs and Existence." Unpublished, Department of Economics, Hitotsubashi University.

Yor, M. 1991. "On Some Exponential Functionals of Brownian Motion." Unpublished, Laboratoire de Probabilités, Université de Paris VI.

Zariphopoulou, T. 1989. "Investment/Consumption Model with Transactions Costs and Markov-Chain Parameters." Unpublished, LCDC/CCS Number 89-16, Department of Applied Mathematics, Brown University.

Symbol Glossary

Z^n, xv

$x \geq 0$, xv

$x > 0$, xv

$x \gg 0$, xv

$X = Y$, xv

$x \mapsto F(x)$, xvi

$\partial U(c^*)$, 6

$\text{corr}(\,\cdot\,)$, 12

$\partial^2 U(c^i)$, 14

C^k, 14

$\partial f(a, b)$, 14

$(\,\cdot \mid \cdot\,)$, 17

δ^θ, 22

$\nabla U(c^*; c)$, 25, 229

$\nabla U(c^*)$, 25, 162, 229

$(x - K)^+$, 33

$\max(x, y)$, 51

$B(D)$, 60

$\mathcal{U}F$, 61

$d(F, G) = 0$, 61

L^*, 65

$\#A$, 67

$\int \theta\, dB$, 78, 236

$\mathcal{H}^1$, 80, 87

$\mathcal{H}^2$, 80, 87

$\mathcal{H}^2(S)$, 81, 89, 115

$\mathcal{L}^1$, 80, 87

$\mathcal{L}^2$, 78, 87

$\mathcal{L}(S)$, 81, 89

$\int \theta\, dS$, 81, 89

Φ, 83

$\text{tr}(A)$, 88

$\mathcal{D}$, 88

X^Y, 96

W^θ, 99

R^θ, 99

$\|Z\| \equiv [E(Z^2)]^{1/2}$, 111

$\mathcal{L}^\infty$, 149

$\emptyset$, 223

$\frac{dQ}{dP}$, 224, 234

E^Q, 224

$\sigma(Z)$, 224

$X^+ \equiv \max(X, 0)$, 232

Author Index

Subject Index